MARVEL
VOICES
HERITAGE

MARVEL VOICES HERITAGE

START HERE

MARVEL'S VOICES: INDIGENOUS VOICES

"THE WATCHER"
JEFFREY VEREGGE // writer, artist & colorist

"HITTING BACK"
REBECCA ROANHORSE // writer
WESHOYOT ALVITRE // artist
LEE LOUGHRIDGE // colorist

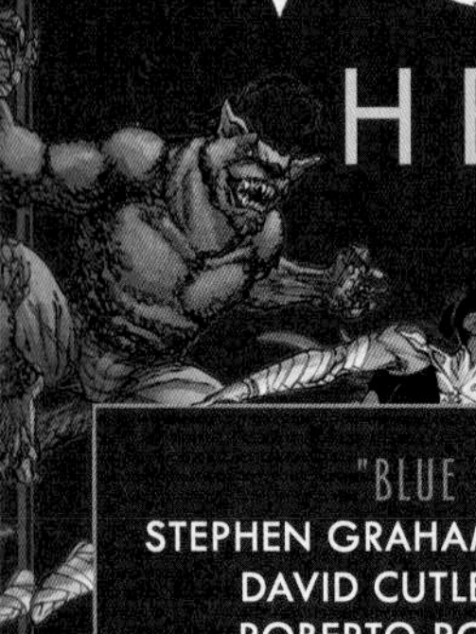

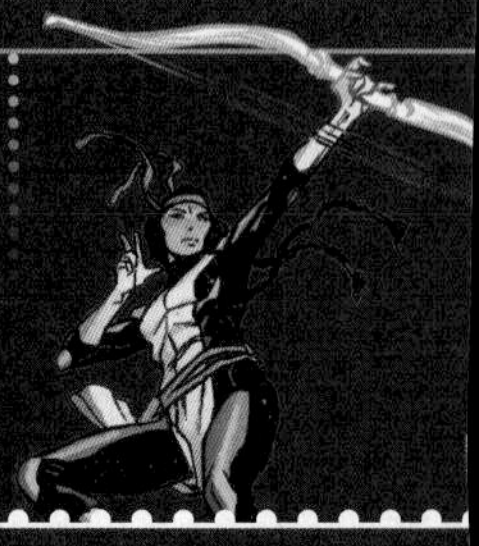

"BLUE MOON"
STEPHEN GRAHAM JONES // writer
DAVID CUTLER // penciller
ROBERTO POGGI // inker
CRIS PETER // colorist

"MULTIFACETED"
DARCIE LITTLE BADGER // writer
KYLE CHARLES // artist
FELIPE SOBREIRO // colorist

AFTERWORD BY TABOO & B. EARL

VC's ARIANA MAHER // letterer
JIM TERRY & BRIAN REBER // cover art
SARAH BRUNSTAD // editor
TOM BREVOORT // executive editor
Special Thanks to ANGÉLIQUE ROCHÉ

MARVEL'S VOICES: HERITAGE

"THE UNEXPECTED"
JIM TERRY // writer & artist
BRITTANY PEER // colorist

"THE TUURNGAIT'S SONG"
NYLA INNUKSUK // writer
NATASHA DONOVAN // artist
RACHELLE ROSENBERG // colorist

"NOT DEAD YET"
STEVEN PAUL JUDD // writer
DAVID CUTLER // penciller
JOSÉ MARZAN JR. // inker
PARIS ALLEYNE // colorist

"A FRIEND IN NEED"
REBECCA ROANHORSE // writers
SHAUN BEYALE // penciller
BELARDINO BRABO // inker
MORRY HOLLOWELL // colorist

AN INTERVIEW WITH WRITER REBECCA ROANHORSE

VC's ARIANA MAHER // letterer
KYLE CHARLES & RACHELLE ROSENBERG // cover art
ANITA OKOYE // assistant editor
SARAH BRUNSTAD // editor
ANGÉLIQUE ROCHÉ // consulting editor
Special Thanks to BOBBY WILSON

CHAMPIONS ANNUAL #1

JIM ZUB & NYLA INNUKSUK // writers
MARCUS TO // artist
JORDAN BOYD // colorist
VC's CLAYTON COWLES // letterer
R.B. SILVA & MARCIO MENYZ // cover art
ALANNA SMITH // associate editor
TOM BREVOORT // editor

MARVEL'S VOICES: HERITAGE. Contains material originally published in magazine form as MARVEL'S VOICES: INDIGENOUS VOICES (2020) #1, MARVEL'S VOICES: HERITAGE (2021) #1, CHAMPIONS ANNUAL (2018) #1, MARVEL COMICS (20 #1000, WEREWOLF BY NIGHT (2020) #1, UNITED STATES OF CAPTAIN AMERICA (2021) #3 and PHOENIX SONG: ECHO (2021) #1. First printing 2022. ISBN 978-1-302-93271-8. Published by MARVEL WORLDWIDE, INC., a subsidiary of MAR ENTERTAINMENT, LLC. OFFICE OF PUBLICATION: 1290 Avenue of the Americas, New York, NY 10104. © 2022 MARVEL No similarity between any of the names, characters, persons, and/or institutions in this book with those of any living dead person or institution is intended, and any such similarity which may exist is purely coincidental. **Printed in Canada.** KEVIN FEIGE, Chief Creative Officer; DAN BUCKLEY, President, Marvel Entertainment; DAVID BOGART, Associate Publis & SVP of Talent Affairs; TOM BREVOORT, VP, Executive Editor; NICK LOWE, Executive Editor, VP of Content, Digital Publishing; DAVID GABRIEL, VP of Print & Digital Publishing; SVEN LARSEN, VP of Licensed Publishing; MARK ANNUNZIATO of Planning & Forecasting; JEFF YOUNGQUIST, VP of Production & Special Projects; ALEX MORALES, Director of Publishing Operations; DAN EDINGTON, Director of Editorial Operations; RICKEY PURDIN, Director of Talent Relations; JENNI GRÜNWALD, Director of Production & Special Projects; SUSAN CRESPI, Production Manager; STAN LEE, Chairman Emeritus. For information regarding advertising in Marvel Comics or on Marvel.com, please contact Vit DeBellis, Custom Soluti & Integrated Advertising Manager, at vdebellis@marvel.com. For Marvel subscription inquiries, please call 888-511-5480. **Manufactured between 8/12/2022 and 9/13/2022 by SOLISCO PRINTERS, SCOTT, QC, CANADA.**

10 9 8 7 6 5 4 3 2 1

Read more and listen at **Marvel.com/Voices.**

WEREWOLF BY NIGHT #1

TABOO & B. EARL // *writers*
SCOT EATON // *penciller*
SCOTT HANNA // *inker*
MIROSLAV MRVA // *colorist*
VC's JOE SABINO // *letterer*
MIKE McKONE & JASON KEITH // *cover art*
LINDSEY COHICK // *assistant editor*
JAKE THOMAS // *editor*
Special Thanks to VINCE & DOLORES SCHILLING *and* JAY C. SHELTON JR.

THE UNITED STATES OF CAPTAIN AMERICA #3

"PEOPLE LIKE US"
DARCIE LITTLE BADGER // *writer*
DAVID CUTLER // *penciller*
ROBERTO POGGI // *inker*
MATT MILLA // *colorist*
VC's JOE CARAMAGNA // *letterer*
GERALD PAREL // *cover art*
KEITH BLUECLOUD & MOSIAH BLUECLOUD // *consultants*
MARTIN BIRO // *assistant editor*
ALANNA SMITH // *editor*
TOM BREVOORT // *executive editor*

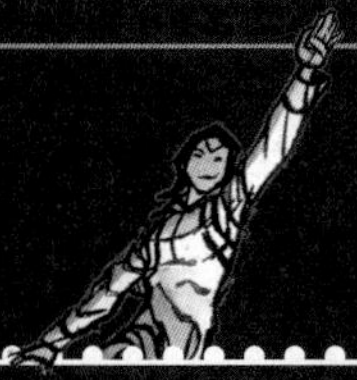

PHOENIX SONG: ECHO #1

REBECCA ROANHORSE // *writer*
LUCA MARESCA // *artist*
CARLOS LOPEZ // *colorist*
VC's ARIANA MAHER // *letterer*
CORY SMITH & ALEJANDRO SÁNCHEZ // *cover art*
SARAH BRUNSTAD // *editor*
TOM BREVOORT // *executive editor*
special thanks to JASON AARON

MARVEL COMICS #1000

"HONOR THE SACRED"
TABOO & B. EARL // *writers*
JEFFREY VEREGGE // *artist & colorist*
VC's TRAVIS LANHAM // *letterer*
SHANNON ANDREWS BALLESTEROS // *assistant editor*
ALANNA SMITH // *associate editor*
TOM BREVOORT // *editor*

"MARVEL'S VOICES" ESSAYS

INTRODUCTION BY LEE FRANCIS IV
ESSAY BY DARCIE LITTLE BADGER
ESSAY BY KARLA PACHECO
AFTERWORD BY AMANDA R. TACHINE

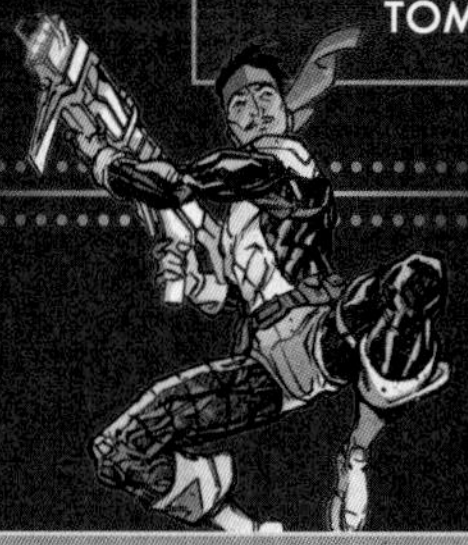

ANGÉLIQUE ROCHÉ // *consulting editor*
JENNIFER GRÜNWALD // *collection editor*
DANIEL KIRCHHOFFER // *assistant editor*
MAIA LOY // *assistant managing editor*
LISA MONTALBANO // *associate manager, talent relations*
JOE HOCHSTEIN // *associate manager, digital assets*
JEFF YOUNGQUIST // *vp production & special projects*
JESS HARROLD // *research*
STACIE ZUCKER // *book designer*
ADAM DEL RE // *senior designer*
DAVID GABRIEL // *svp print, sales & marketing*
C.B. CEBULSKI // *editor in chief*

Special thanks to SARAH AMOS, BRAD BARTON, ROBYN BELT, BRENDON BIGLEY, ANTHONY BLACKWOOD, TIM CHENG, HALEY CONATSER, PATRICK COTNOIR, ADRI COWAN, MR DANIEL, CHRISTINE DINH, JILL DUBOFF, JON-MICHAEL ENNIS, JASMINE ESTRADA, HARRY GO, BRANDON GRUGLE, MARIKA HASHIMOTO, TUCKER MARKUS, KARA McGUIRK-ALLISON, RON RICHARDS, ISABEL ROBERTSON, LARISSA ROSEN, WALT SCHWENK, STEPHEN WACKER, ALEXIS WILLIAMS & PERCIA VERLIN

END HERE

INTRODUCTION

BY LEE FRANCIS IV

When we tell stories, we build relationships with each other, our ancestors and Creation as a whole. So let me tell you a story about the power of stories.

My love of comics is deeply rooted in Pueblo tradition. My dad was from the Pueblo of Laguna, 45 miles west of my hometown of Albuquerque, New Mexico. Because of him, I grew up hearing incredible stories of star wanderers, monster hunters, tricksters and heroes.

While many of the characters in comics were white and came from different cultural and family traditions, I fell in love with the medium as it was filled with the same wanderers, tricksters and heroes I grew up with. For me, there was nothing more exciting than heading down to Duran's Central Pharmacy and hitting the spinner rack looking for the newest releases. While I was partial to *Thor* and *Iron Man* in those days, *The Official Handbook of the Marvel Universe* was always a prized choice because I could learn more about the backstories of the panoply of characters.

Over the years, I formed bonds with many of these said characters. I related to their stories, their flaws, their perseverance and their heroism, but most of all, their humanity. They were endowed by their mortal creators with accessible traits, relatable quirks, unique talents and ample humor that made them more than figures on a page.

The same could not be said about the Native characters at the time.

Native and Indigenous People occupy a unique place in pop culture. No group of People have been illustrated and written about as much as the Indigenous Peoples of the Americas and yet have so little input in developing said media, effectively erasing not just our history and culture but also our identities. Until the 1960s, there were only a handful of published Native writers, let alone illustrators, in modern literature.

Mainstream comics were no different. Similar to other people of color, Native and Indigenous stereotypes saturated the pages of Westerns and super hero comics from the very beginning. Even though there were attempts at creating more positive representation over the decades, as Caddo scholar and writer Michael Sheyahshe writes in *Native Americans in Comics* (2012), "[i]ndispensable to picturesque or pastoral illustrations of historical times, Indigenous characters nevertheless continued to be flat, two-dimensional characters who were mere caricatures of real Native people."

Largely absent from pop media for hundreds of years, including many years when our community and culture were faced with genocide and ethnocide, whenever Indigenous People have been "represented," you are grateful for any — ANY — representation at all. But these images are a mirage and continue to marginalize Native and Indigenous voices. As we emerge into an uncertain decade, it's not enough to simply show a character who is Indigenous — we need to know their stories. It is clear that representation alone is not enough. We need relationships. We need to form the same bond with these characters as I did with Iron Man and Thor when I was little

There are exceptions, including Maya Lopez, A.K.A. Echo. For one of the first times, a Native character was presented with multiple dimensions. Her story didn't focus exclusively on her cultural trappings but rather on the individual, which gave Native and non-Native readers alike the opportunity to have a deeper bond with her and her adventures.

We also see this in the work of foundational Native comic creators Timothy Truman, Jon Proudstar, Arigon Starr and Jay Odjick, all of whom cleared the path with work dating back to the 1980s. In their comics, the characters not only exist but have authenticity. While their culture is a part of who they are, the stories focus on the humanity of their characters, not just their cultural elements.

This brings me back to my story about the power of stories and why Marvel's Voices: Heritage is not just powerful but necessary. Not only does Marvel's Voices: Heritage's global platform center on the stories of Native and Indigenous characters, it goes beyond just highlighting cultural elements. Written and illustrated by Native and Indigenous writers and artists, this book provides a necessary authenticity and essential humanness that has been missing from Marvel's Native characters. Characters who have often been overlooked and underutilized appear on these pages not just as heroes but in their full multidimensional identities. In addition, and most importantly, these stories move the characters and their stories from hollow representations to deeper and more authentic relationships, which, from an Indigenous perspective, are about the connections we share with each other and all of Creation.

These relationships are present in the bold lines of Jeffrey Veregge, perfectly synthesizing his tradition and pop culture.

These relationships are in the energy and power that Rebecca Roanhorse imbues Echo with in her stories of empowerment and action.

These relationships are in the cover art by Jim Terry, flying off the page with each Native character in movement, in momentum — a stark contrast to so many of those aforementioned comics of yesteryear.

These relationships exist in the art of each Native and Indigenous contributor in this volume. Every one of them brings their own depth and dynamism and an irrefutable authenticity that can be felt. It is the core of the relationship that is being built. The being of a story that has only begun.

A story that Native youth can pick up and see themselves in, not just as caricatures but in their full humanity. Moving forward, these young readers will be able to find themselves not only in flat images but at the center of all of Creation. In the end, isn't that what comics should be about — bonding with our heroes and sharing in their wins, failures, conflicts, heartbreaks and growth so that one day, we too can make the world better, more engaging, more authentic, more human, more connected? Here's to making the Marvel Universe and the world outside our window a little (A LOT) more indigenous.

Albuquerque-based activist, educator and comic creator Dr. Lee Francis IV is the Executive Director of Wordcraft Circle of Native Writers and Storytellers, owner and C.E.O. of Native Realities Publishing and founder of the Indigenous Comic Con and Red Planet Books and Comics. Dr. Francis is an award-winning poet and writer, whose work revolves around education and how Native Peoples and Indigenous communities are represented in popular culture.

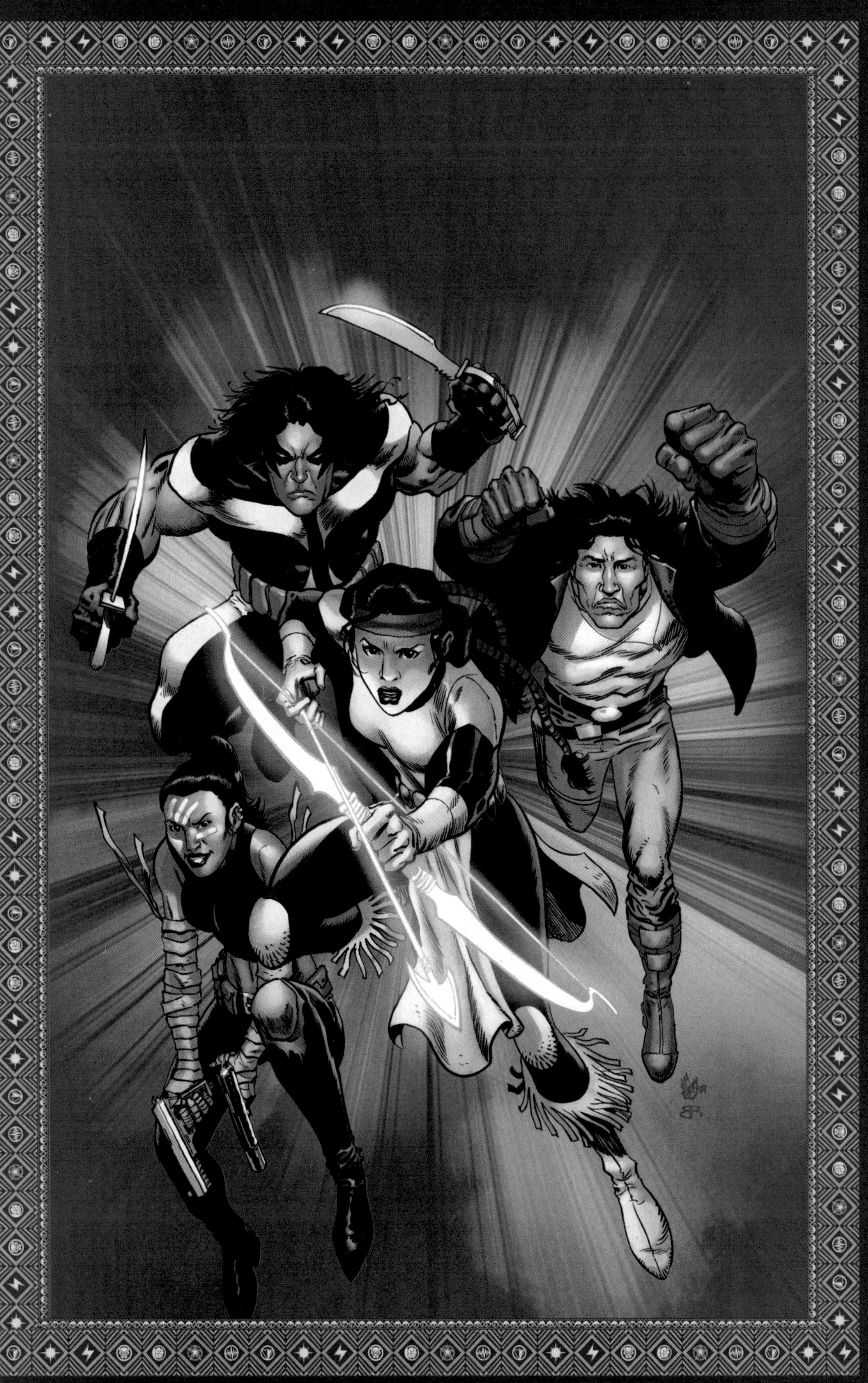

MARVEL'S VOICES: INDIGENOUS VOICES

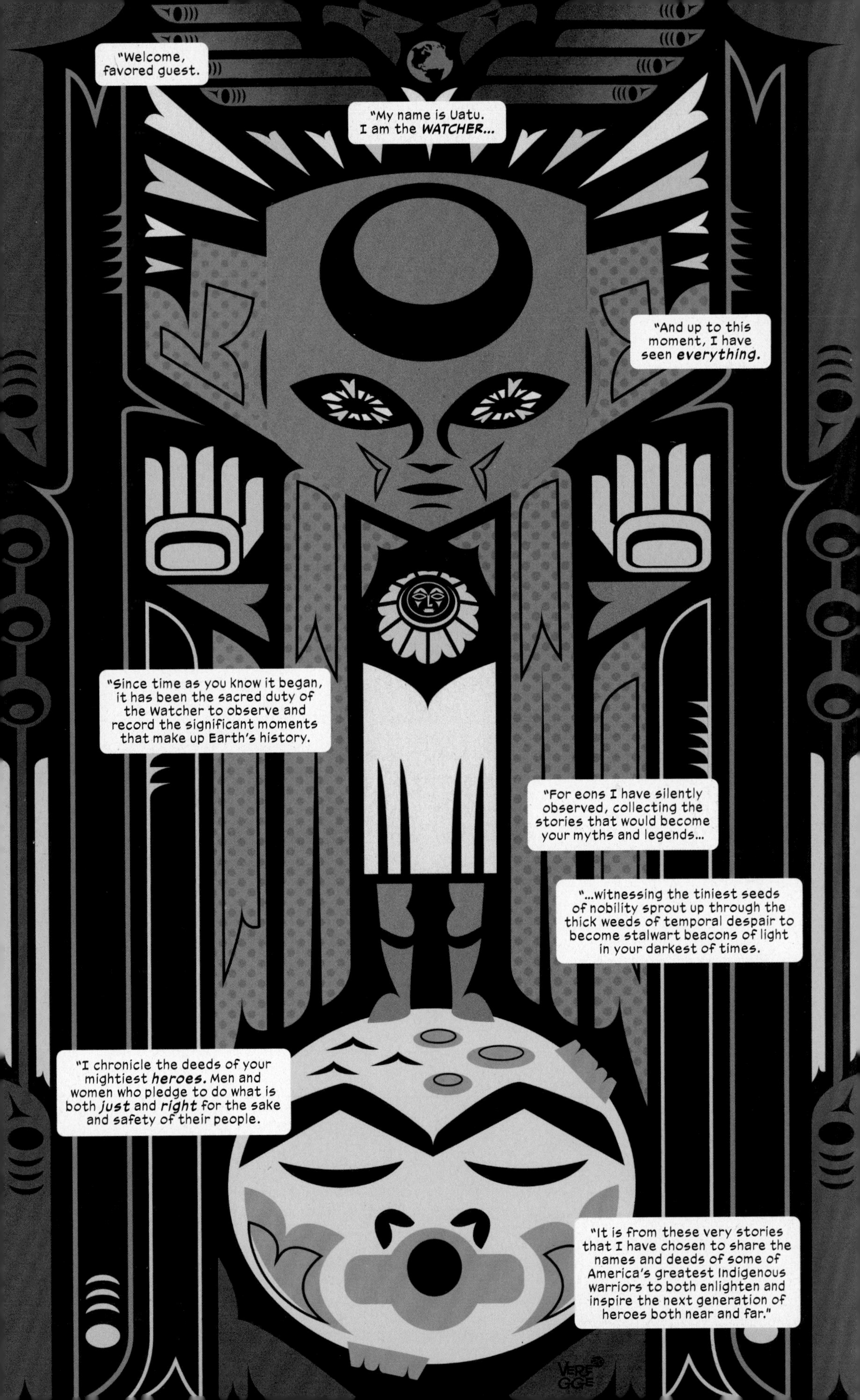
"Welcome, favored guest.
"My name is Uatu. I am the WATCHER...
"And up to this moment, I have seen everything.
"Since time as you know it began, it has been the sacred duty of the Watcher to observe and record the significant moments that make up Earth's history.
"For eons I have silently observed, collecting the stories that would become your myths and legends...
"...witnessing the tiniest seeds of nobility sprout up through the thick weeds of temporal despair to become stalwart beacons of light in your darkest of times.
"I chronicle the deeds of your mightiest heroes. Men and women who pledge to do what is both just and right for the sake and safety of their people.
"It is from these very stories that I have chosen to share the names and deeds of some of America's greatest Indigenous warriors to both enlighten and inspire the next generation of heroes both near and far."
VERAGGE

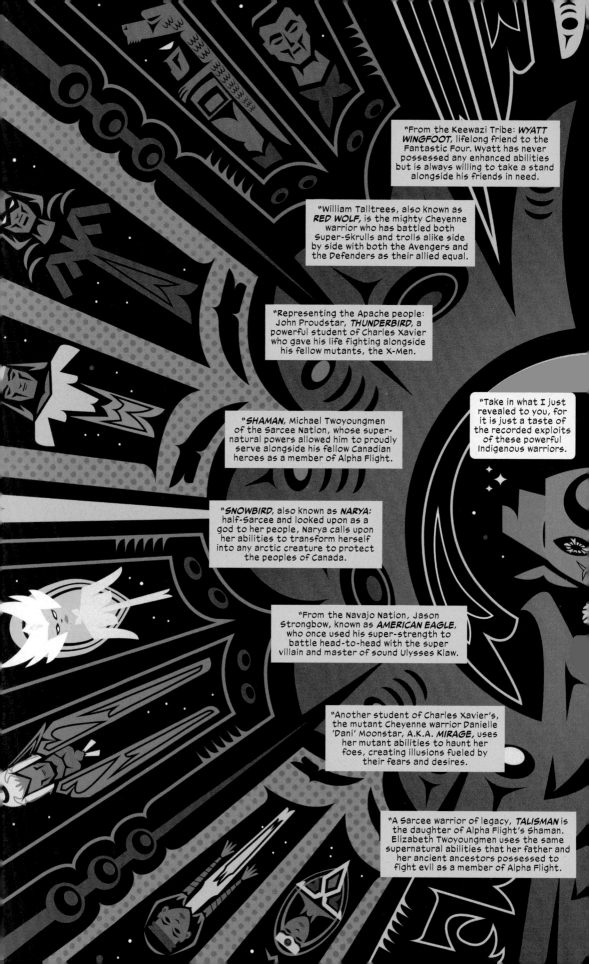

"From the Keewazi Tribe: *WYATT WINGFOOT*, lifelong friend to the Fantastic Four. Wyatt has never possessed any enhanced abilities but is always willing to take a stand alongside his friends in need.

"William Talltrees, also known as *RED WOLF*, is the mighty Cheyenne warrior who has battled both Super-Skrulls and trolls alike side by side with both the Avengers and the Defenders as their allied equal.

"Representing the Apache people: John Proudstar, *THUNDERBIRD*, a powerful student of Charles Xavier who gave his life fighting alongside his fellow mutants, the X-Men.

"*SHAMAN*, Michael Twoyoungmen of the Sarcee Nation, whose super-natural powers allowed him to proudly serve alongside his fellow Canadian heroes as a member of Alpha Flight.

"Take in what I just revealed to you, for it is just a taste of the recorded exploits of these powerful Indigenous warriors.

"*SNOWBIRD*, also known as *NARYA*: half-Sarcee and looked upon as a god to her people, Narya calls upon her abilities to transform herself into any arctic creature to protect the peoples of Canada.

"From the Navajo Nation, Jason Strongbow, known as *AMERICAN EAGLE*, who once used his super-strength to battle head-to-head with the super villain and master of sound Ulysses Klaw.

"Another student of Charles Xavier's, the mutant Cheyenne warrior Danielle 'Dani' Moonstar, A.K.A. *MIRAGE*, uses her mutant abilities to haunt her foes, creating illusions fueled by their fears and desires.

"A Sarcee warrior of legacy, *TALISMAN* is the daughter of Alpha Flight's Shaman. Elizabeth Twoyoungmen uses the same supernatural abilities that her father and her ancient ancestors possessed to fight evil as a member of Alpha Flight.

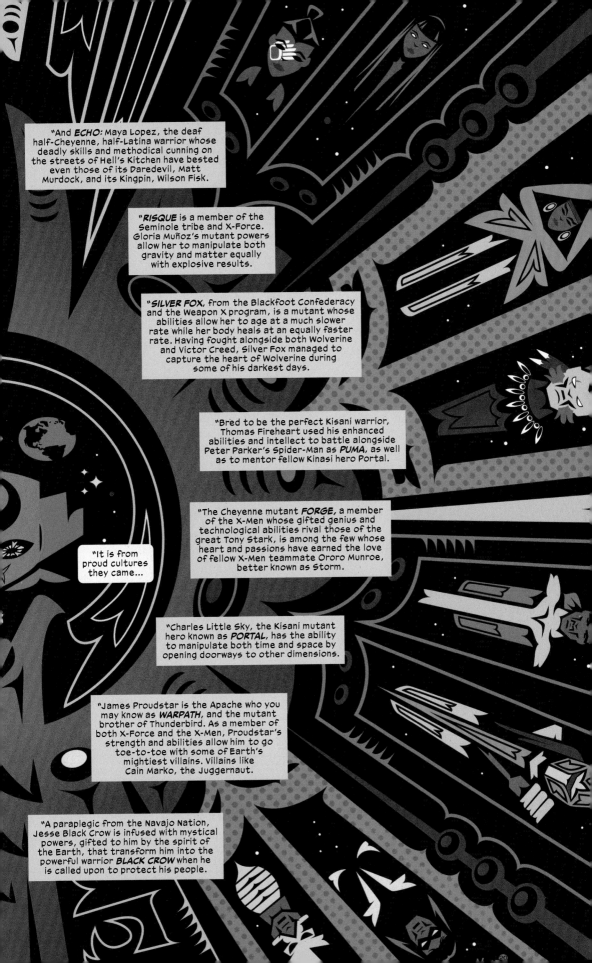

"And *ECHO:* Maya Lopez, the deaf half-Cheyenne, half-Latina warrior whose deadly skills and methodical cunning on the streets of Hell's Kitchen have bested even those of its Daredevil, Matt Murdock, and its Kingpin, Wilson Fisk.

"*RISQUE* is a member of the Seminole tribe and X-Force. Gloria Muñoz's mutant powers allow her to manipulate both gravity and matter equally with explosive results.

"*SILVER FOX*, from the Blackfoot Confederacy and the Weapon X program, is a mutant whose abilities allow her to age at a much slower rate while her body heals at an equally faster rate. Having fought alongside both Wolverine and Victor Creed, Silver Fox managed to capture the heart of Wolverine during some of his darkest days.

"Bred to be the perfect Kisani warrior, Thomas Fireheart used his enhanced abilities and intellect to battle alongside Peter Parker's Spider-Man as *PUMA*, as well as to mentor fellow Kinasi hero Portal.

"The Cheyenne mutant *FORGE,* a member of the X-Men whose gifted genius and technological abilities rival those of the great Tony Stark, is among the few whose heart and passions have earned the love of fellow X-Men teammate Ororo Munroe, better known as Storm.

"It is from proud cultures they came...

"Charles Little Sky, the Kisani mutant hero known as *PORTAL*, has the ability to manipulate both time and space by opening doorways to other dimensions.

"James Proudstar is the Apache who you may know as *WARPATH*, and the mutant brother of Thunderbird. As a member of both X-Force and the X-Men, Proudstar's strength and abilities allow him to go toe-to-toe with some of Earth's mightiest villains. Villains like Cain Marko, the Juggernaut.

"A paraplegic from the Navajo Nation, Jesse Black Crow is infused with mystical powers, gifted to him by the spirit of the Earth, that transform him into the powerful warrior *BLACK CROW* when he is called upon to protect his people.

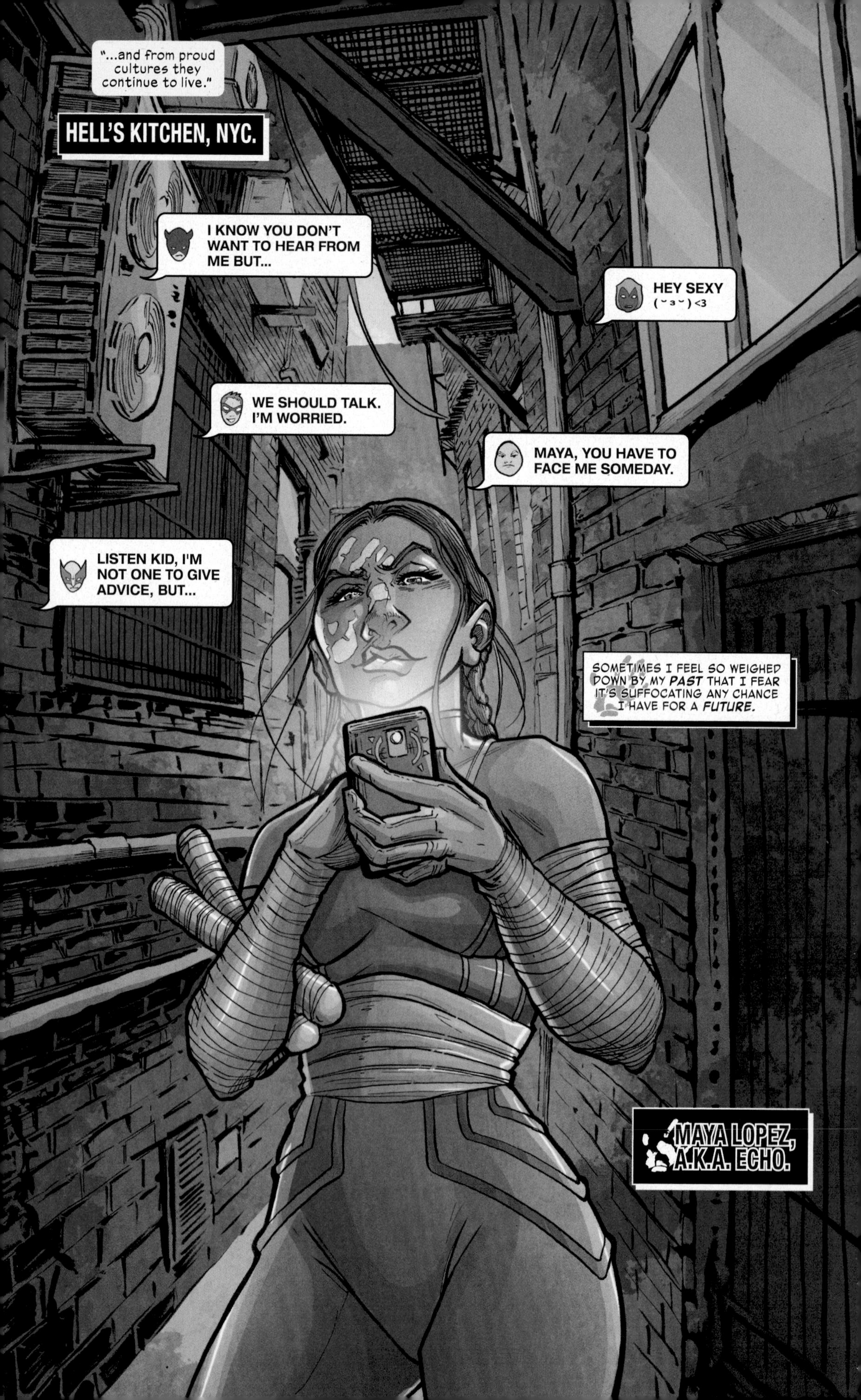
"...and from proud cultures they continue to live."
HELL'S KITCHEN, NYC.
I KNOW YOU DON'T WANT TO HEAR FROM ME BUT...
HEY SEXY (˘³˘) <3
WE SHOULD TALK. I'M WORRIED.
MAYA, YOU HAVE TO FACE ME SOMEDAY.
LISTEN KID, I'M NOT ONE TO GIVE ADVICE, BUT...
SOMETIMES I FEEL SO WEIGHED DOWN BY MY PAST THAT I FEAR IT'S SUFFOCATING ANY CHANCE I HAVE FOR A FUTURE.
MAYA LOPEZ, A.K.A. ECHO.

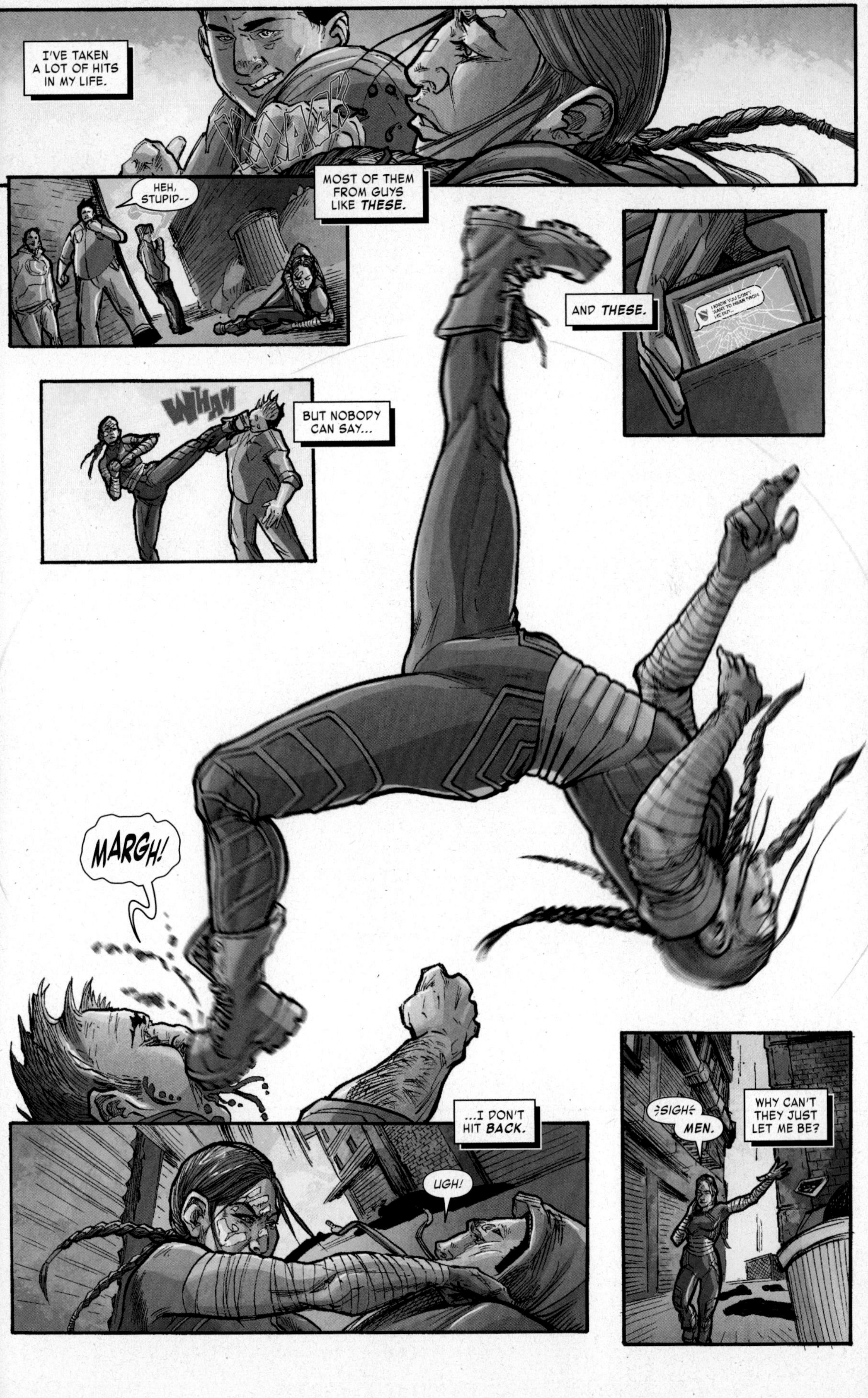
I'VE TAKEN A LOT OF HITS IN MY LIFE.
HEH, STUPID--
MOST OF THEM FROM GUYS LIKE THESE.
AND THESE.
I KNOW YOU DON'T WANT TO HEAR FROM ME BUT...
WHAM
BUT NOBODY CAN SAY...
MARGH!
...I DON'T HIT BACK.
UGH!
SIGH MEN.
WHY CAN'T THEY JUST LET ME BE?

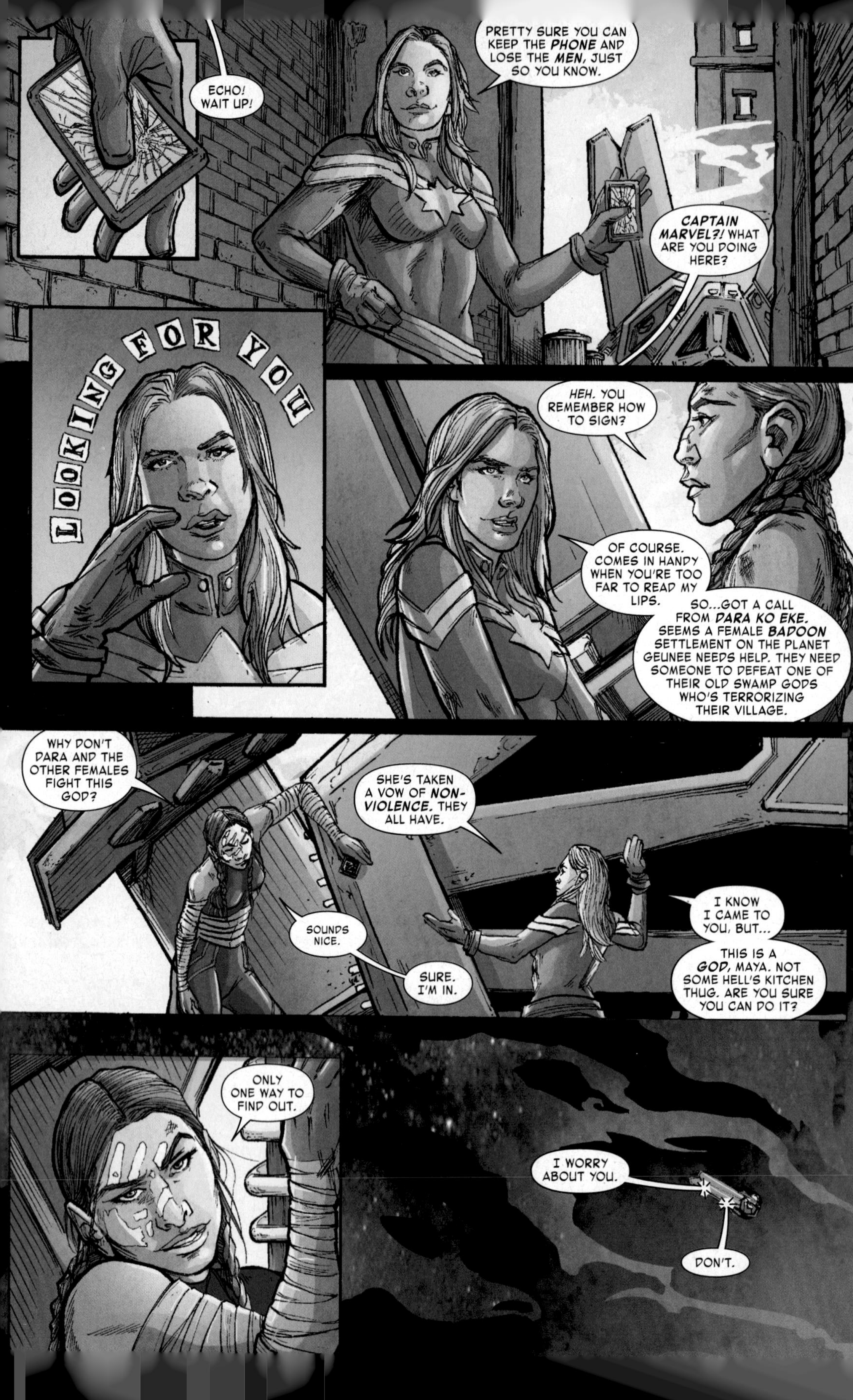
ECHO! WAIT UP!
PRETTY SURE YOU CAN KEEP THE PHONE AND LOSE THE MEN, JUST SO YOU KNOW.
CAPTAIN MARVEL?! WHAT ARE YOU DOING HERE?
LOOKING FOR YOU
HEH. YOU REMEMBER HOW TO SIGN?
OF COURSE. COMES IN HANDY WHEN YOU'RE TOO FAR TO READ MY LIPS.
SO...GOT A CALL FROM DARA KO EKE. SEEMS A FEMALE BADOON SETTLEMENT ON THE PLANET GEUNEE NEEDS HELP. THEY NEED SOMEONE TO DEFEAT ONE OF THEIR OLD SWAMP GODS WHO'S TERRORIZING THEIR VILLAGE.
WHY DON'T DARA AND THE OTHER FEMALES FIGHT THIS GOD?
SHE'S TAKEN A VOW OF NON-VIOLENCE. THEY ALL HAVE.
SOUNDS NICE.
SURE. I'M IN.
I KNOW I CAME TO YOU, BUT...
THIS IS A GOD, MAYA. NOT SOME HELL'S KITCHEN THUG. ARE YOU SURE YOU CAN DO IT?
ONLY ONE WAY TO FIND OUT.
I WORRY ABOUT YOU.
DON'T.

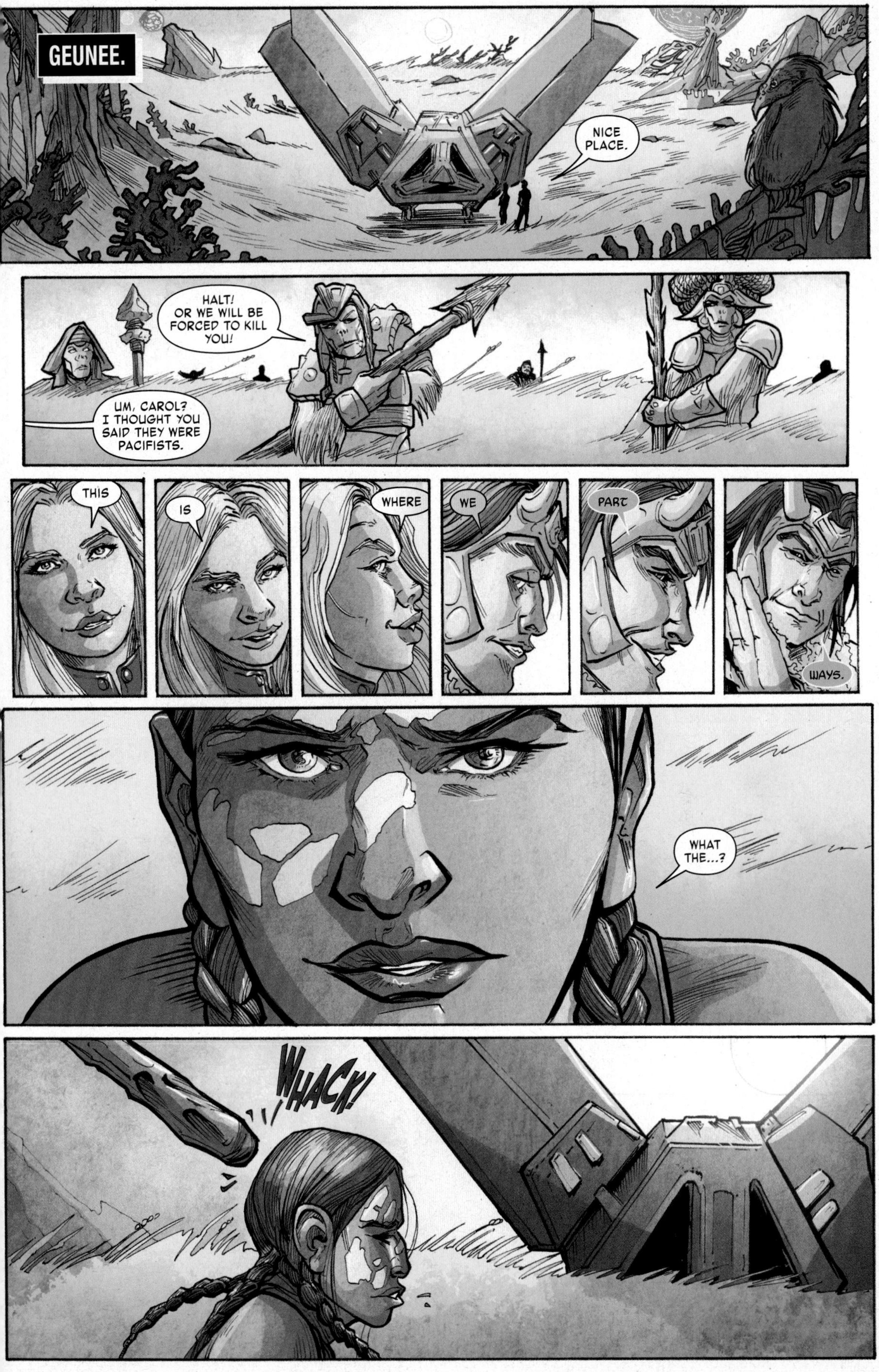
GEUNEE.
NICE PLACE.
HALT! OR WE WILL BE FORCED TO KILL YOU!
UM, CAROL? I THOUGHT YOU SAID THEY WERE PACIFISTS.
THIS
IS
WHERE
WE
PART
WAYS.
WHAT THE...?
WHACK!

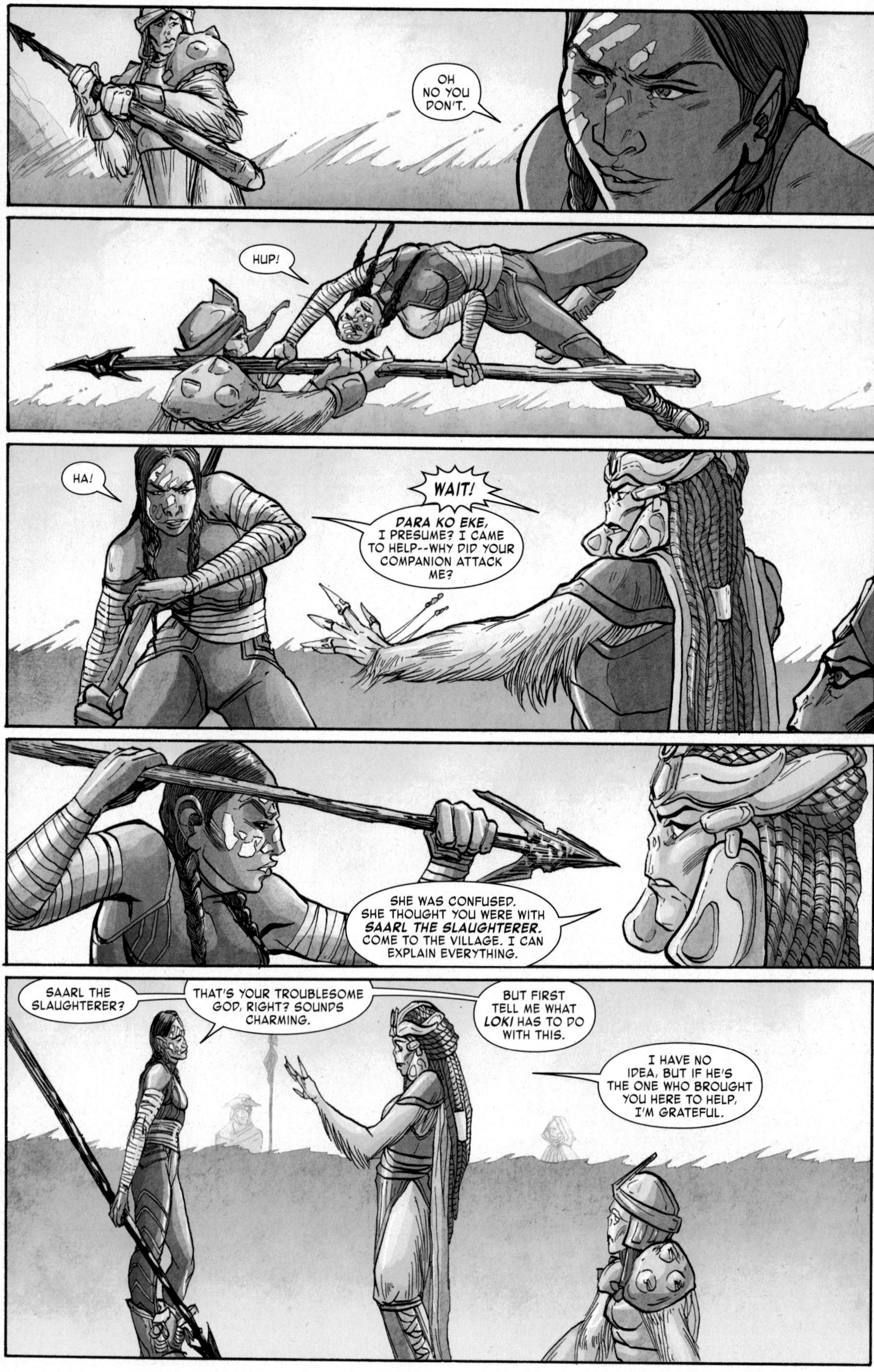
OH NO YOU DON'T.
HUP!
HA!
WAIT!
DARA KO EKE, I PRESUME? I CAME TO HELP--WHY DID YOUR COMPANION ATTACK ME?
SHE WAS CONFUSED. SHE THOUGHT YOU WERE WITH SAARL THE SLAUGHTERER. COME TO THE VILLAGE. I CAN EXPLAIN EVERYTHING.
SAARL THE SLAUGHTERER?
THAT'S YOUR TROUBLESOME GOD, RIGHT? SOUNDS CHARMING.
BUT FIRST TELL ME WHAT LOKI HAS TO DO WITH THIS.
I HAVE NO IDEA, BUT IF HE'S THE ONE WHO BROUGHT YOU HERE TO HELP, I'M GRATEFUL.

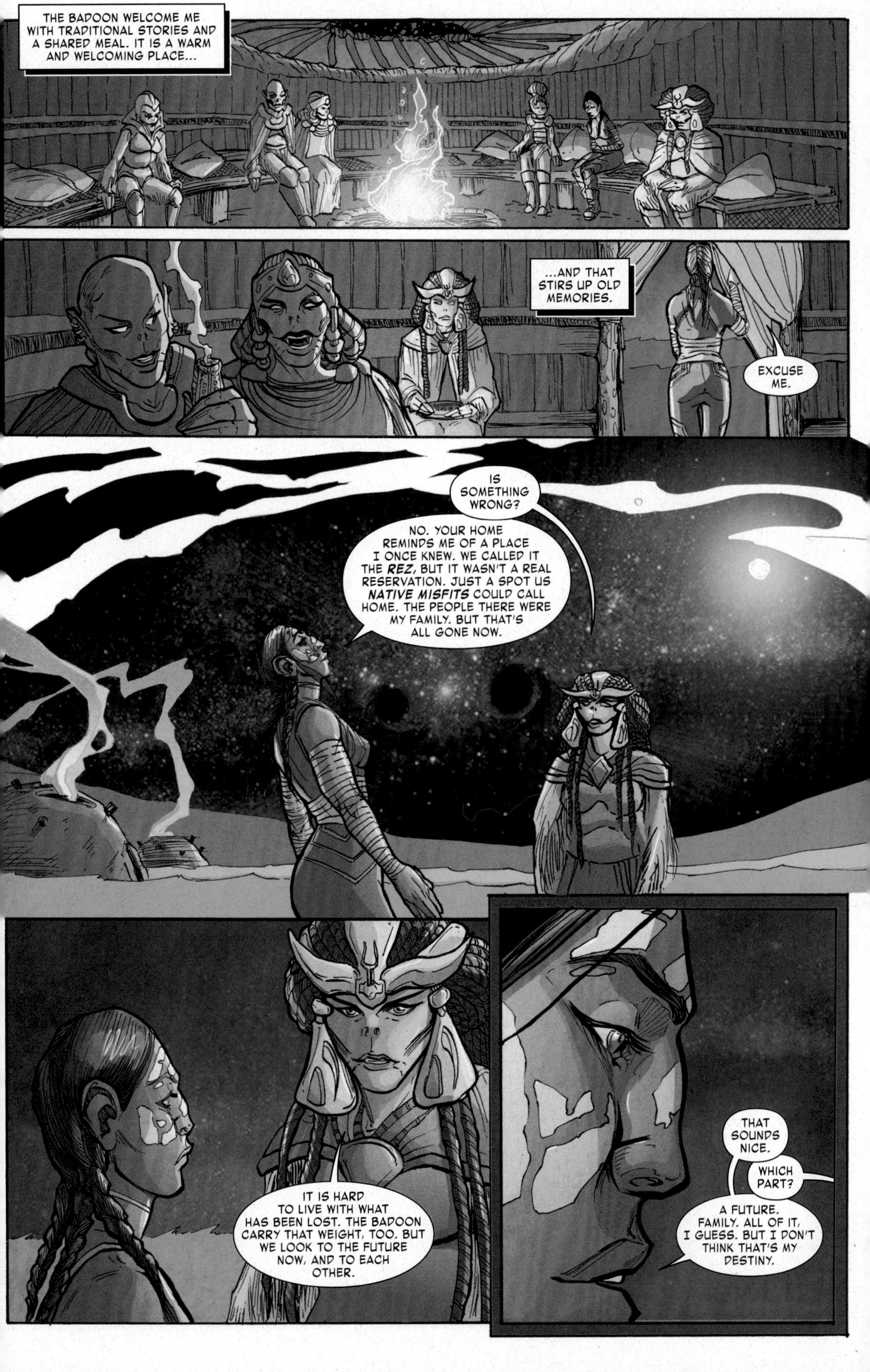
THE BADOON WELCOME ME WITH TRADITIONAL STORIES AND A SHARED MEAL. IT IS A WARM AND WELCOMING PLACE...
...AND THAT STIRS UP OLD MEMORIES.
EXCUSE ME.
IS SOMETHING WRONG?
NO. YOUR HOME REMINDS ME OF A PLACE I ONCE KNEW. WE CALLED IT THE REZ, BUT IT WASN'T A REAL RESERVATION. JUST A SPOT US NATIVE MISFITS COULD CALL HOME. THE PEOPLE THERE WERE MY FAMILY. BUT THAT'S ALL GONE NOW.
IT IS HARD TO LIVE WITH WHAT HAS BEEN LOST. THE BADOON CARRY THAT WEIGHT, TOO. BUT WE LOOK TO THE FUTURE NOW, AND TO EACH OTHER.
THAT SOUNDS NICE.
WHICH PART?
A FUTURE. FAMILY. ALL OF IT, I GUESS. BUT I DON'T THINK THAT'S MY DESTINY.

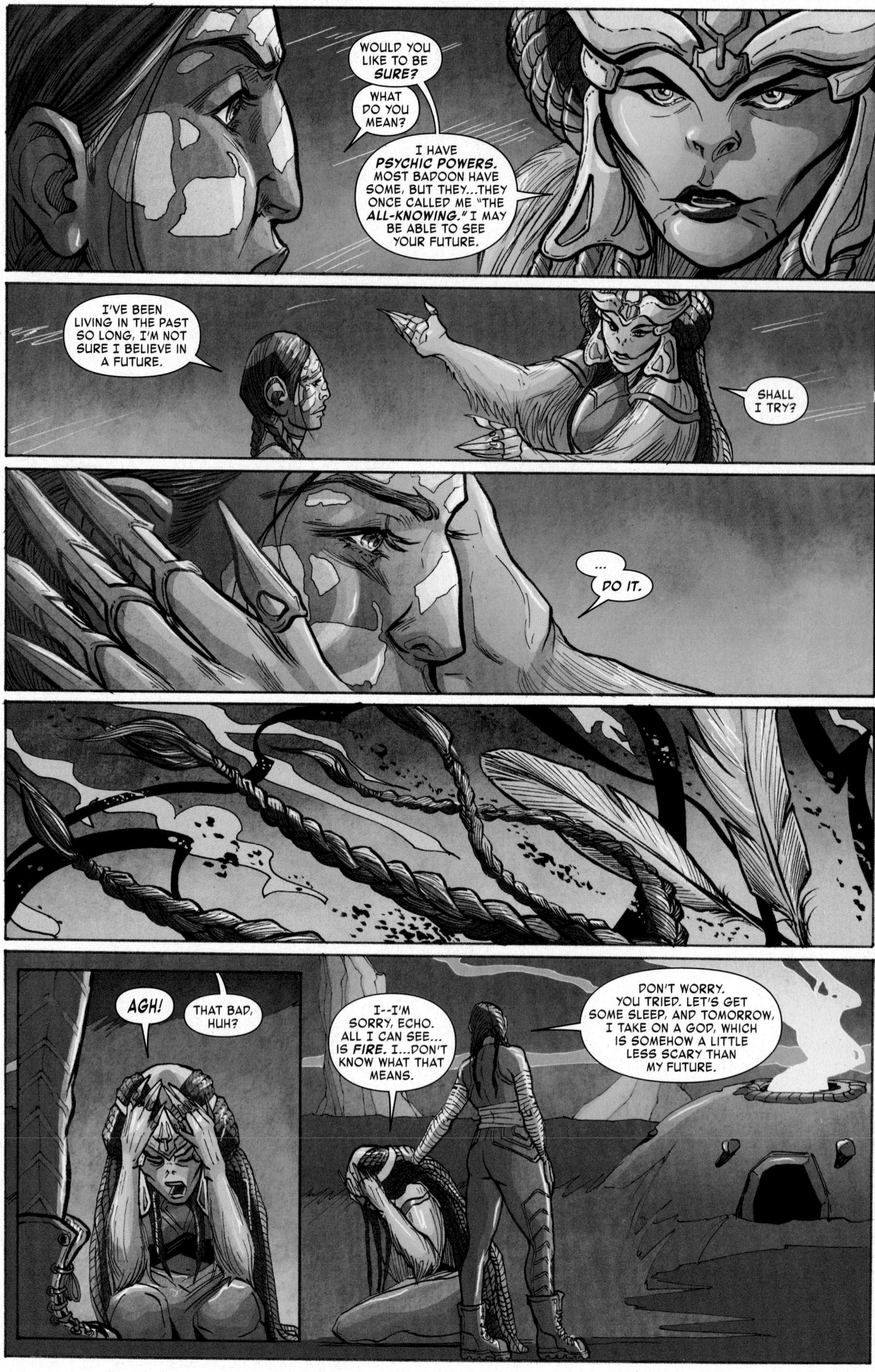

WOULD YOU LIKE TO BE *SURE?*
WHAT DO YOU MEAN?
I HAVE *PSYCHIC POWERS.* MOST BADOON HAVE SOME, BUT THEY...THEY ONCE CALLED ME "THE *ALL-KNOWING.*" I MAY BE ABLE TO SEE YOUR FUTURE.
I'VE BEEN LIVING IN THE PAST SO LONG, I'M NOT SURE I BELIEVE IN A FUTURE.
SHALL I TRY?
...
DO IT.
AGH!
THAT BAD, HUH?
I--I'M SORRY, ECHO. ALL I CAN SEE... IS *FIRE.* I...DON'T KNOW WHAT THAT MEANS.
DON'T WORRY. YOU TRIED. LET'S GET SOME SLEEP, AND TOMORROW, I TAKE ON A GOD, WHICH IS SOMEHOW A LITTLE LESS SCARY THAN MY FUTURE.

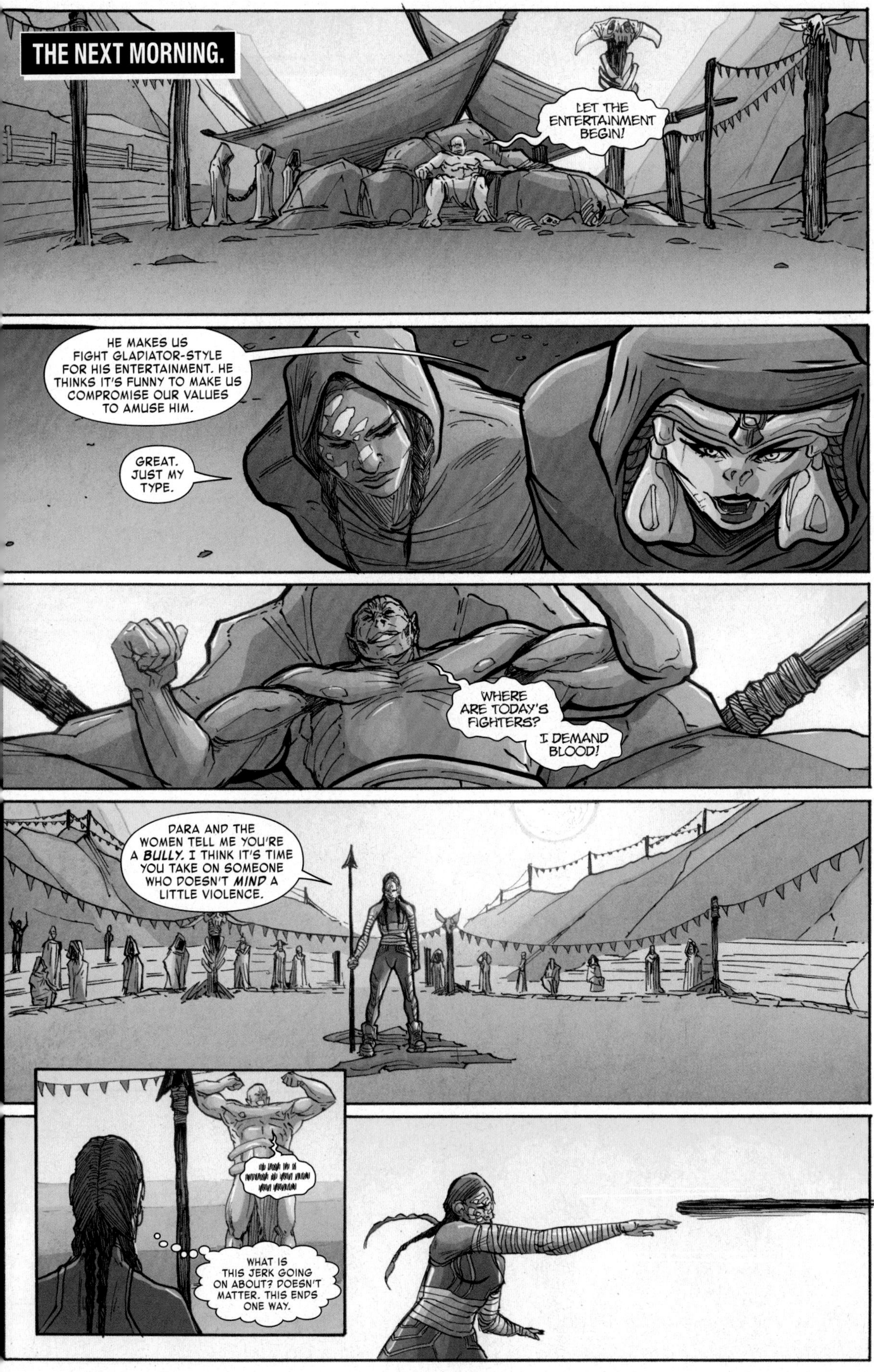
THE NEXT MORNING.
LET THE ENTERTAINMENT BEGIN!
HE MAKES US FIGHT GLADIATOR-STYLE FOR HIS ENTERTAINMENT. HE THINKS IT'S FUNNY TO MAKE US COMPROMISE OUR VALUES TO AMUSE HIM.
GREAT. JUST MY TYPE.
WHERE ARE TODAY'S FIGHTERS?
I DEMAND BLOOD!
DARA AND THE WOMEN TELL ME YOU'RE A BULLY. I THINK IT'S TIME YOU TAKE ON SOMEONE WHO DOESN'T MIND A LITTLE VIOLENCE.
WHAT IS THIS JERK GOING ON ABOUT? DOESN'T MATTER. THIS ENDS ONE WAY.

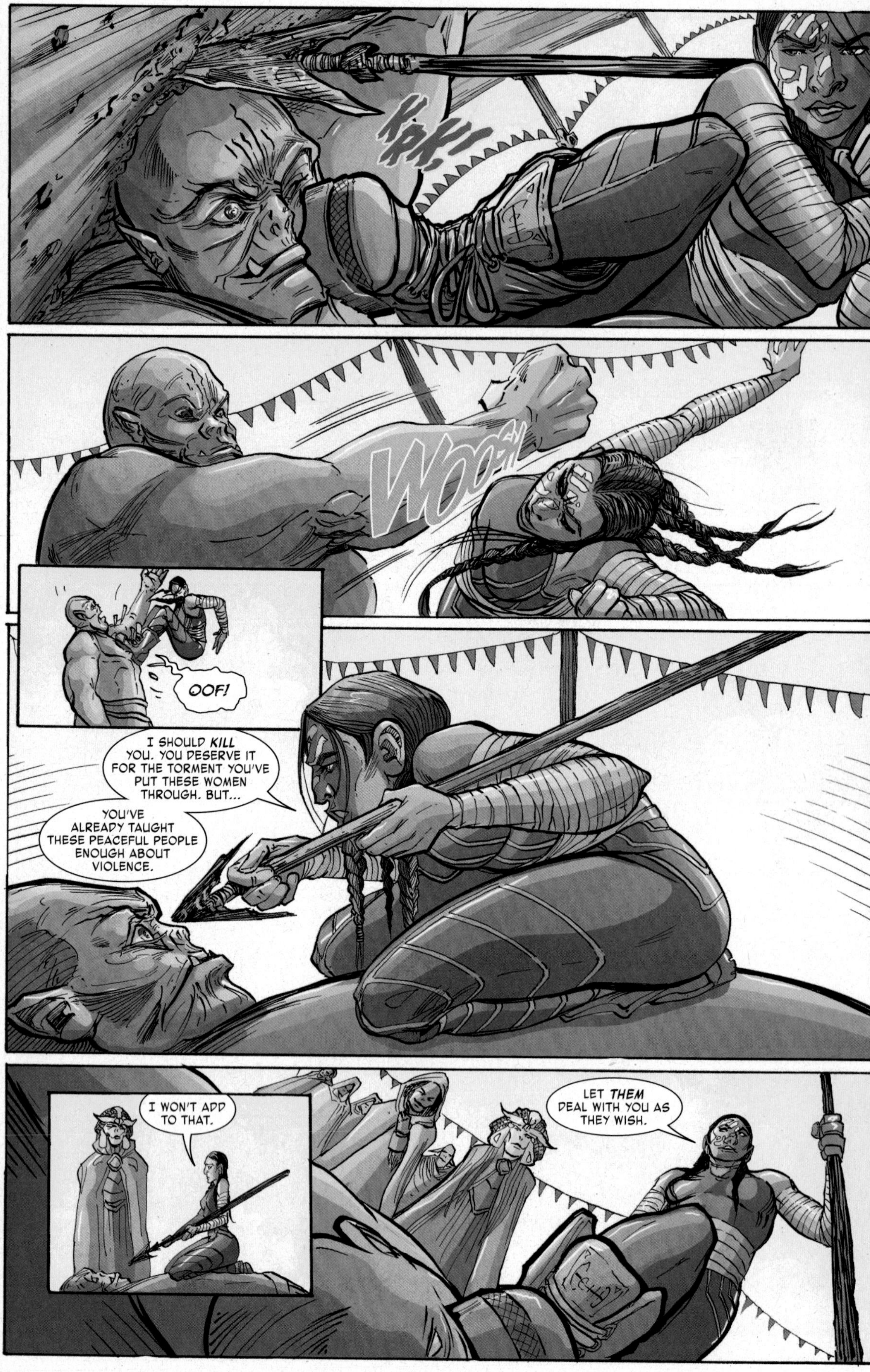
KRAK!!
WOOSH
OOF!
I SHOULD KILL YOU. YOU DESERVE IT FOR THE TORMENT YOU'VE PUT THESE WOMEN THROUGH. BUT...
YOU'VE ALREADY TAUGHT THESE PEACEFUL PEOPLE ENOUGH ABOUT VIOLENCE.
I WON'T ADD TO THAT.
LET THEM DEAL WITH YOU AS THEY WISH.

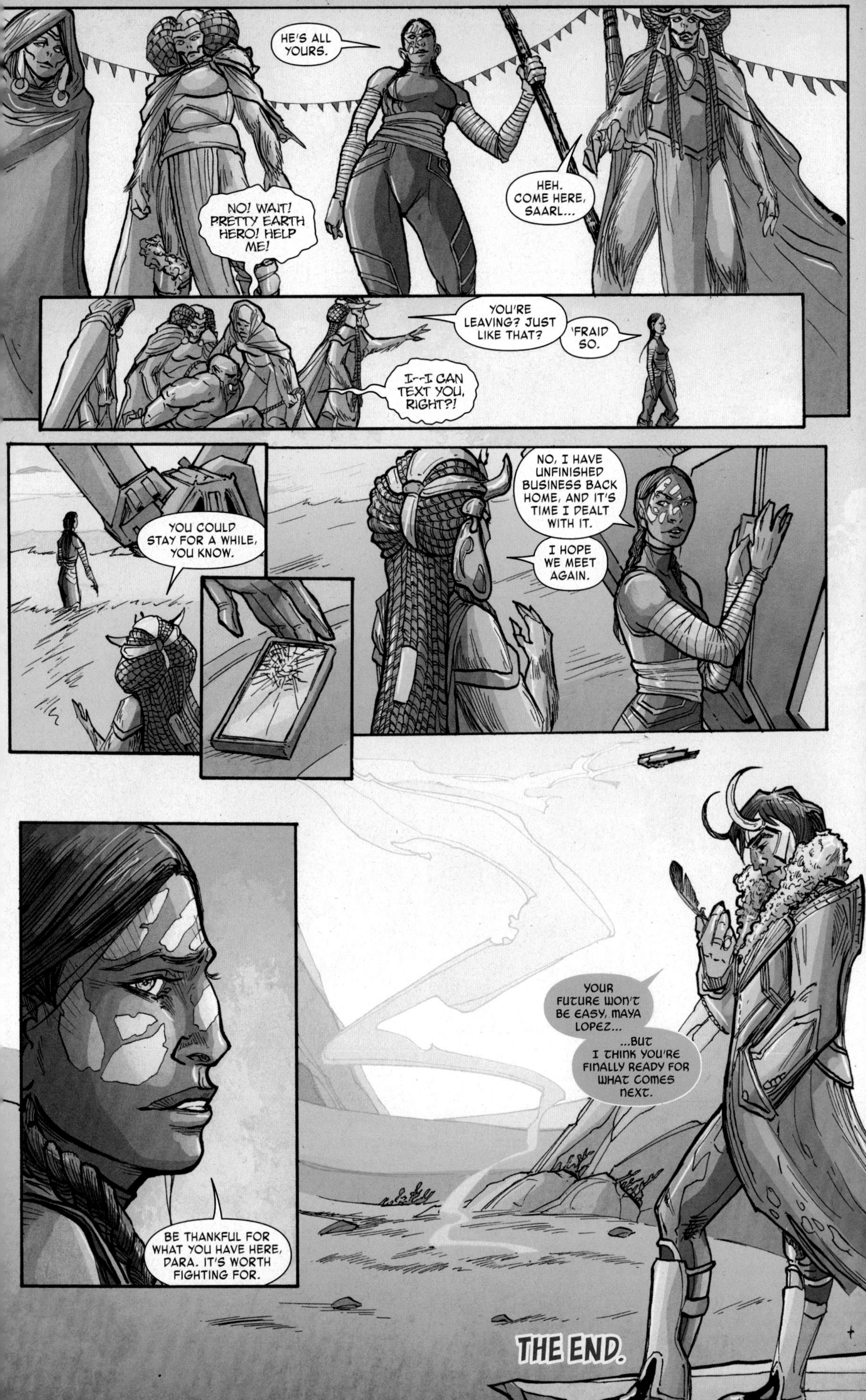
HE'S ALL YOURS.
NO! WAIT! PRETTY EARTH HERO! HELP ME!
HEH. COME HERE, SAARL...
YOU'RE LEAVING? JUST LIKE THAT?
'FRAID SO.
I--I CAN TEXT YOU, RIGHT?!
YOU COULD STAY FOR A WHILE, YOU KNOW.
NO, I HAVE UNFINISHED BUSINESS BACK HOME, AND IT'S TIME I DEALT WITH IT.
I HOPE WE MEET AGAIN.
BE THANKFUL FOR WHAT YOU HAVE HERE, DARA. IT'S WORTH FIGHTING FOR.
YOUR FUTURE WON'T BE EASY, MAYA LOPEZ...
...BUT I THINK YOU'RE FINALLY READY FOR WHAT COMES NEXT.
THE END.

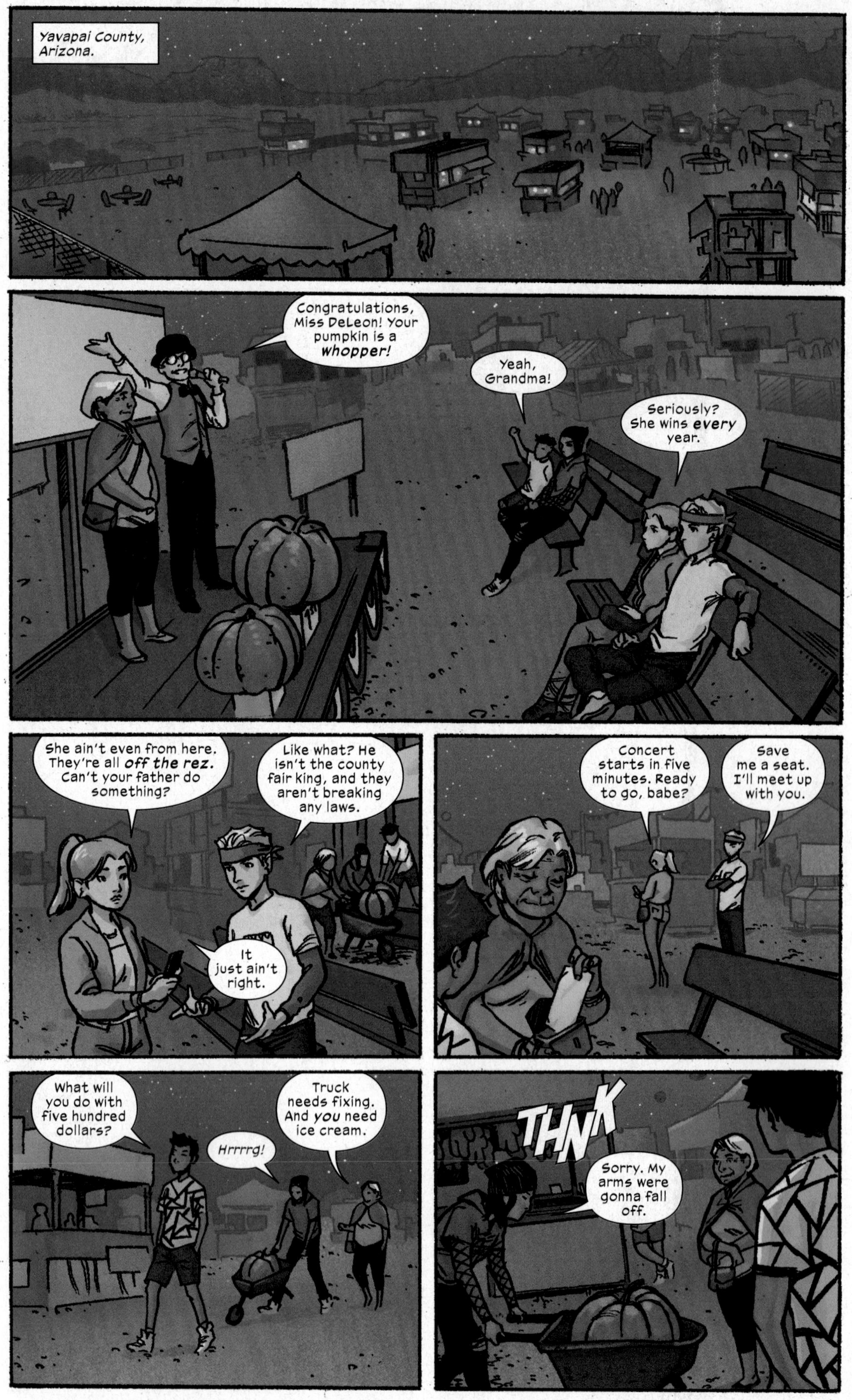
Yavapai County, Arizona.
Congratulations, Miss DeLeon! Your pumpkin is a whopper!
Yeah, Grandma!
Seriously? She wins every year.
She ain't even from here. They're all off the rez. Can't your father do something?
Like what? He isn't the county fair king, and they aren't breaking any laws.
It just ain't right.
Concert starts in five minutes. Ready to go, babe?
Save me a seat. I'll meet up with you.
What will you do with five hundred dollars?
Hrrrrg!
Truck needs fixing. And you need ice cream.
THNK
Sorry. My arms were gonna fall off.

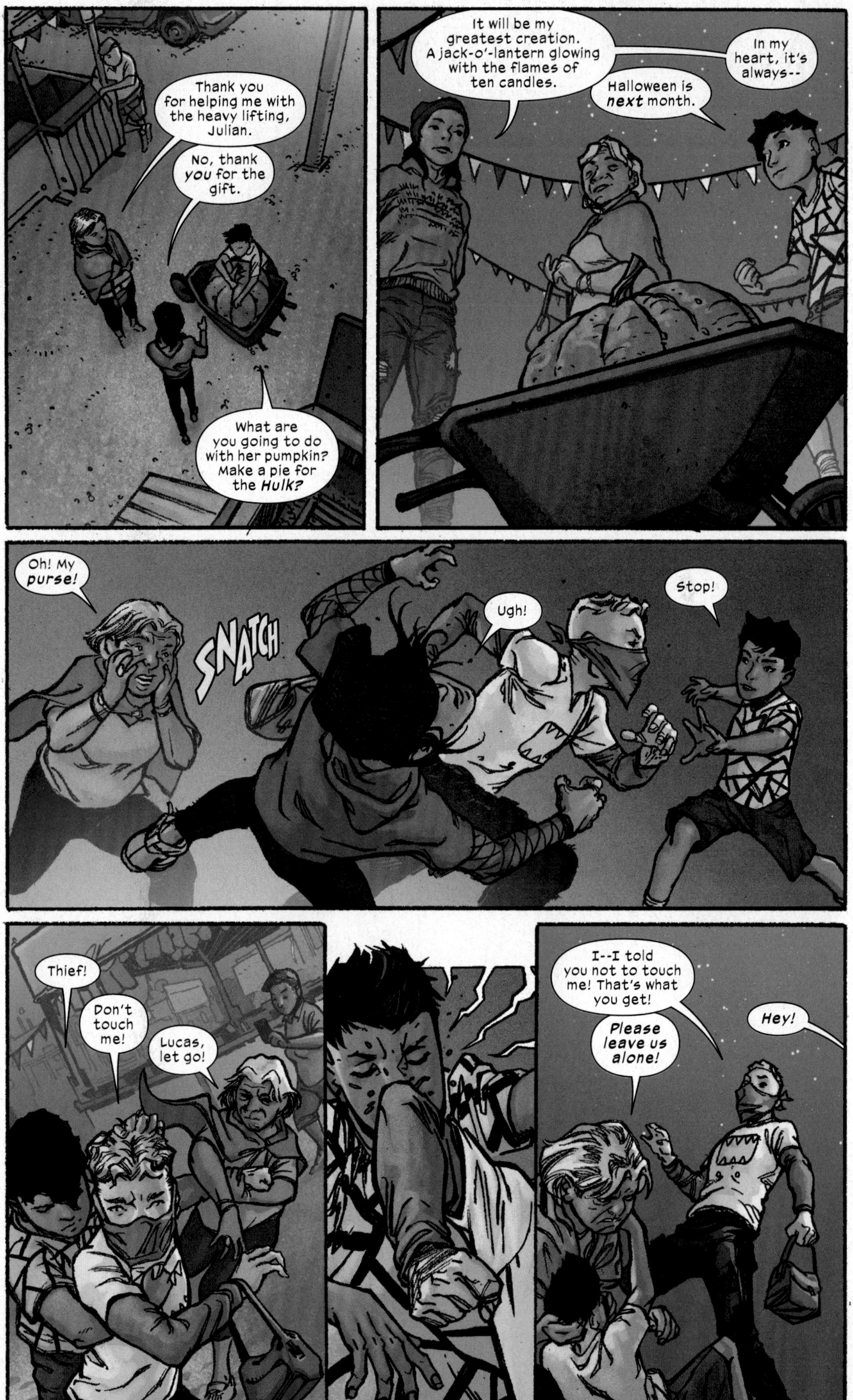
Thank you for helping me with the heavy lifting, Julian.
No, thank *you* for the gift.
What are you going to do with her pumpkin? Make a pie for the *Hulk?*
It will be my greatest creation. A jack-o'-lantern glowing with the flames of ten candles.
Halloween is *next* month.
In my heart, it's always--
Oh! My *purse!*
SNATCH
Ugh!
Stop!
Thief!
Don't touch me!
Lucas, let go!
I--I told you not to touch me! That's what you get!
Please leave us alone!
Hey!

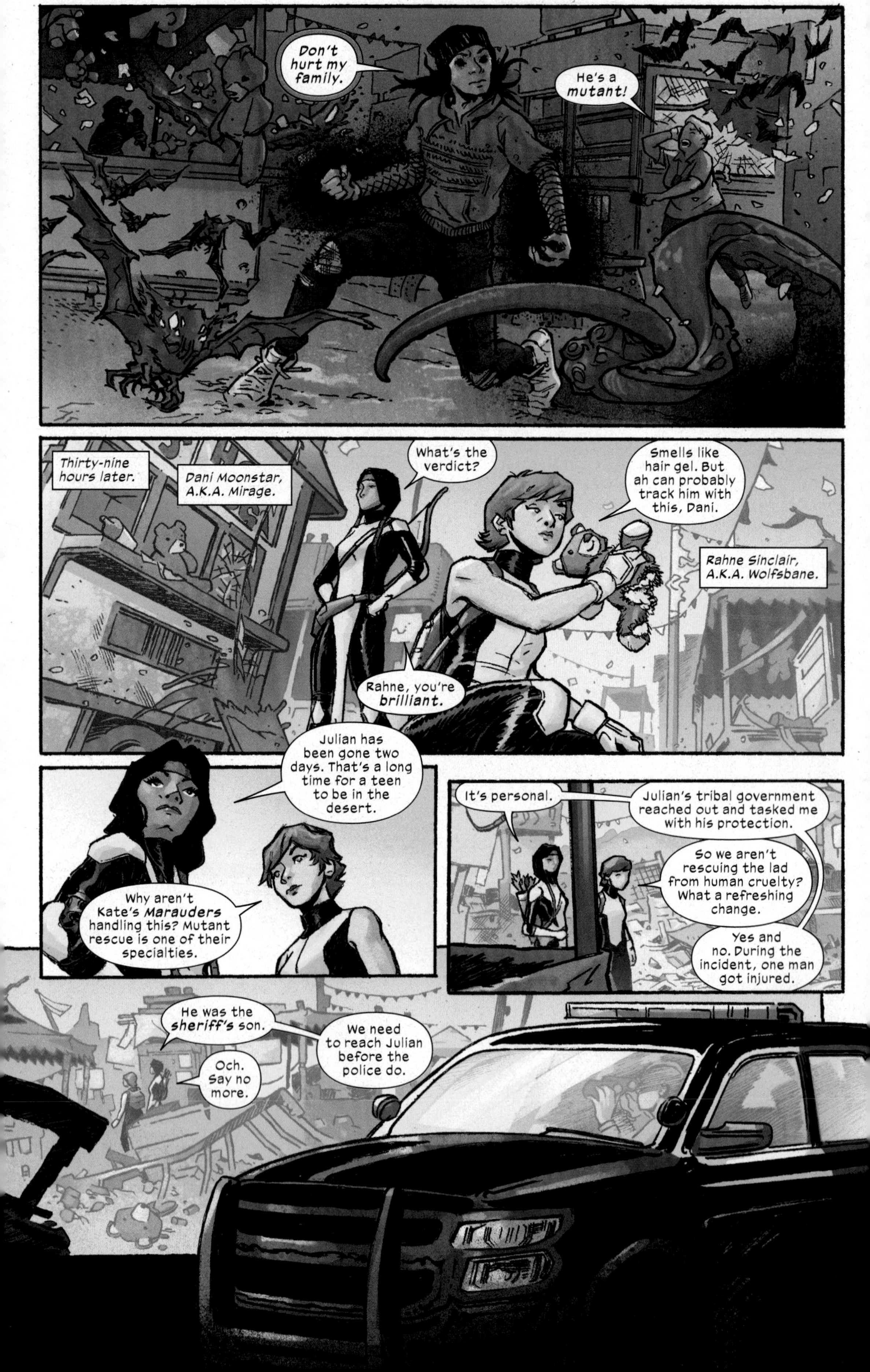

Don't hurt my family.
He's a mutant!
Thirty-nine hours later.
Dani Moonstar, A.K.A. Mirage.
What's the verdict?
Smells like hair gel. But ah can probably track him with this, Dani.
Rahne Sinclair, A.K.A. Wolfsbane.
Rahne, you're brilliant.
Julian has been gone two days. That's a long time for a teen to be in the desert.
Why aren't Kate's Marauders handling this? Mutant rescue is one of their specialties.
It's personal.
Julian's tribal government reached out and tasked me with his protection.
So we aren't rescuing the lad from human cruelty? What a refreshing change.
Yes and no. During the incident, one man got injured.
He was the sheriff's son.
Och. Say no more.
We need to reach Julian before the police do.

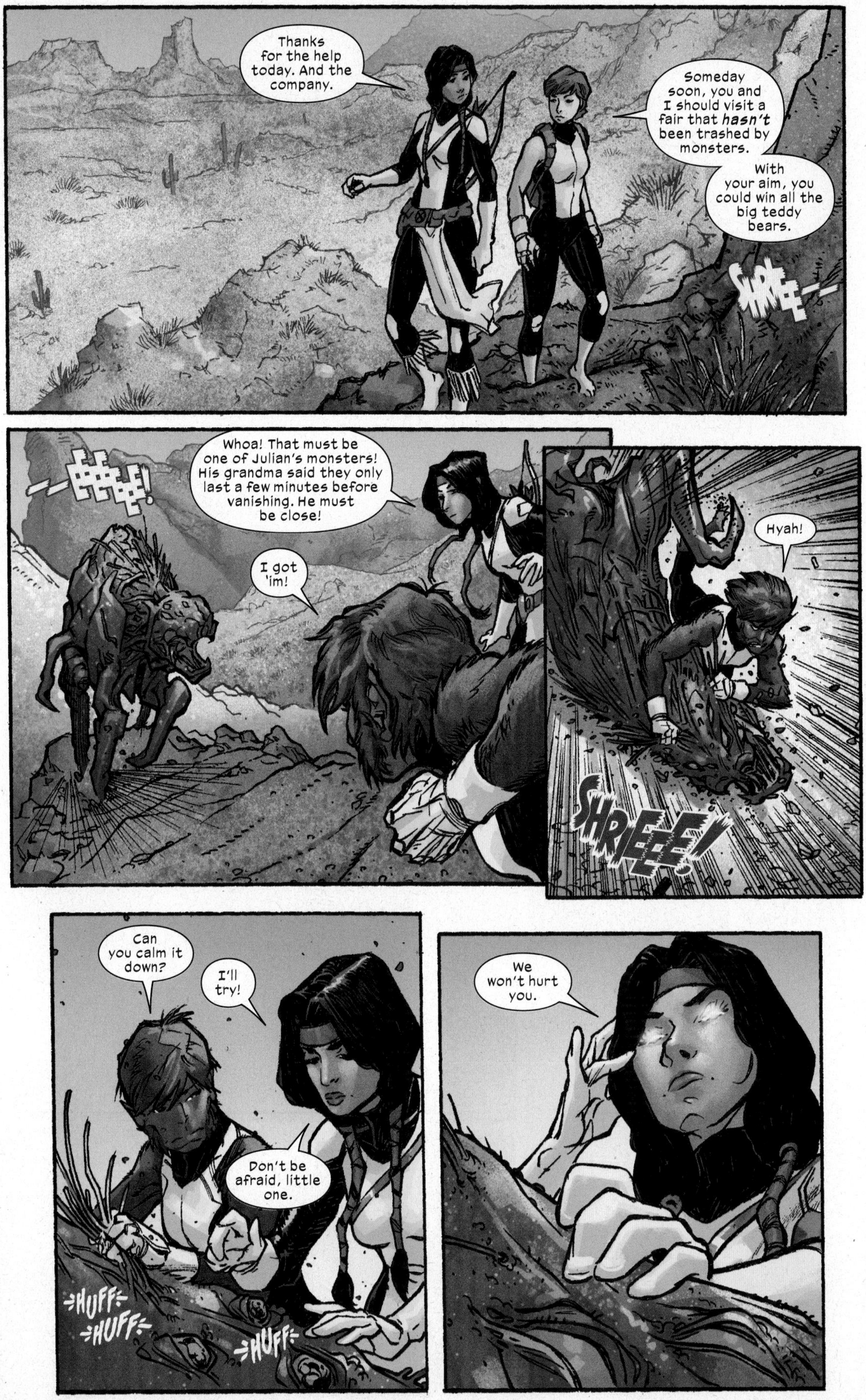
Thanks for the help today. And the company.
Someday soon, you and I should visit a fair that *hasn't* been trashed by monsters.
With your aim, you could win all the big teddy bears.
SHRIEE--
Whoa! That must be one of Julian's monsters! His grandma said they only last a few minutes before vanishing. He must be close!
I got 'im!
Hyah!
SHRIEEE!
Can you calm it down?
I'll try!
Don't be afraid, little one.
HUFF
HUFF
HUFF
We won't hurt you.

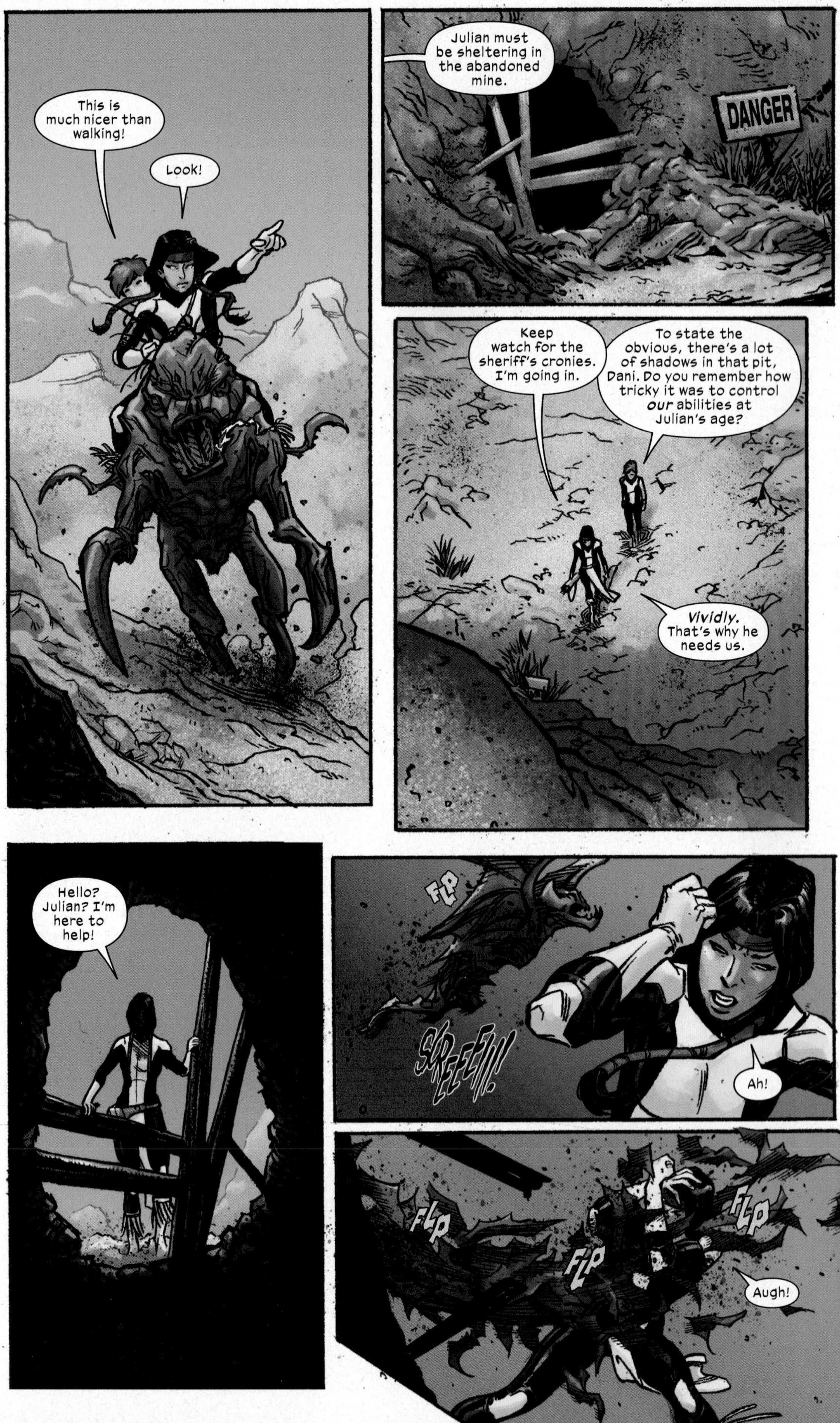
This is much nicer than walking!
Look!
Julian must be sheltering in the abandoned mine.
DANGER
Keep watch for the sheriff's cronies. I'm going in.
To state the obvious, there's a lot of shadows in that pit, Dani. Do you remember how tricky it was to control our abilities at Julian's age?
Vividly. That's why he needs us.
Hello? Julian? I'm here to help!
FLP
SCREEEE!!!
Ah!
FLP
FLP
FLP
Augh!

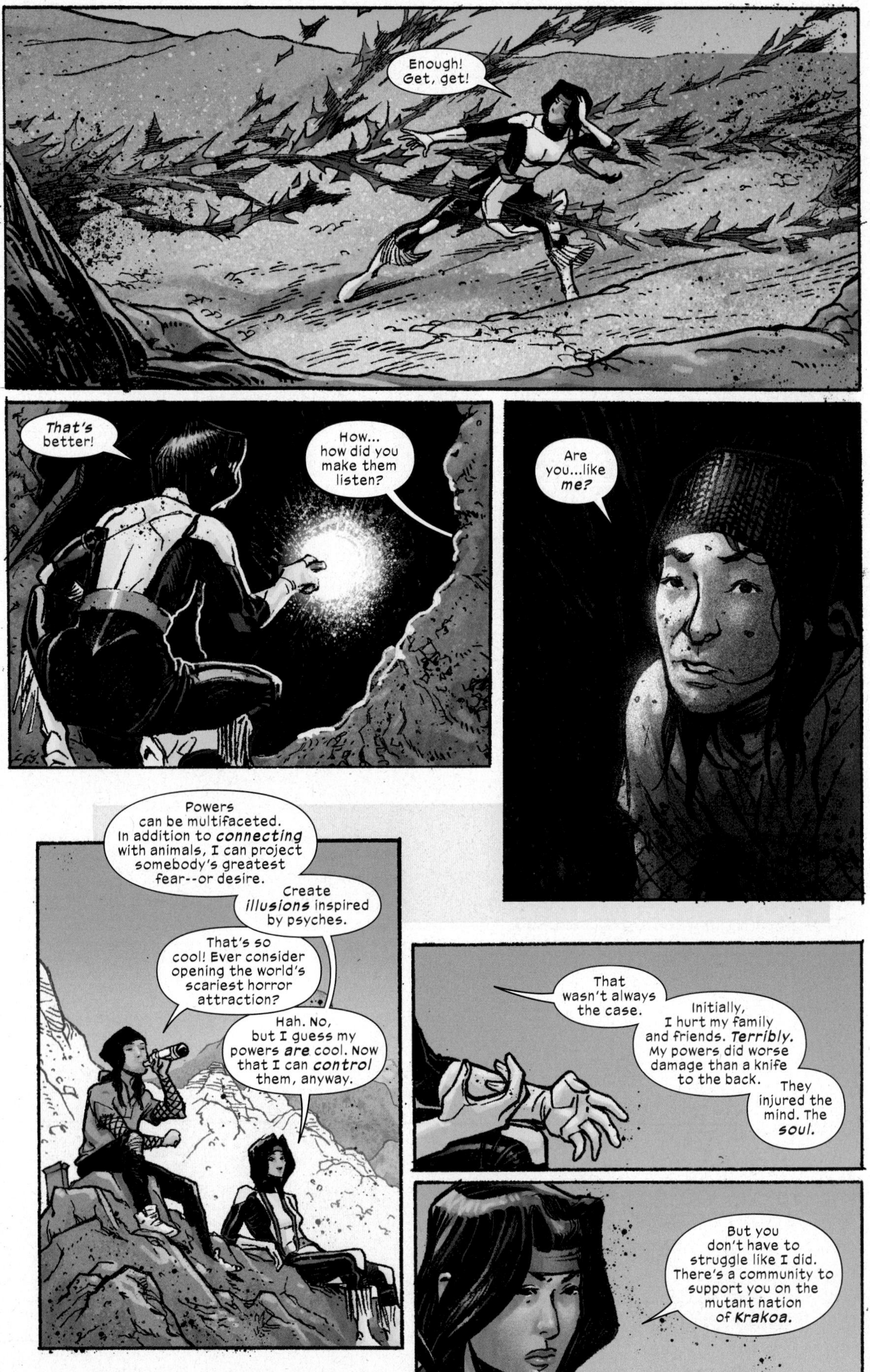

Enough! Get, get!
That's better!
How... how did you make them listen?
Are you...like me?
Powers can be multifaceted. In addition to connecting with animals, I can project somebody's greatest fear--or desire.
Create illusions inspired by psyches.
That's so cool! Ever consider opening the world's scariest horror attraction?
Hah. No, but I guess my powers are cool. Now that I can control them, anyway.
That wasn't always the case.
Initially, I hurt my family and friends. Terribly. My powers did worse damage than a knife to the back.
They injured the mind. The soul.
But you don't have to struggle like I did. There's a community to support you on the mutant nation of Krakoa.

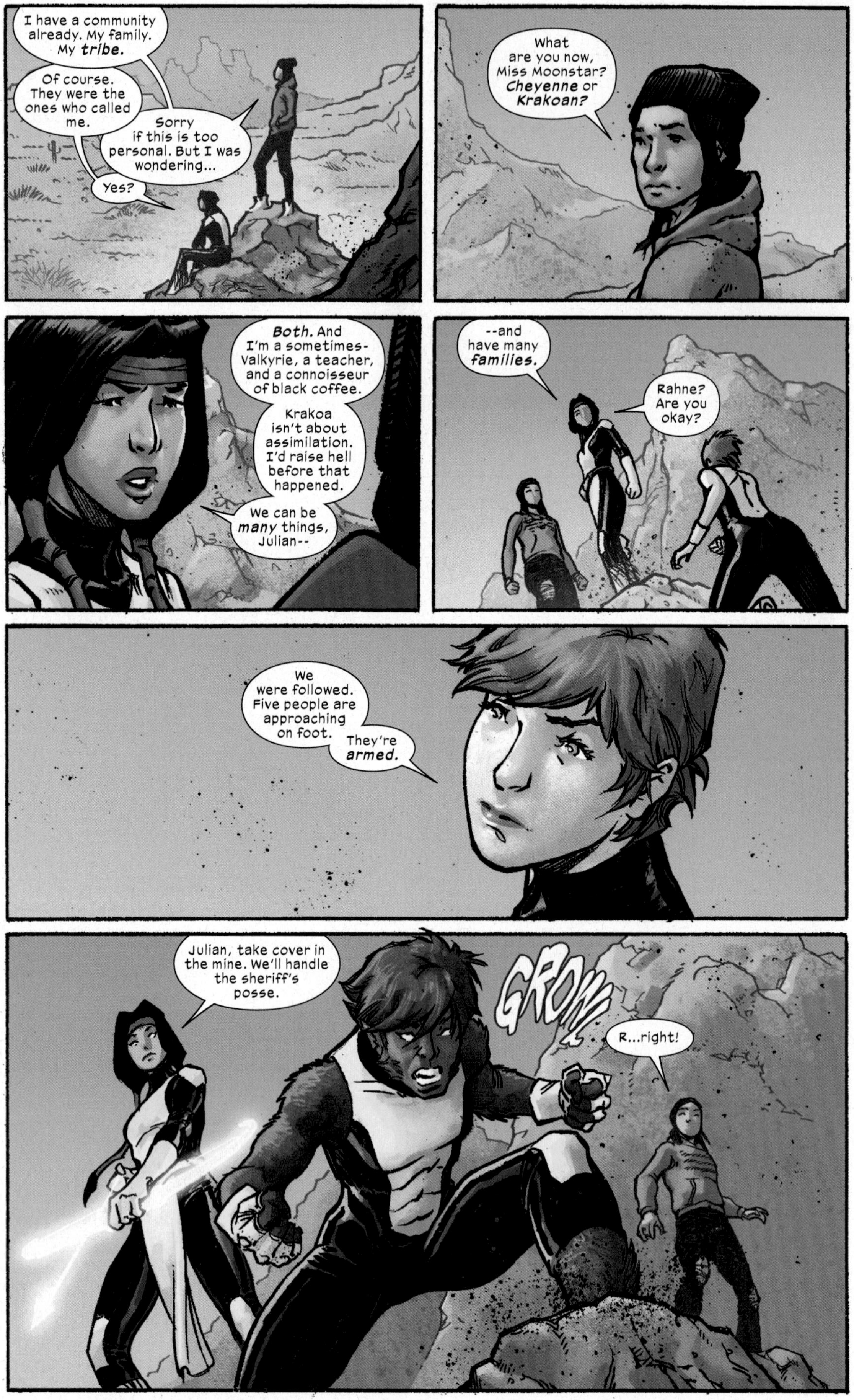
I have a community already. My family. My tribe.
Of course. They were the ones who called me.
Sorry if this is too personal. But I was wondering...
Yes?
What are you now, Miss Moonstar? Cheyenne or Krakoan?
Both. And I'm a sometimes-Valkyrie, a teacher, and a connoisseur of black coffee.
Krakoa isn't about assimilation. I'd raise hell before that happened.
We can be many things, Julian--
--and have many families.
Rahne? Are you okay?
We were followed. Five people are approaching on foot.
They're armed.
Julian, take cover in the mine. We'll handle the sheriff's posse.
GROWL
R...right!

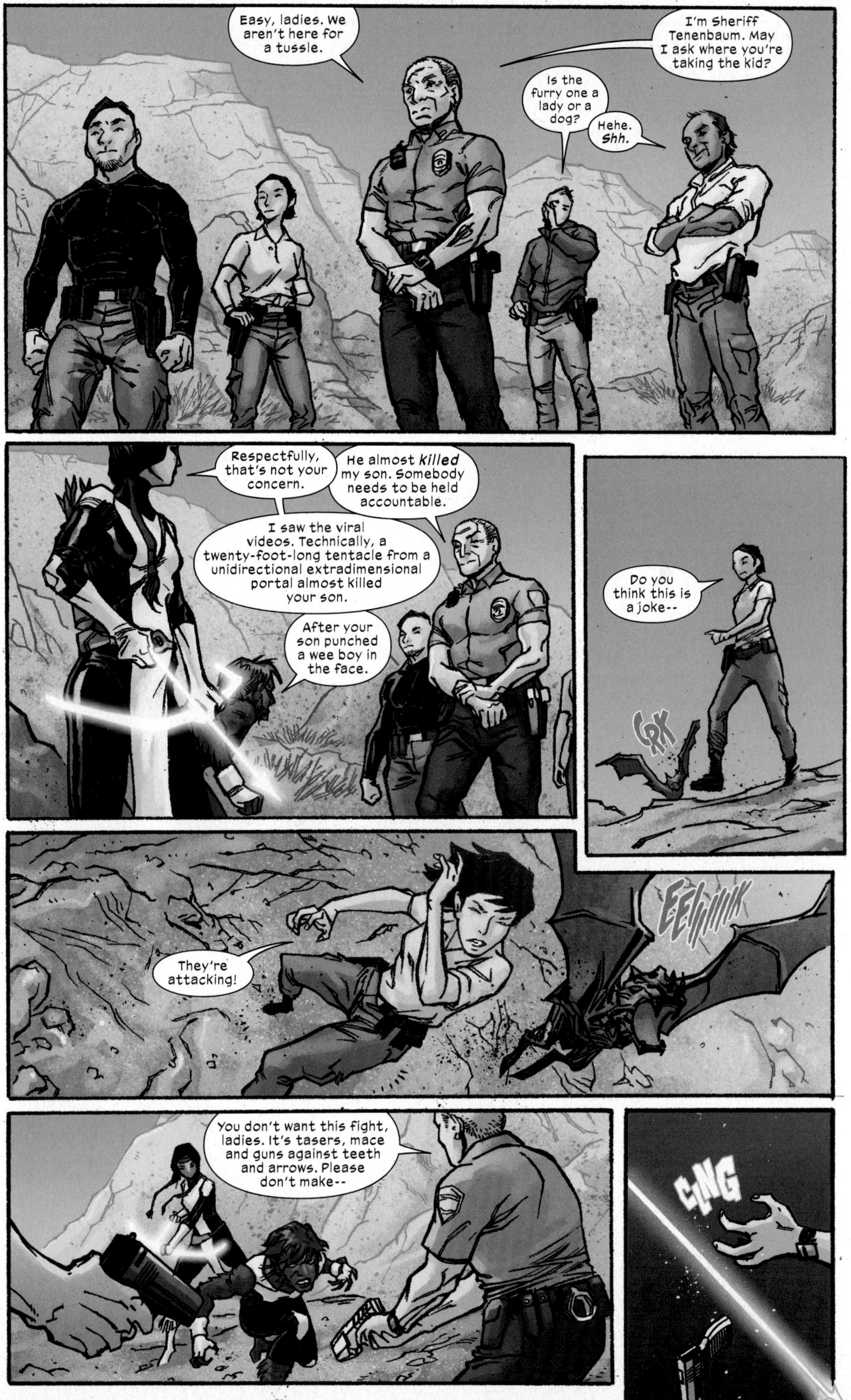
Easy, ladies. We aren't here for a tussle.
I'm Sheriff Tenenbaum. May I ask where you're taking the kid?
Is the furry one a lady or a dog?
Hehe. Shh.
Respectfully, that's not your concern.
He almost killed my son. Somebody needs to be held accountable.
I saw the viral videos. Technically, a twenty-foot-long tentacle from a unidirectional extradimensional portal almost killed your son.
After your son punched a wee boy in the face.
Do you think this is a joke--
CRK
EEIIIIIIK
They're attacking!
You don't want this fight, ladies. It's tasers, mace and guns against teeth and arrows. Please don't make--
CLNG

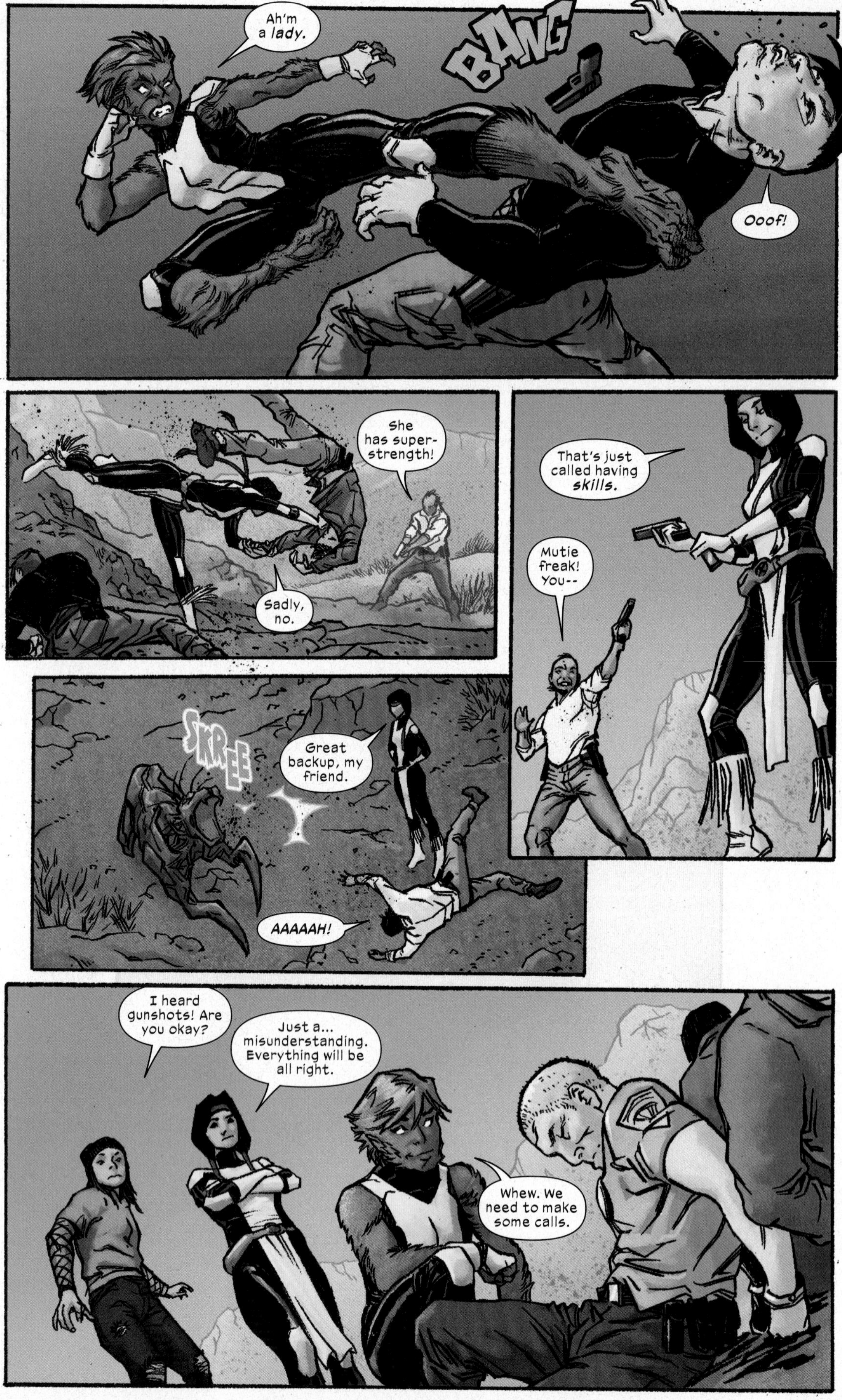
Ah'm a *lady.*
BANG
Ooof!
Sadly, no.
She has super-strength!
That's just called having *skills.*
Mutie freak! You--
SKREE
Great backup, my friend.
AAAAAH!
I heard gunshots! Are you okay?
Just a... misunderstanding. Everything will be all right.
Whew. We need to make some calls.

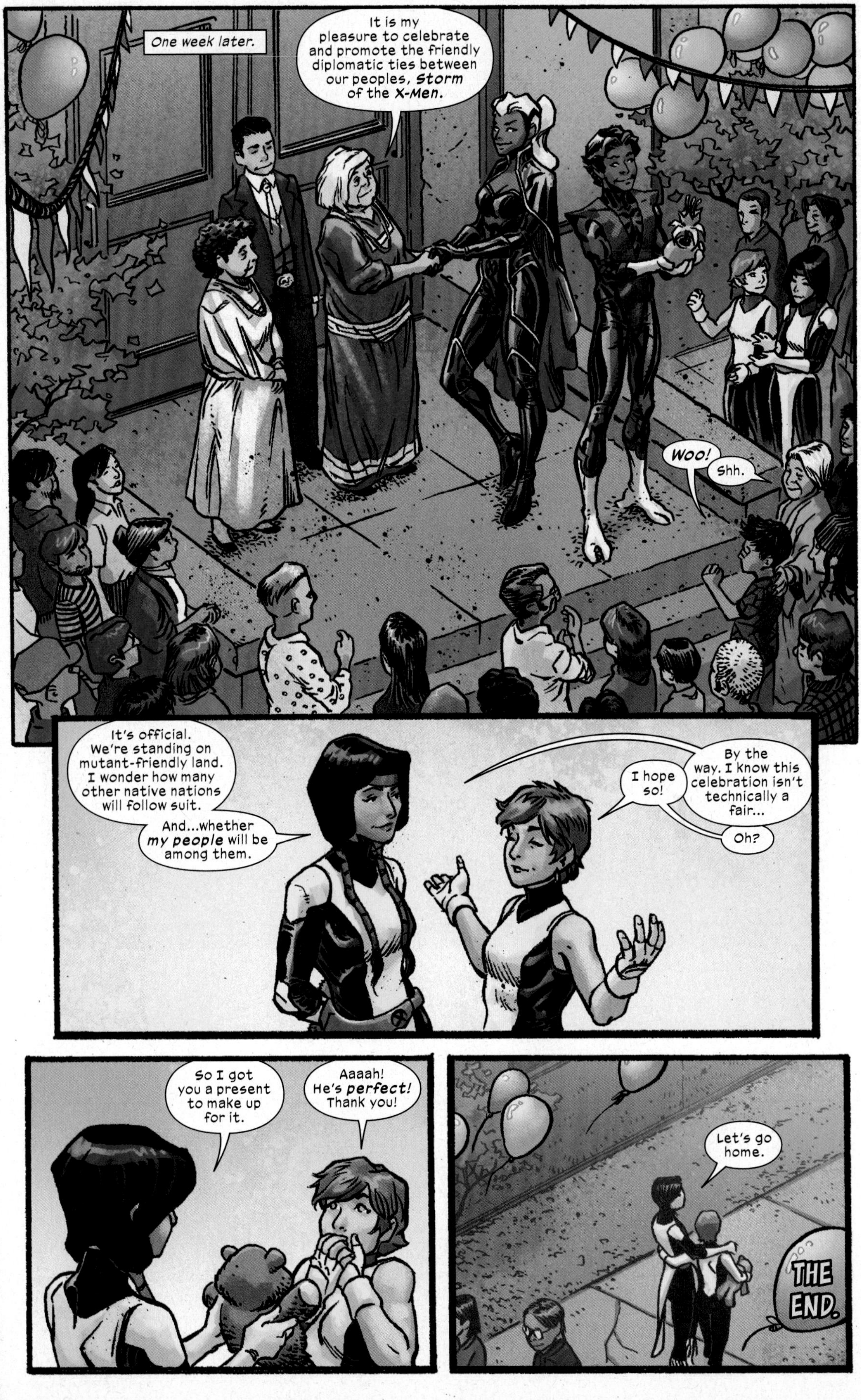
One week later.
It is my pleasure to celebrate and promote the friendly diplomatic ties between our peoples, Storm of the X-Men.
Woo!
Shh.
It's official. We're standing on mutant-friendly land. I wonder how many other native nations will follow suit.
And...whether my people will be among them.
I hope so!
By the way. I know this celebration isn't technically a fair...
Oh?
So I got you a present to make up for it.
Aaaah! He's perfect! Thank you!
Let's go home.
THE END.

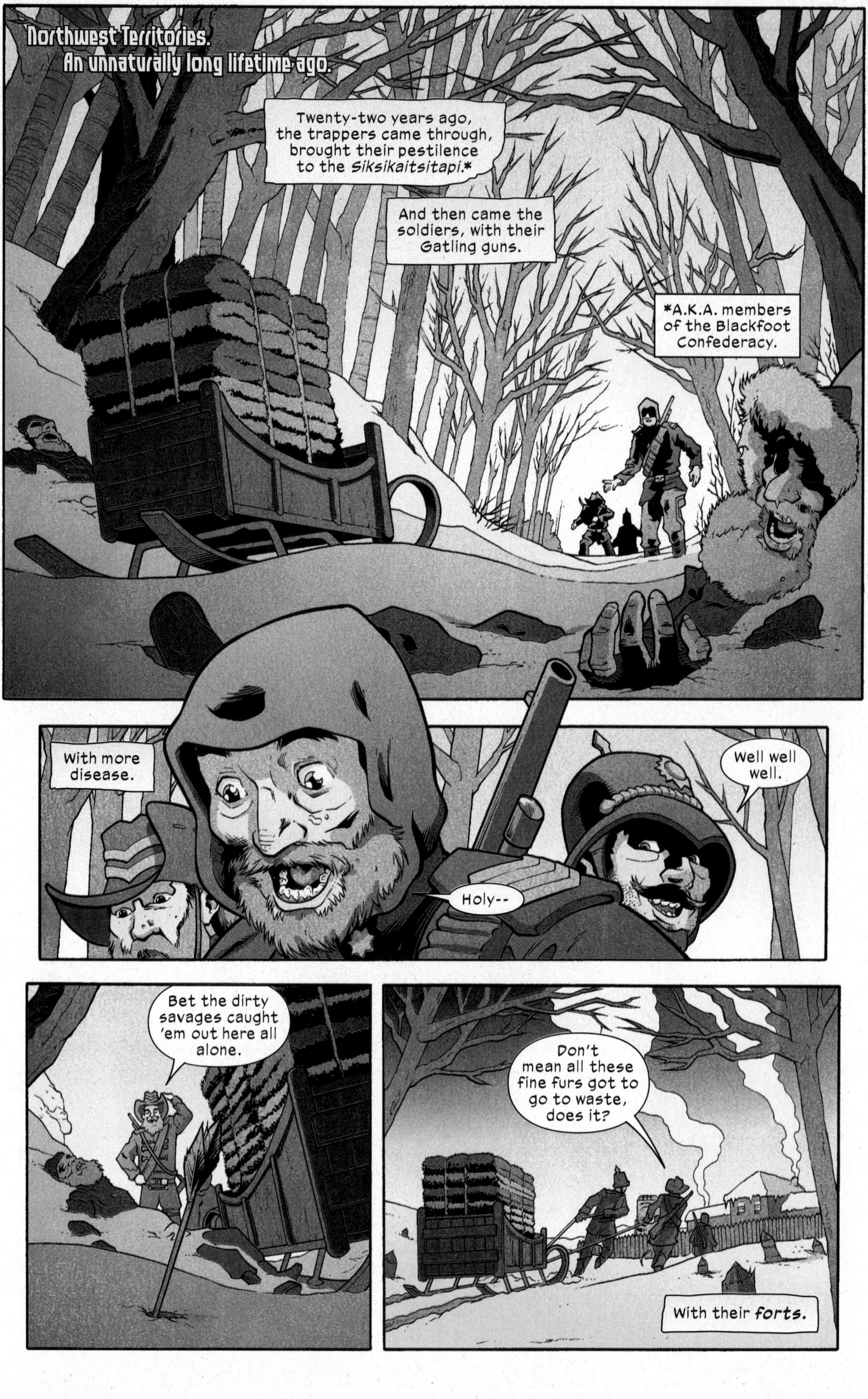

Northwest Territories.
An unnaturally long lifetime ago.
Twenty-two years ago, the trappers came through, brought their pestilence to the *Siksikaitsitapi.**
And then came the soldiers, with their Gatling guns.
*A.K.A. members of the Blackfoot Confederacy.
With more disease.
Holy--
Well well well.
Bet the dirty savages caught 'em out here all alone.
Don't mean all these fine furs got to go to waste, does it?
With their *forts.*

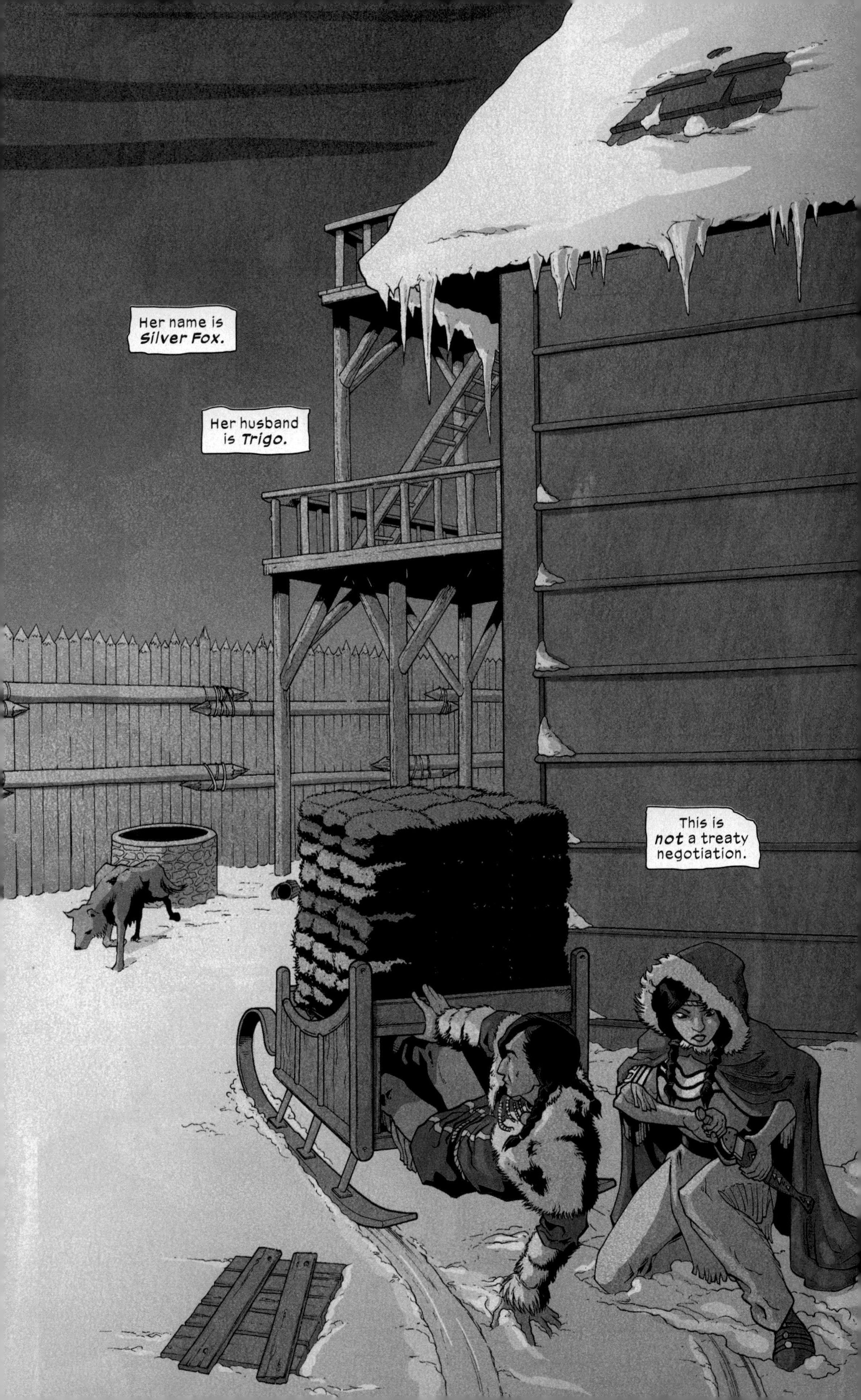
Her name is *Silver Fox.*
Her husband is *Trigo.*
This is *not* a treaty negotiation.

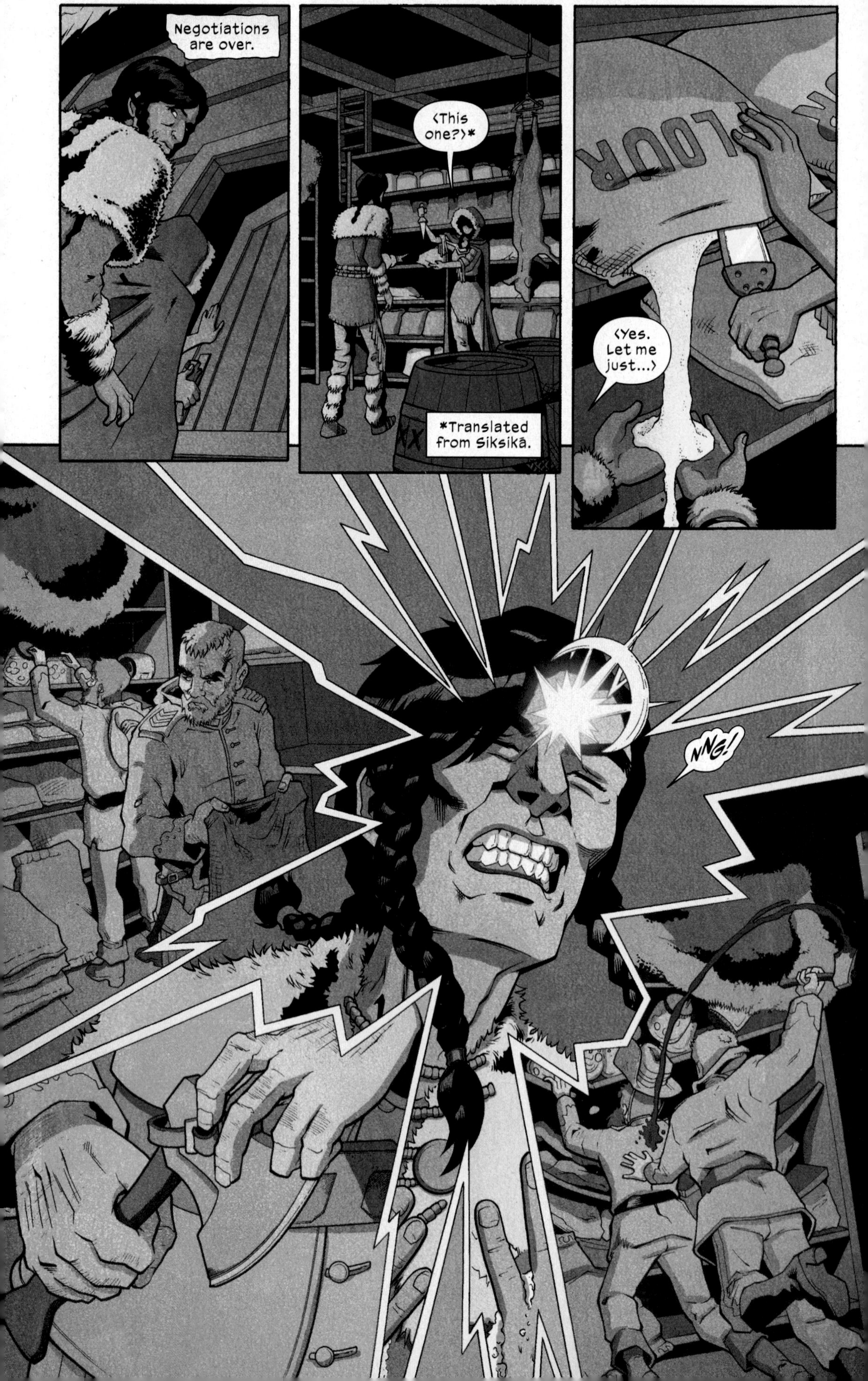
Negotiations are over.
‹This one?›*
*Translated from Siksikā.
‹Yes. Let me just...›
NNG!

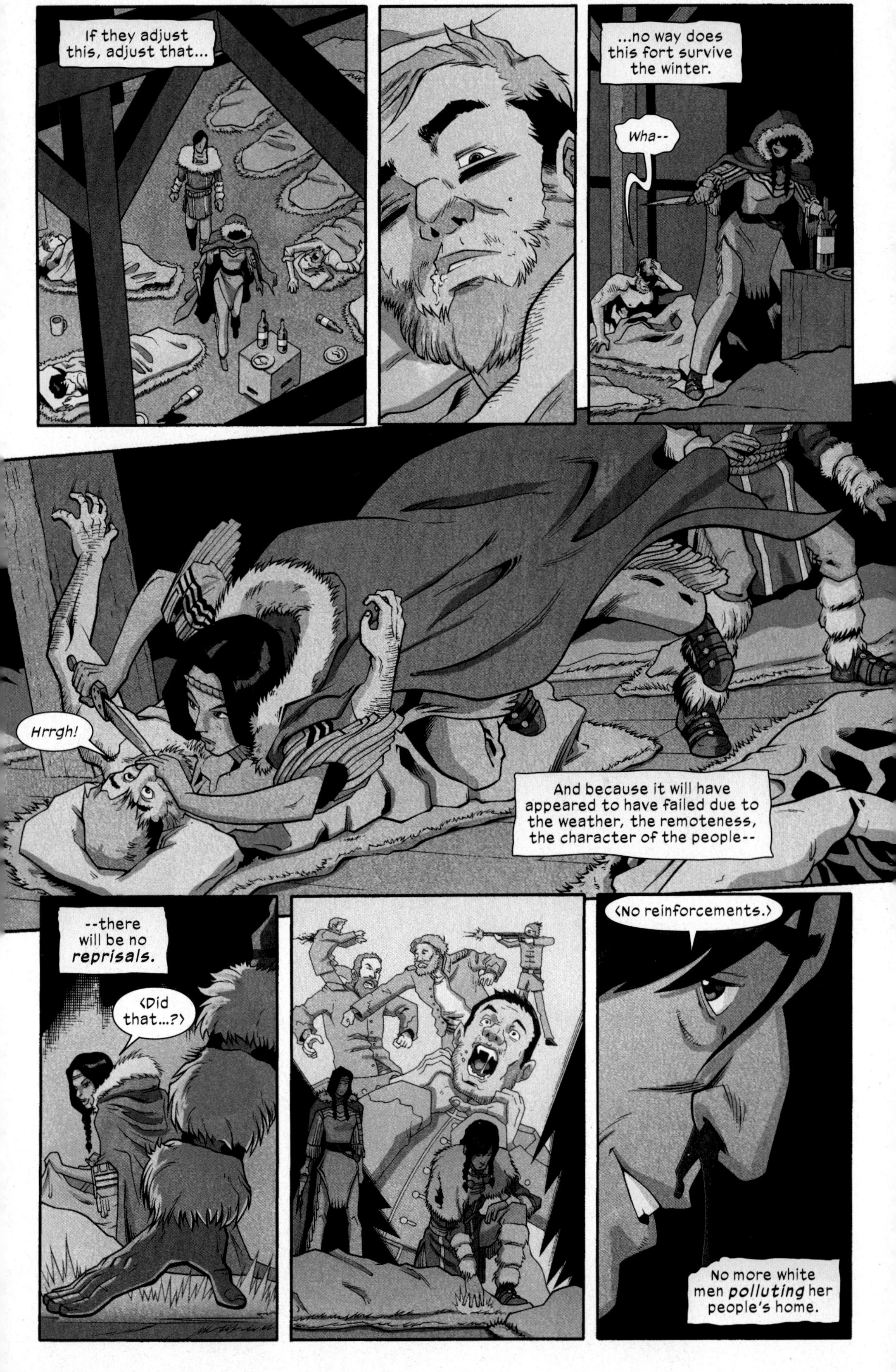
If they adjust this, adjust that...
...no way does this fort survive the winter.
Wha--
Hrrgh!
And because it will have appeared to have failed due to the weather, the remoteness, the character of the people--
--there will be no *reprisals.*
<Did that...?>
<No reinforcements.>
No more white men *polluting* her people's home.

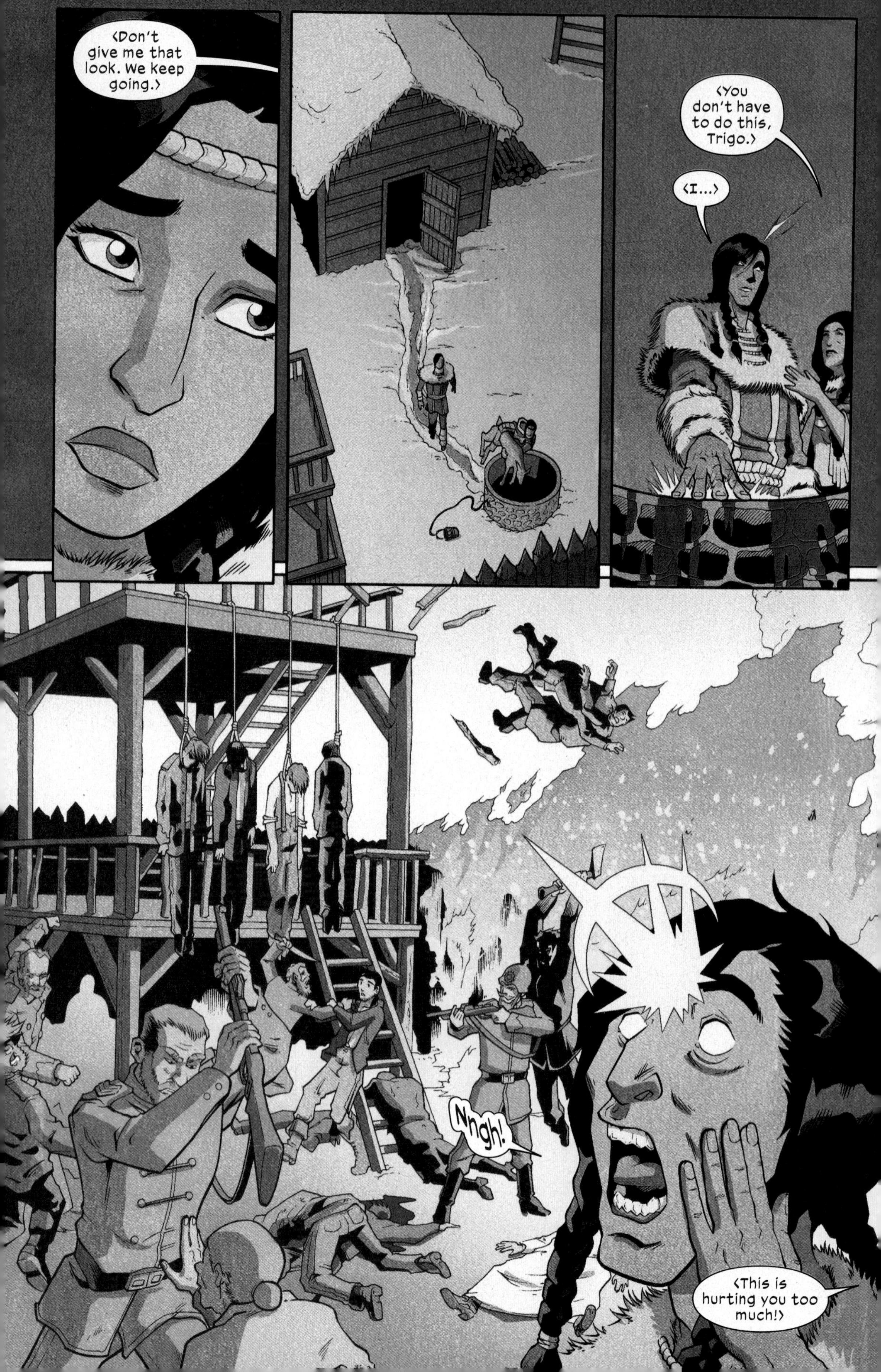
‹Don't give me that look. We keep going.›
‹You don't have to do this, Trigo.›
‹I...›
Nngh!
‹This is hurting you too much!›

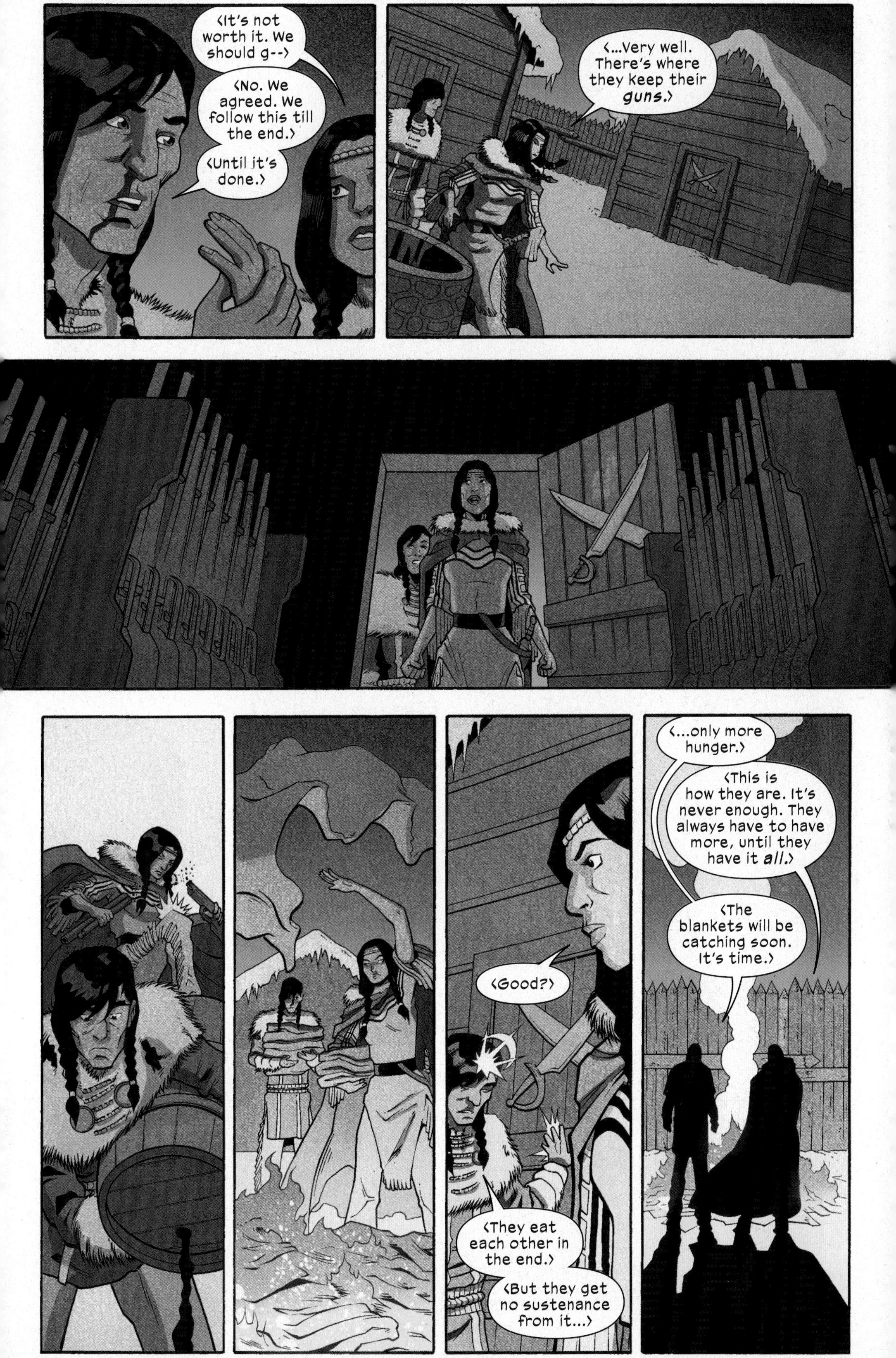
‹It's not worth it. We should g--›
‹No. We agreed. We follow this till the end.›
‹Until it's done.›
‹...Very well. There's where they keep their *guns.*›
‹Good?›
‹They eat each other in the end.›
‹But they get no sustenance from it...›
‹...only more hunger.›
‹This is how they are. It's never enough. They always have to have more, until they have it *all.*›
‹The blankets will be catching soon. It's time.›

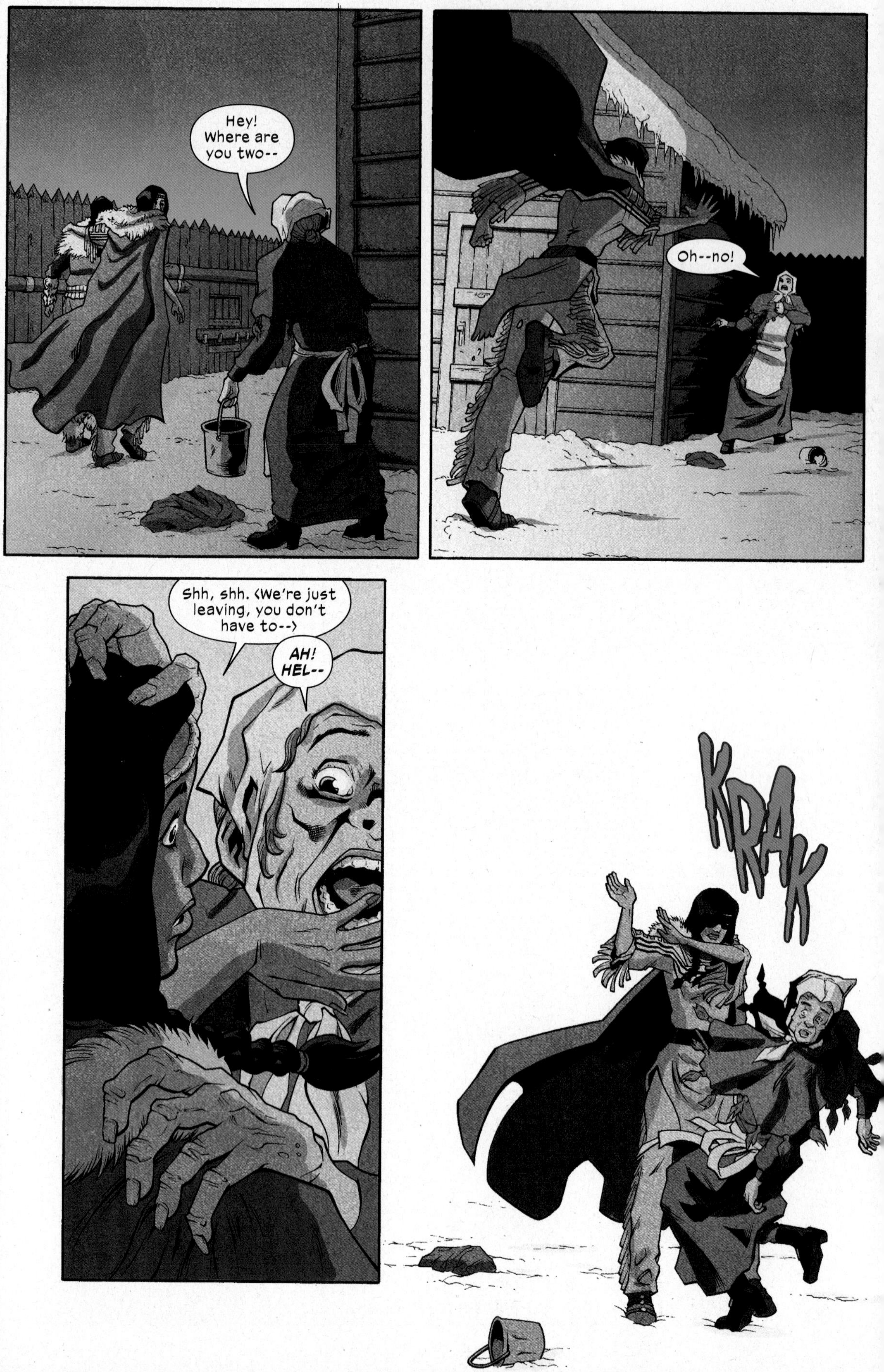

Hey! Where are you two--
Oh--no!
Shh, shh. <We're just leaving, you don't have to-->
AH! HEL--
KRAK

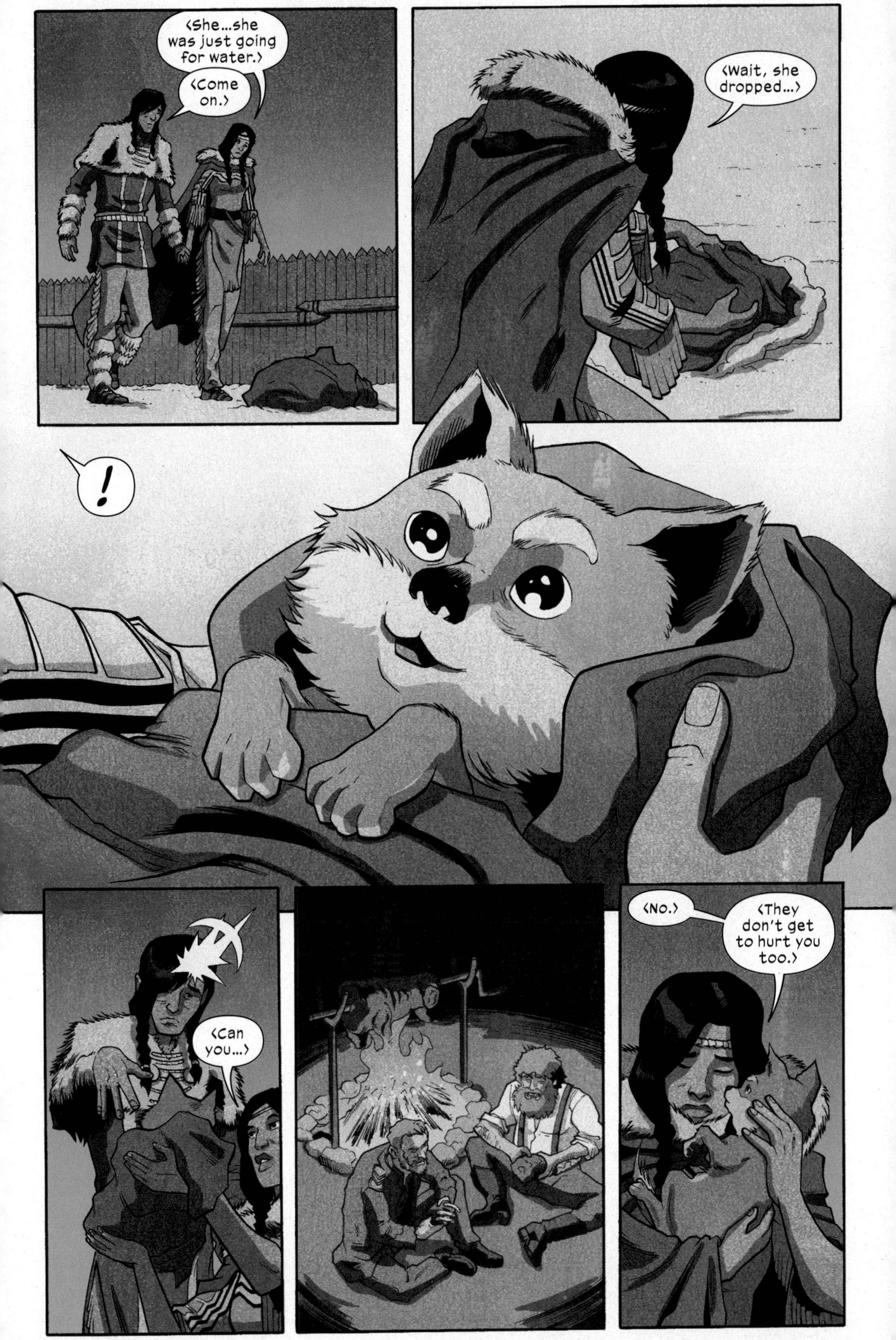

‹She...she was just going for water.›
‹Come on.›
‹Wait, she dropped...›
!
‹Can you...›
‹No.›
‹They don't get to hurt you too.›

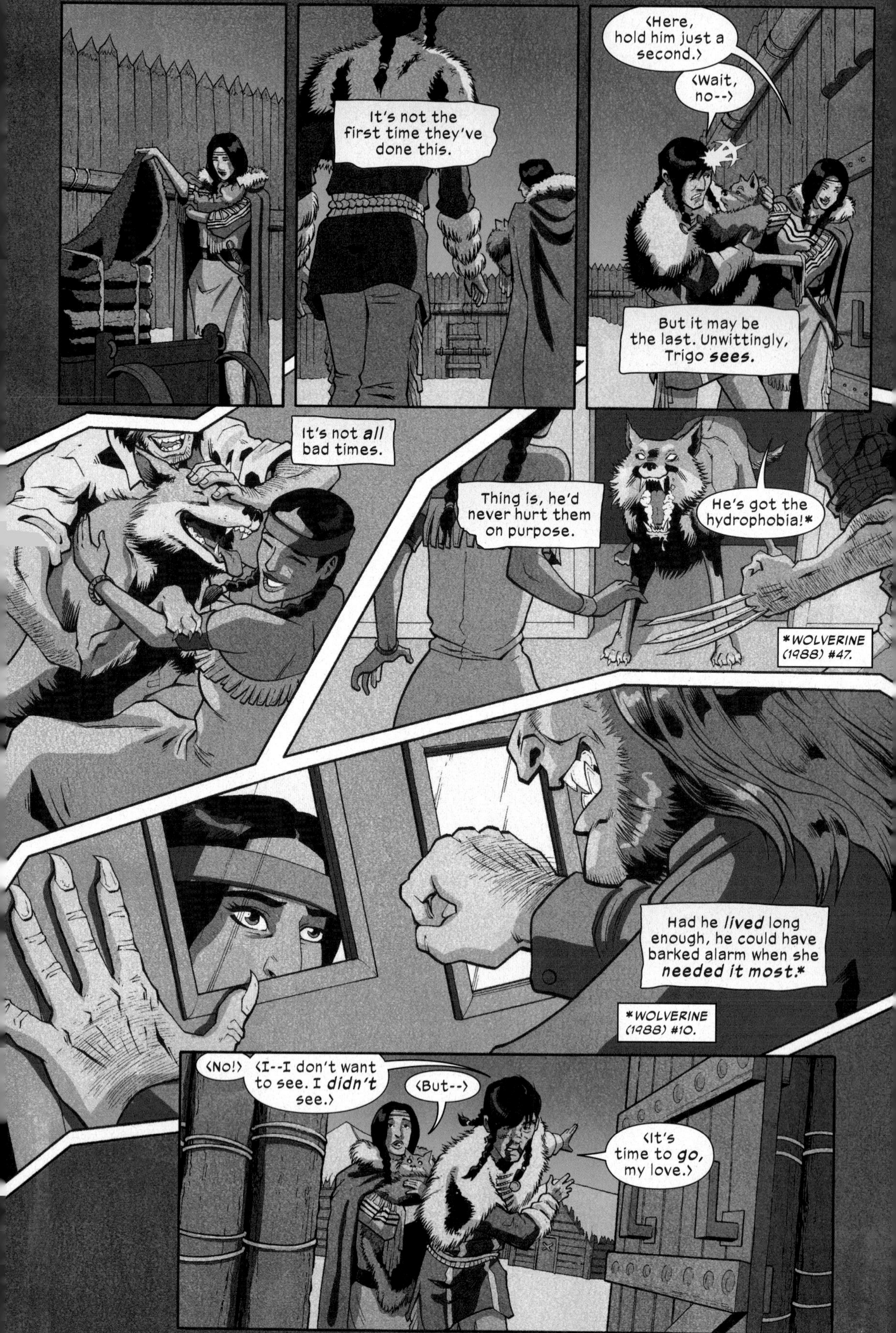
It's not the first time they've done this.
‹Here, hold him just a second.›
‹Wait, no--›
But it may be the last. Unwittingly, Trigo *sees.*
It's not *all* bad times.
Thing is, he'd never hurt them on purpose.
He's got the hydrophobia!*
*WOLVERINE (1988) #47.
Had he *lived* long enough, he could have barked alarm when she *needed it most.**
*WOLVERINE (1988) #10.
‹No!›
‹I--I don't want to see. I *didn't* see.›
‹But--›
‹It's time to *go,* my love.›

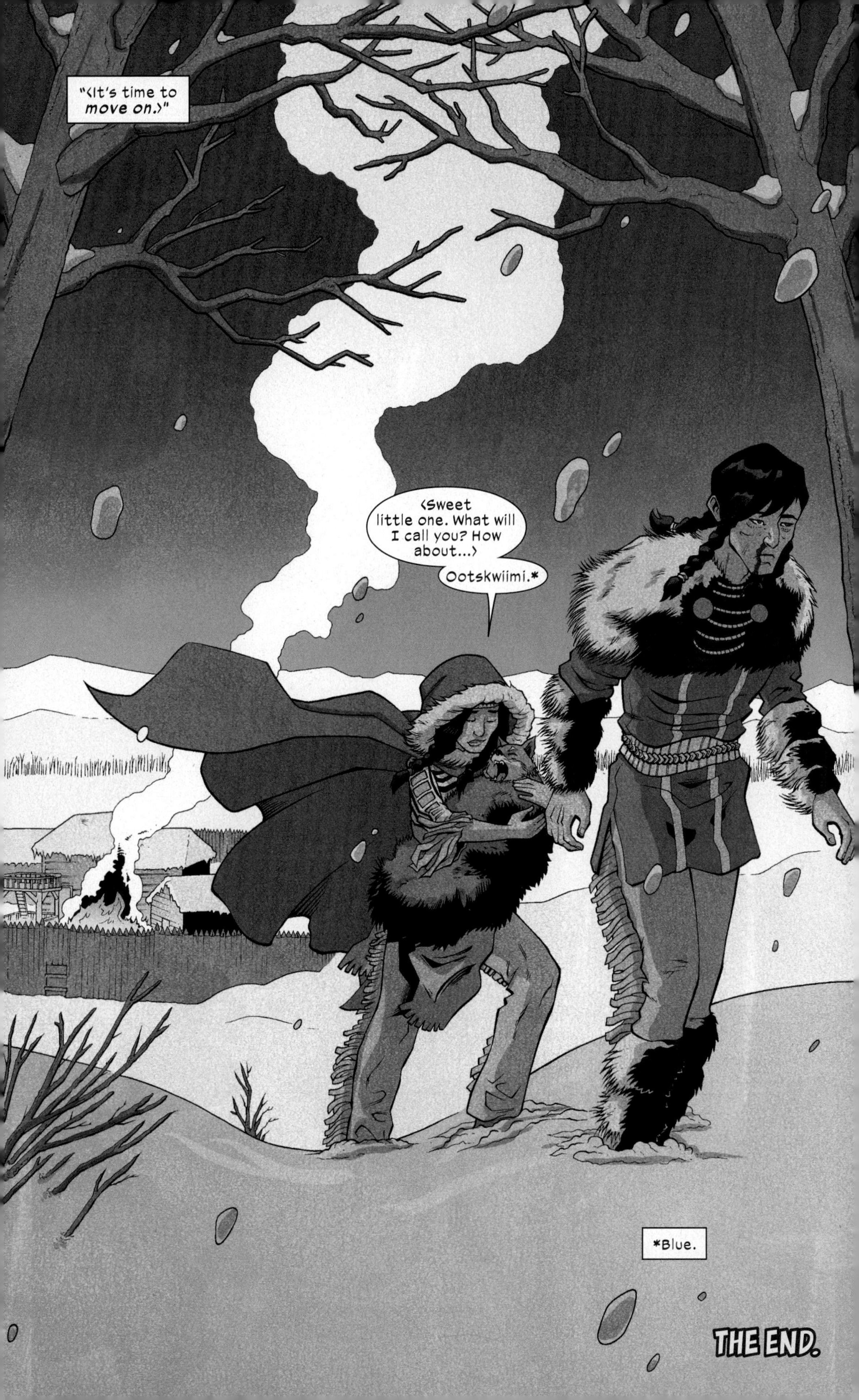
"<It's time to *move on.*>"
<Sweet little one. What will I call you? How about...>
Ootskwiimi.*
*Blue.
THE END.

AFTERWORD

Time is a strange entity. We know time is real because every day we feel its effects. But time isn't something we can touch or control. Okay, there is that thing called Daylight Savings Time, but it's really just everyone agreeing to turn their clocks back or push them forward so we can all stay outside later for barbecues. It's not like we have some agreement with the sun so we can throw horseshoes or play lawn darts for an extra hour.

But time exists differently when you're a reader. You can jump entire spans of time by turning the page! Which you, dear reader, just did, jumping from the past to the present to the future...from a barren frontier to a modern-day Rez to a far-off planet. There is a very visceral connection to time since you physically have to turn the page in order to advance it or rewind it. It's you and the page. That's it. Which is why reading is a far more personal experience than movies or TV shows. It is you, the reader, who moves the story forward and chooses how quickly or slowly it progresses. How long do you sit there with that amazing two-page spread, or how quickly do you flip the pages to see how the story ends?!

There is a magic to storytelling in how a story relates to space and time. Comics are an amazing medium to explore and experiment with how an audience interacts with these concepts. From panel-to-panel pacing or two-page splashes, time is constantly being manipulated through the use of space. And Jeffrey Veregge, one of the people behind this amazing book you hold in your hands, is a master of both time and space.

Taboo and I first met Jeffrey on the MARVEL #1000 one-shot, when we were asked to write a one-page Red Wolf story. Taboo had been championing Red Wolf for some time, and when we got the call we had the green light to reintroduce the character in the milestone *Marvel #1000*, we were beyond excited. We started ping-ponging (it's what we call our creative sessions!), and we came up with this really cool idea of how to build out the page while telling the story. We wanted the reader to see Red Wolf throughout time (there's that word again!) but also jump out at you when you flipped through the book. Who could do something like this yet maintain the visual Native integrity rooted in the Red Wolf character?

The next day Tab called me up and goes, "Yo, Benny, check out this cat Jeffrey Veregge. He's so dope." Now to be honest, I wasn't entirely familiar with Jeffrey's work. I did what anyone in this era would do...I pulled out my laptop and leaped onto the interwebs. Lo and behold, I was greeted with page after page of Jeffrey's work as well as a wonderful article detailing his exhibition in the Smithsonian Museum. This was the guy who could bring our vision to life.

Red Wolf was our first time working with Jeffrey, as well as our first time creating for Marvel. What Jeffrey created based off a rough little thumbnail idea and some text blocks was a masterpiece. A couple months later we got the call to reboot *Werewolf by Night* through a Native lens. Our task, should we accept it, was to tell the origins of a teenager who has the werewolf curse running through his blood. Of course we told our editor we had to work with Jeffrey again. The wish was granted, and as we speak, Jeffrey is crafting a masterpiece to elevate our new werewolf mythology in a beautiful two-page spread!

Jeffrey is an amazing and humble human being. He is the mastermind behind this book, giving storytellers who otherwise might not have had an opportunity or the platform to tell their stories. It is something that Taboo and I work toward in everything we do for our company, SkyView Way. We believe this journey is one we are all taking together. We see this same kindred spirit in Jeffrey and are blessed to call him both friend and collaborator.

Thank you, Jeffrey. Keep doing what you do as you advance the story one page at a time.

Taboo & B. Earl
September 10, 2020

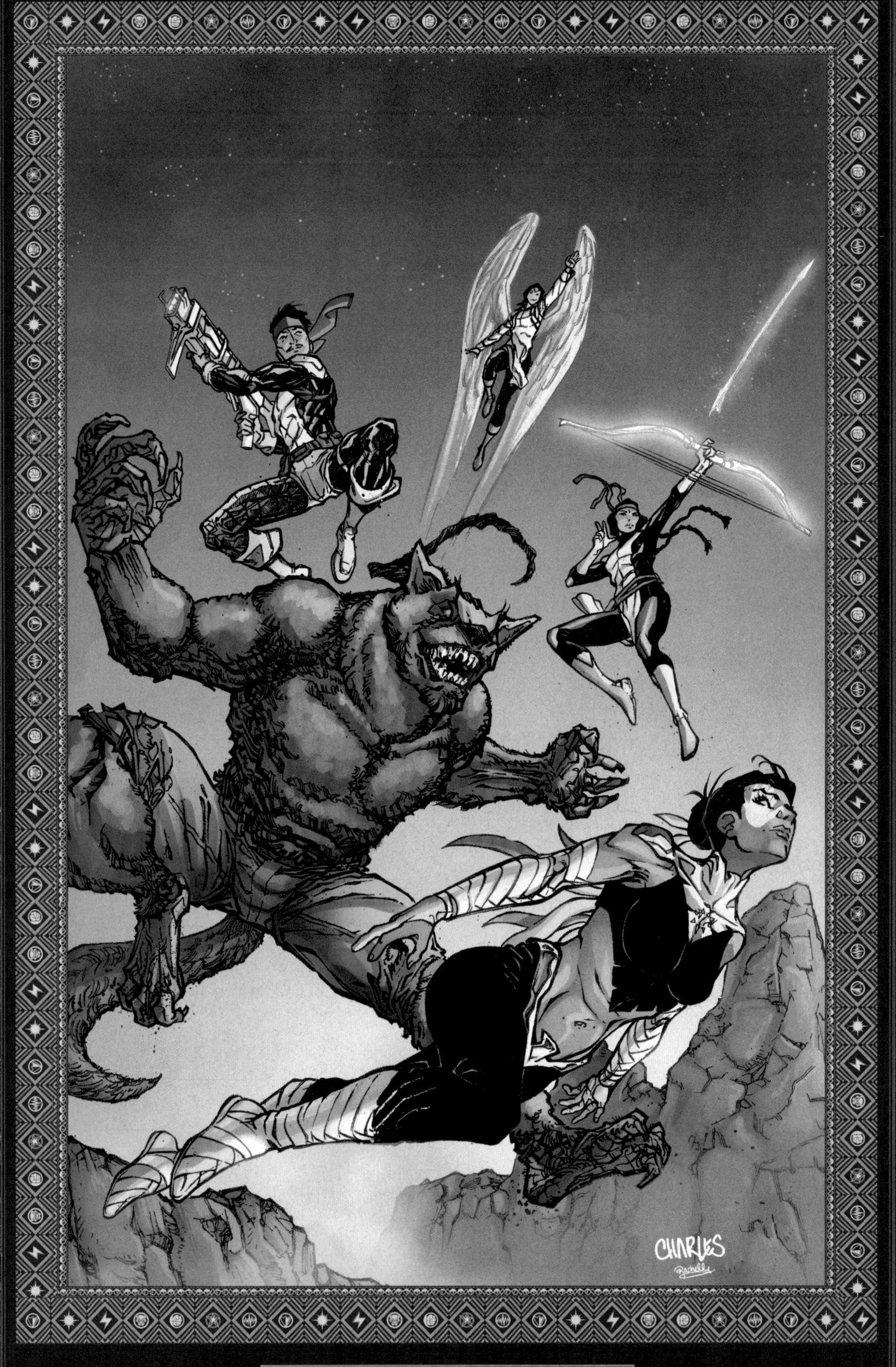
CHARLES

MARVEL'S VOICES: HERITAGE

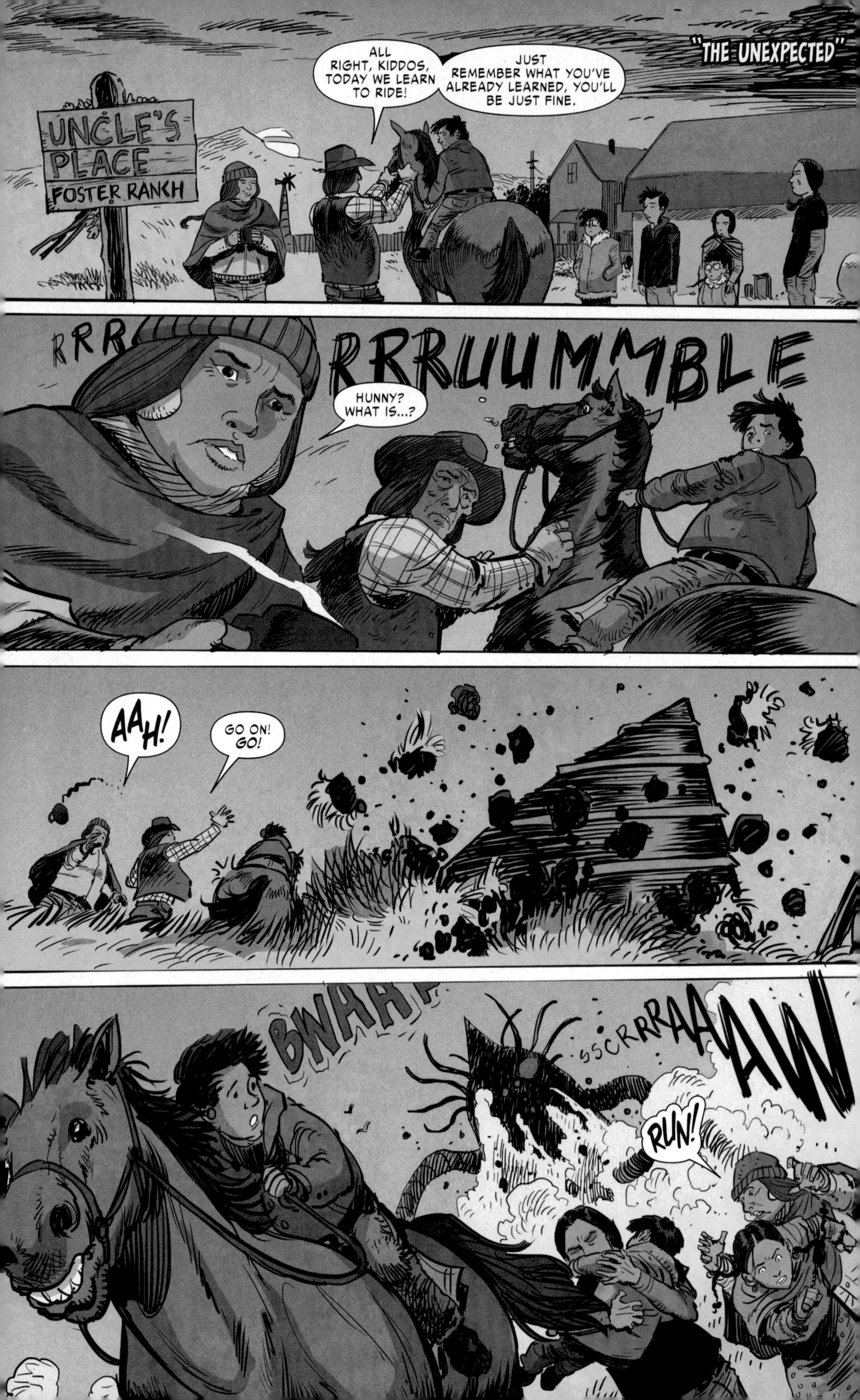
"THE UNEXPECTED"
UNCLE'S PLACE
FOSTER RANCH
ALL RIGHT, KIDDOS, TODAY WE LEARN TO RIDE!
JUST REMEMBER WHAT YOU'VE ALREADY LEARNED, YOU'LL BE JUST FINE.
RRRRRRUUMMBLE
HUNNY? WHAT IS...?
AAH!
GO ON! GO!
BWAAP
SSCRRRAAAW
RUN!

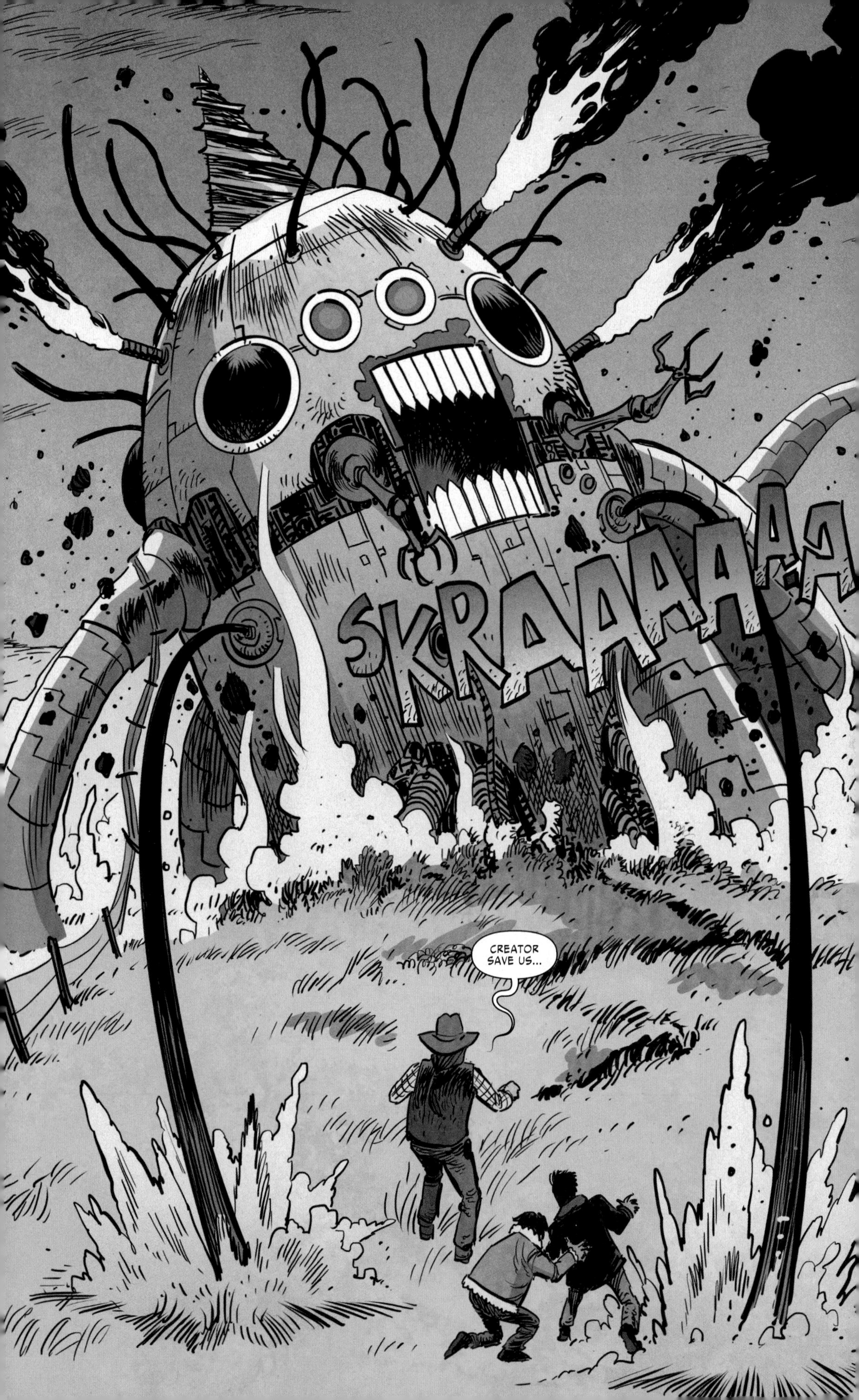
SKRAAAAAAA
CREATOR SAVE US...

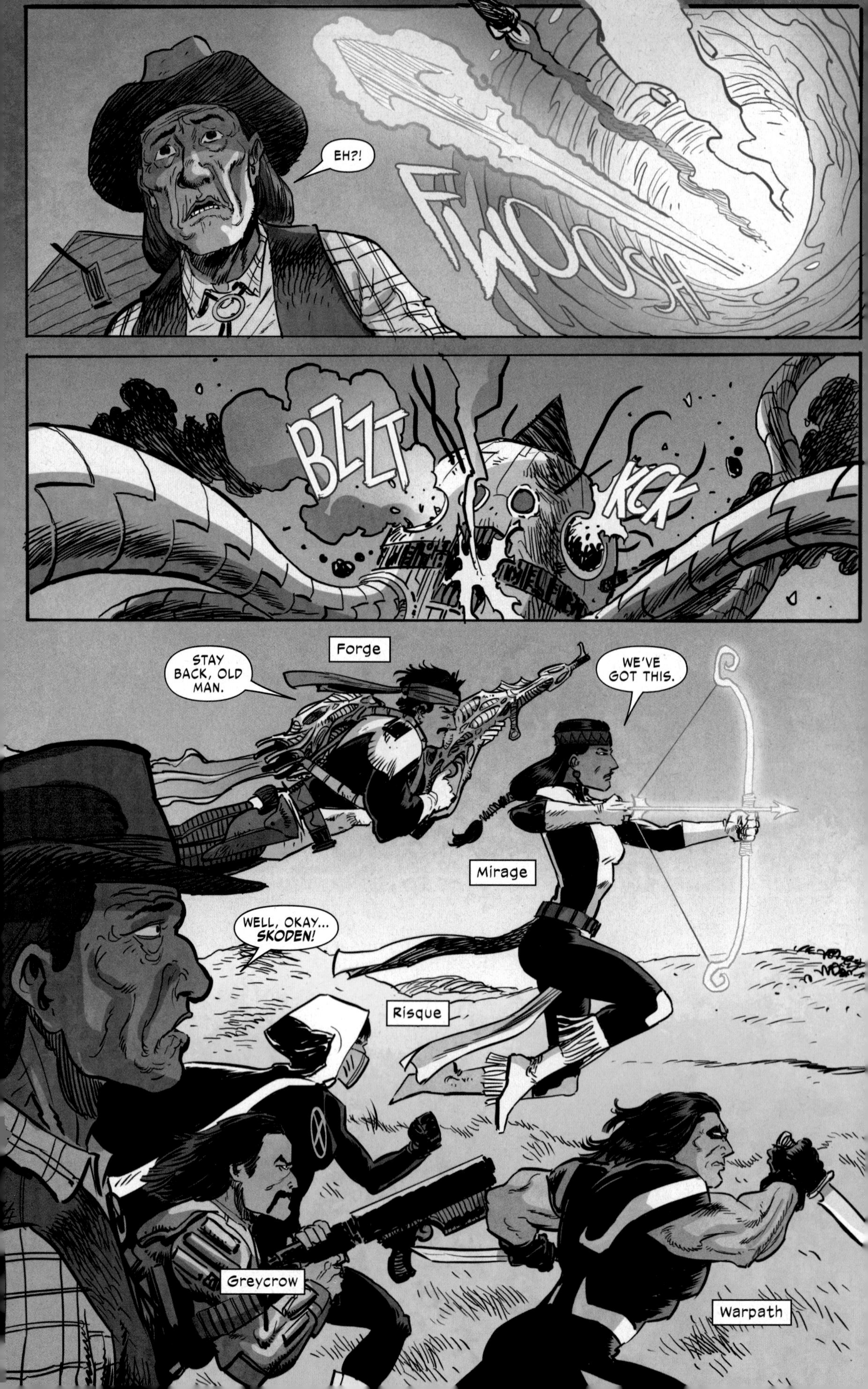
EH?!
FWOOSH
BZZT
KCK
Forge
STAY BACK, OLD MAN.
WE'VE GOT THIS.
Mirage
WELL, OKAY... **SKODEN!**
Risque
Greycrow
Warpath

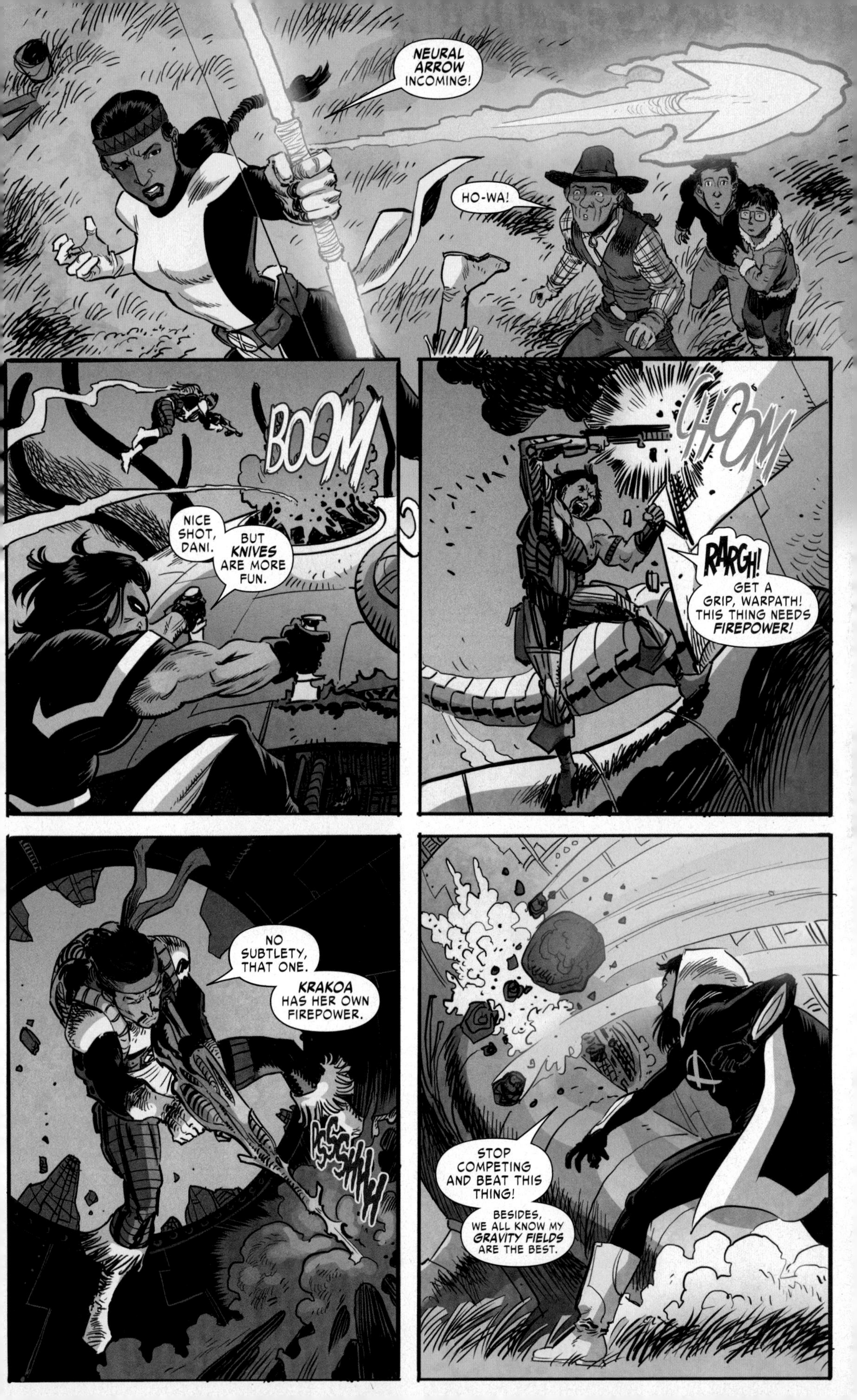
NEURAL ARROW INCOMING!
HO-WA!
BOOM
NICE SHOT, DANI.
BUT KNIVES ARE MORE FUN.
CHOOM
RARGH!
GET A GRIP, WARPATH! THIS THING NEEDS FIREPOWER!
NO SUBTLETY, THAT ONE.
KRAKOA HAS HER OWN FIREPOWER.
PSSSHHH
STOP COMPETING AND BEAT THIS THING!
BESIDES, WE ALL KNOW MY GRAVITY FIELDS ARE THE BEST.

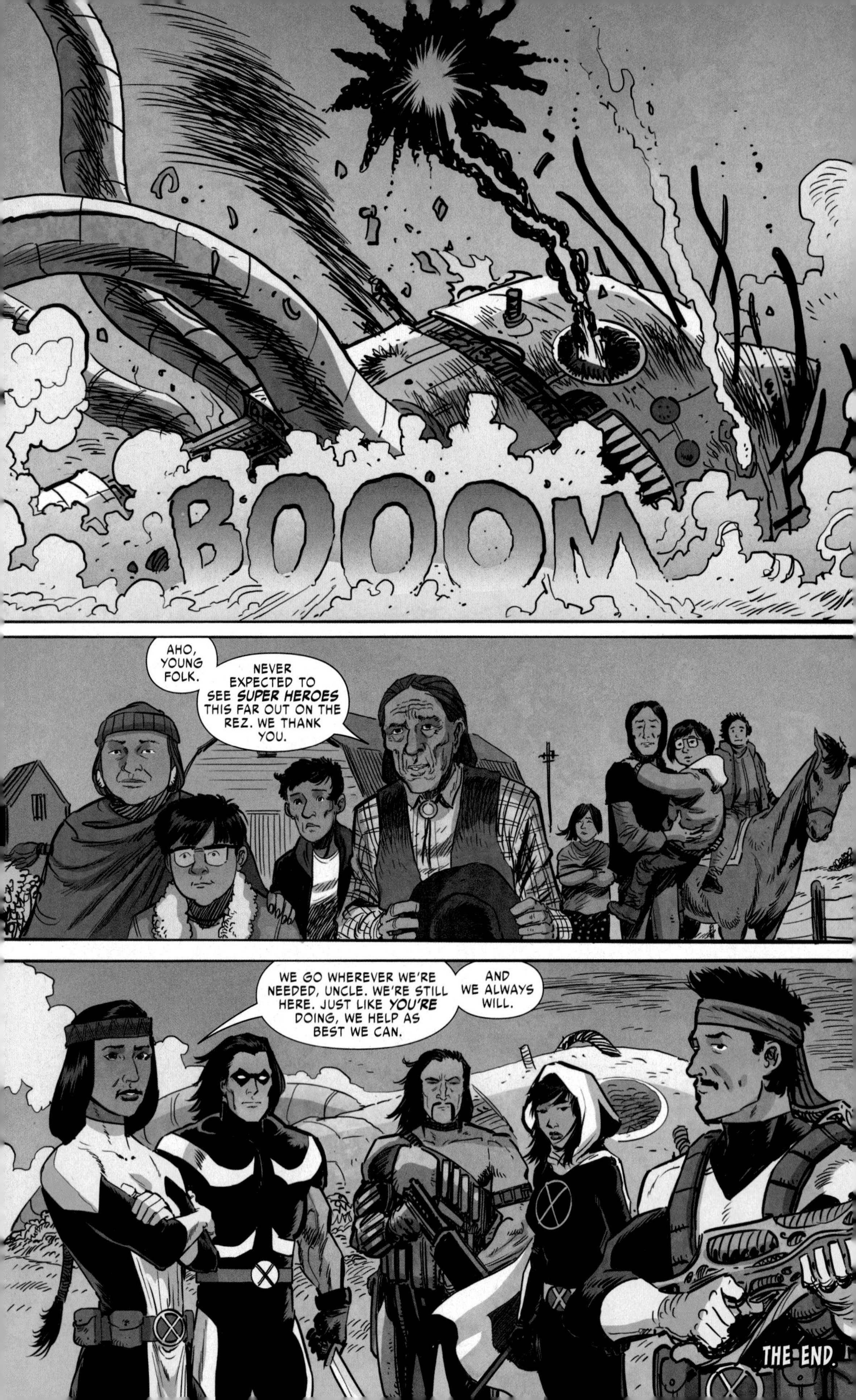
BOOOM
AHO, YOUNG FOLK.
NEVER EXPECTED TO SEE SUPER HEROES THIS FAR OUT ON THE REZ. WE THANK YOU.
WE GO WHEREVER WE'RE NEEDED, UNCLE. WE'RE STILL HERE. JUST LIKE YOU'RE DOING, WE HELP AS BEST WE CAN.
AND WE ALWAYS WILL.
THE END.

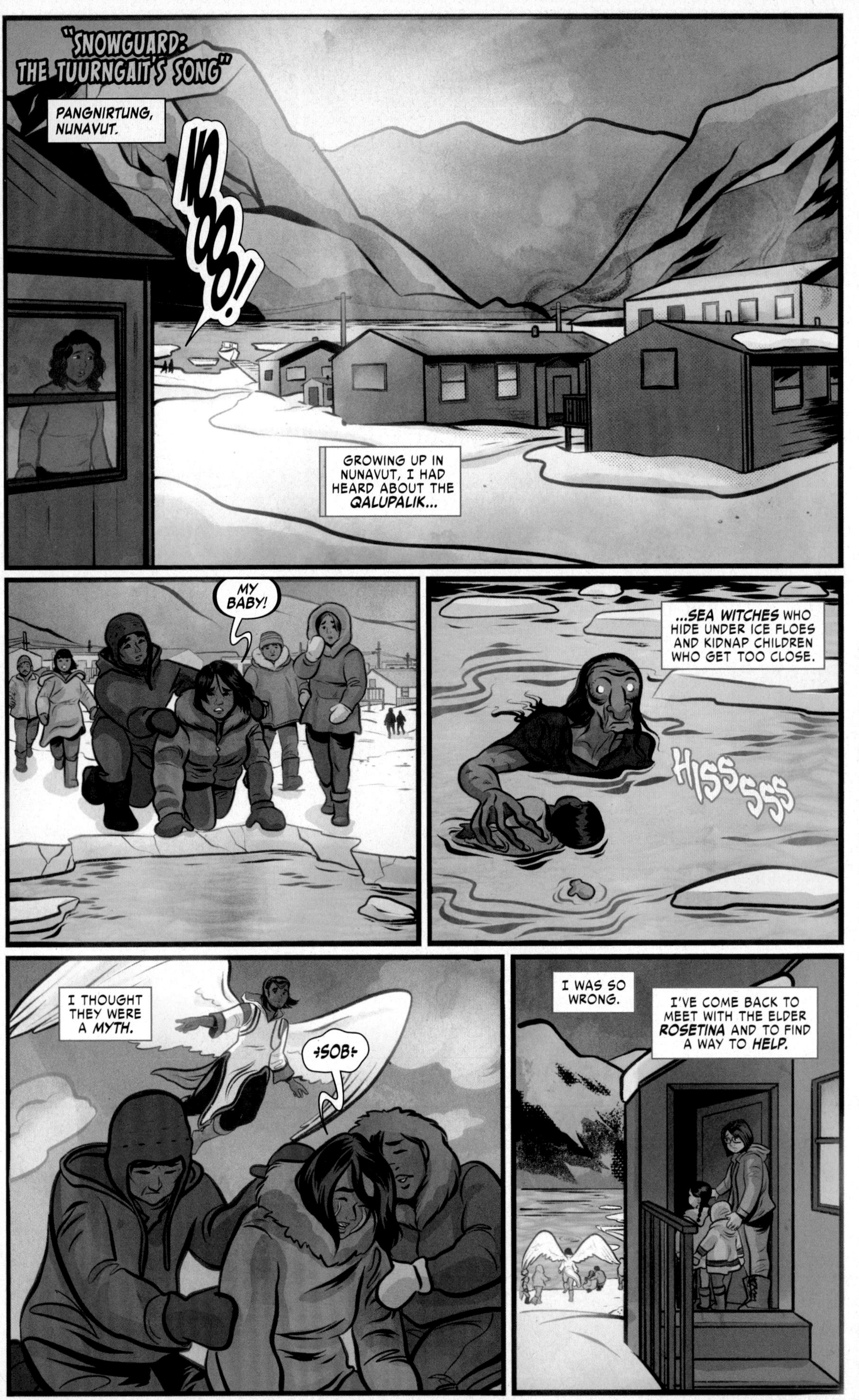
"SNOWGUARD: THE TUURNGAIT'S SONG"
PANGNIRTUNG, NUNAVUT.
NOOOO!
GROWING UP IN NUNAVUT, I HAD HEARD ABOUT THE QALUPALIK...
MY BABY!
...SEA WITCHES WHO HIDE UNDER ICE FLOES AND KIDNAP CHILDREN WHO GET TOO CLOSE.
HISSSSS
I THOUGHT THEY WERE A MYTH.
SOB
I WAS SO WRONG.
I'VE COME BACK TO MEET WITH THE ELDER ROSETINA AND TO FIND A WAY TO HELP.

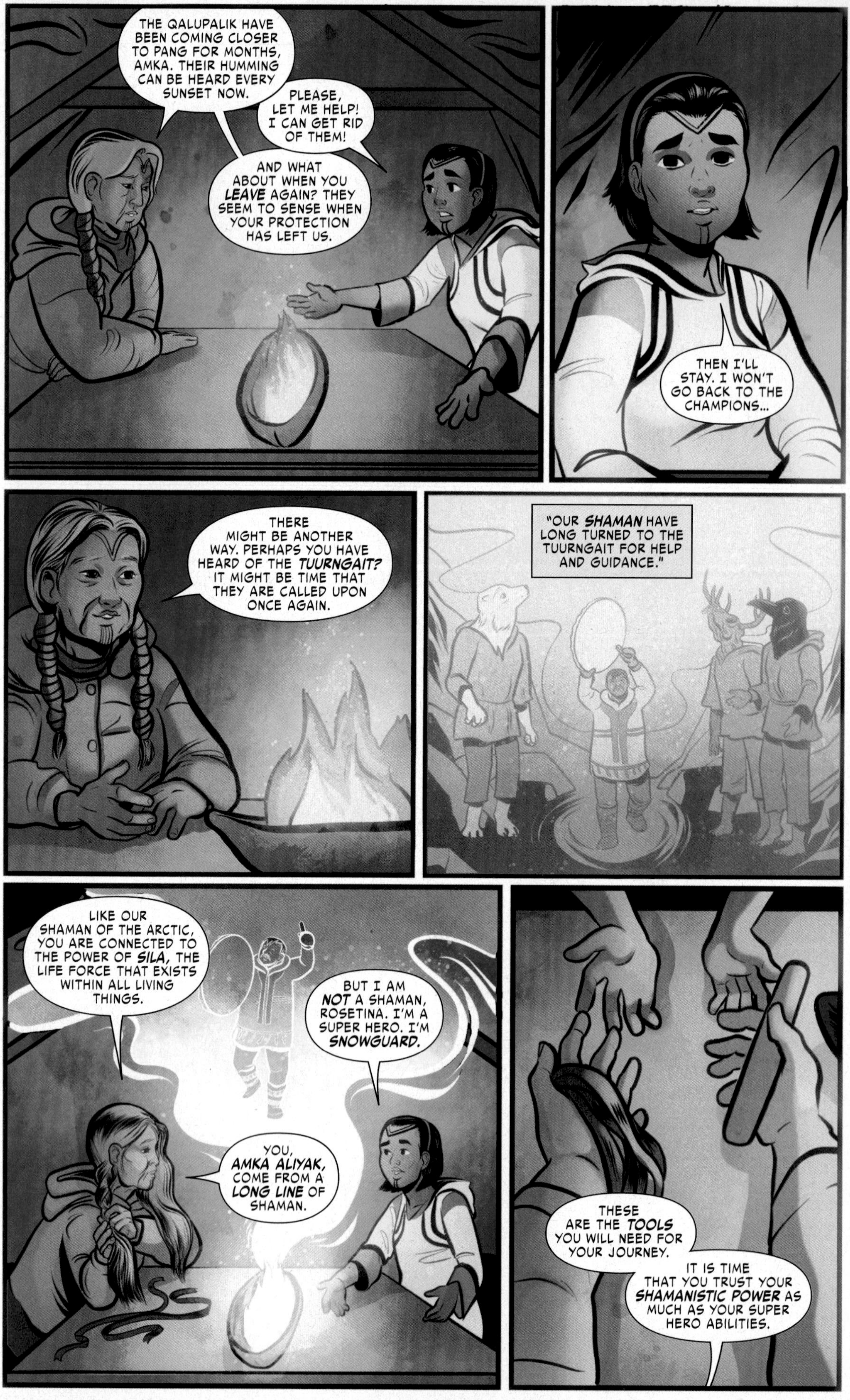
THE QALUPALIK HAVE BEEN COMING CLOSER TO PANG FOR MONTHS, AMKA. THEIR HUMMING CAN BE HEARD EVERY SUNSET NOW.
PLEASE, LET ME HELP! I CAN GET RID OF THEM!
AND WHAT ABOUT WHEN YOU LEAVE AGAIN? THEY SEEM TO SENSE WHEN YOUR PROTECTION HAS LEFT US.
THEN I'LL STAY. I WON'T GO BACK TO THE CHAMPIONS...
THERE MIGHT BE ANOTHER WAY. PERHAPS YOU HAVE HEARD OF THE TUURNGAIT? IT MIGHT BE TIME THAT THEY ARE CALLED UPON ONCE AGAIN.
"OUR SHAMAN HAVE LONG TURNED TO THE TUURNGAIT FOR HELP AND GUIDANCE."
LIKE OUR SHAMAN OF THE ARCTIC, YOU ARE CONNECTED TO THE POWER OF SILA, THE LIFE FORCE THAT EXISTS WITHIN ALL LIVING THINGS.
BUT I AM NOT A SHAMAN, ROSETINA. I'M A SUPER HERO. I'M SNOWGUARD.
YOU, AMKA ALIYAK, COME FROM A LONG LINE OF SHAMAN.
THESE ARE THE TOOLS YOU WILL NEED FOR YOUR JOURNEY.
IT IS TIME THAT YOU TRUST YOUR SHAMANISTIC POWER AS MUCH AS YOUR SUPER HERO ABILITIES.

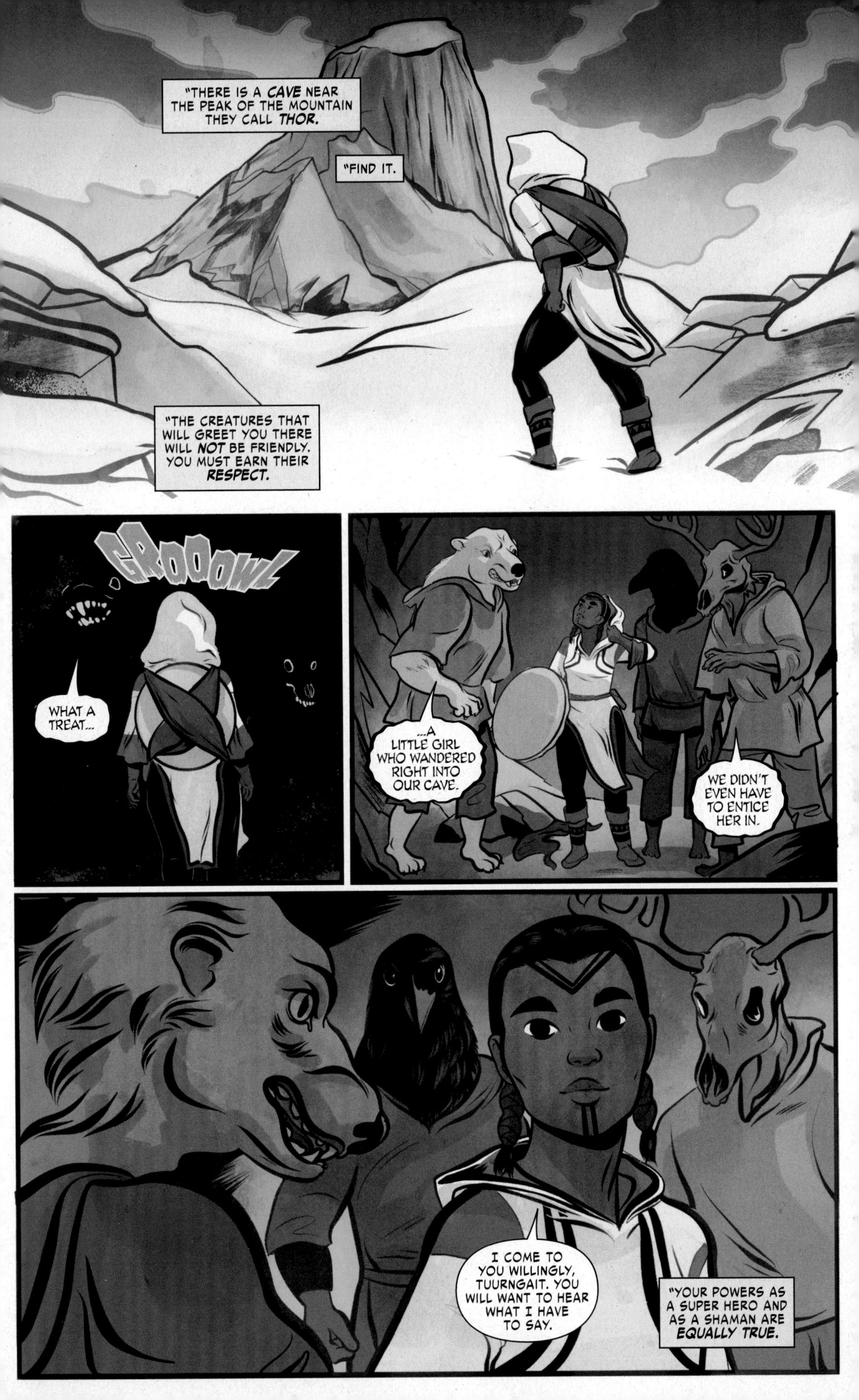
"THERE IS A CAVE NEAR THE PEAK OF THE MOUNTAIN THEY CALL THOR.
"FIND IT.
"THE CREATURES THAT WILL GREET YOU THERE WILL NOT BE FRIENDLY. YOU MUST EARN THEIR RESPECT.
GROOOWL
WHAT A TREAT...
...A LITTLE GIRL WHO WANDERED RIGHT INTO OUR CAVE.
WE DIDN'T EVEN HAVE TO ENTICE HER IN.
I COME TO YOU WILLINGLY, TUURNGAIT. YOU WILL WANT TO HEAR WHAT I HAVE TO SAY.
"YOUR POWERS AS A SUPER HERO AND AS A SHAMAN ARE EQUALLY TRUE.

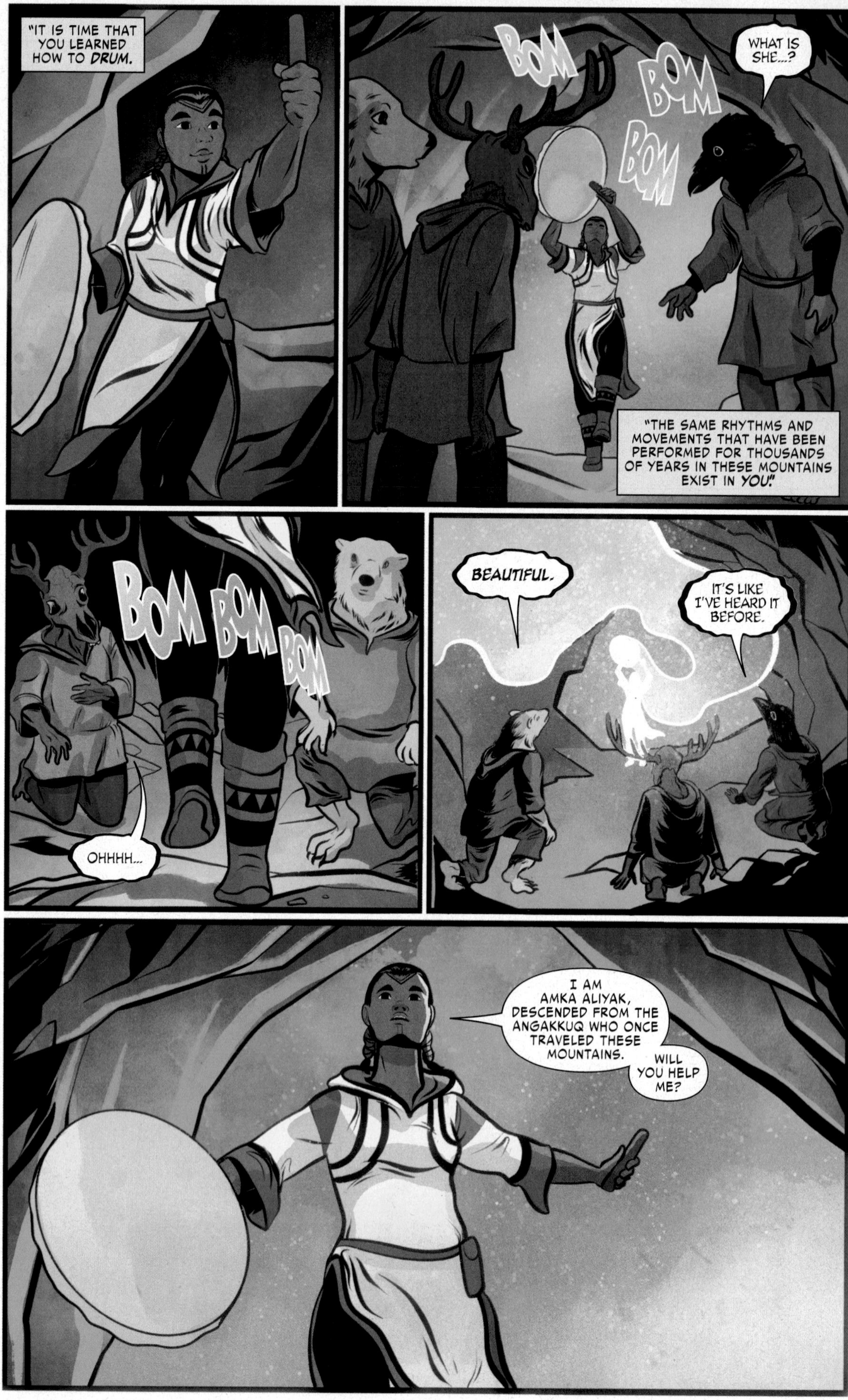
"IT IS TIME THAT YOU LEARNED HOW TO DRUM.
BOM
BOM
BOM
WHAT IS SHE...?
"THE SAME RHYTHMS AND MOVEMENTS THAT HAVE BEEN PERFORMED FOR THOUSANDS OF YEARS IN THESE MOUNTAINS EXIST IN YOU."
BOM BOM BOM
OHHHH...
BEAUTIFUL.
IT'S LIKE I'VE HEARD IT BEFORE.
I AM AMKA ALIYAK, DESCENDED FROM THE ANGAKKUQ WHO ONCE TRAVELED THESE MOUNTAINS.
WILL YOU HELP ME?

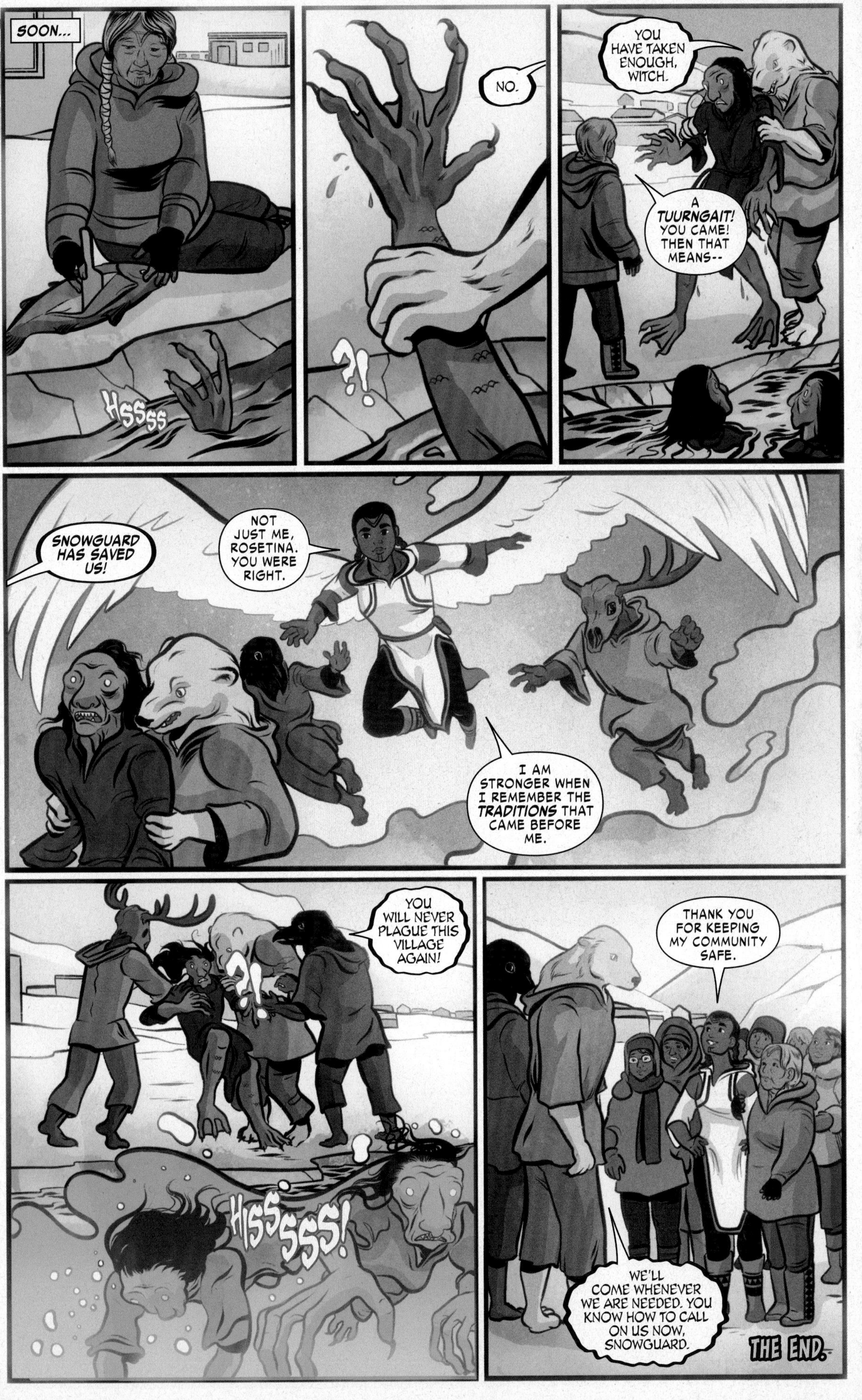
SOON...
HSSSS
NO.
?!
YOU HAVE TAKEN ENOUGH, WITCH.
A TUURNGAIT! YOU CAME! THEN THAT MEANS--
SNOWGUARD HAS SAVED US!
NOT JUST ME, ROSETINA. YOU WERE RIGHT.
I AM STRONGER WHEN I REMEMBER THE TRADITIONS THAT CAME BEFORE ME.
YOU WILL NEVER PLAGUE THIS VILLAGE AGAIN!
?!
HISSSSS!
THANK YOU FOR KEEPING MY COMMUNITY SAFE.
WE'LL COME WHENEVER WE ARE NEEDED. YOU KNOW HOW TO CALL ON US NOW, SNOWGUARD.
THE END.

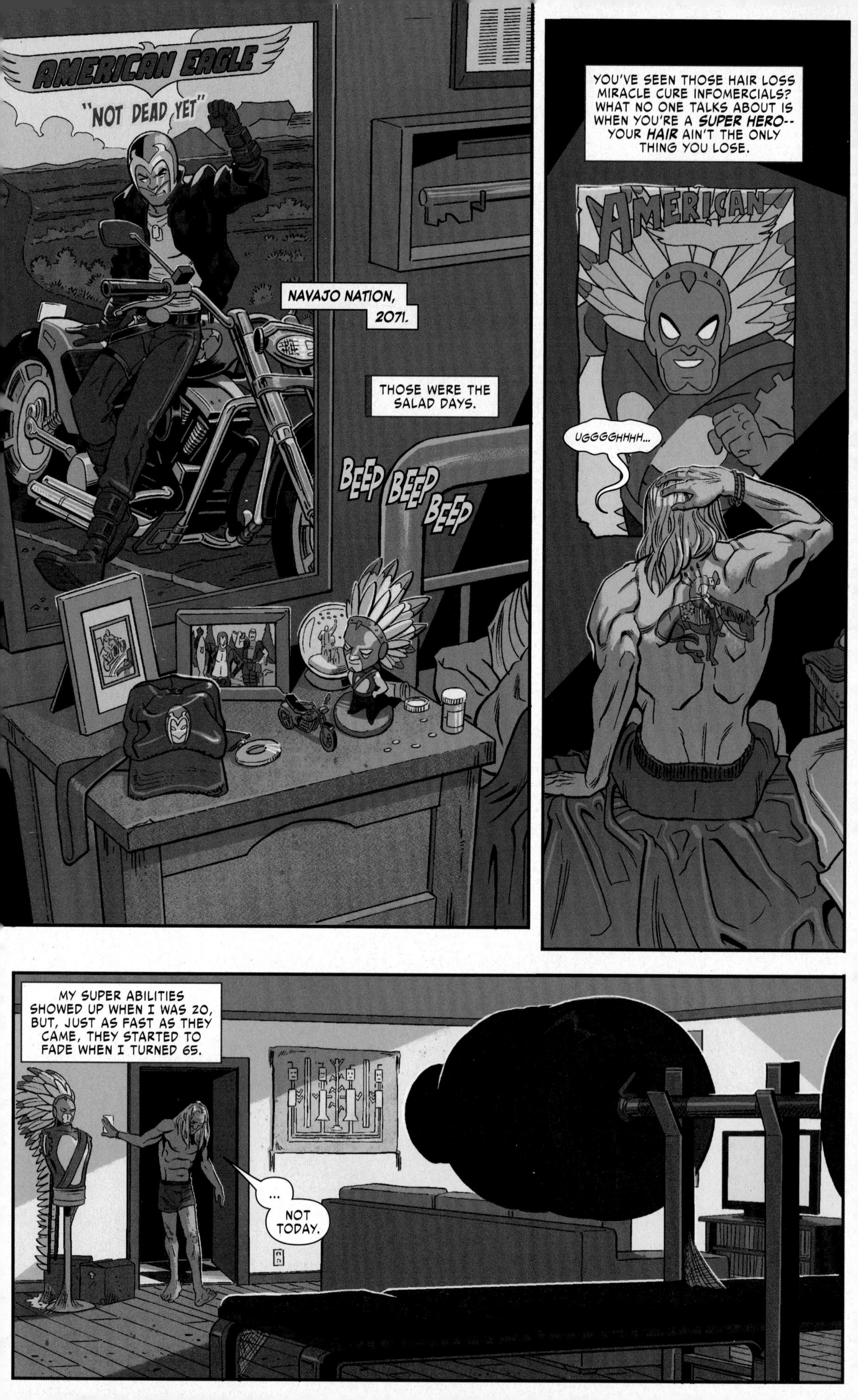

AMERICAN EAGLE
"NOT DEAD YET"
NAVAJO NATION, 2071.
THOSE WERE THE SALAD DAYS.
BEEP BEEP BEEP
YOU'VE SEEN THOSE HAIR LOSS MIRACLE CURE INFOMERCIALS? WHAT NO ONE TALKS ABOUT IS WHEN YOU'RE A SUPER HERO-- YOUR HAIR AIN'T THE ONLY THING YOU LOSE.
AMERICAN
UGGGGHHHH...
MY SUPER ABILITIES SHOWED UP WHEN I WAS 20, BUT, JUST AS FAST AS THEY CAME, THEY STARTED TO FADE WHEN I TURNED 65.
... NOT TODAY.

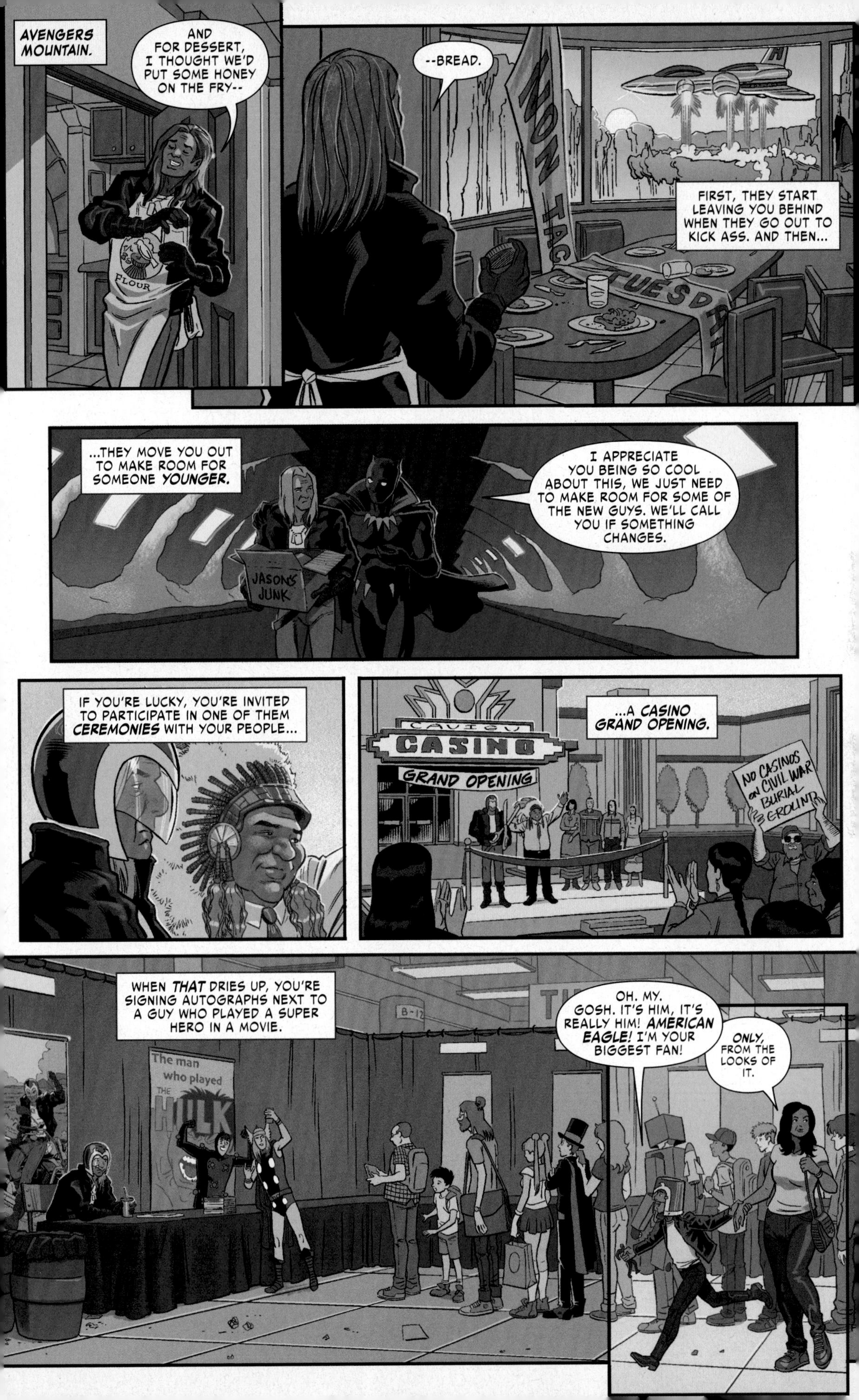
AVENGERS MOUNTAIN.
AND FOR DESSERT, I THOUGHT WE'D PUT SOME HONEY ON THE FRY--
FLOUR
--BREAD.
TUESD
FIRST, THEY START LEAVING YOU BEHIND WHEN THEY GO OUT TO KICK ASS. AND THEN...
...THEY MOVE YOU OUT TO MAKE ROOM FOR SOMEONE YOUNGER.
I APPRECIATE YOU BEING SO COOL ABOUT THIS, WE JUST NEED TO MAKE ROOM FOR SOME OF THE NEW GUYS. WE'LL CALL YOU IF SOMETHING CHANGES.
JASON'S JUNK
IF YOU'RE LUCKY, YOU'RE INVITED TO PARTICIPATE IN ONE OF THEM CEREMONIES WITH YOUR PEOPLE...
...A CASINO GRAND OPENING.
CASINO
GRAND OPENING
NO CASINOS on CIVIL WAR BURIAL GROUND
WHEN THAT DRIES UP, YOU'RE SIGNING AUTOGRAPHS NEXT TO A GUY WHO PLAYED A SUPER HERO IN A MOVIE.
The man who played THE HULK
B-12
OH. MY. GOSH. IT'S HIM, IT'S REALLY HIM! AMERICAN EAGLE! I'M YOUR BIGGEST FAN!
ONLY, FROM THE LOOKS OF IT.

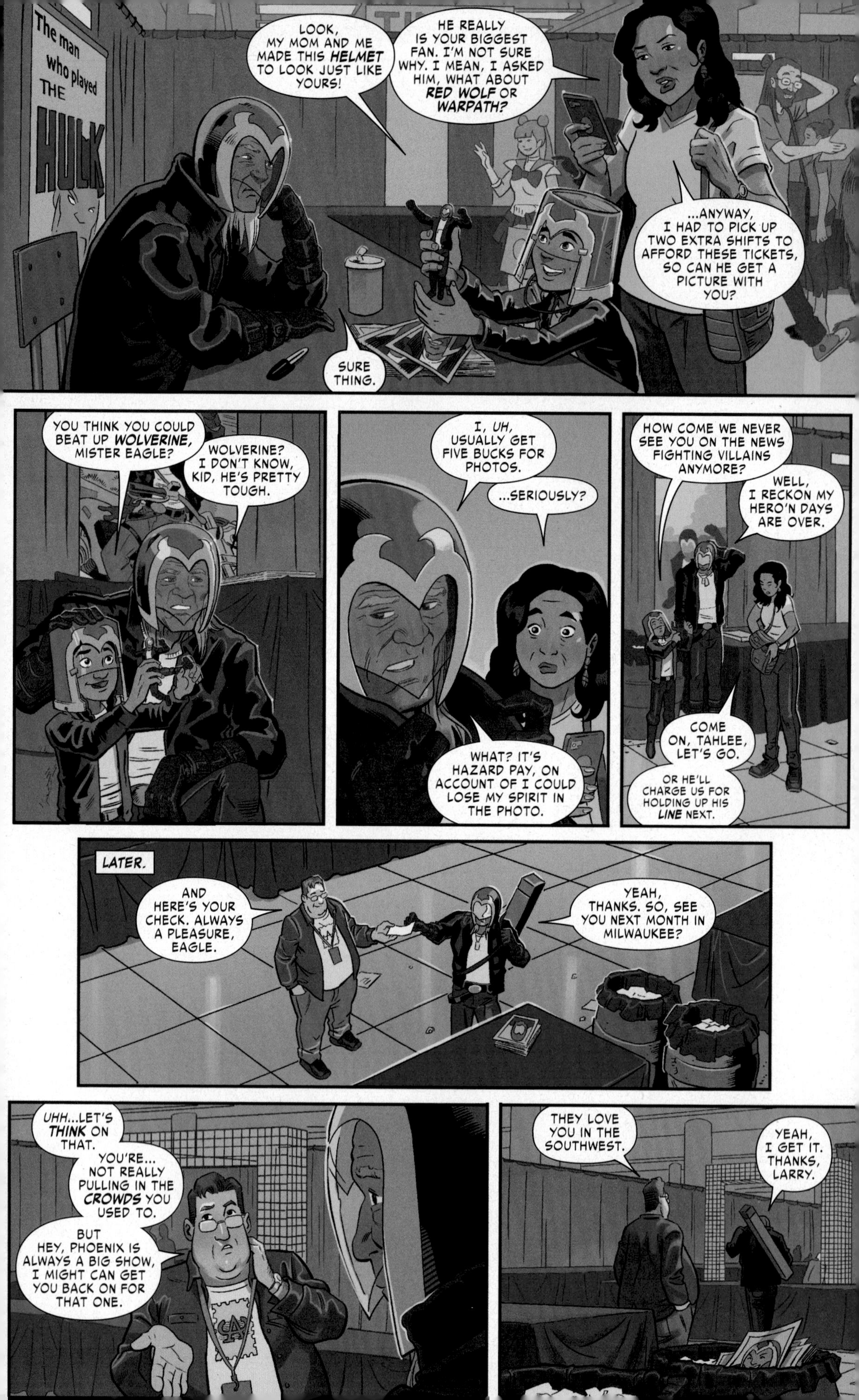
The man who played THE HULK
LOOK, MY MOM AND ME MADE THIS *HELMET* TO LOOK JUST LIKE YOURS!
HE REALLY IS YOUR BIGGEST FAN. I'M NOT SURE WHY. I MEAN, I ASKED HIM, WHAT ABOUT **RED WOLF** OR **WARPATH?**
...ANYWAY, I HAD TO PICK UP TWO EXTRA SHIFTS TO AFFORD THESE TICKETS, SO CAN HE GET A PICTURE WITH YOU?
SURE THING.
YOU THINK YOU COULD BEAT UP ***WOLVERINE,*** MISTER EAGLE?
WOLVERINE? I DON'T KNOW, KID, HE'S PRETTY TOUGH.
I, *UH,* USUALLY GET FIVE BUCKS FOR PHOTOS.
...SERIOUSLY?
WHAT? IT'S HAZARD PAY, ON ACCOUNT OF I COULD LOSE MY SPIRIT IN THE PHOTO.
HOW COME WE NEVER SEE YOU ON THE NEWS FIGHTING VILLAINS ANYMORE?
WELL, I RECKON MY HERO'N DAYS ARE OVER.
COME ON, TAHLEE, LET'S GO.
OR HE'LL CHARGE US FOR HOLDING UP HIS ***LINE*** NEXT.
LATER.
AND HERE'S YOUR CHECK. ALWAYS A PLEASURE, EAGLE.
YEAH, THANKS. SO, SEE YOU NEXT MONTH IN MILWAUKEE?
UHH...LET'S ***THINK*** ON THAT.
YOU'RE... NOT REALLY PULLING IN THE ***CROWDS*** YOU USED TO.
BUT HEY, PHOENIX IS ALWAYS A BIG SHOW, I MIGHT CAN GET YOU BACK ON FOR THAT ONE.
THEY LOVE YOU IN THE SOUTHWEST.
YEAH, I GET IT. THANKS, LARRY.

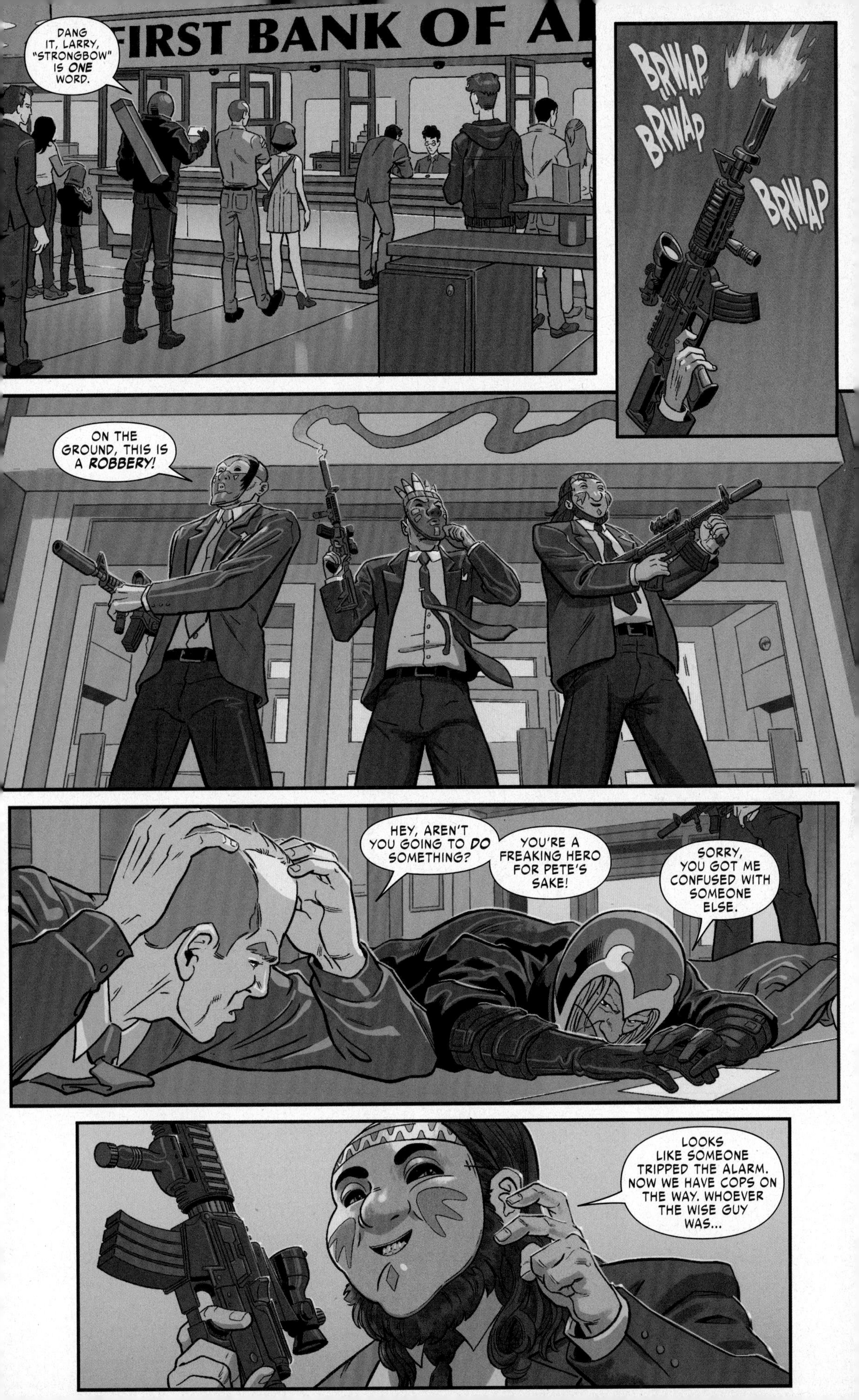
FIRST BANK OF A
DANG IT, LARRY, "STRONGBOW" IS ONE WORD.
BRWAP BRWAP BRWAP
ON THE GROUND, THIS IS A ROBBERY!
HEY, AREN'T YOU GOING TO DO SOMETHING?
YOU'RE A FREAKING HERO FOR PETE'S SAKE!
SORRY, YOU GOT ME CONFUSED WITH SOMEONE ELSE.
LOOKS LIKE SOMEONE TRIPPED THE ALARM. NOW WE HAVE COPS ON THE WAY. WHOEVER THE WISE GUY WAS...

...THEY JUST TURNED THIS INTO A *HOSTAGE* SITUATION.

AH!

PLEASE DON'T HURT MY SON!

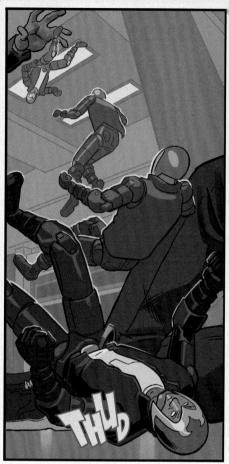

THUD

HELP!

FIRST BANK OF
JASON S
FOUR HUND
302 0497 38

CLENCH

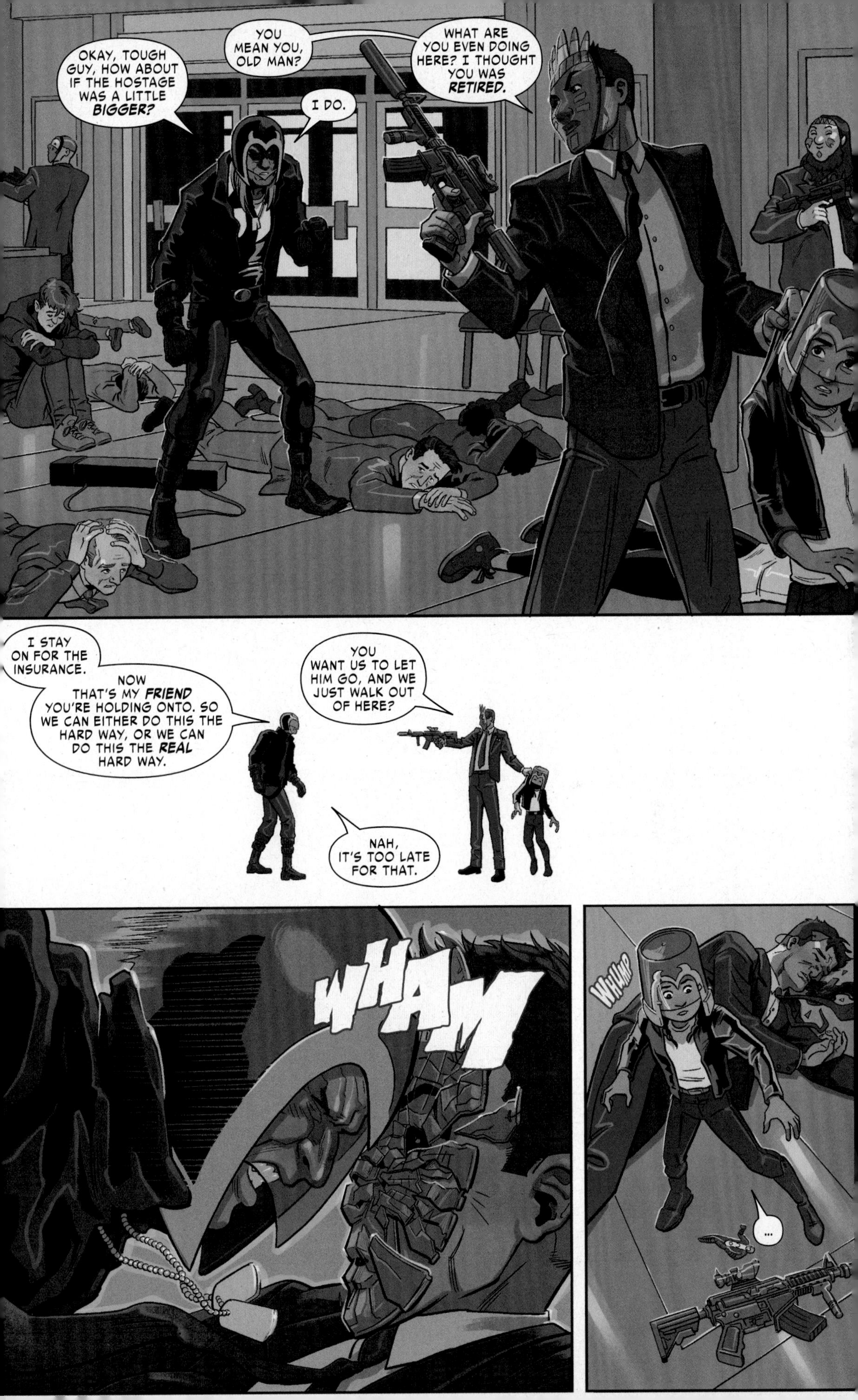
OKAY, TOUGH GUY, HOW ABOUT IF THE HOSTAGE WAS A LITTLE *BIGGER?*
YOU MEAN YOU, OLD MAN?
I DO.
WHAT ARE YOU EVEN DOING HERE? I THOUGHT YOU WAS *RETIRED.*
I STAY ON FOR THE INSURANCE.
NOW THAT'S MY *FRIEND* YOU'RE HOLDING ONTO. SO WE CAN EITHER DO THIS THE HARD WAY, OR WE CAN DO THIS THE *REAL* HARD WAY.
YOU WANT US TO LET HIM GO, AND WE JUST WALK OUT OF HERE?
NAH, IT'S TOO LATE FOR THAT.
WHAM
WHUMP
...

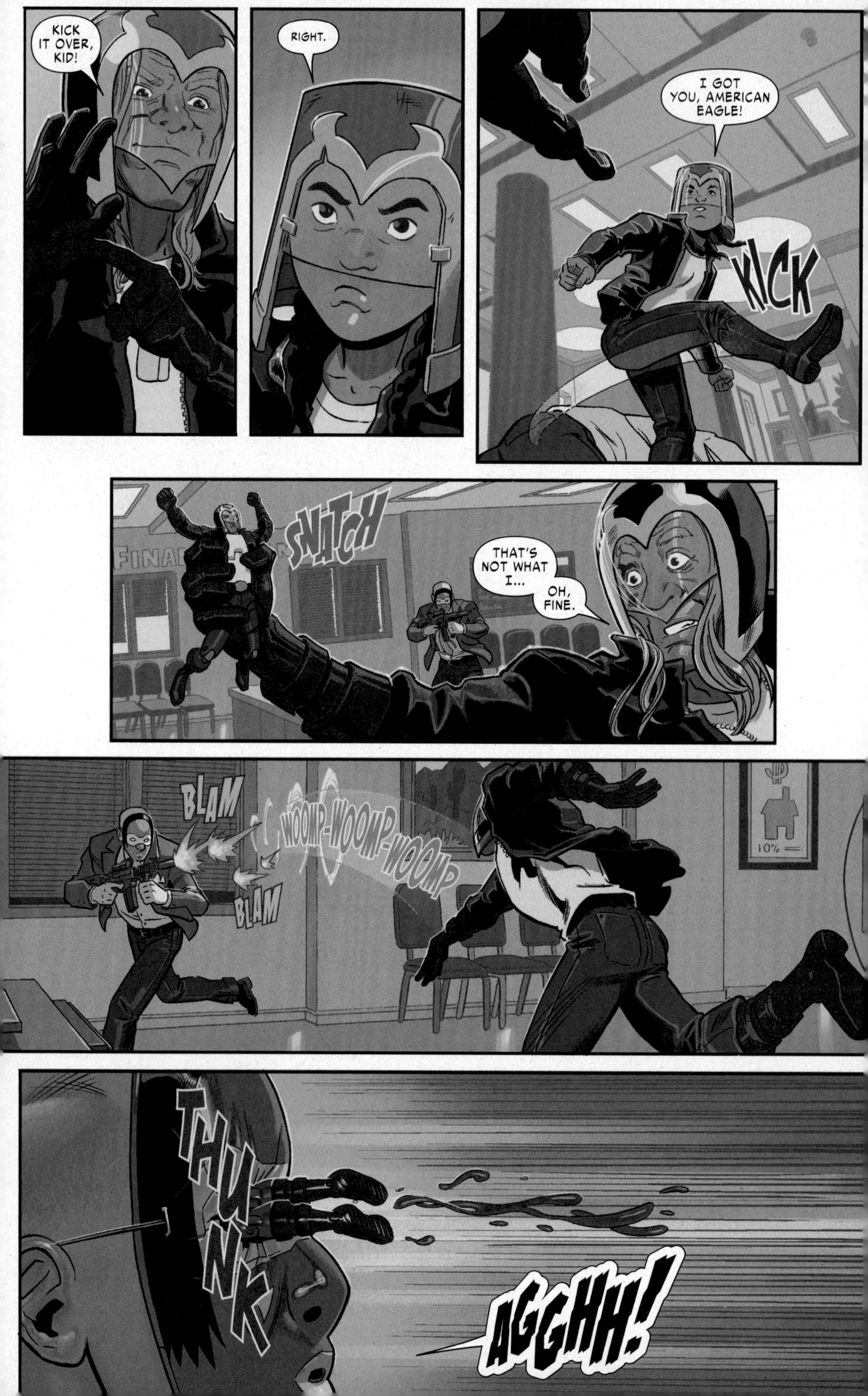
KICK IT OVER, KID!
RIGHT.
I GOT YOU, AMERICAN EAGLE!
KICK
SNATCH
THAT'S NOT WHAT I...
OH, FINE.
BLAM
WOOMP-WOOMP-WOOMP
BLAM
10%
THUNK
AGGHH!

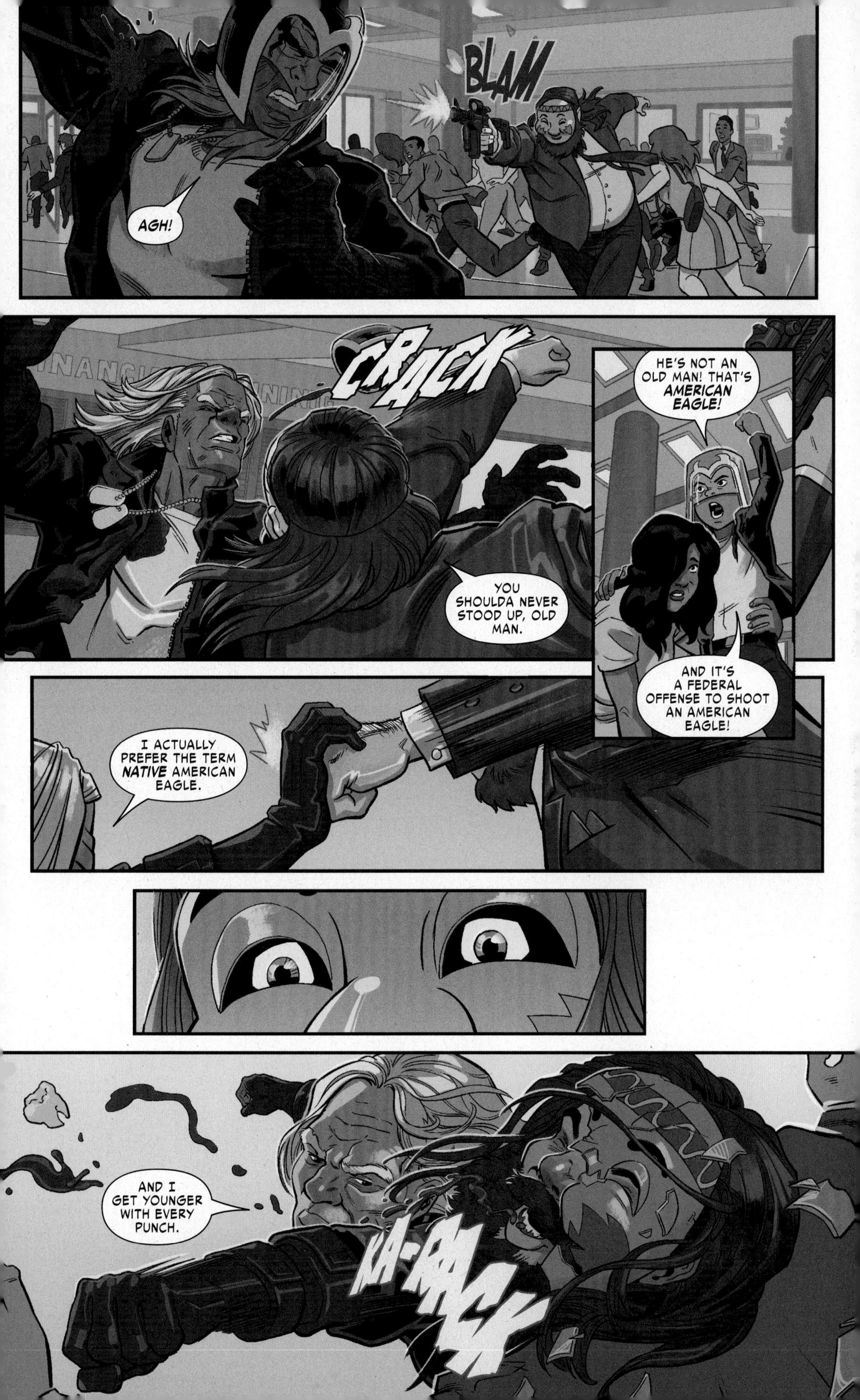
BLAM
AGH!
CRACK
YOU SHOULDA NEVER STOOD UP, OLD MAN.
HE'S NOT AN OLD MAN! THAT'S AMERICAN EAGLE!
AND IT'S A FEDERAL OFFENSE TO SHOOT AN AMERICAN EAGLE!
I ACTUALLY PREFER THE TERM NATIVE AMERICAN EAGLE.
AND I GET YOUNGER WITH EVERY PUNCH.
KA-RACK

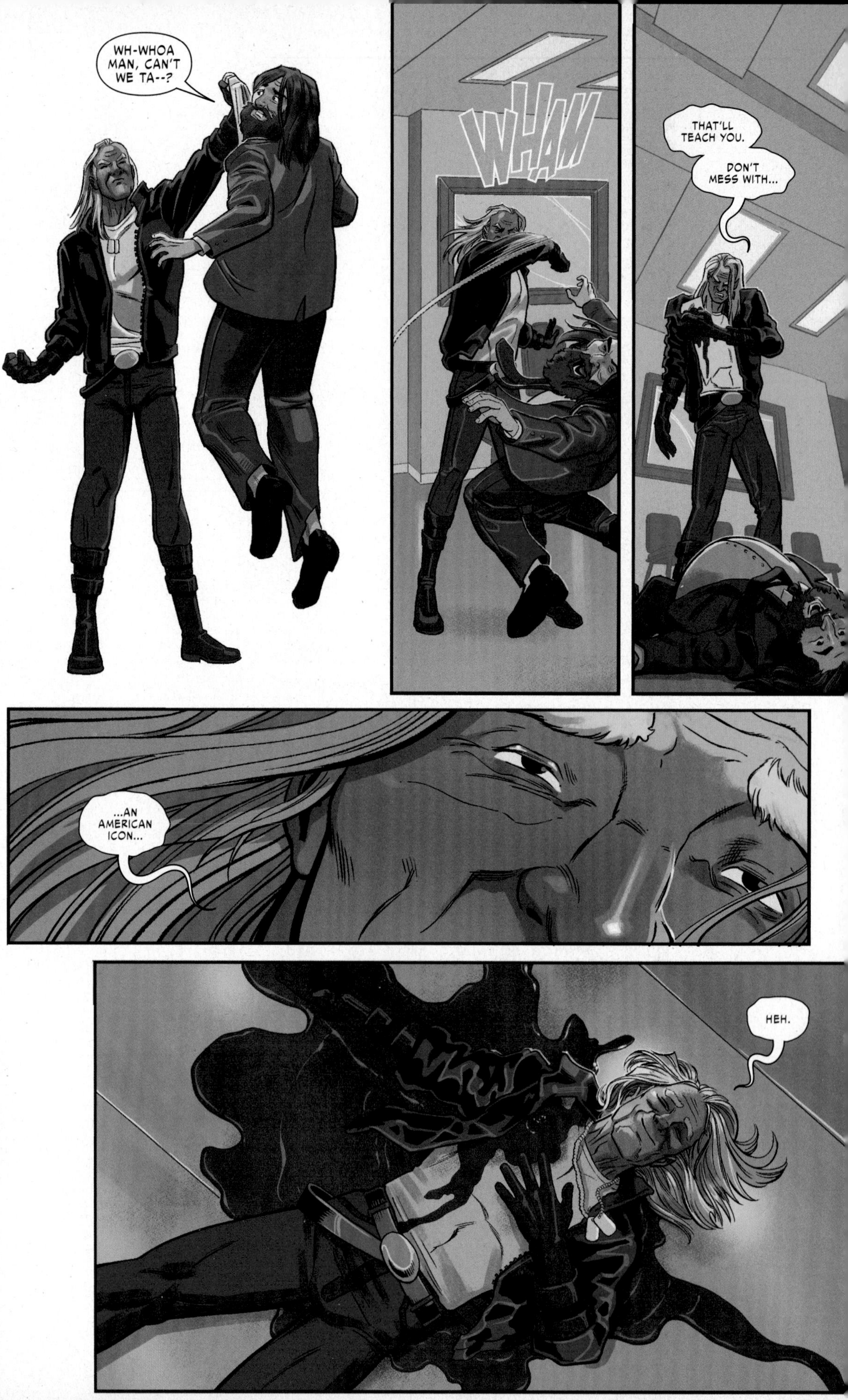
WH-WHOA MAN, CAN'T WE TA--?
WHAM
THAT'LL TEACH YOU.
DON'T MESS WITH...
...AN AMERICAN ICON...
HEH.

HEY, KID--

--HERE.

÷GASP÷

YOU DID IT! I KNEW YOUR HERO'N DAYS WEREN'T OVER!

I AIN'T NO HERO, KID. I'M JUST A GUY WHO CAN TAKE A PUNCH TO THE FACE.

THE NEXT DAY.

...

GUESS I'M NOT DONE AFTER ALL.

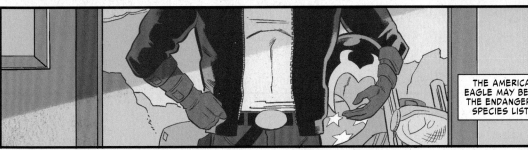

THE AMERICAN EAGLE MAY BE ON THE ENDANGERED SPECIES LIST...

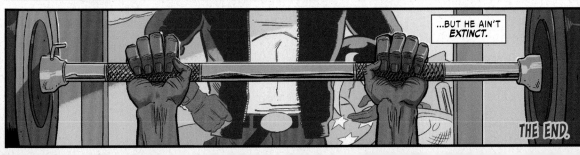

...BUT HE AIN'T EXTINCT.

THE END.

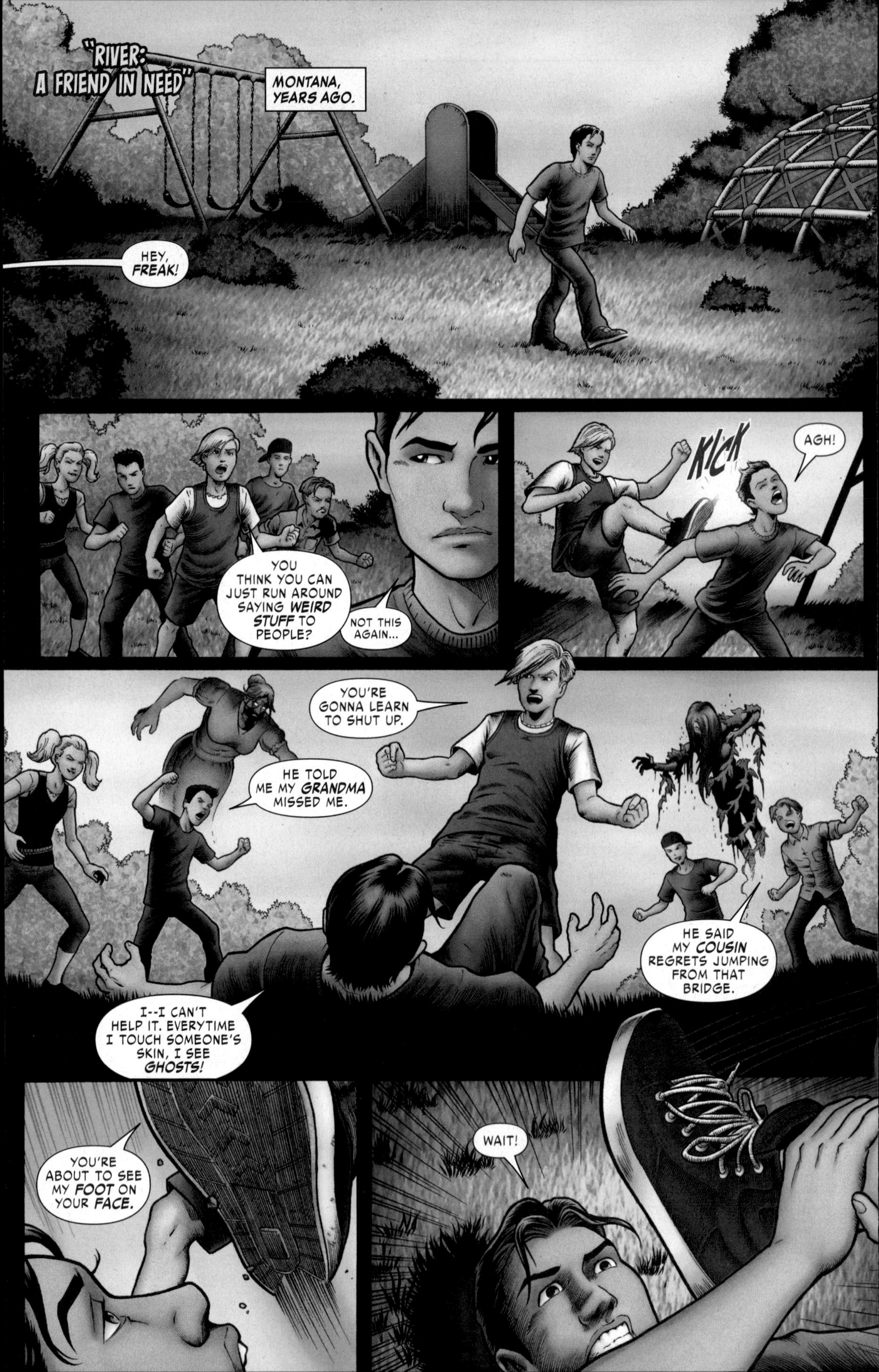
"RIVER: A FRIEND IN NEED"
MONTANA, YEARS AGO.
HEY, FREAK!
YOU THINK YOU CAN JUST RUN AROUND SAYING WEIRD STUFF TO PEOPLE?
NOT THIS AGAIN...
KICK
AGH!
YOU'RE GONNA LEARN TO SHUT UP.
HE TOLD ME MY GRANDMA MISSED ME.
HE SAID MY COUSIN REGRETS JUMPING FROM THAT BRIDGE.
I--I CAN'T HELP IT. EVERYTIME I TOUCH SOMEONE'S SKIN, I SEE GHOSTS!
YOU'RE ABOUT TO SEE MY FOOT ON YOUR FACE.
WAIT!

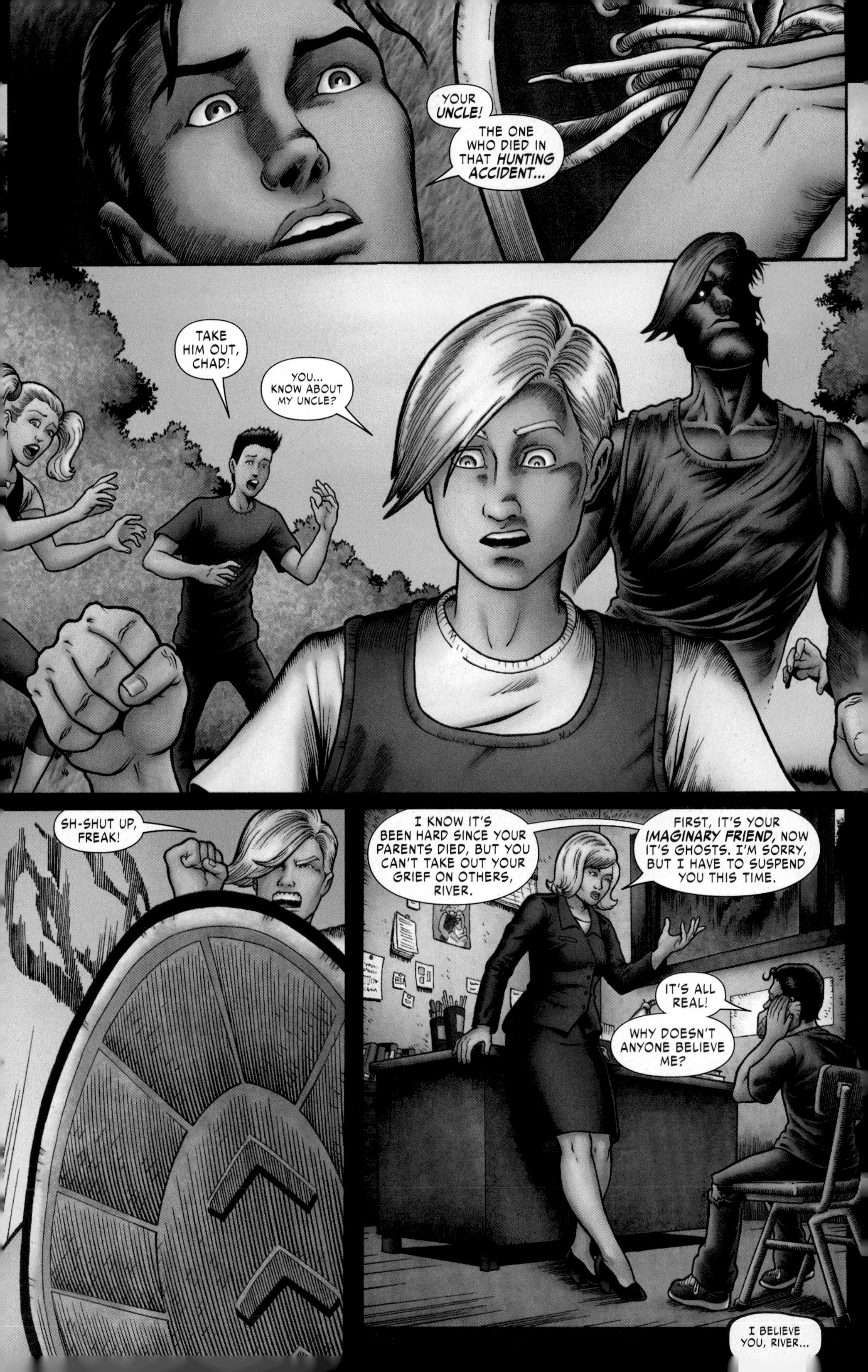
YOUR UNCLE!
THE ONE WHO DIED IN THAT HUNTING ACCIDENT...
TAKE HIM OUT, CHAD!
YOU... KNOW ABOUT MY UNCLE?
SH-SHUT UP, FREAK!
I KNOW IT'S BEEN HARD SINCE YOUR PARENTS DIED, BUT YOU CAN'T TAKE OUT YOUR GRIEF ON OTHERS, RIVER.
FIRST, IT'S YOUR IMAGINARY FRIEND, NOW IT'S GHOSTS. I'M SORRY, BUT I HAVE TO SUSPEND YOU THIS TIME.
IT'S ALL REAL!
WHY DOESN'T ANYONE BELIEVE ME?
I BELIEVE YOU, RIVER...

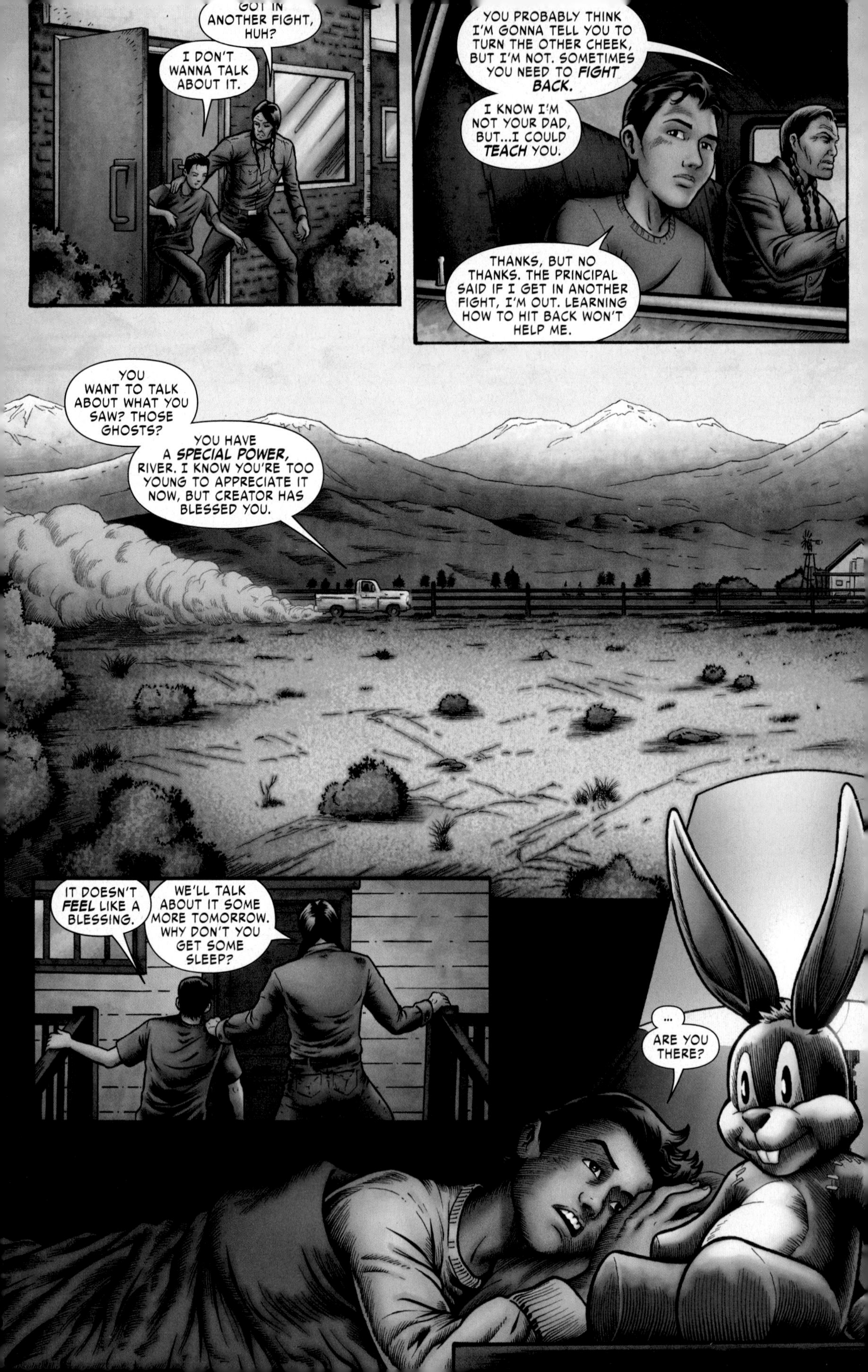
GOT IN ANOTHER FIGHT, HUH?
I DON'T WANNA TALK ABOUT IT.
YOU PROBABLY THINK I'M GONNA TELL YOU TO TURN THE OTHER CHEEK, BUT I'M NOT. SOMETIMES YOU NEED TO FIGHT BACK.
I KNOW I'M NOT YOUR DAD, BUT...I COULD TEACH YOU.
THANKS, BUT NO THANKS. THE PRINCIPAL SAID IF I GET IN ANOTHER FIGHT, I'M OUT. LEARNING HOW TO HIT BACK WON'T HELP ME.
YOU WANT TO TALK ABOUT WHAT YOU SAW? THOSE GHOSTS?
YOU HAVE A SPECIAL POWER, RIVER. I KNOW YOU'RE TOO YOUNG TO APPRECIATE IT NOW, BUT CREATOR HAS BLESSED YOU.
IT DOESN'T FEEL LIKE A BLESSING.
WE'LL TALK ABOUT IT SOME MORE TOMORROW. WHY DON'T YOU GET SOME SLEEP?
... ARE YOU THERE?

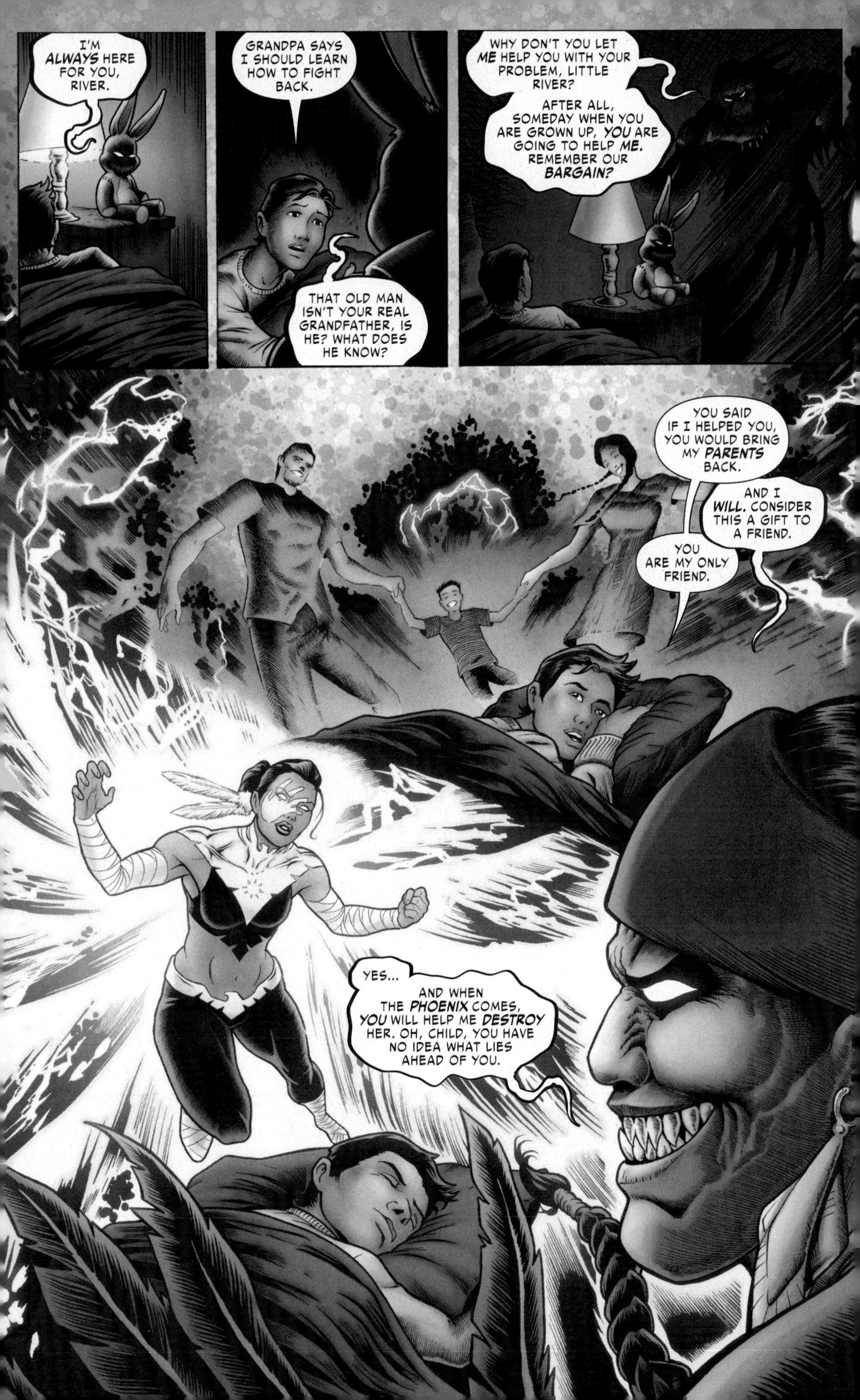
I'M ALWAYS HERE FOR YOU, RIVER.
GRANDPA SAYS I SHOULD LEARN HOW TO FIGHT BACK.
THAT OLD MAN ISN'T YOUR REAL GRANDFATHER, IS HE? WHAT DOES HE KNOW?
WHY DON'T YOU LET ME HELP YOU WITH YOUR PROBLEM, LITTLE RIVER?
AFTER ALL, SOMEDAY WHEN YOU ARE GROWN UP, YOU ARE GOING TO HELP ME. REMEMBER OUR BARGAIN?
YOU SAID IF I HELPED YOU, YOU WOULD BRING MY PARENTS BACK.
YOU ARE MY ONLY FRIEND.
AND I WILL. CONSIDER THIS A GIFT TO A FRIEND.
YES...
AND WHEN THE PHOENIX COMES, YOU WILL HELP ME DESTROY HER. OH, CHILD, YOU HAVE NO IDEA WHAT LIES AHEAD OF YOU.

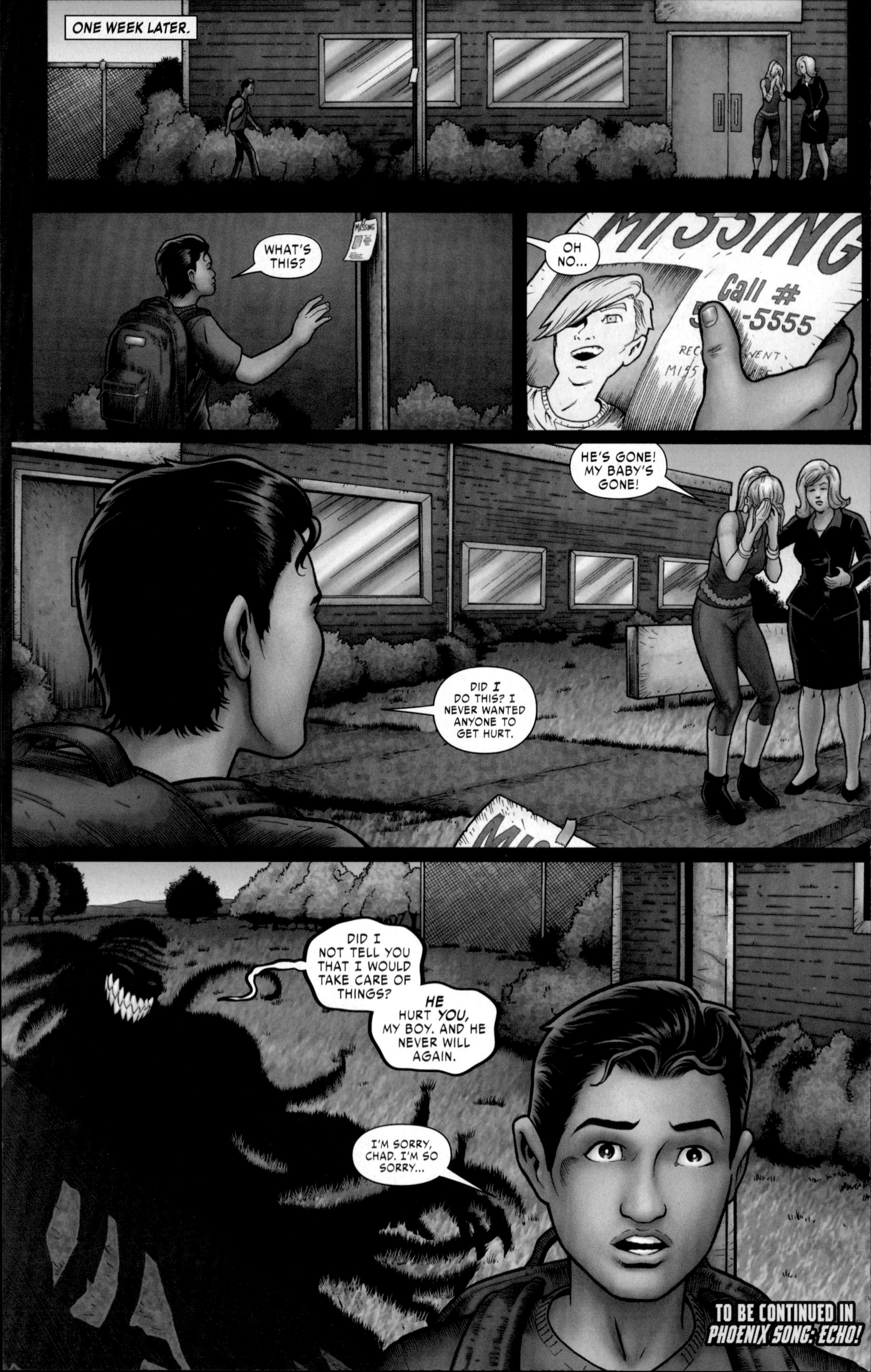
ONE WEEK LATER.
WHAT'S THIS?
MISSING
OH NO...
MISSING
Call #
-5555
HE'S GONE! MY BABY'S GONE!
DID I DO THIS? I NEVER WANTED ANYONE TO GET HURT.
DID I NOT TELL YOU THAT I WOULD TAKE CARE OF THINGS?
HE HURT YOU, MY BOY. AND HE NEVER WILL AGAIN.
I'M SORRY, CHAD. I'M SO SORRY...
TO BE CONTINUED IN PHOENIX SONG: ECHO!

AN INTERVIEW WITH WRITER REBECCA ROANHORSE

BY ANGÉLIQUE ROCHÉ

THE FOLLOWING HAS BEEN EDITED FOR
BREVITY AND CONTEXT.

Best-selling and Hugo Award-winning novelist Rebecca Roanhorse made her debut as a comic book writer with a ten-page short story featuring Super Hero Maya Lopez, A.K.A. Echo, in last year's *Marvel's Voices: Indigenous Voices #1*. A writer of stories about magic, super-powers, and "badass women taking control," Rebecca has continued her work with Marvel with the newly released *Phoenix Song: Echo* miniseries. This series follows Echo as she learns about her new cosmic abilities and struggles with the Phoenix's overwhelming personality. I sat down with the novelist and now screenwriter to talk about her career, passion for storytelling, and what is next for Echo.

Let's start at the beginning. How did you get into comics?

My first comics were more graphic novels like *Preacher* and *League of Extraordinary Gentlemen*. I do have to admit, I hadn't been a massive comic book fan, but I've fallen in love with the storytelling abilities of comics over novels. There's something really cool, collaborative, and exciting about comics and the visual elements—about working with an artist who brings your vision and your words to life, often in ways that you hadn't expected.

What has been kind of important for you going about writing these narratives and being able to craft literary spaces?

It's an incredible thing that I get to do this for a living, and I am very aware of that and very grateful to people who have given me the opportunity and to the fans who continue to read my work. I think my real mission in life is to bring Indigenous presence in a myriad of iterations into popular culture.

Why Echo's story?

Initially, Marvel came to me and asked me if I wanted to write an Echo story and I absolutely fell in love with the character. She's so cool. She's very much in my wheelhouse of characters that I like to write.

What does it mean for you now to be spearheading an Echo solo series?

I was very excited to tell her story. I wanted it to be something that stood on its own. In the past, Echo has often been a supporting character or attached to a love interest rather than standing in her own. I wanted this to be about her and who she is.

As an Indigenous Super Hero, in particular—Latina and Indigenous—I really wanted her to be the star of her own show. Of course, in this book, she also has the Phoenix power, which let me tell you, when you're trying to write one of the most powerful beings in the universe it's challenging story to come up with.

Fans might be interested to know that there was a deaf consultant involved in crafting Echo's story.

[Yes] we wanted to incorporate sign language. We wanted to catch things like making sure that the characters were speaking face-to-face, since Echo reads lips, small things like that.

You're introducing an important new character in *Phoenix Song: Echo*. Talk to us about River.

River was created for the series. You actually get a little bit of his backstory in this anthology. He's a fascinating character. He's quite complex. He has a really unusual power. And, quite frankly, we don't know exactly whose side he's on. So he was a lot of fun to write.

What has been your approach to comics and how has that differed from your other writing?

I am a visual writer. When I'm writing, the scene plays out in my head. Usually, it's my job just to get it down on paper. And so I was absolutely thrilled to be paired with an artist.

Why do you think it was so important for you as a writer to have also really used your career to change the narrative about what Indigenous and First Nations people look like in fiction?

There are so many stories of Natives from the 1800s. We seem stuck in the 1800s. It was important for me to create Native characters that exist now, in contemporary times, and in the future. My first novel was set in a postapocalyptic near future where Natives are thriving. It was important for me to bring forward those stories and the stories of the people I see around me every day.

And not just these stereotypes, these one-dimensional characters where there's always a spirit animal or someone's changing into an animal. I wanted complexity. I wanted heroes, but I wanted villains, too. I wanted a love interest. I wanted characters who are difficult to love as well. The whole sort of panoply of human emotion that we don't often get to see in Native characters. We're often so limited in the cultural imagination to the past, the one-dimensional characters, and the stereotypes. We're not all just Pocahontas. There are so many other stories that can be told.

Listen to more of my conversation with Rebecca on a very special bonus episode of the Marvel's Voices *Podcast available on Marvel Podcasts Unlimited.*

◇ ◇ ◇

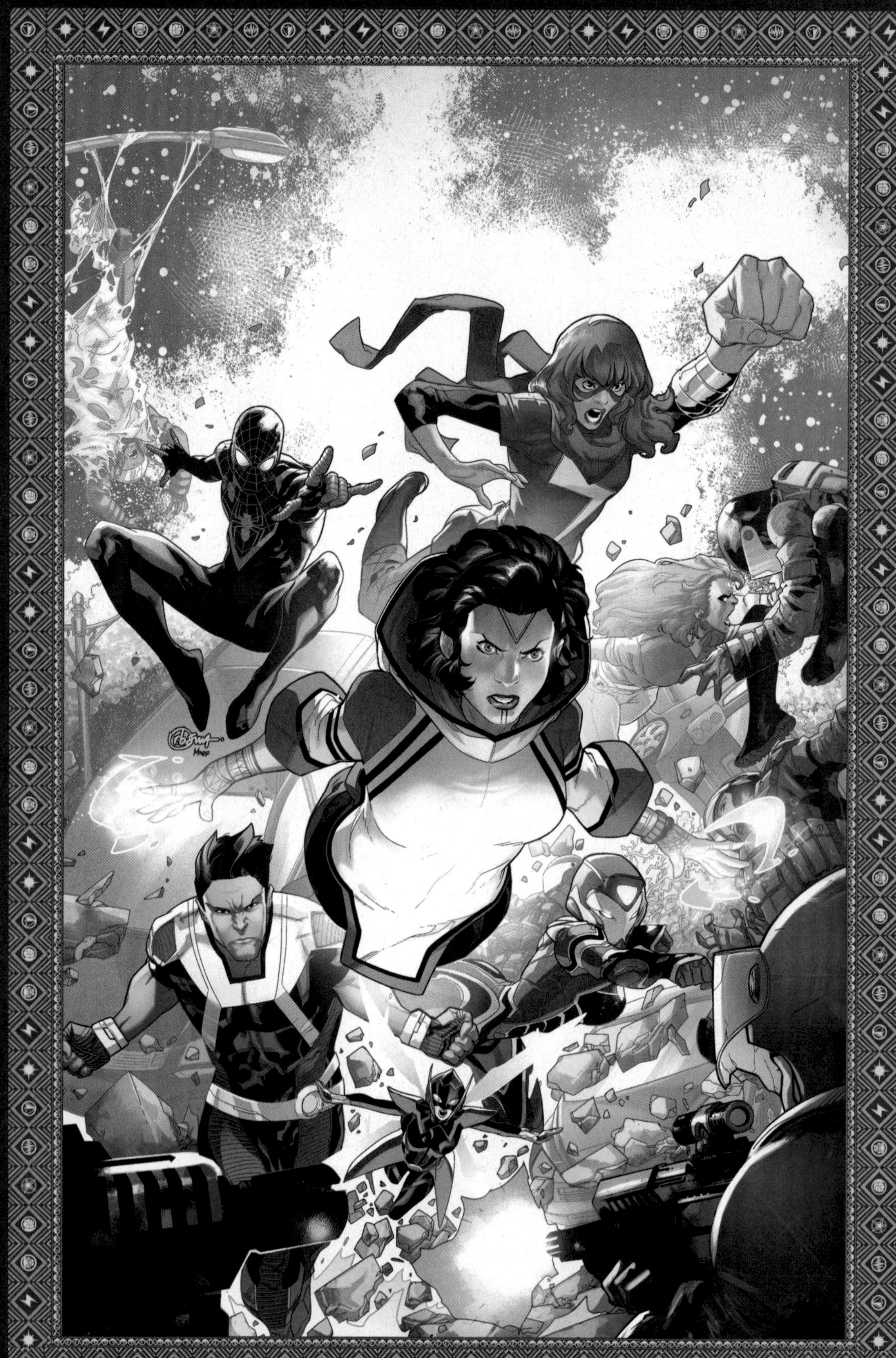

CHAMPIONS ANNUAL #1

When society became disillusioned with its heroes, the next generation made a vow to do better. To make a difference. To change the world. They are the...

CHAMPIONS

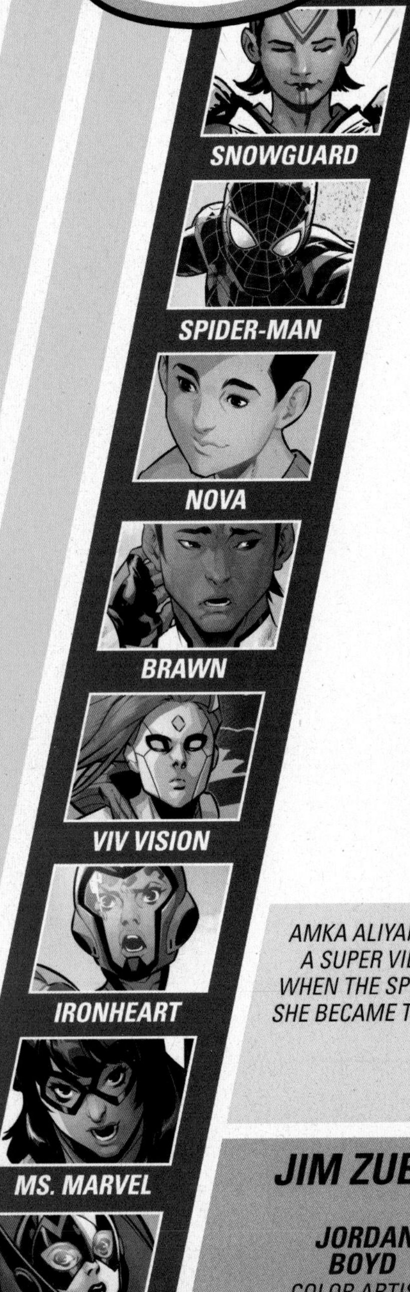
SNOWGUARD
SPIDER-MAN
NOVA
BRAWN
VIV VISION
IRONHEART
MS. MARVEL
WASP

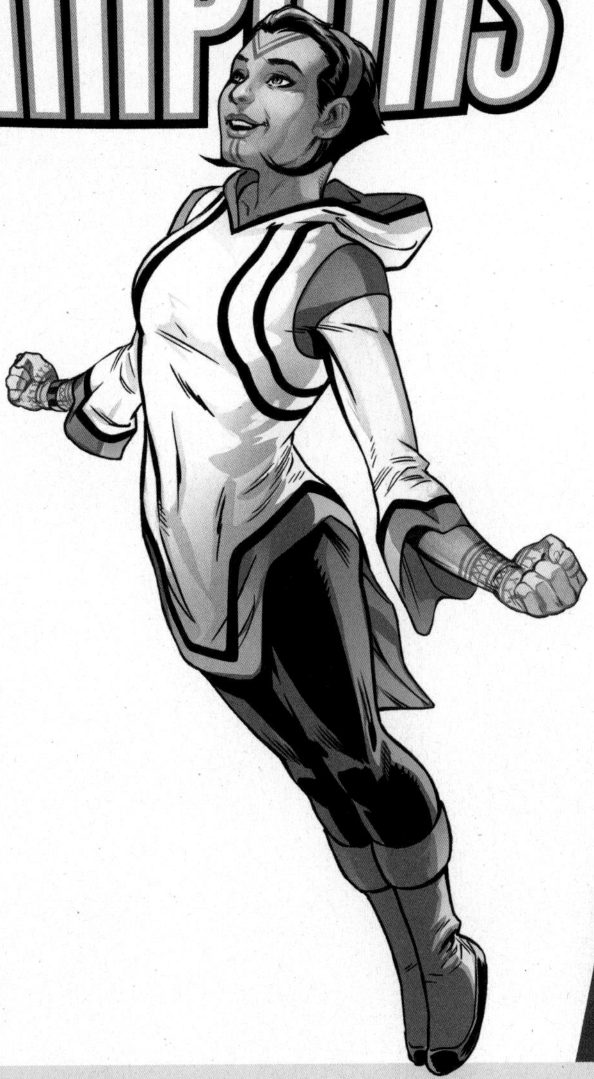

AMKA ALIYAK IS AN INUK TEENAGER WHO FIRST ENCOUNTERED THE CHAMPIONS WHEN A SUPER VILLAIN THREATENED HER HOME OF PANGNIRTUNG IN NORTHERN CANADA. WHEN THE SPIRITS OF THE NORTH KNOWN AS THE SILAP INUA SAVED HER FROM DEATH, SHE BECAME THE SHAPE-SHIFTING SUPER HERO SNOWGUARD, AND LEFT PANGNIRTUNG TO EXPLORE THE WORLD WITH THE CHAMPIONS!

BUT EVERYONE HAS TO GO HOME EVENTUALLY...

JIM ZUB & NYLA INNUKSUK WRITERS
MARCUS TO ARTIST
JORDAN BOYD COLOR ARTIST
VC's CLAYTON COWLES LETTERER & PRODUCTION
R.B. SILVA & MARCIO MENYZ COVER ARTISTS

BABS TARR VARIANT COVER ARTIST **ALANNA SMITH** ASSOC. EDITOR
TOM BREVOORT EDITOR **C.B. CEBULSKI** EDITOR IN CHIEF
JOE QUESADA CHIEF CREATIVE OFFICER **DAN BUCKLEY** PRESIDENT **ALAN FINE** EXEC. PRODUCER

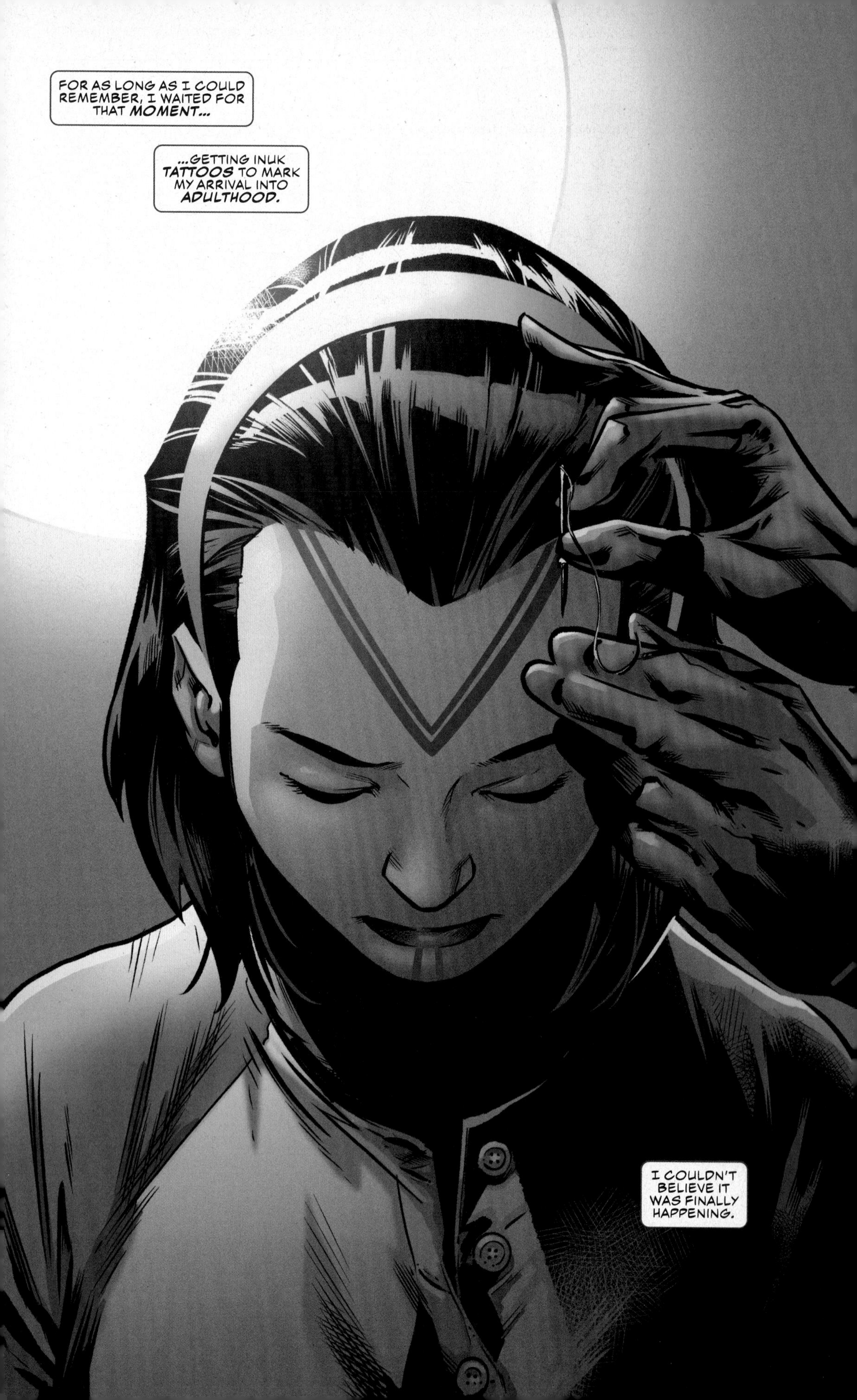
FOR AS LONG AS I COULD REMEMBER, I WAITED FOR THAT MOMENT...
...GETTING INUK TATTOOS TO MARK MY ARRIVAL INTO ADULTHOOD.
I COULDN'T BELIEVE IT WAS FINALLY HAPPENING.

I WAS SHAKING FROM THE ADRENALINE. I COULDN'T STOP CRYING.

MOM WAS SO PROUD.

<NOW YOU ARE A WOMAN!>*

<THANK YOU, THANK YOU!>

*TRANSLATED FROM INUKTITUT.

BUT THE EUPHORIA PASSED AND I DIDN'T FEEL ANY DIFFERENT.

THERE WAS NO SPECIAL INSIGHT. I WASN'T ANY CLOSER TO MY ANCESTORS.

I WAS STILL JUST...ME, AMKA ALIYAK...ONLY NOW I HAD PRETTY LINES ON MY FACE AND HANDS.

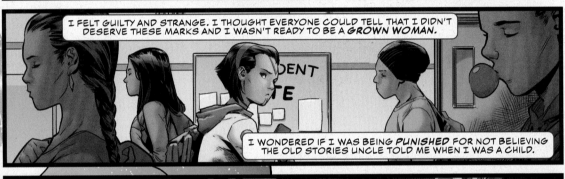

I FELT GUILTY AND STRANGE. I THOUGHT EVERYONE COULD TELL THAT I DIDN'T DESERVE THESE MARKS AND I WASN'T READY TO BE A GROWN WOMAN.

I WONDERED IF I WAS BEING PUNISHED FOR NOT BELIEVING THE OLD STORIES UNCLE TOLD ME WHEN I WAS A CHILD.

THREE YEARS LATER, I STUMBLED ACROSS SILA...SOUL OF THE NORTH AND SPIRIT OF THE SKY, WIND AND WEATHER.

I FREED SILA FROM A HIGH-TECH PRISON AND WAS CAUGHT IN AN EXPLOSION.*

<YOU ARE A WARRIOR, AMKA ALIYAK...>

*AS SHOWN IN CHAMPIONS #20. --TOM

I SHOULD HAVE DIED, BUT SILA GAVE ME A PIECE OF THEIR ENERGY...

<...AND THOUGH I DO NOT KNOW WHAT THE FUTURE HOLDS, I DO KNOW THIS...>

<...YOU WILL NOT DIE THIS DAY.>

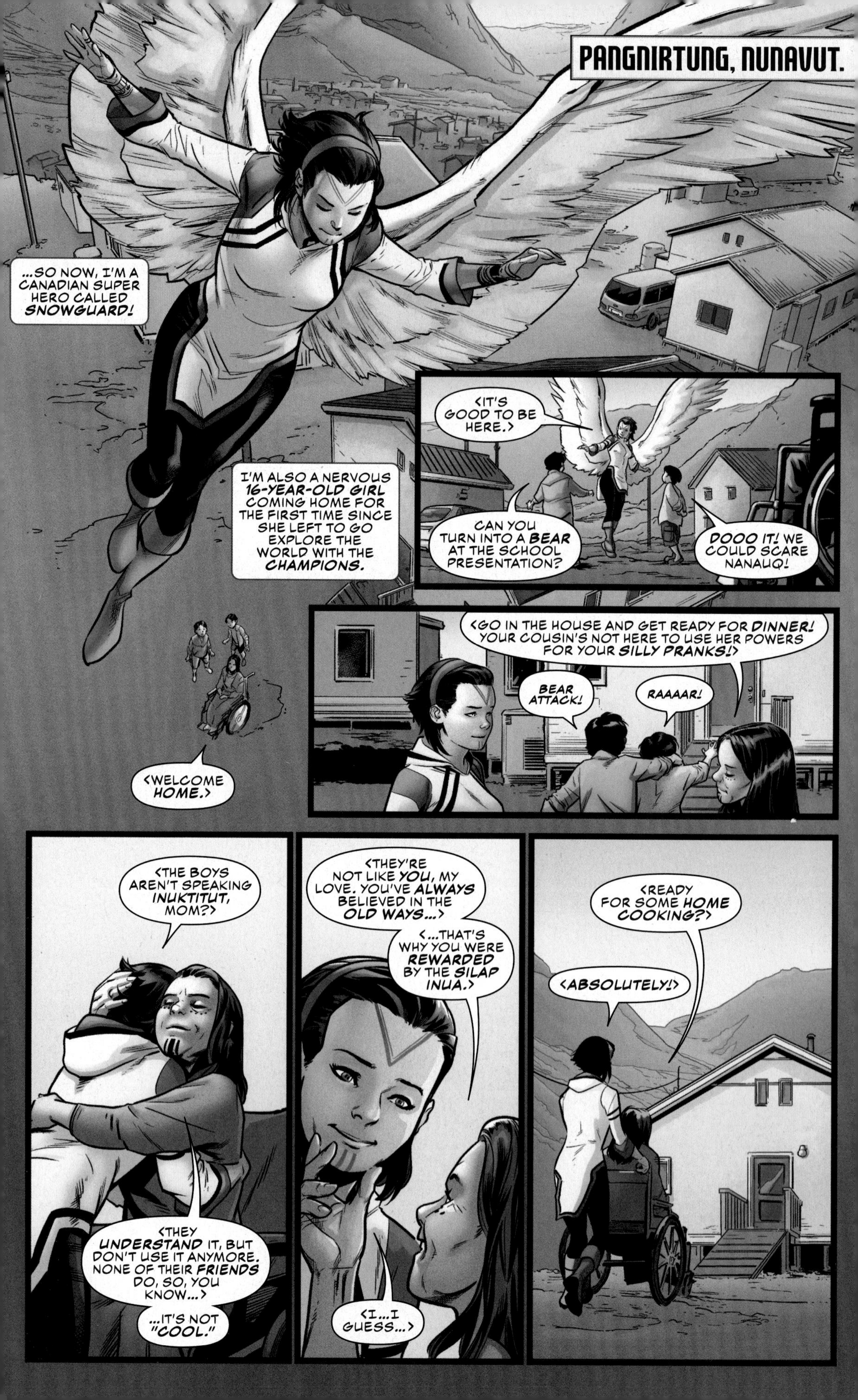
PANGNIRTUNG, NUNAVUT.
...SO NOW, I'M A CANADIAN SUPER HERO CALLED SNOWGUARD!
I'M ALSO A NERVOUS 16-YEAR-OLD GIRL COMING HOME FOR THE FIRST TIME SINCE SHE LEFT TO GO EXPLORE THE WORLD WITH THE CHAMPIONS.
<WELCOME HOME.>
<IT'S GOOD TO BE HERE.>
CAN YOU TURN INTO A BEAR AT THE SCHOOL PRESENTATION?
DOOO IT! WE COULD SCARE NANAUQ!
<GO IN THE HOUSE AND GET READY FOR DINNER! YOUR COUSIN'S NOT HERE TO USE HER POWERS FOR YOUR SILLY PRANKS!>
BEAR ATTACK!
RAAAAR!
<THE BOYS AREN'T SPEAKING INUKTITUT, MOM?>
<THEY UNDERSTAND IT, BUT DON'T USE IT ANYMORE. NONE OF THEIR FRIENDS DO, SO, YOU KNOW...>
...IT'S NOT "COOL."
<THEY'RE NOT LIKE YOU, MY LOVE. YOU'VE ALWAYS BELIEVED IN THE OLD WAYS...>
<...THAT'S WHY YOU WERE REWARDED BY THE SILAP INUA.>
<I...I GUESS...>
<READY FOR SOME HOME COOKING?>
<ABSOLUTELY!>

<THANK YOU, EVERYONE!>

THE *CHATTER*, THE *GOSSIP*...IN SOME WAYS IT FEELS LIKE I NEVER LEFT.

EXCEPT THE THINGS THEY'RE TALKING *ABOUT*-- I'M A BIT LOST. IT'S ALL PASSED ME BY AS I--

...BUT THEY CAN'T IGNORE US *NOW!* WE'VE GOT A *SUPER HERO* IN *ALPHA FLIGHT!*

EH?

NO, NO, PILIP... I JOINED THE *CHAMPIONS.*

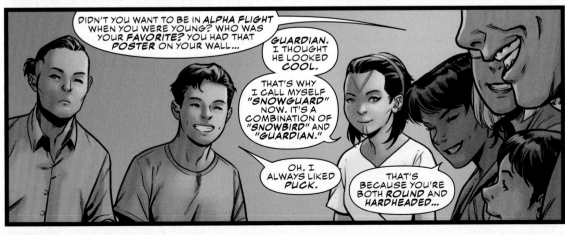

DIDN'T YOU WANT TO BE IN *ALPHA FLIGHT* WHEN YOU WERE YOUNG? WHO WAS YOUR *FAVORITE?* YOU HAD THAT *POSTER* ON YOUR WALL...

GUARDIAN. I THOUGHT HE LOOKED *COOL.*

THAT'S WHY I CALL MYSELF *"SNOWGUARD"* NOW. IT'S A COMBINATION OF *"SNOWBIRD"* AND *"GUARDIAN."*

OH. I ALWAYS LIKED *PUCK.*

THAT'S BECAUSE YOU'RE BOTH *ROUND* AND *HARDHEADED...*

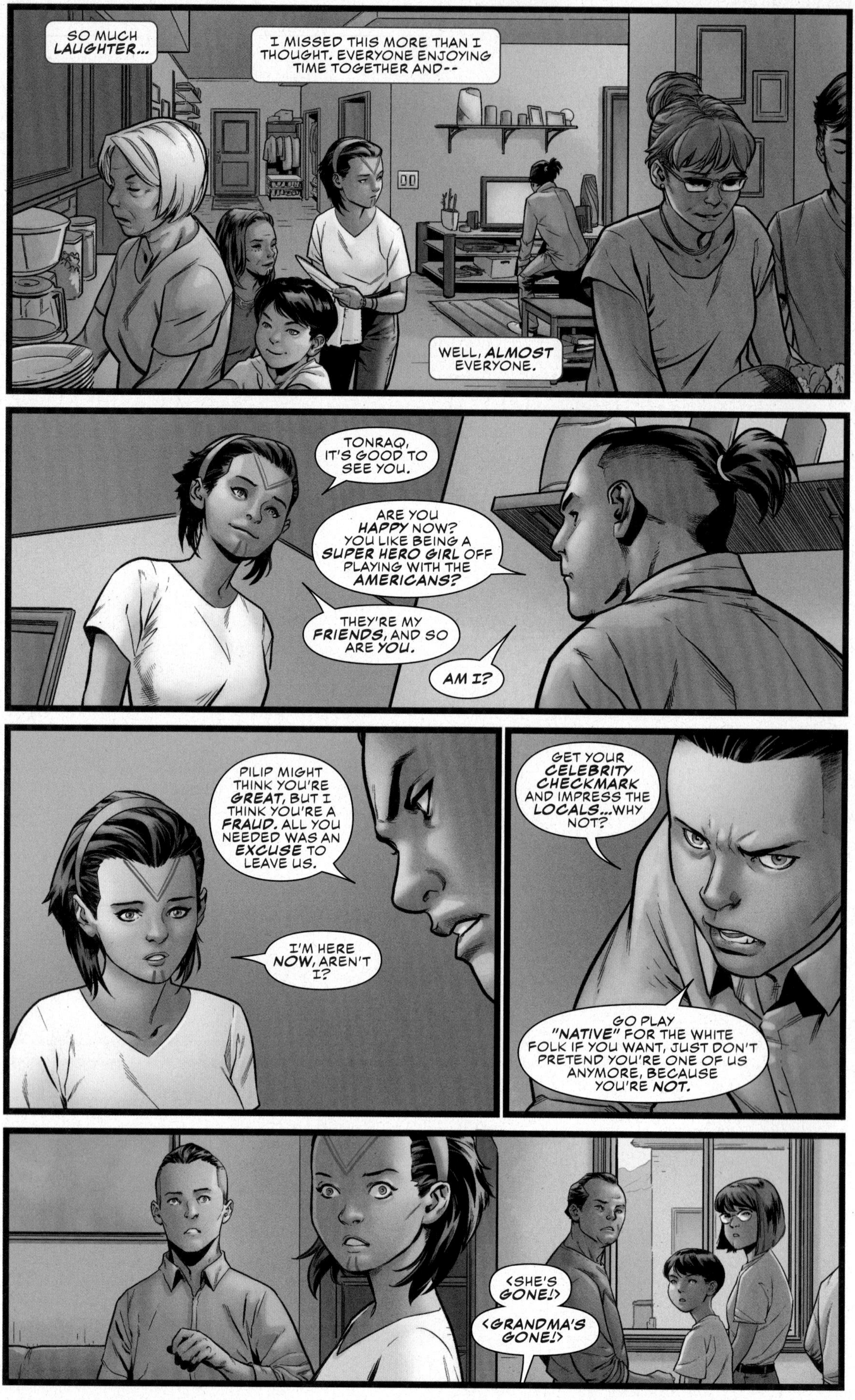
SO MUCH LAUGHTER...
I MISSED THIS MORE THAN I THOUGHT. EVERYONE ENJOYING TIME TOGETHER AND--
WELL, ALMOST EVERYONE.
TONRAQ, IT'S GOOD TO SEE YOU.
ARE YOU HAPPY NOW? YOU LIKE BEING A SUPER HERO GIRL OFF PLAYING WITH THE AMERICANS?
THEY'RE MY FRIENDS, AND SO ARE YOU.
AM I?
PILIP MIGHT THINK YOU'RE GREAT, BUT I THINK YOU'RE A FRAUD. ALL YOU NEEDED WAS AN EXCUSE TO LEAVE US.
I'M HERE NOW, AREN'T I?
GET YOUR CELEBRITY CHECKMARK AND IMPRESS THE LOCALS...WHY NOT?
GO PLAY "NATIVE" FOR THE WHITE FOLK IF YOU WANT, JUST DON'T PRETEND YOU'RE ONE OF US ANYMORE, BECAUSE YOU'RE NOT.
<SHE'S GONE!>
<GRANDMA'S GONE!>

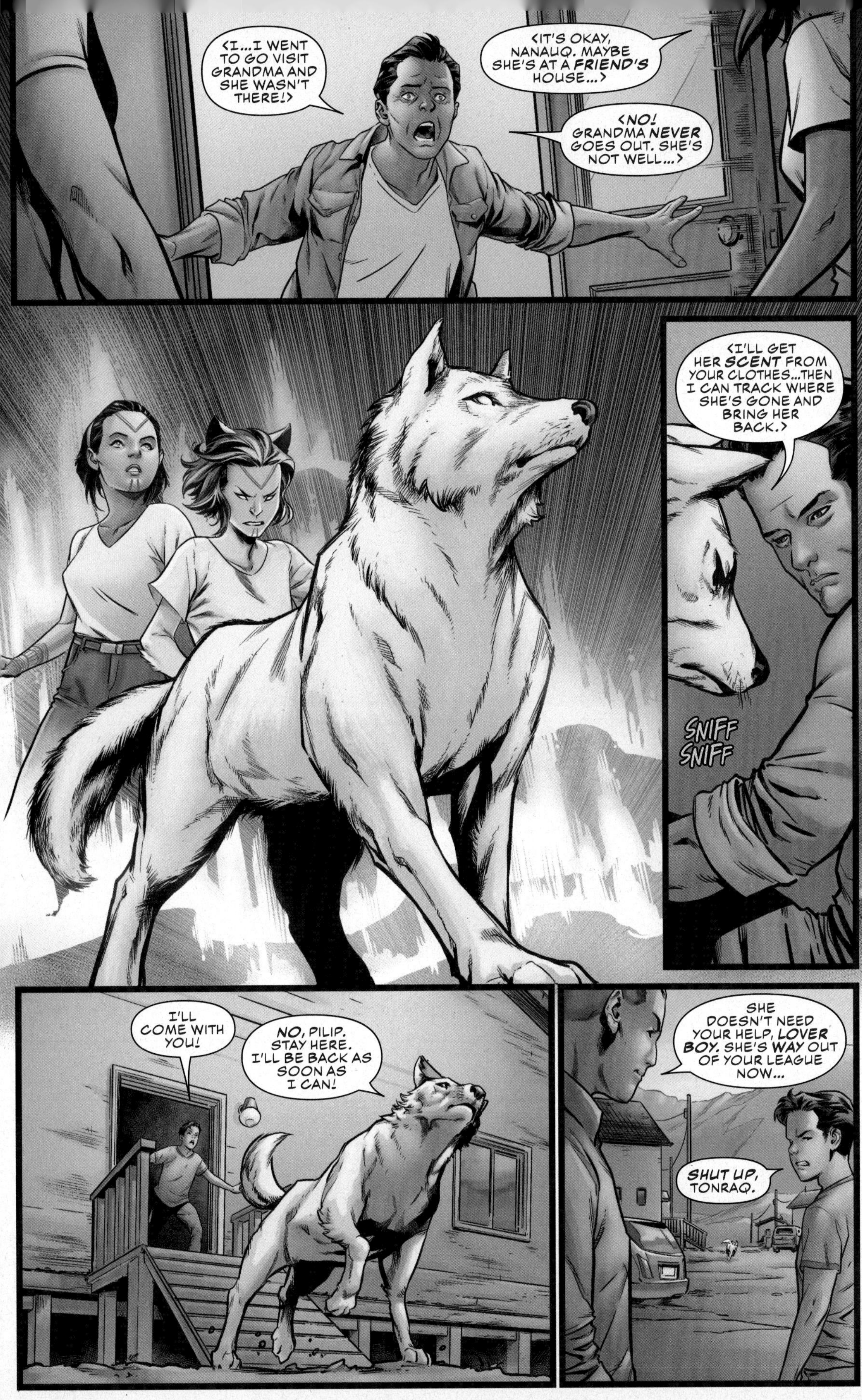

<I...I WENT TO GO VISIT GRANDMA AND SHE WASN'T THERE!>
<IT'S OKAY, NANAUQ. MAYBE SHE'S AT A FRIEND'S HOUSE...>
<NO! GRANDMA NEVER GOES OUT. SHE'S NOT WELL...>
<I'LL GET HER SCENT FROM YOUR CLOTHES...THEN I CAN TRACK WHERE SHE'S GONE AND BRING HER BACK.>
SNIFF SNIFF
I'LL COME WITH YOU!
NO, PILIP. STAY HERE. I'LL BE BACK AS SOON AS I CAN!
SHE DOESN'T NEED YOUR HELP, LOVER BOY. SHE'S WAY OUT OF YOUR LEAGUE NOW...
SHUT UP, TONRAQ.

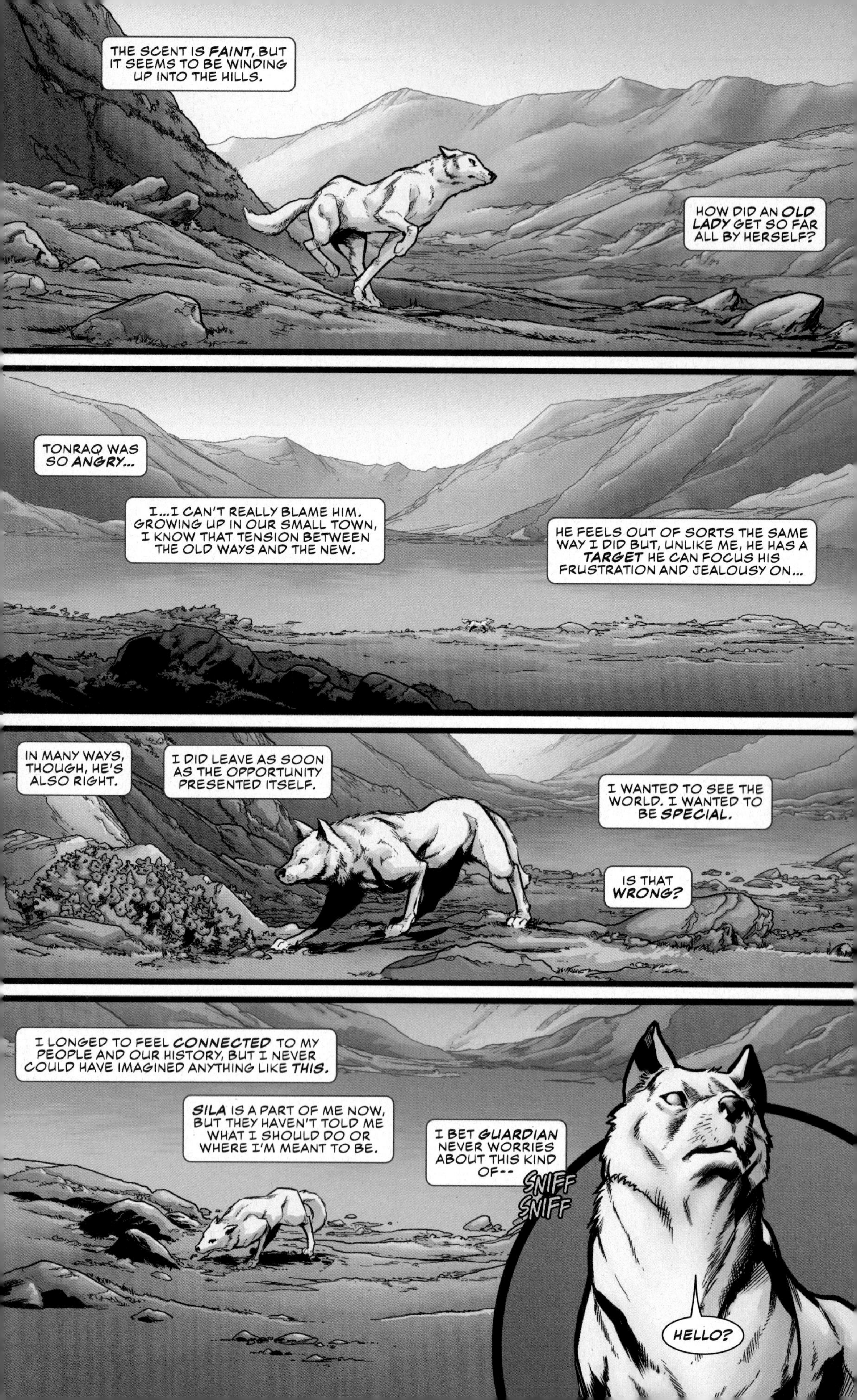
THE SCENT IS FAINT, BUT IT SEEMS TO BE WINDING UP INTO THE HILLS.
HOW DID AN OLD LADY GET SO FAR ALL BY HERSELF?
TONRAQ WAS SO ANGRY...
I...I CAN'T REALLY BLAME HIM. GROWING UP IN OUR SMALL TOWN, I KNOW THAT TENSION BETWEEN THE OLD WAYS AND THE NEW.
HE FEELS OUT OF SORTS THE SAME WAY I DID BUT, UNLIKE ME, HE HAS A TARGET HE CAN FOCUS HIS FRUSTRATION AND JEALOUSY ON...
IN MANY WAYS, THOUGH, HE'S ALSO RIGHT.
I DID LEAVE AS SOON AS THE OPPORTUNITY PRESENTED ITSELF.
I WANTED TO SEE THE WORLD. I WANTED TO BE SPECIAL.
IS THAT WRONG?
I LONGED TO FEEL CONNECTED TO MY PEOPLE AND OUR HISTORY, BUT I NEVER COULD HAVE IMAGINED ANYTHING LIKE THIS.
SILA IS A PART OF ME NOW, BUT THEY HAVEN'T TOLD ME WHAT I SHOULD DO OR WHERE I'M MEANT TO BE.
I BET GUARDIAN NEVER WORRIES ABOUT THIS KIND OF--
SNIFF SNIFF
HELLO?

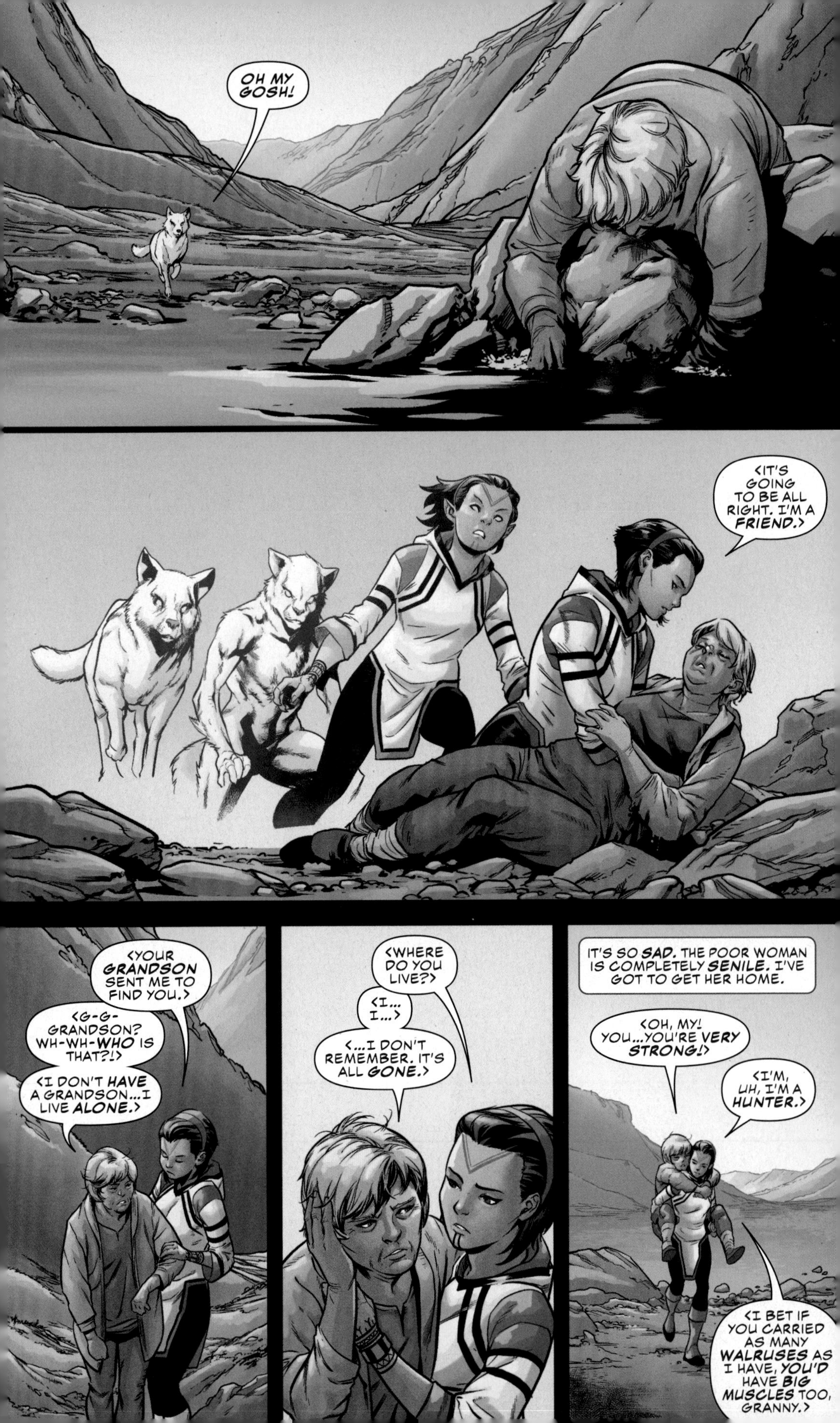
OH MY GOSH!
<IT'S GOING TO BE ALL RIGHT. I'M A FRIEND.>
<YOUR GRANDSON SENT ME TO FIND YOU.>
<G-G-GRANDSON? WH-WH-WHO IS THAT?!>
<I DON'T HAVE A GRANDSON...I LIVE ALONE.>
<WHERE DO YOU LIVE?>
<I... I...>
<...I DON'T REMEMBER. IT'S ALL GONE.>
IT'S SO SAD. THE POOR WOMAN IS COMPLETELY SENILE. I'VE GOT TO GET HER HOME.
<OH, MY! YOU...YOU'RE VERY STRONG!>
<I'M, UH, I'M A HUNTER.>
<I BET IF YOU CARRIED AS MANY WALRUSES AS I HAVE, YOU'D HAVE BIG MUSCLES TOO, GRANNY.>

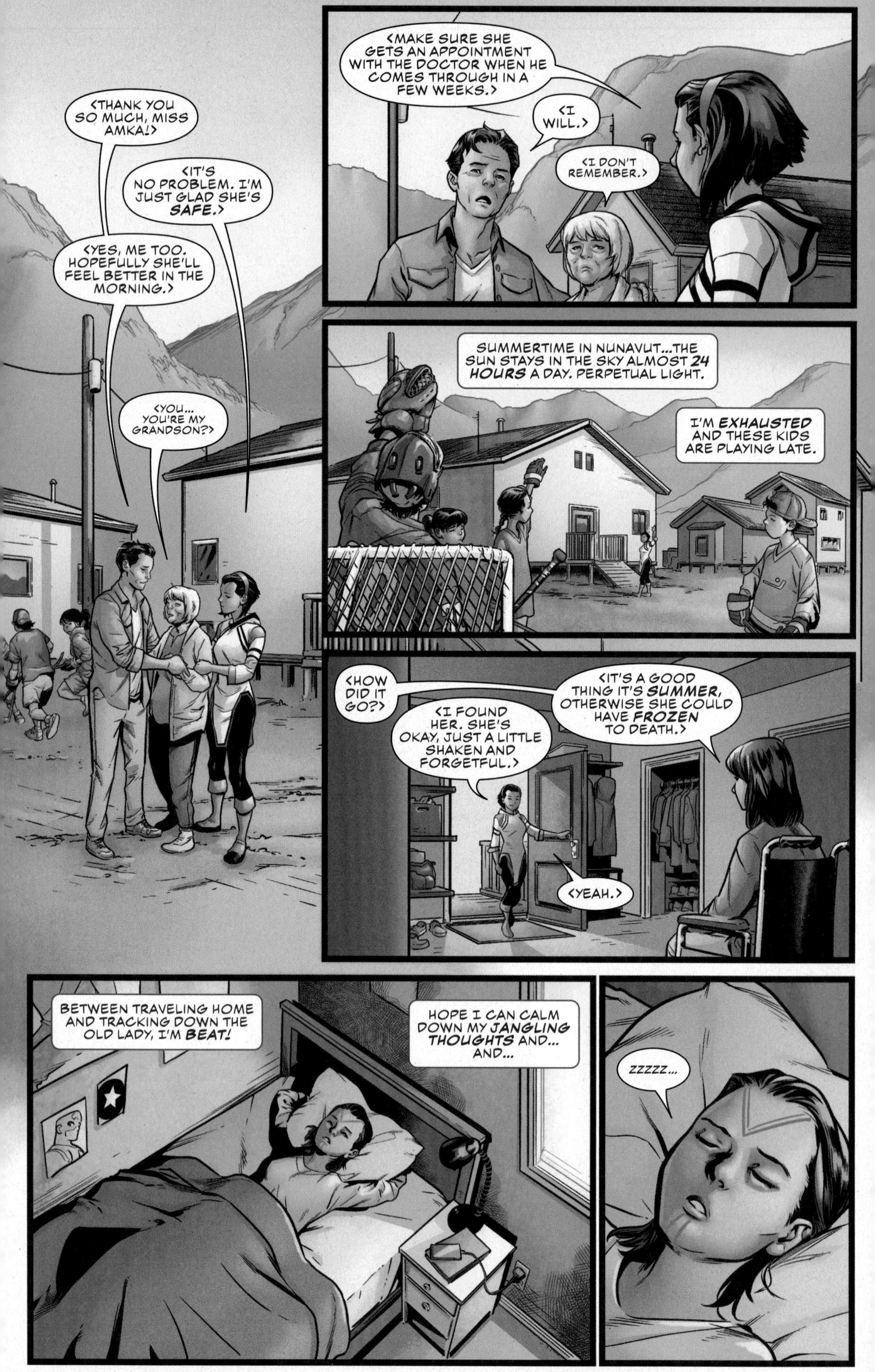
<THANK YOU SO MUCH, MISS AMKA!>
<IT'S NO PROBLEM. I'M JUST GLAD SHE'S SAFE.>
<YES, ME TOO. HOPEFULLY SHE'LL FEEL BETTER IN THE MORNING.>
<YOU... YOU'RE MY GRANDSON?>
<MAKE SURE SHE GETS AN APPOINTMENT WITH THE DOCTOR WHEN HE COMES THROUGH IN A FEW WEEKS.>
<I WILL.>
<I DON'T REMEMBER.>
SUMMERTIME IN NUNAVUT...THE SUN STAYS IN THE SKY ALMOST 24 HOURS A DAY. PERPETUAL LIGHT.
I'M EXHAUSTED AND THESE KIDS ARE PLAYING LATE.
<HOW DID IT GO?>
<I FOUND HER. SHE'S OKAY, JUST A LITTLE SHAKEN AND FORGETFUL.>
<IT'S A GOOD THING IT'S SUMMER, OTHERWISE SHE COULD HAVE FROZEN TO DEATH.>
<YEAH.>
BETWEEN TRAVELING HOME AND TRACKING DOWN THE OLD LADY, I'M BEAT!
HOPE I CAN CALM DOWN MY JANGLING THOUGHTS AND... AND...
ZZZZZ...

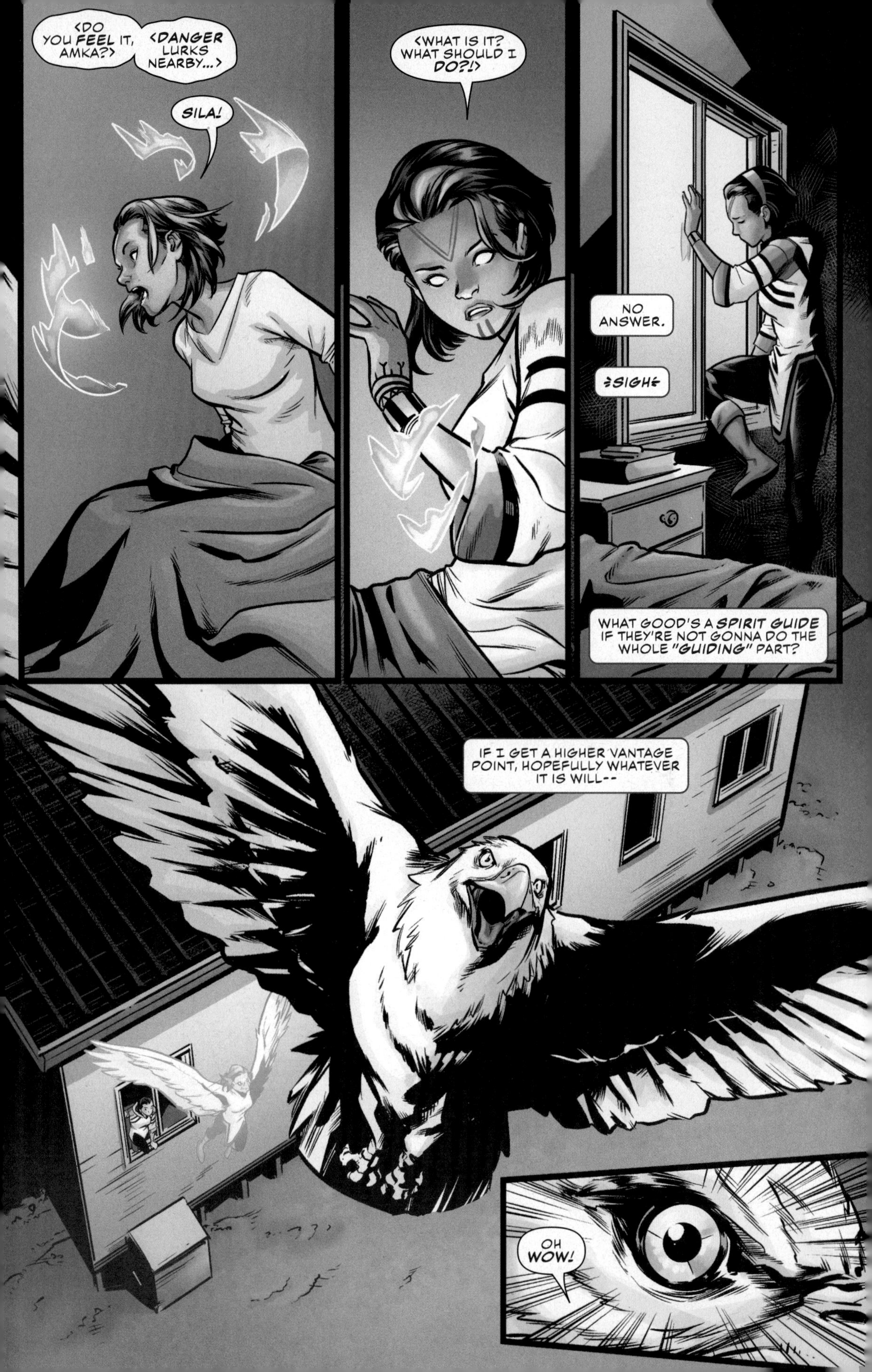

<DO YOU FEEL IT, AMKA?>
<DANGER LURKS NEARBY...>
SILA!
<WHAT IS IT? WHAT SHOULD I DO?!>
NO ANSWER.
SIGH
WHAT GOOD'S A SPIRIT GUIDE IF THEY'RE NOT GONNA DO THE WHOLE "GUIDING" PART?
IF I GET A HIGHER VANTAGE POINT, HOPEFULLY WHATEVER IT IS WILL--
OH WOW!

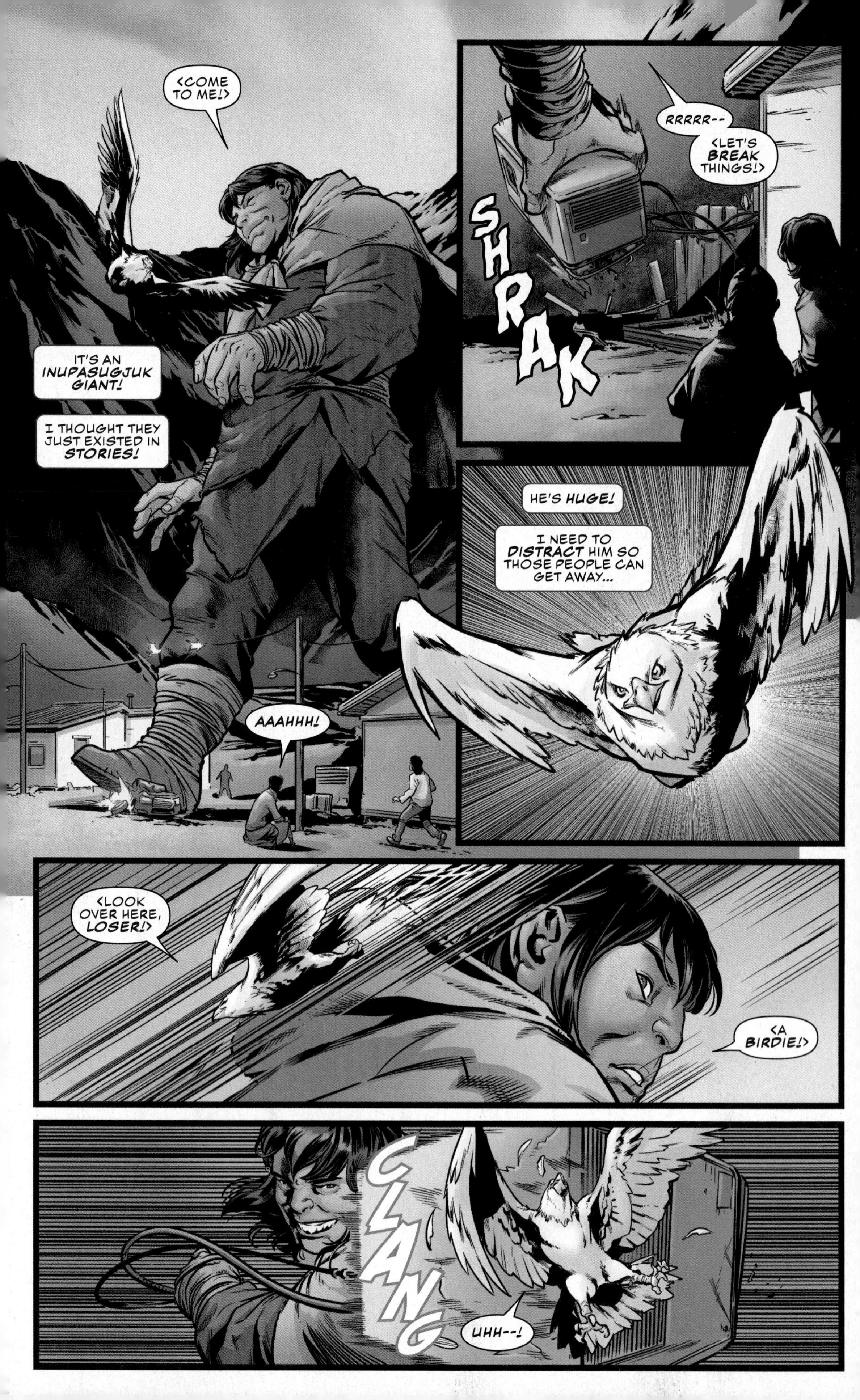

<COME TO ME!>
IT'S AN INUPASUGJUK GIANT!
I THOUGHT THEY JUST EXISTED IN STORIES!
AAAHHH!
RRRRR--
<LET'S BREAK THINGS!>
SHRAK
HE'S HUGE!
I NEED TO DISTRACT HIM SO THOSE PEOPLE CAN GET AWAY...
<LOOK OVER HERE, LOSER!>
<A BIRDIE!>
CLANG
UHH--!

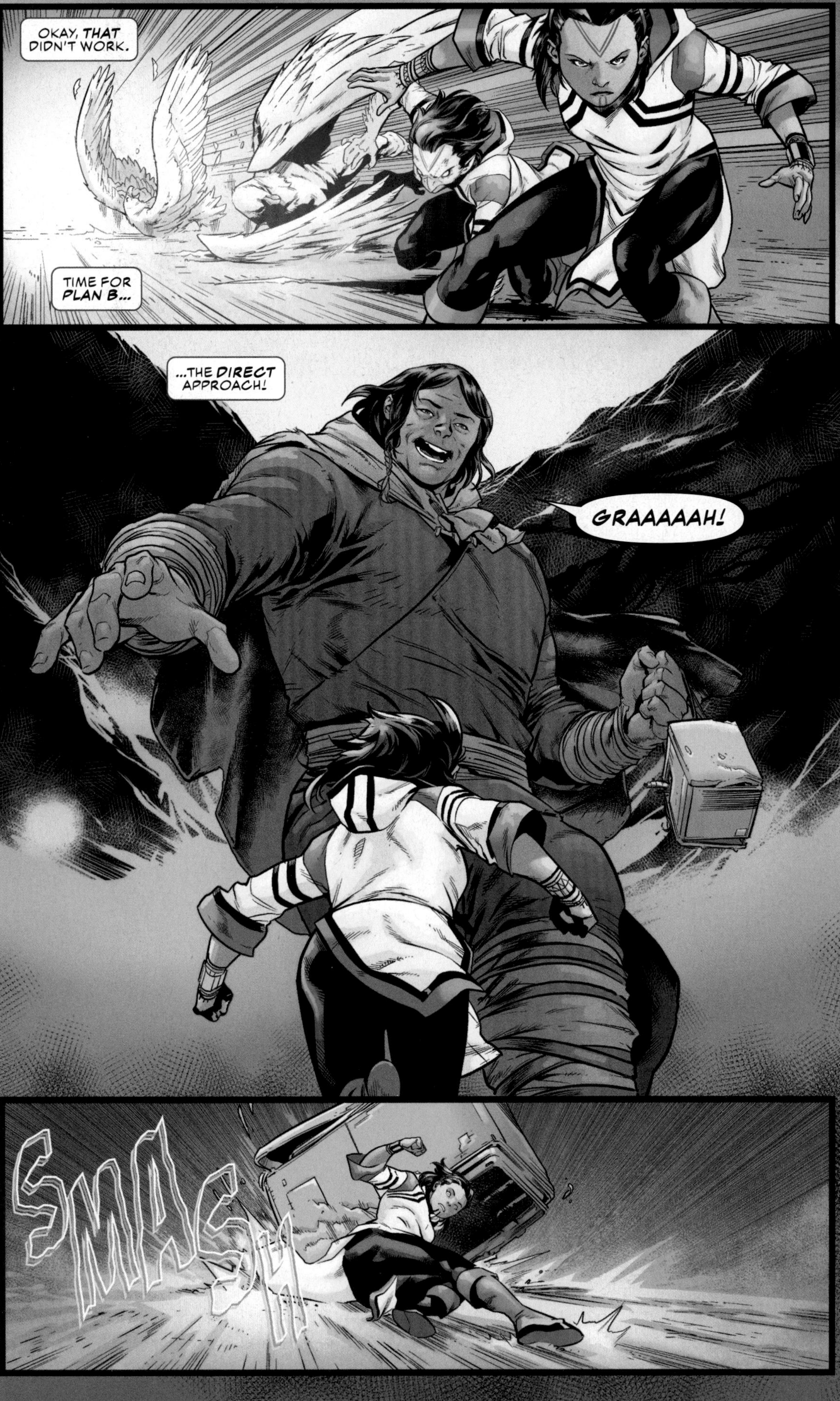
OKAY, THAT DIDN'T WORK.
TIME FOR PLAN B...
...THE DIRECT APPROACH!
GRAAAAAH!
SMASH

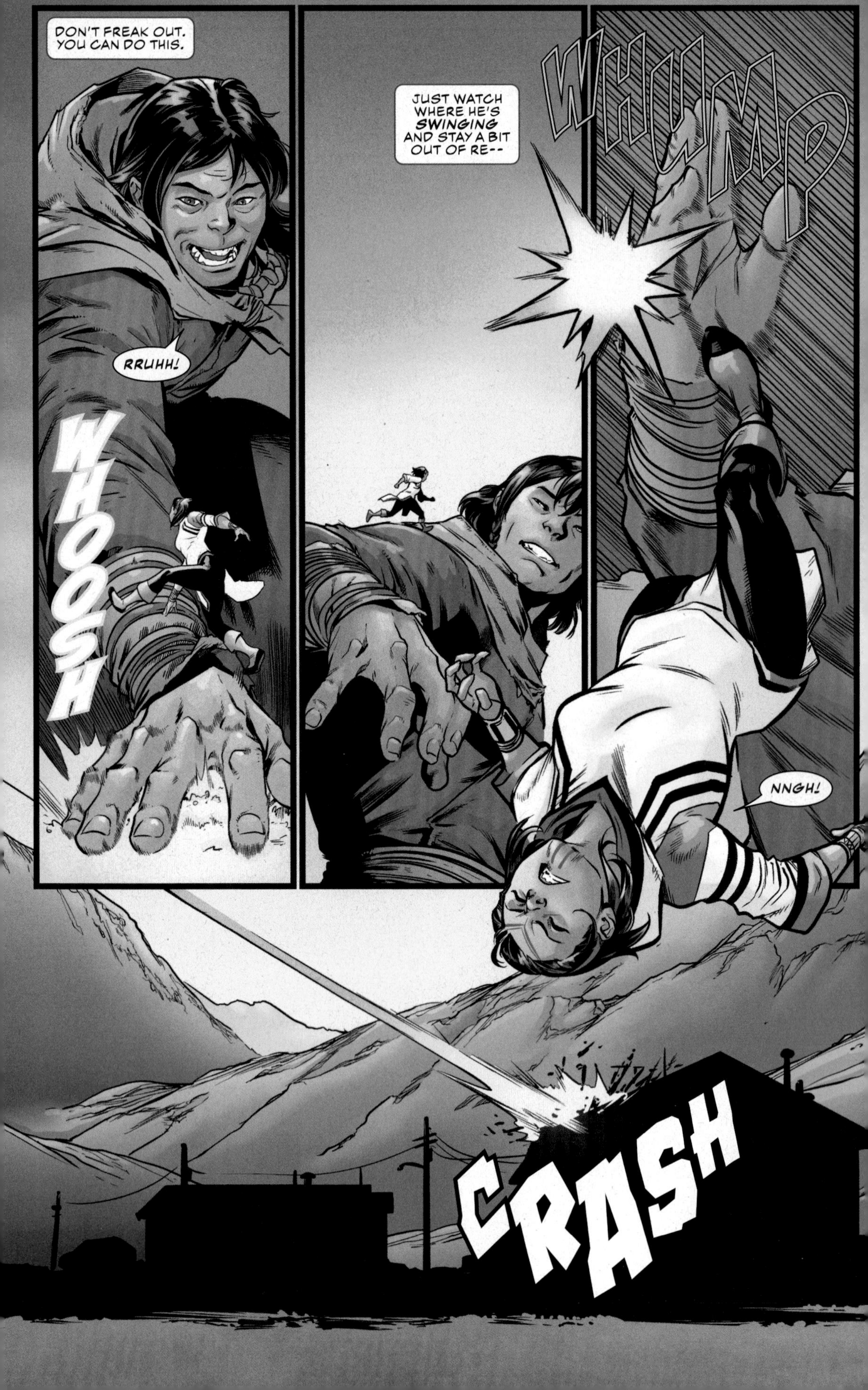
DON'T FREAK OUT. YOU CAN DO THIS.
RRUHH!
WHOOOSH
JUST WATCH WHERE HE'S SWINGING AND STAY A BIT OUT OF RE--
WHUMP
NNGH!
CRASH

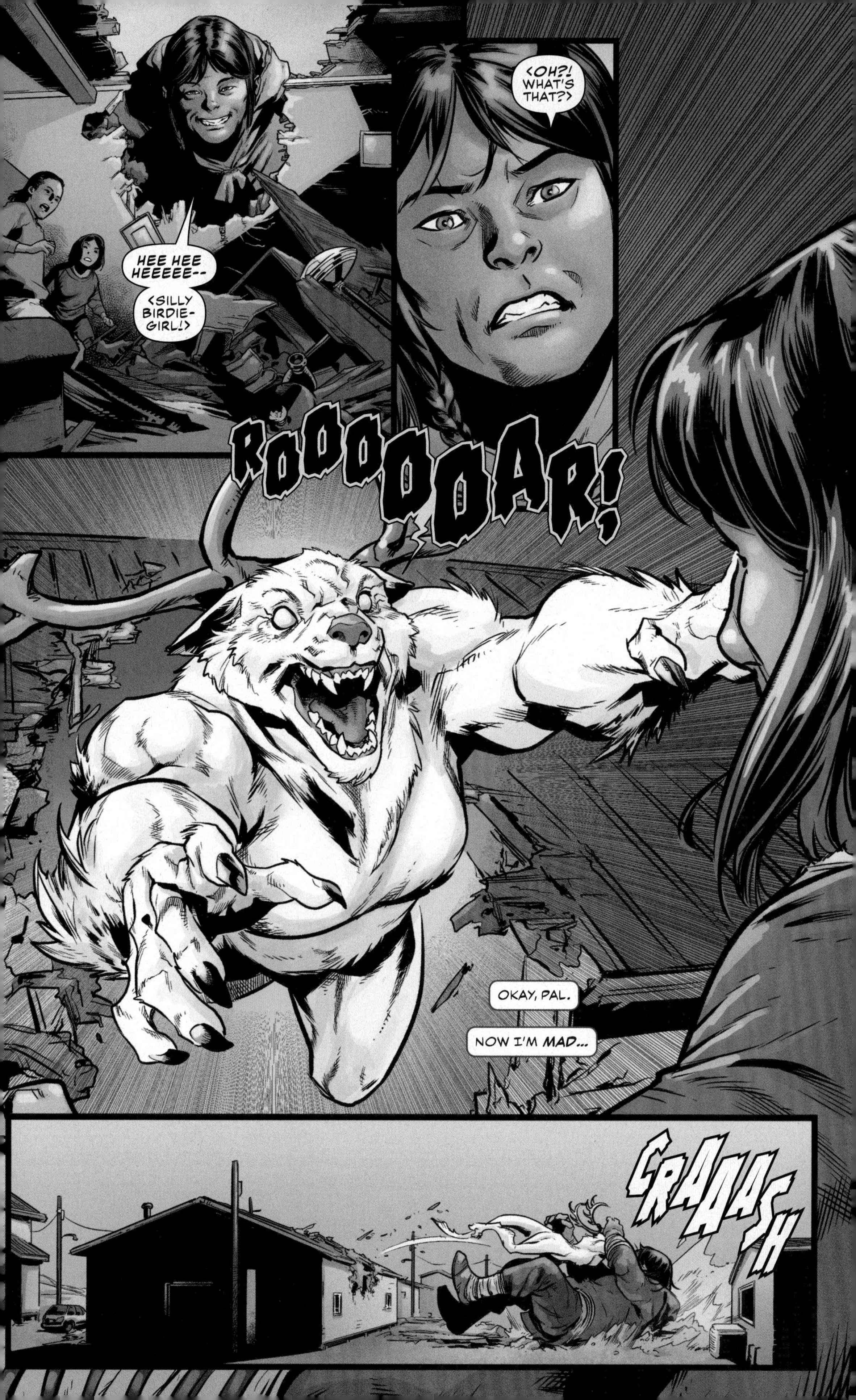

HEE HEE HEEEEE--
<SILLY BIRDIE-GIRL!>
<OH?! WHAT'S THAT?>
ROOOOOAR!
OKAY, PAL.
NOW I'M MAD...
CRAAASH

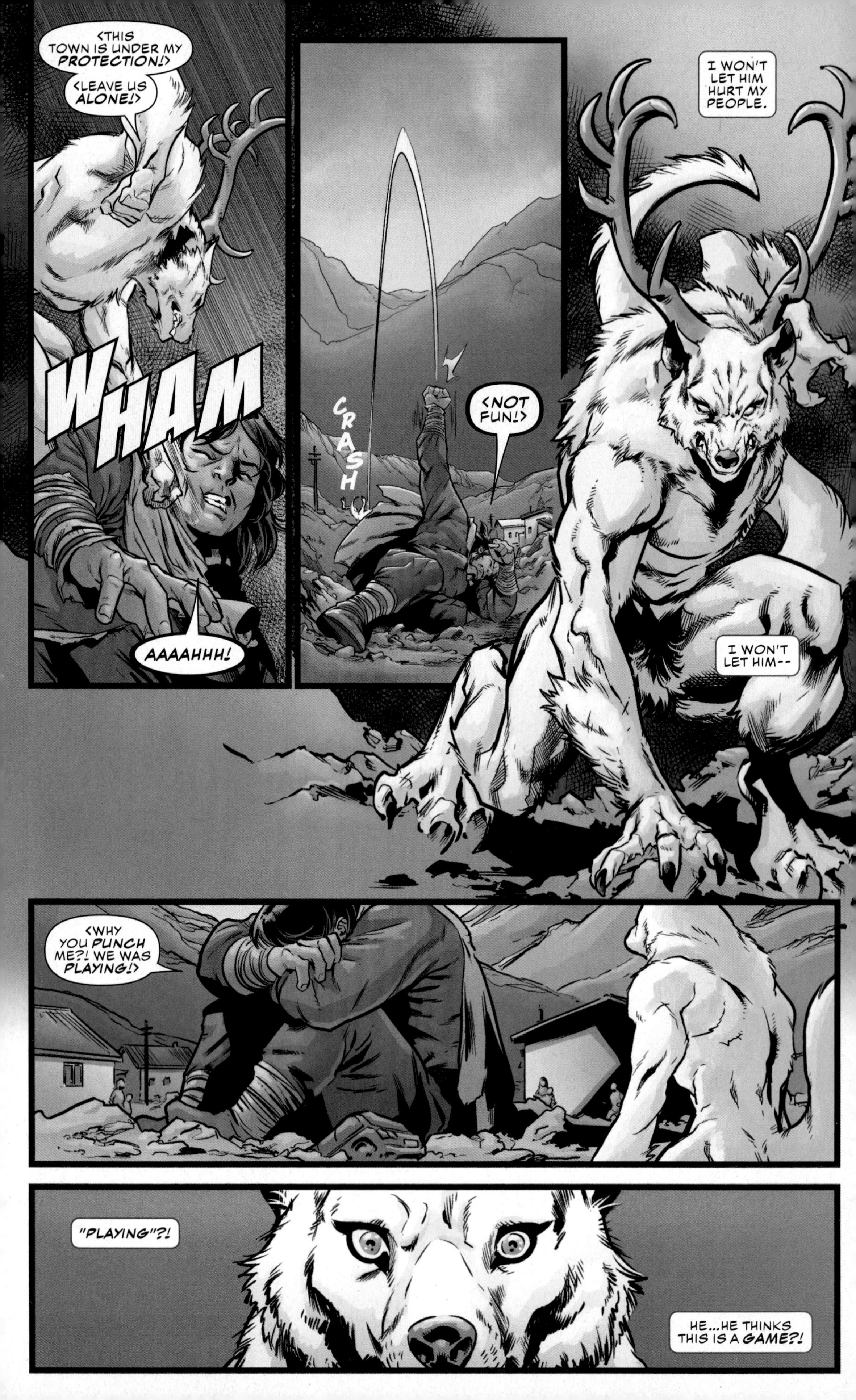
<THIS TOWN IS UNDER MY PROTECTION!>
<LEAVE US ALONE!>
WHAM
AAAAHHH!
CRASH
<NOT FUN!>
I WON'T LET HIM HURT MY PEOPLE.
I WON'T LET HIM--
<WHY YOU PUNCH ME?! WE WAS PLAYING!>
"PLAYING"?!
HE...HE THINKS THIS IS A GAME?!

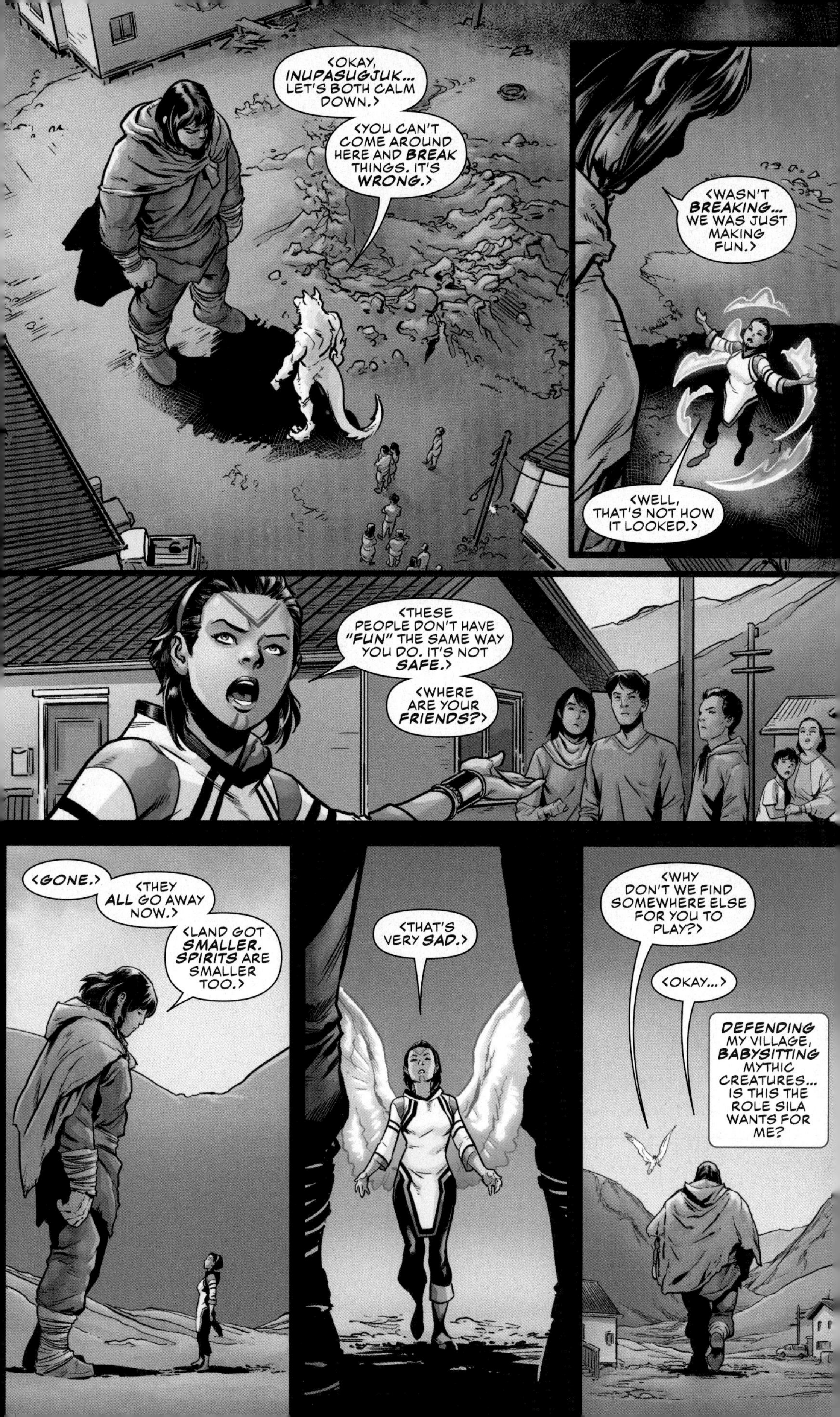

<OKAY, INUPASUGJUK... LET'S BOTH CALM DOWN.>
<YOU CAN'T COME AROUND HERE AND BREAK THINGS. IT'S WRONG.>
<WASN'T BREAKING... WE WAS JUST MAKING FUN.>
<WELL, THAT'S NOT HOW IT LOOKED.>
<THESE PEOPLE DON'T HAVE "FUN" THE SAME WAY YOU DO. IT'S NOT SAFE.>
<WHERE ARE YOUR FRIENDS?>
<GONE.>
<THEY ALL GO AWAY NOW.>
<LAND GOT SMALLER. SPIRITS ARE SMALLER TOO.>
<THAT'S VERY SAD.>
<WHY DON'T WE FIND SOMEWHERE ELSE FOR YOU TO PLAY?>
<OKAY...>
DEFENDING MY VILLAGE, BABYSITTING MYTHIC CREATURES... IS THIS THE ROLE SILA WANTS FOR ME?

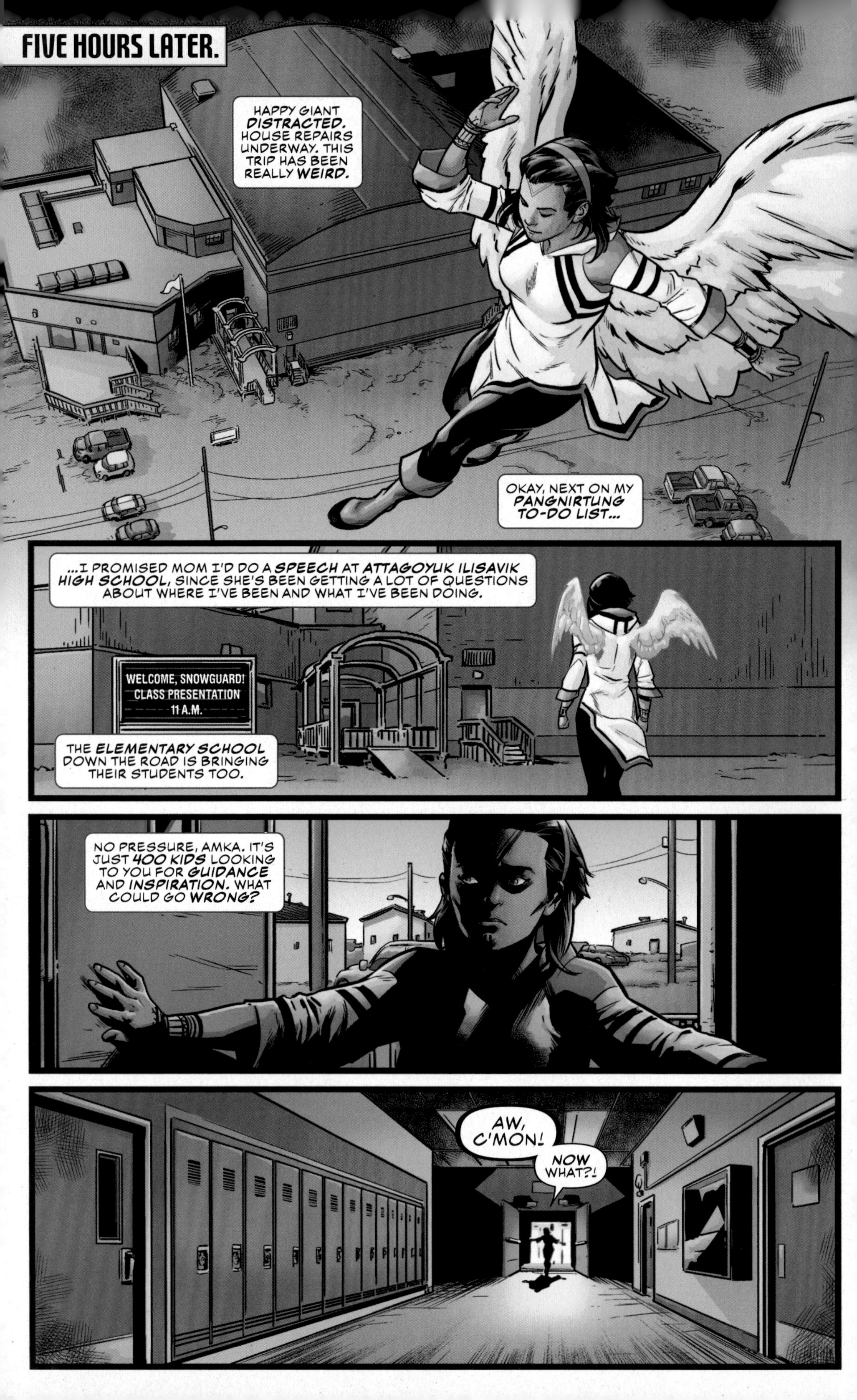
FIVE HOURS LATER.
HAPPY GIANT DISTRACTED. HOUSE REPAIRS UNDERWAY. THIS TRIP HAS BEEN REALLY WEIRD.
OKAY, NEXT ON MY PANGNIRTUNG TO-DO LIST...
...I PROMISED MOM I'D DO A SPEECH AT ATTAGOYUK ILISAVIK HIGH SCHOOL, SINCE SHE'S BEEN GETTING A LOT OF QUESTIONS ABOUT WHERE I'VE BEEN AND WHAT I'VE BEEN DOING.
WELCOME, SNOWGUARD! CLASS PRESENTATION 11 A.M.
THE ELEMENTARY SCHOOL DOWN THE ROAD IS BRINGING THEIR STUDENTS TOO.
NO PRESSURE, AMKA. IT'S JUST 400 KIDS LOOKING TO YOU FOR GUIDANCE AND INSPIRATION. WHAT COULD GO WRONG?
AW, C'MON!
NOW WHAT?!

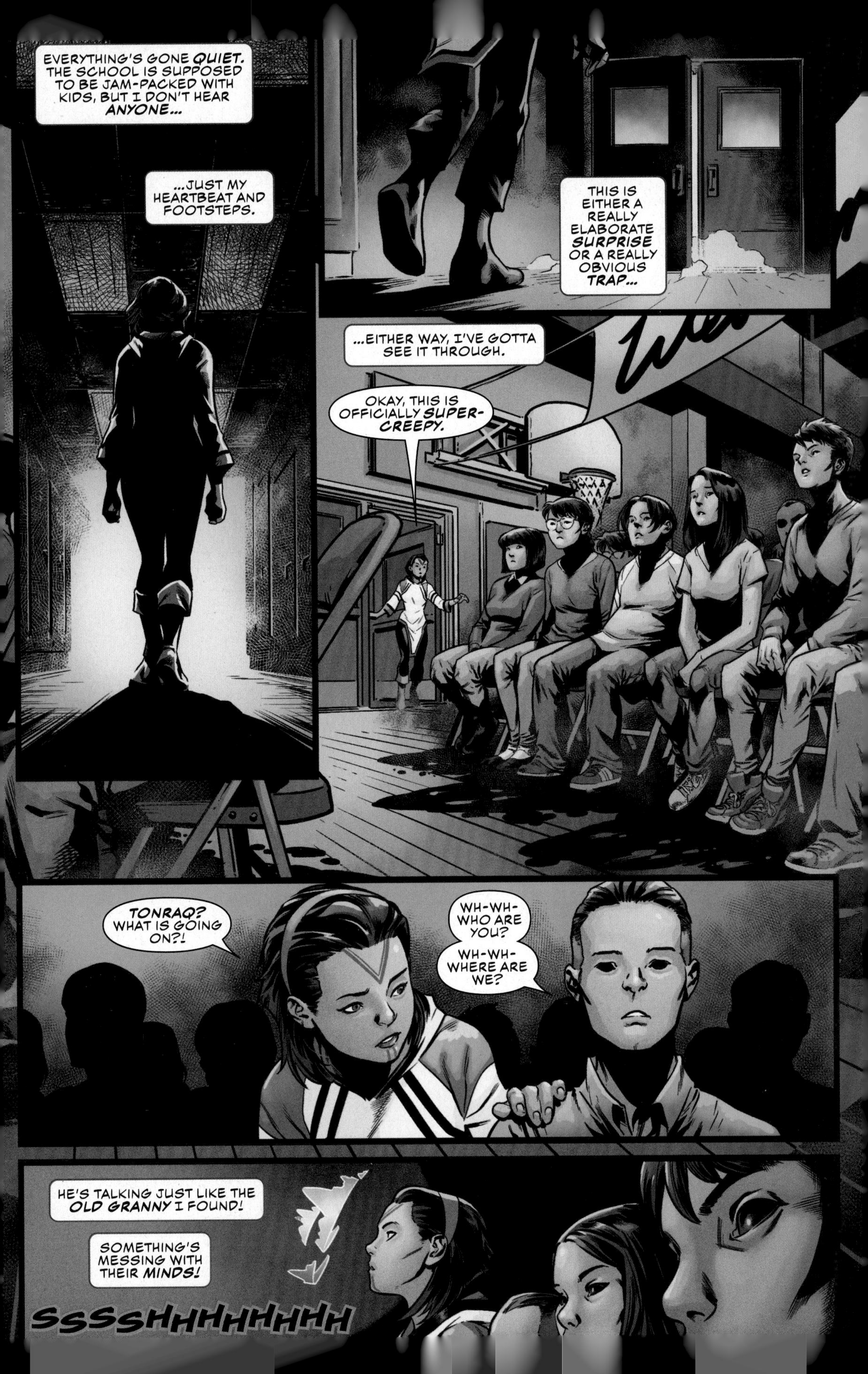
EVERYTHING'S GONE QUIET. THE SCHOOL IS SUPPOSED TO BE JAM-PACKED WITH KIDS, BUT I DON'T HEAR ANYONE...
...JUST MY HEARTBEAT AND FOOTSTEPS.
THIS IS EITHER A REALLY ELABORATE SURPRISE OR A REALLY OBVIOUS TRAP...
...EITHER WAY, I'VE GOTTA SEE IT THROUGH.
OKAY, THIS IS OFFICIALLY SUPER-CREEPY.
TONRAQ? WHAT IS GOING ON?!
WH-WH-WHO ARE YOU?
WH-WH-WHERE ARE WE?
HE'S TALKING JUST LIKE THE OLD GRANNY I FOUND!
SOMETHING'S MESSING WITH THEIR MINDS!
SSSSHHHHHHHH

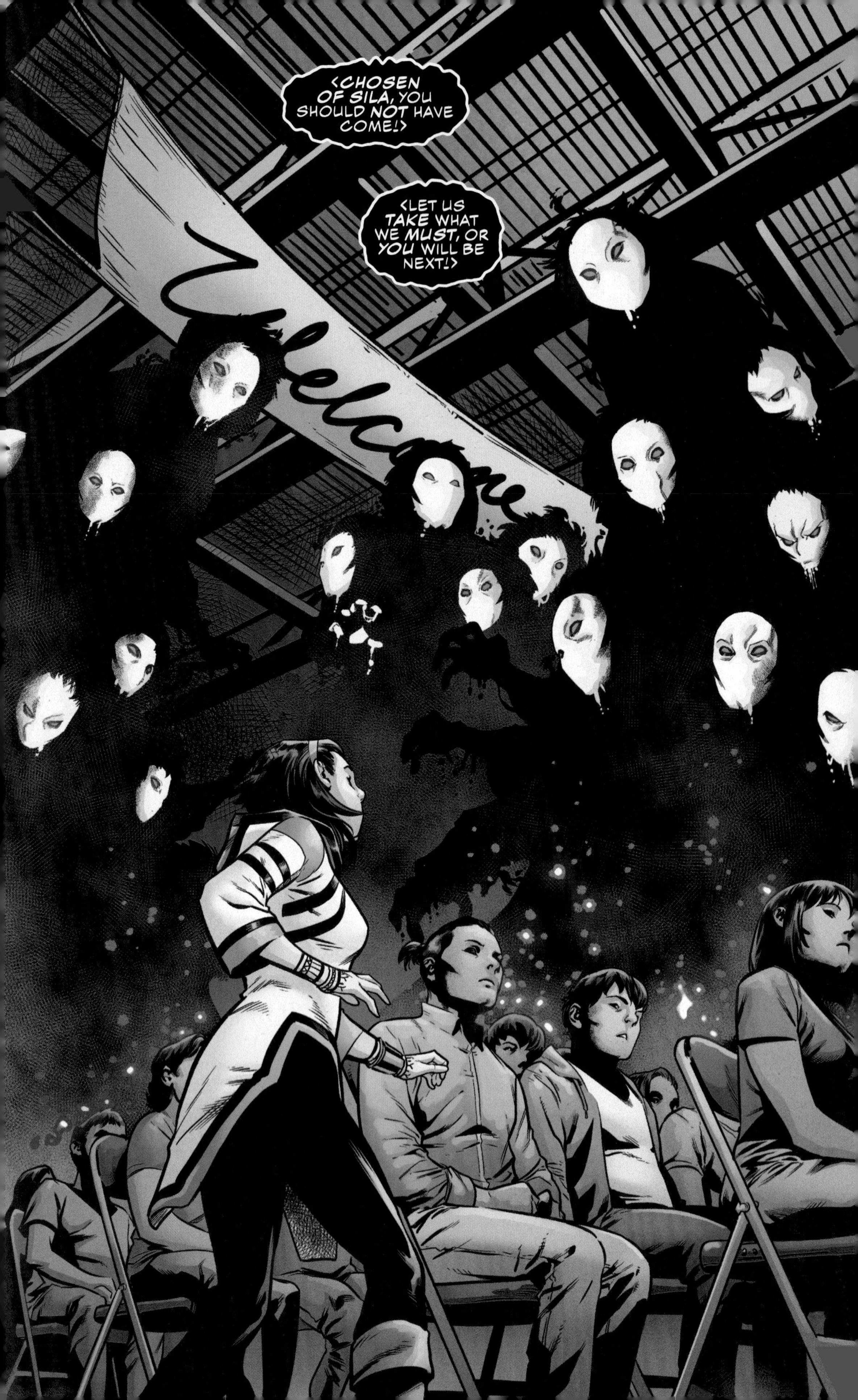
<CHOSEN OF SILA, YOU SHOULD NOT HAVE COME!>
<LET US TAKE WHAT WE MUST, OR YOU WILL BE NEXT!>
Welcome

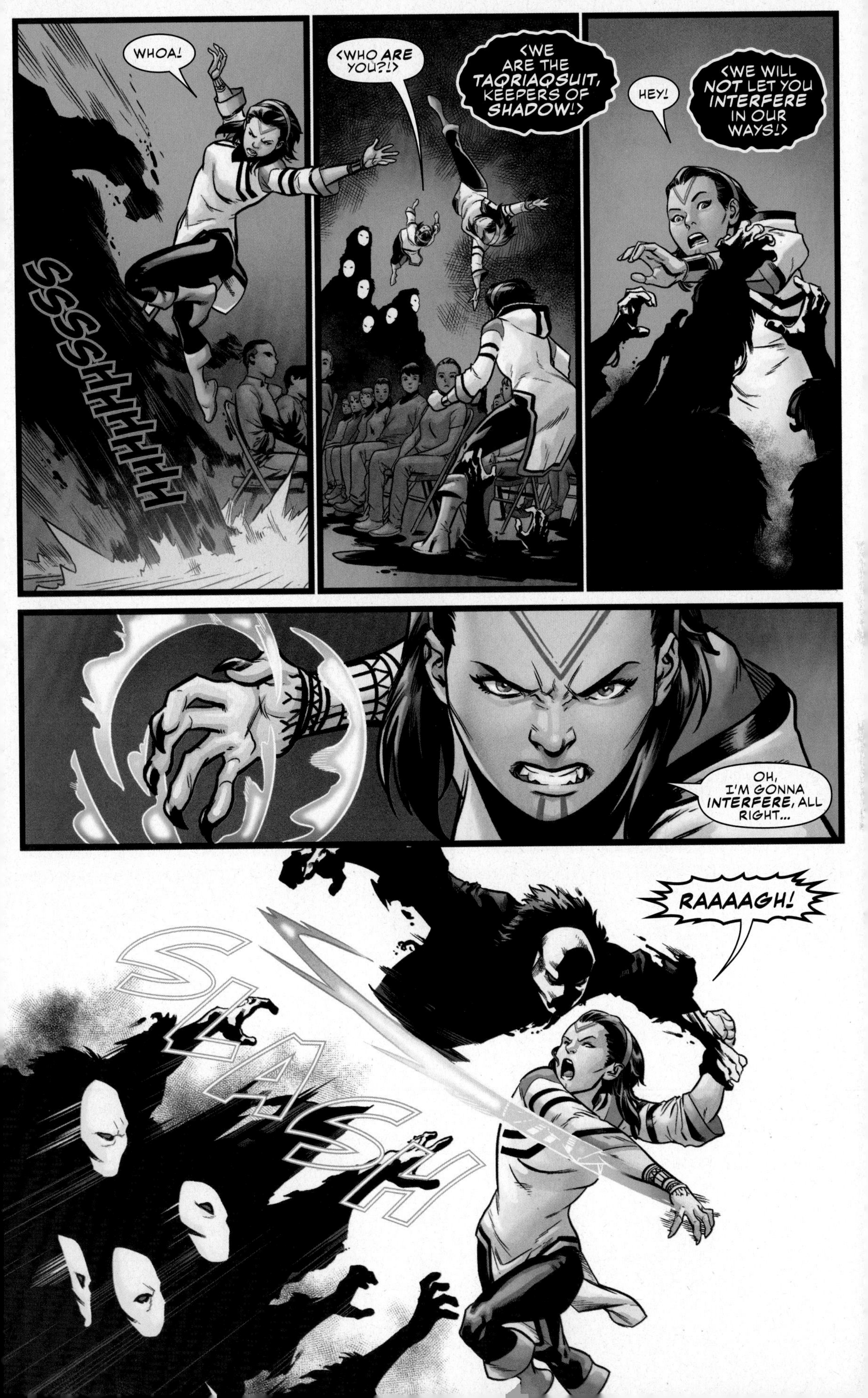
WHOA!
SSSSHHHHHH
<WHO ARE YOU?!>
<WE ARE THE TAQRIAQSUIT, KEEPERS OF SHADOW!>
HEY!
<WE WILL NOT LET YOU INTERFERE IN OUR WAYS!>
OH, I'M GONNA INTERFERE, ALL RIGHT...
RAAAAGH!
SLASH

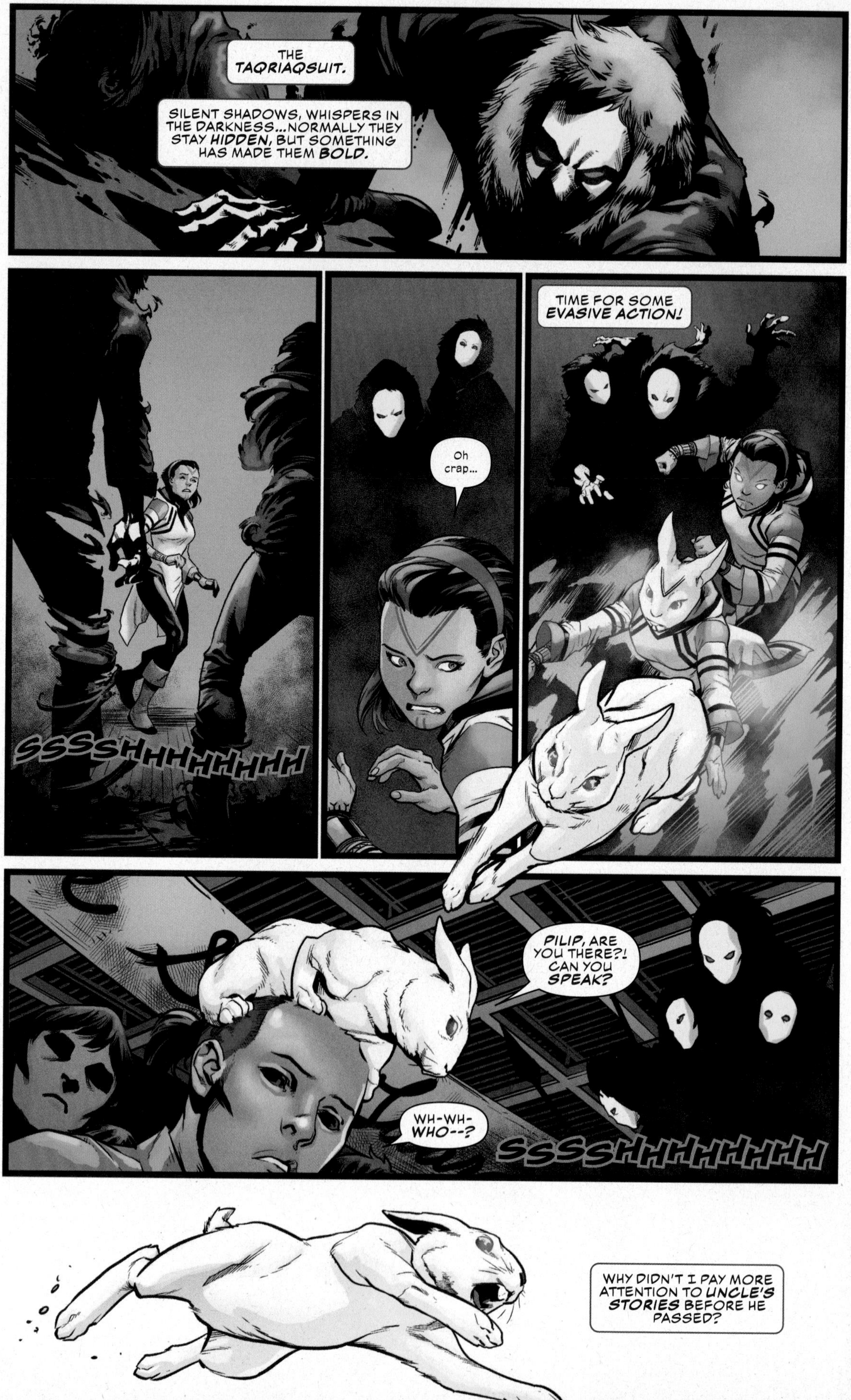
THE TAQRIAQSUIT.
SILENT SHADOWS, WHISPERS IN THE DARKNESS...NORMALLY THEY STAY HIDDEN, BUT SOMETHING HAS MADE THEM BOLD.
SSSSHHHHHHHHH
Oh crap...
TIME FOR SOME EVASIVE ACTION!
PILIP, ARE YOU THERE?! CAN YOU SPEAK?
WH-WH-WHO--?
SSSSHHHHHHHHHH
WHY DIDN'T I PAY MORE ATTENTION TO UNCLE'S STORIES BEFORE HE PASSED?

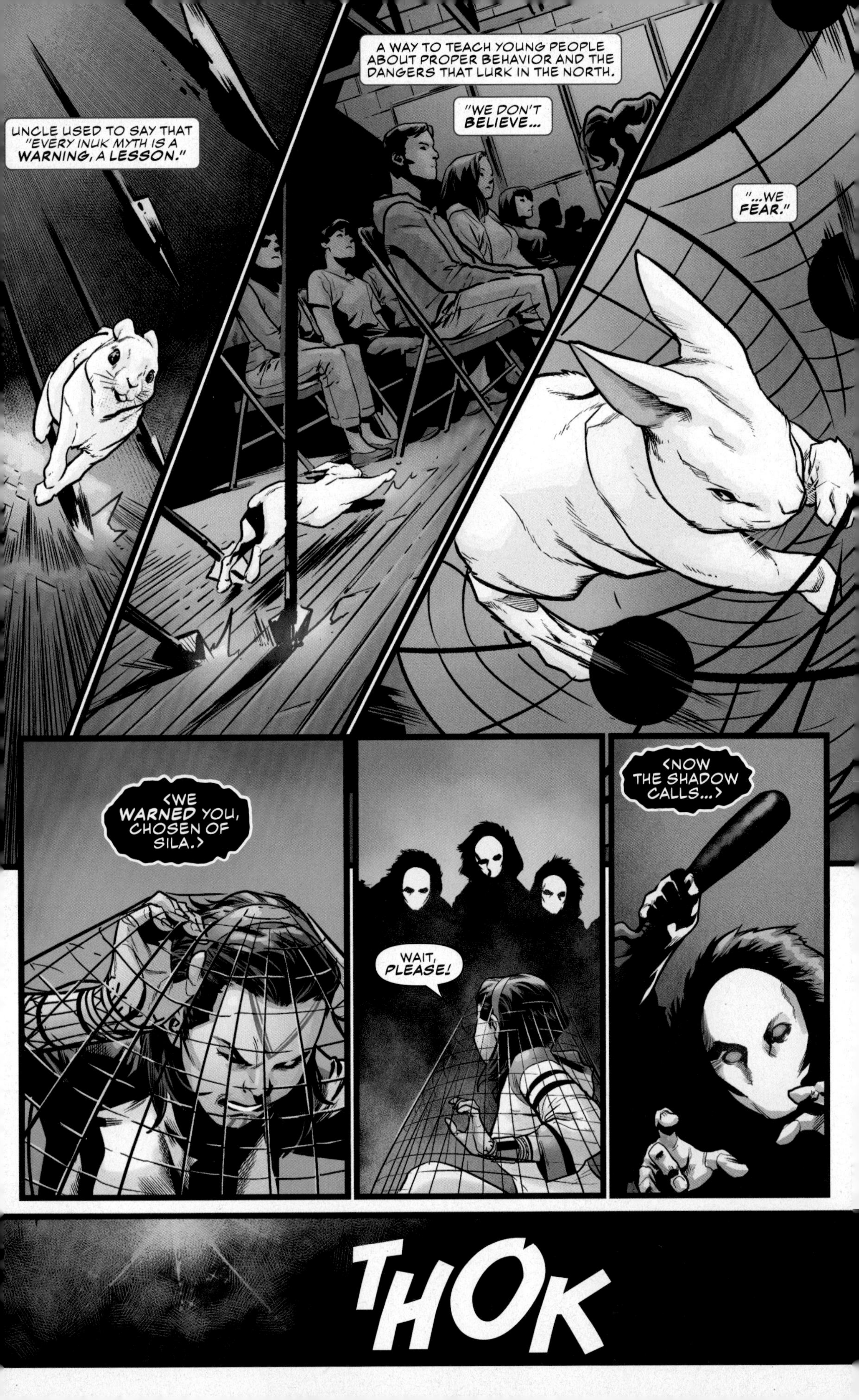
UNCLE USED TO SAY THAT "EVERY INUK MYTH IS A WARNING, A LESSON."
A WAY TO TEACH YOUNG PEOPLE ABOUT PROPER BEHAVIOR AND THE DANGERS THAT LURK IN THE NORTH.
"WE DON'T BELIEVE...
"...WE FEAR."
<WE WARNED YOU, CHOSEN OF SILA.>
WAIT, PLEASE!
<NOW THE SHADOW CALLS...>
THOK

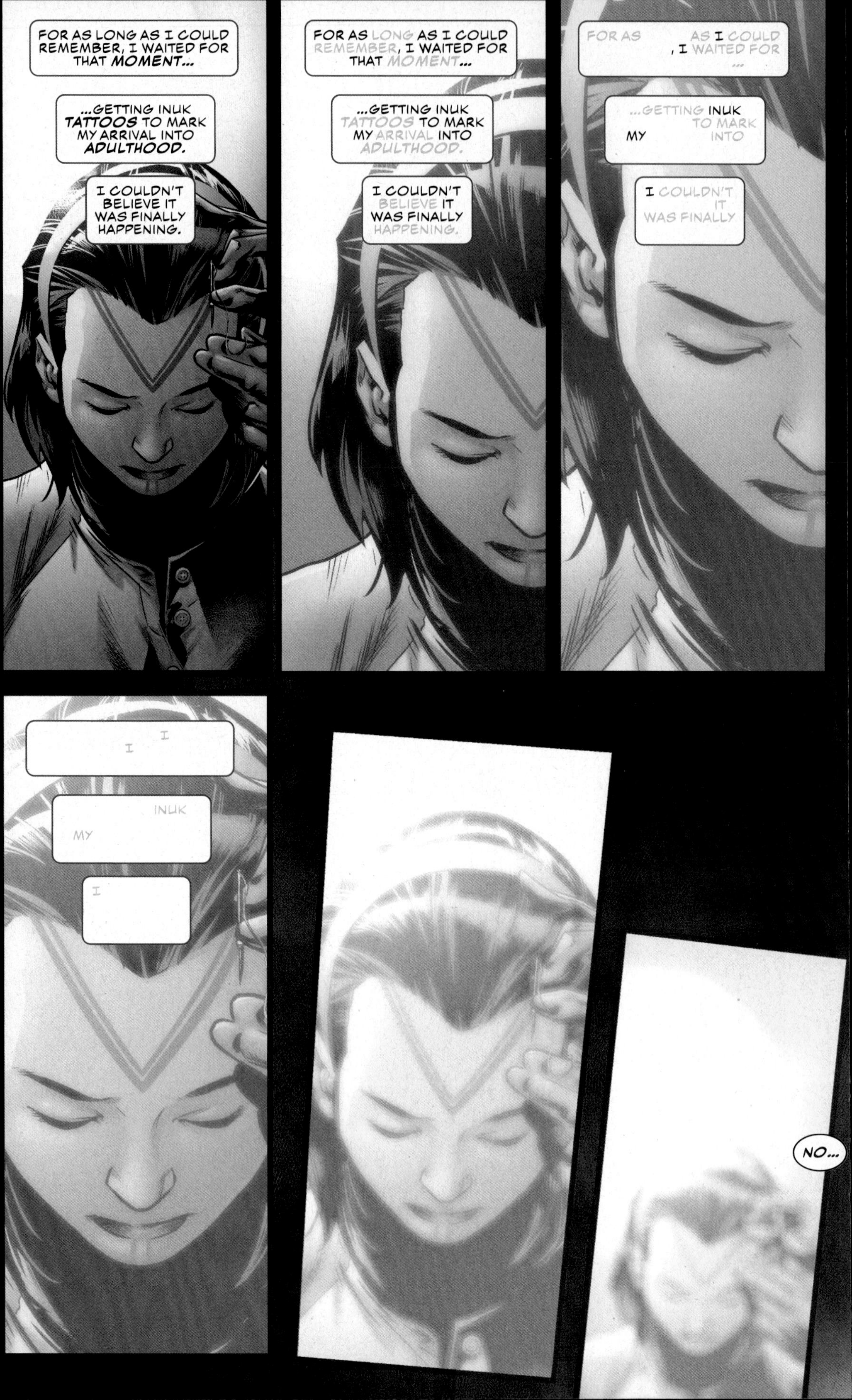
FOR AS LONG AS I COULD REMEMBER, I WAITED FOR THAT MOMENT...
...GETTING INUK TATTOOS TO MARK MY ARRIVAL INTO ADULTHOOD.
I COULDN'T BELIEVE IT WAS FINALLY HAPPENING.
FOR AS LONG AS I COULD REMEMBER, I WAITED FOR THAT MOMENT...
...GETTING INUK TATTOOS TO MARK MY ARRIVAL INTO ADULTHOOD.
I COULDN'T BELIEVE IT WAS FINALLY HAPPENING.
FOR AS AS I COULD , I WAITED FOR ...
...GETTING INUK TO MARK MY INTO
I COULDN'T IT WAS FINALLY
I I
INUK MY
I
NO...

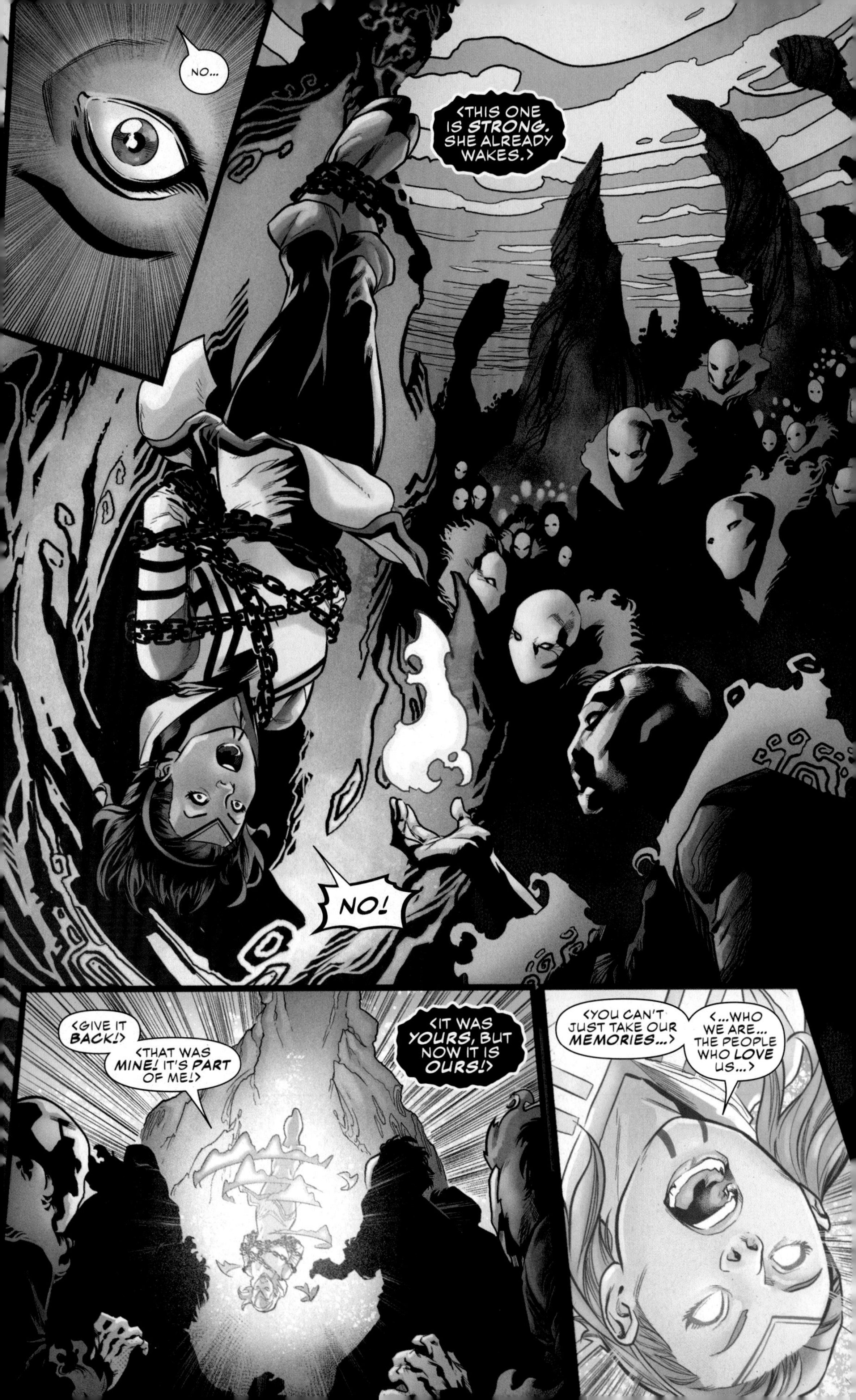
NO...
<THIS ONE IS STRONG. SHE ALREADY WAKES.>
NO!
<GIVE IT BACK!>
<THAT WAS MINE! IT'S PART OF ME!>
<IT WAS YOURS, BUT NOW IT IS OURS!>
<YOU CAN'T JUST TAKE OUR MEMORIES...>
<...WHO WE ARE... THE PEOPLE WHO LOVE US...>

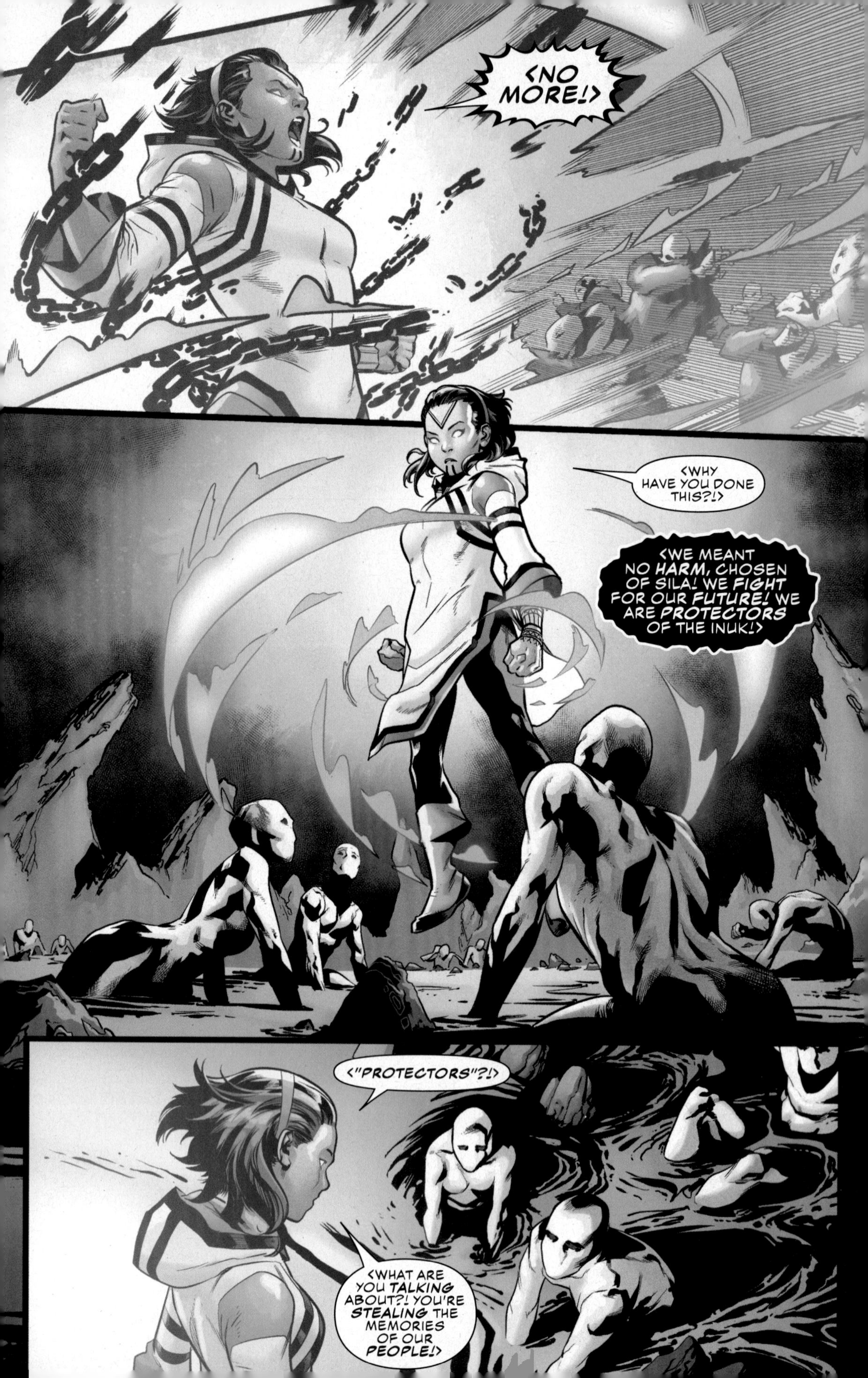
<NO MORE!>
<WHY HAVE YOU DONE THIS?!>
<WE MEANT NO HARM, CHOSEN OF SILA! WE FIGHT FOR OUR FUTURE! WE ARE PROTECTORS OF THE INUK!>
<"PROTECTORS"?!>
<WHAT ARE YOU TALKING ABOUT?! YOU'RE STEALING THE MEMORIES OF OUR PEOPLE!>

<THE NUMBER OF INUK WHO REMEMBER US FALLS EACH YEAR. THE CHILDREN DO NOT CARE ABOUT THE *ANCESTORS* AND THEIR *STORIES*.>

<THEY ALREADY FORGET WHO THEY WERE AND WHERE THEY CAME FROM. WE FEARED IT WOULD ALL BE LOST, SO WE *TOOK* THE MEMORIES TO KEEP THEM *SAFE*.>

<IF WE DO NOT, OUR *HISTORY* WILL FADE...>

<...AND THEN *WE* WILL FADE.>

<YOU...YOU CAN'T JUST TAKE THE PAST FROM PEOPLE AND HIDE IT AWAY. THE *STORIES*, THE *BEAUTY* OF WHO WE ARE...>

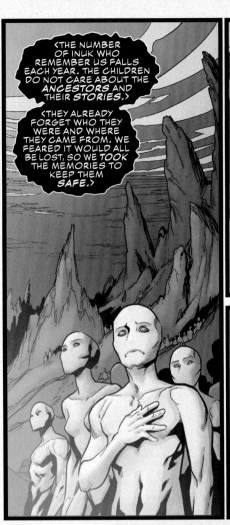

<...WE CAN *SHARE* IT AND MAKE IT *GROW*.>

<BUT HOW?>

<I'LL SHOW YOU.>

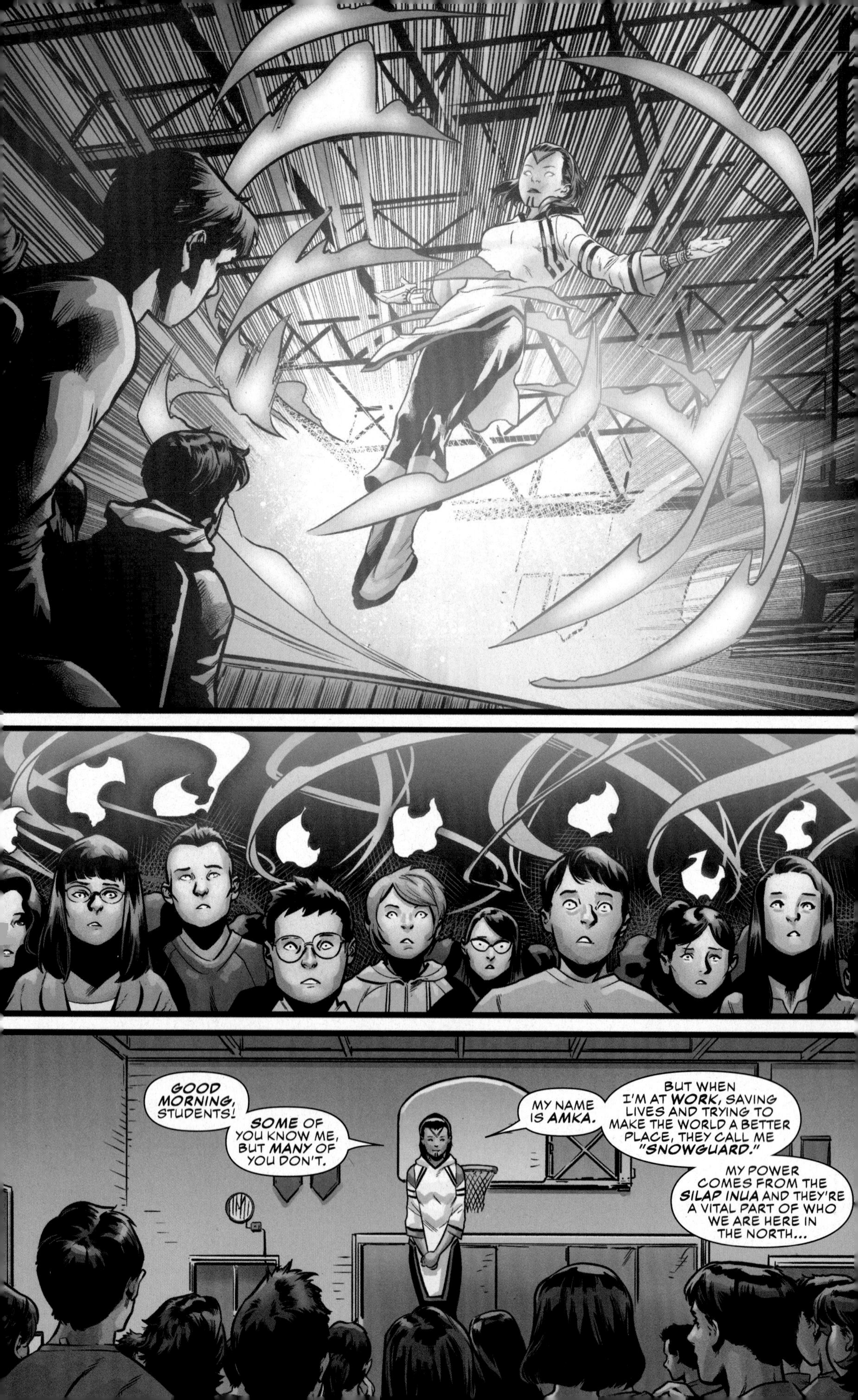
GOOD MORNING, STUDENTS!
SOME OF YOU KNOW ME, BUT MANY OF YOU DON'T.
MY NAME IS AMKA.
BUT WHEN I'M AT WORK, SAVING LIVES AND TRYING TO MAKE THE WORLD A BETTER PLACE, THEY CALL ME "SNOWGUARD."
MY POWER COMES FROM THE SILAP INUA AND THEY'RE A VITAL PART OF WHO WE ARE HERE IN THE NORTH...

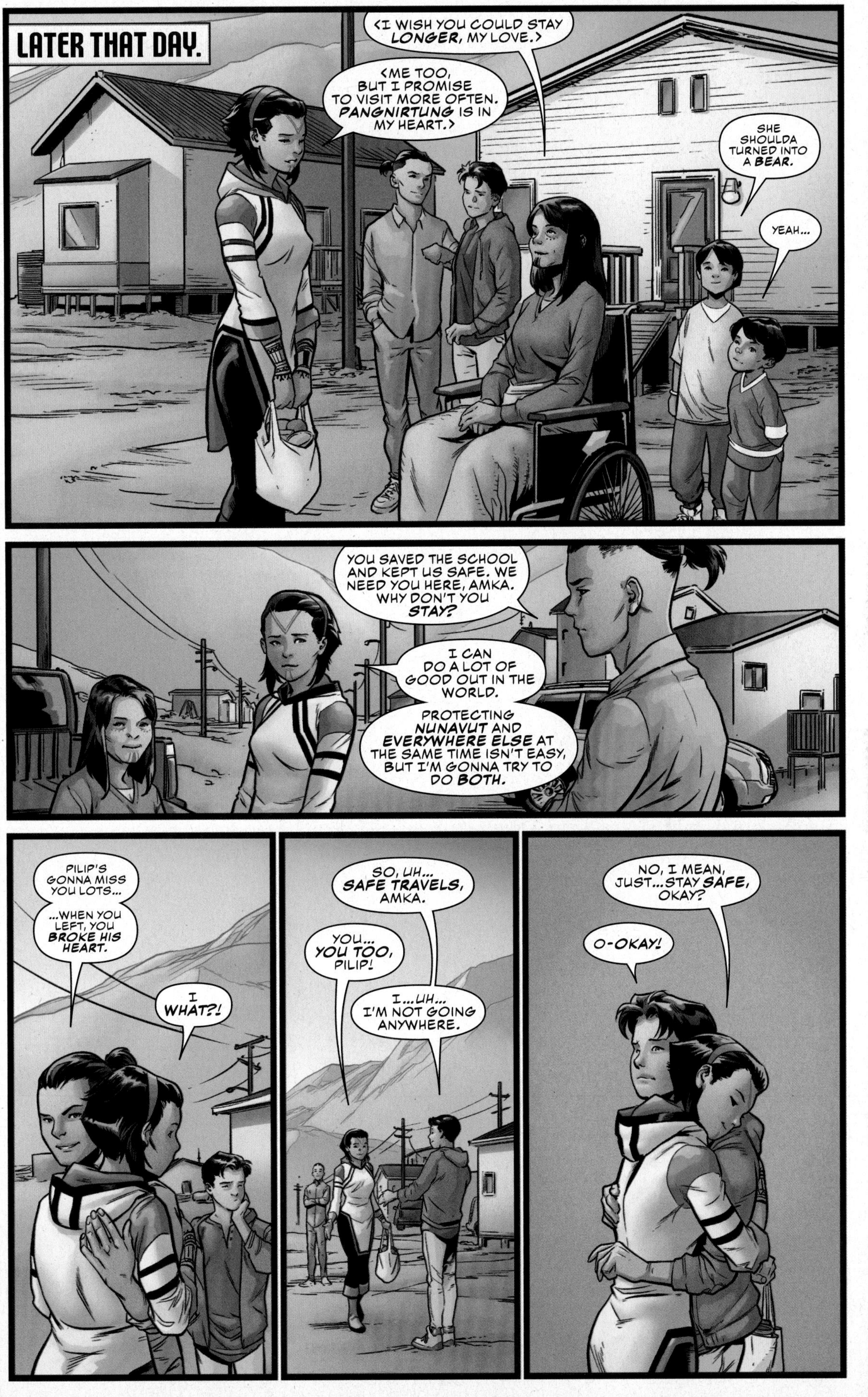
LATER THAT DAY.
<I WISH YOU COULD STAY LONGER, MY LOVE.>
<ME TOO, BUT I PROMISE TO VISIT MORE OFTEN. PANGNIRTUNG IS IN MY HEART.>
SHE SHOULDA TURNED INTO A BEAR.
YEAH...
YOU SAVED THE SCHOOL AND KEPT US SAFE. WE NEED YOU HERE, AMKA. WHY DON'T YOU STAY?
I CAN DO A LOT OF GOOD OUT IN THE WORLD.
PROTECTING NUNAVUT AND EVERYWHERE ELSE AT THE SAME TIME ISN'T EASY, BUT I'M GONNA TRY TO DO BOTH.
PILIP'S GONNA MISS YOU LOTS...
...WHEN YOU LEFT, YOU BROKE HIS HEART.
I WHAT?!
SO, UH... SAFE TRAVELS, AMKA.
YOU... YOU TOO, PILIP!
I...UH... I'M NOT GOING ANYWHERE.
NO, I MEAN, JUST...STAY SAFE, OKAY?
O-OKAY!

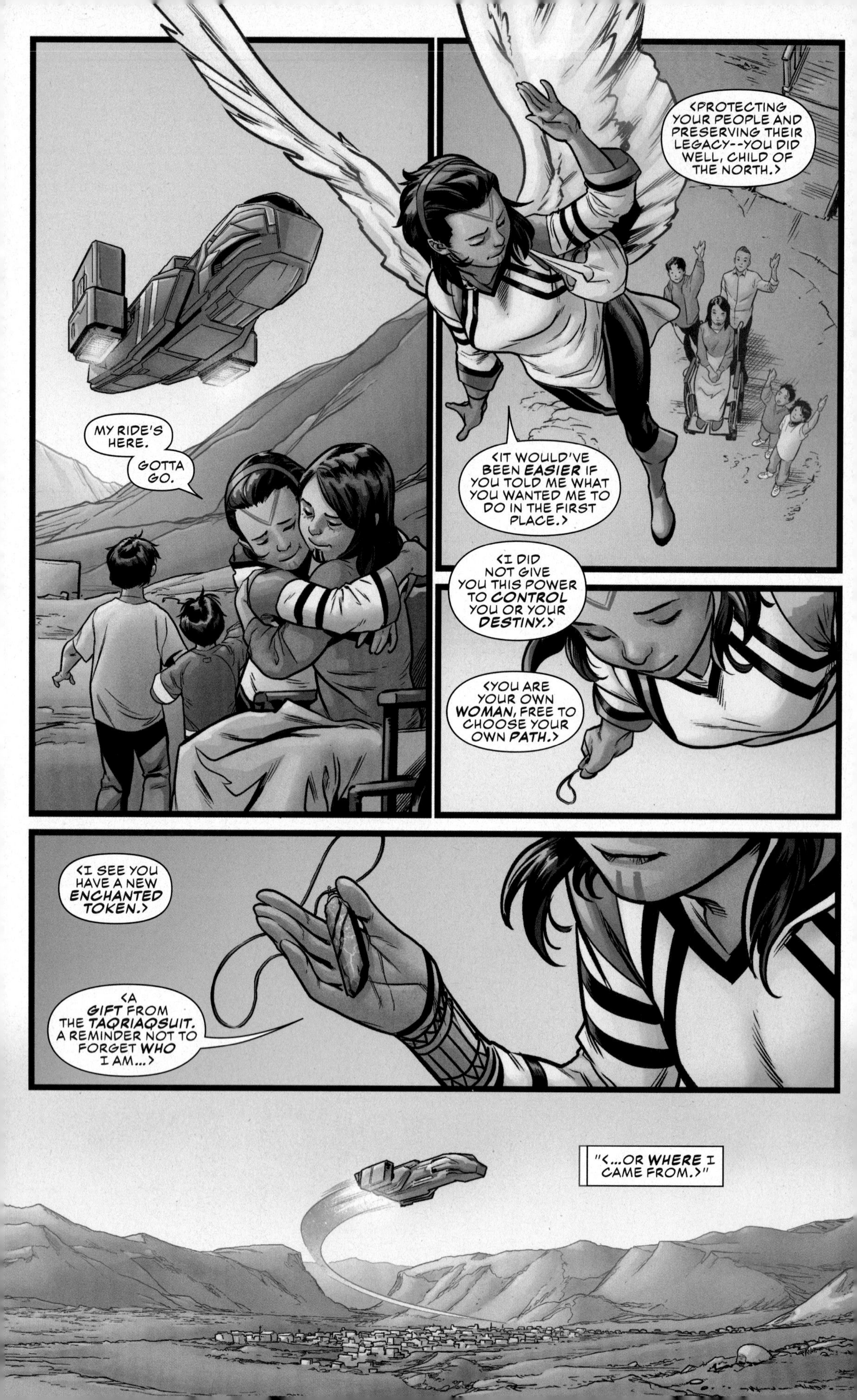
MY RIDE'S HERE.
GOTTA GO.
<PROTECTING YOUR PEOPLE AND PRESERVING THEIR LEGACY--YOU DID WELL, CHILD OF THE NORTH.>
<IT WOULD'VE BEEN EASIER IF YOU TOLD ME WHAT YOU WANTED ME TO DO IN THE FIRST PLACE.>
<I DID NOT GIVE YOU THIS POWER TO CONTROL YOU OR YOUR DESTINY.>
<YOU ARE YOUR OWN WOMAN, FREE TO CHOOSE YOUR OWN PATH.>
<I SEE YOU HAVE A NEW ENCHANTED TOKEN.>
<A GIFT FROM THE TAQRIAQSUIT. A REMINDER NOT TO FORGET WHO I AM...>
"<...OR WHERE I CAME FROM.>"

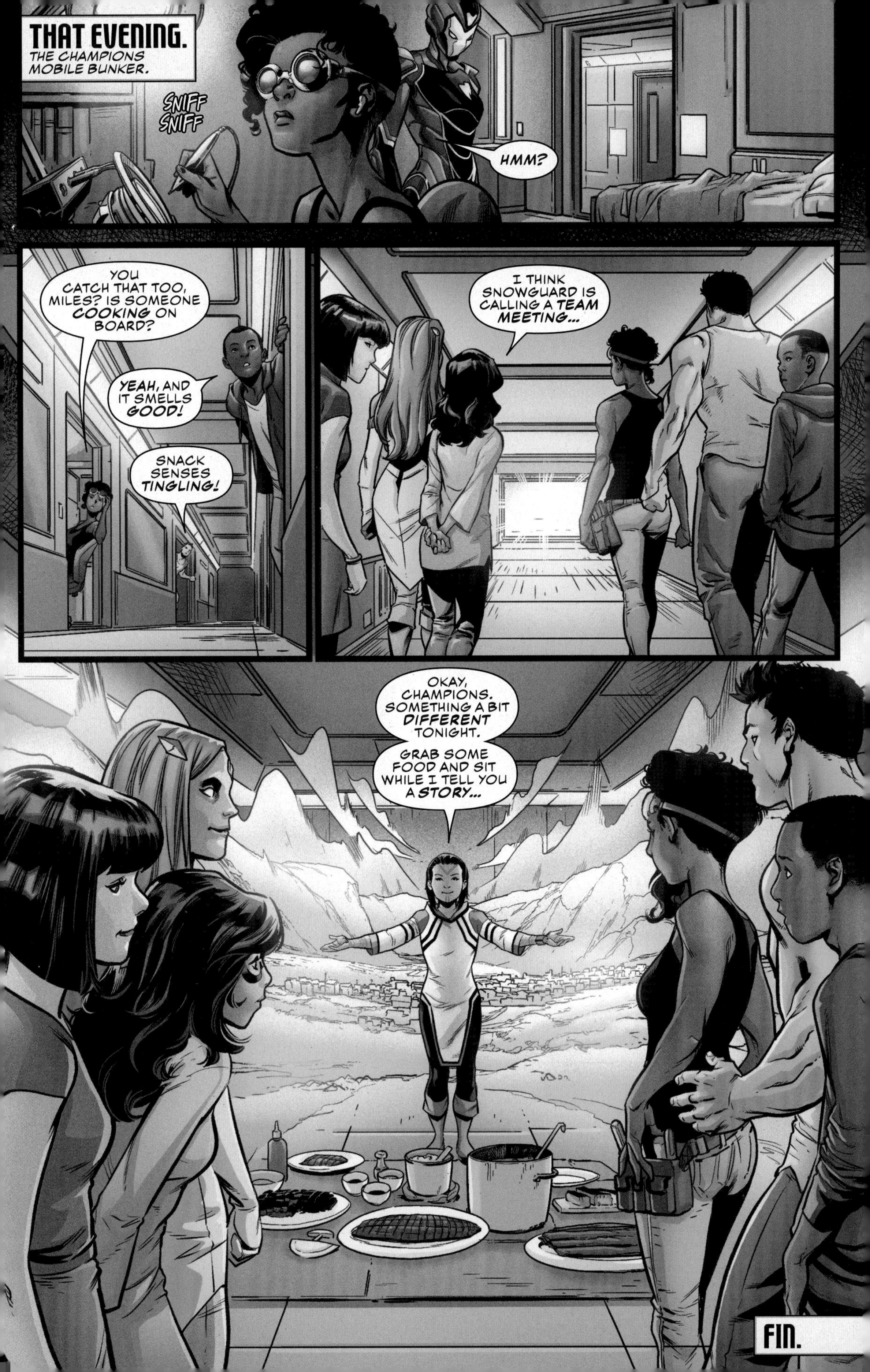
THAT EVENING.
THE CHAMPIONS MOBILE BUNKER.
SNIFF SNIFF
HMM?
YOU CATCH THAT TOO, MILES? IS SOMEONE COOKING ON BOARD?
YEAH, AND IT SMELLS GOOD!
SNACK SENSES TINGLING!
I THINK SNOWGUARD IS CALLING A TEAM MEETING...
OKAY, CHAMPIONS. SOMETHING A BIT DIFFERENT TONIGHT.
GRAB SOME FOOD AND SIT WHILE I TELL YOU A STORY...
FIN.

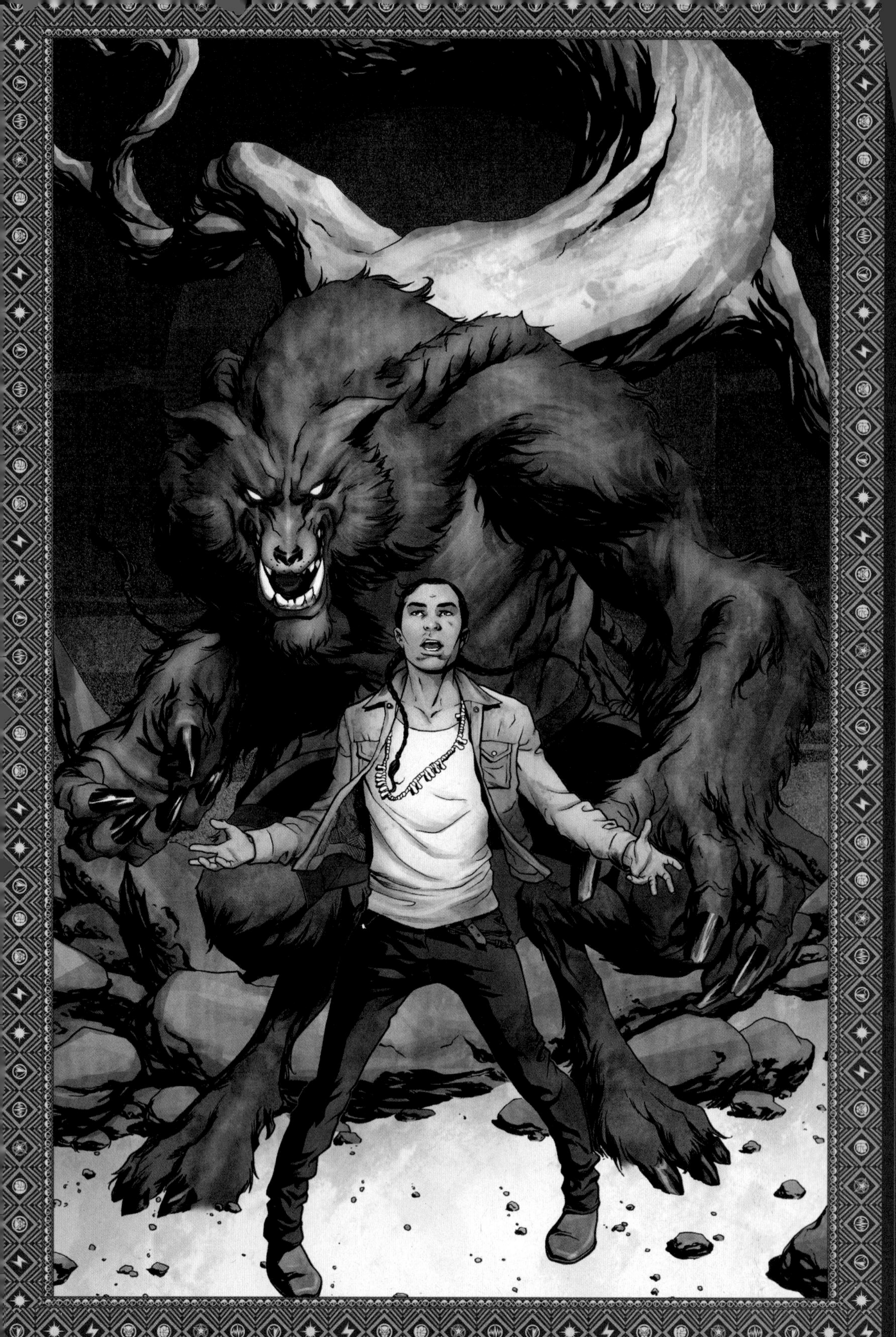

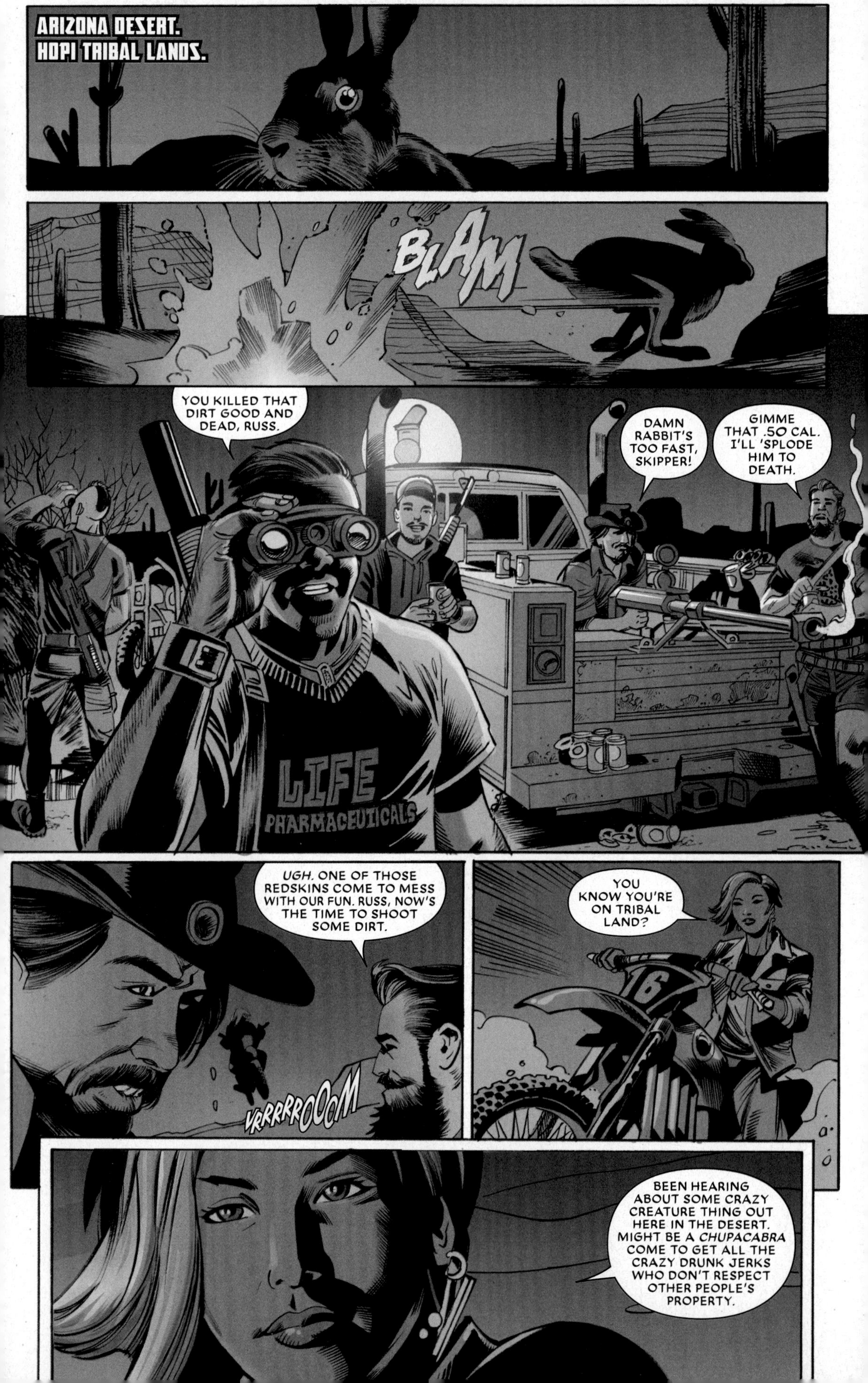
ARIZONA DESERT.
HOPI TRIBAL LANDS.
BLAM
YOU KILLED THAT DIRT GOOD AND DEAD, RUSS.
DAMN RABBIT'S TOO FAST, SKIPPER!
GIMME THAT .50 CAL. I'LL 'SPLODE HIM TO DEATH.
LIFE PHARMACEUTICALS
UGH. ONE OF THOSE REDSKINS COME TO MESS WITH OUR FUN. RUSS, NOW'S THE TIME TO SHOOT SOME DIRT.
VRRRRROOOM
YOU KNOW YOU'RE ON TRIBAL LAND?
BEEN HEARING ABOUT SOME CRAZY CREATURE THING OUT HERE IN THE DESERT. MIGHT BE A *CHUPACABRA* COME TO GET ALL THE CRAZY DRUNK JERKS WHO DON'T RESPECT OTHER PEOPLE'S PROPERTY.

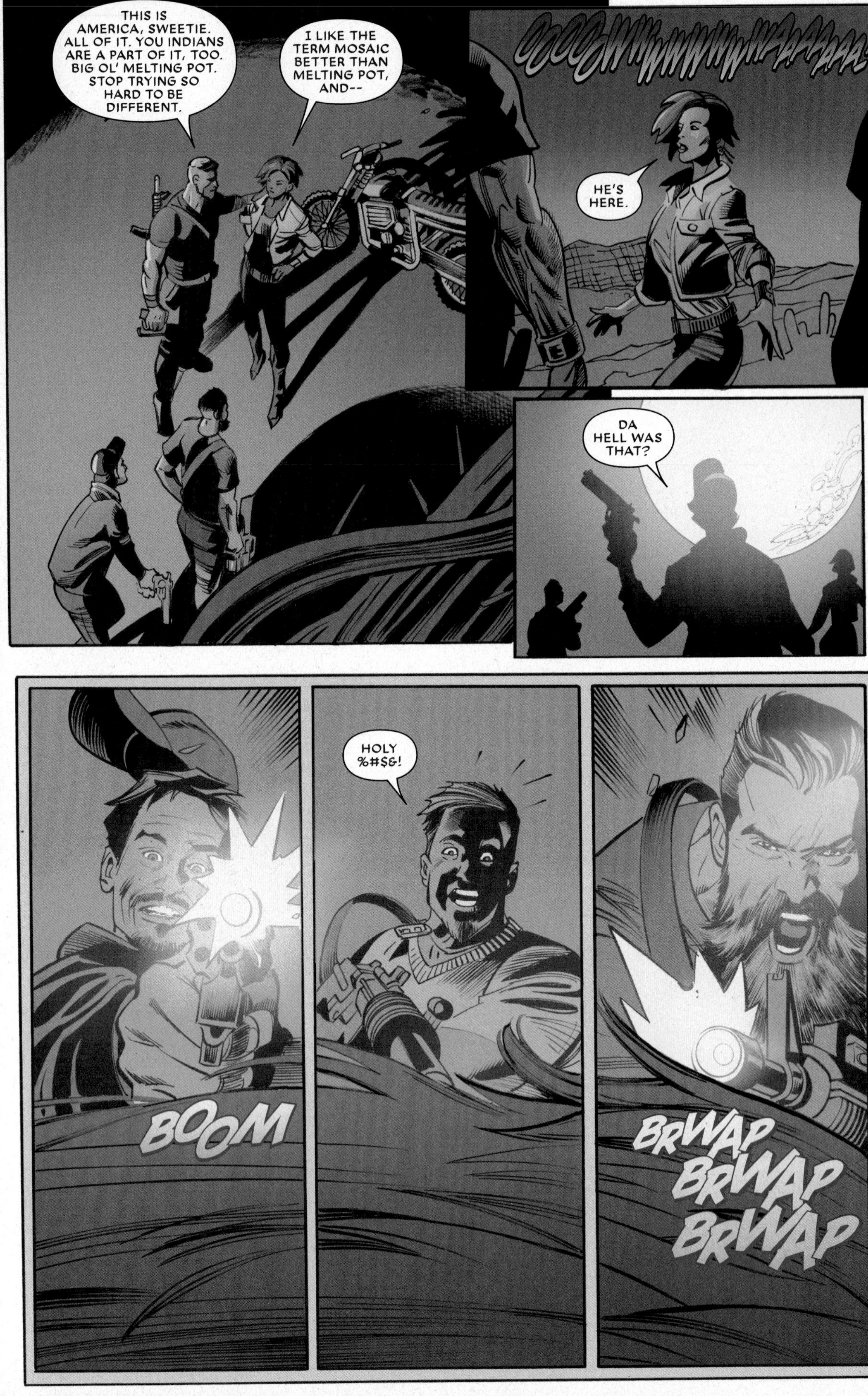
THIS IS AMERICA, SWEETIE. ALL OF IT. YOU INDIANS ARE A PART OF IT, TOO. BIG OL' MELTING POT. STOP TRYING SO HARD TO BE DIFFERENT.
I LIKE THE TERM MOSAIC BETTER THAN MELTING POT, AND--
OOOOWWWWWWWWAAAAAAA!
HE'S HERE.
DA HELL WAS THAT?
BOOM
HOLY %#$&!
BRWAP
BRWAP
BRWAP

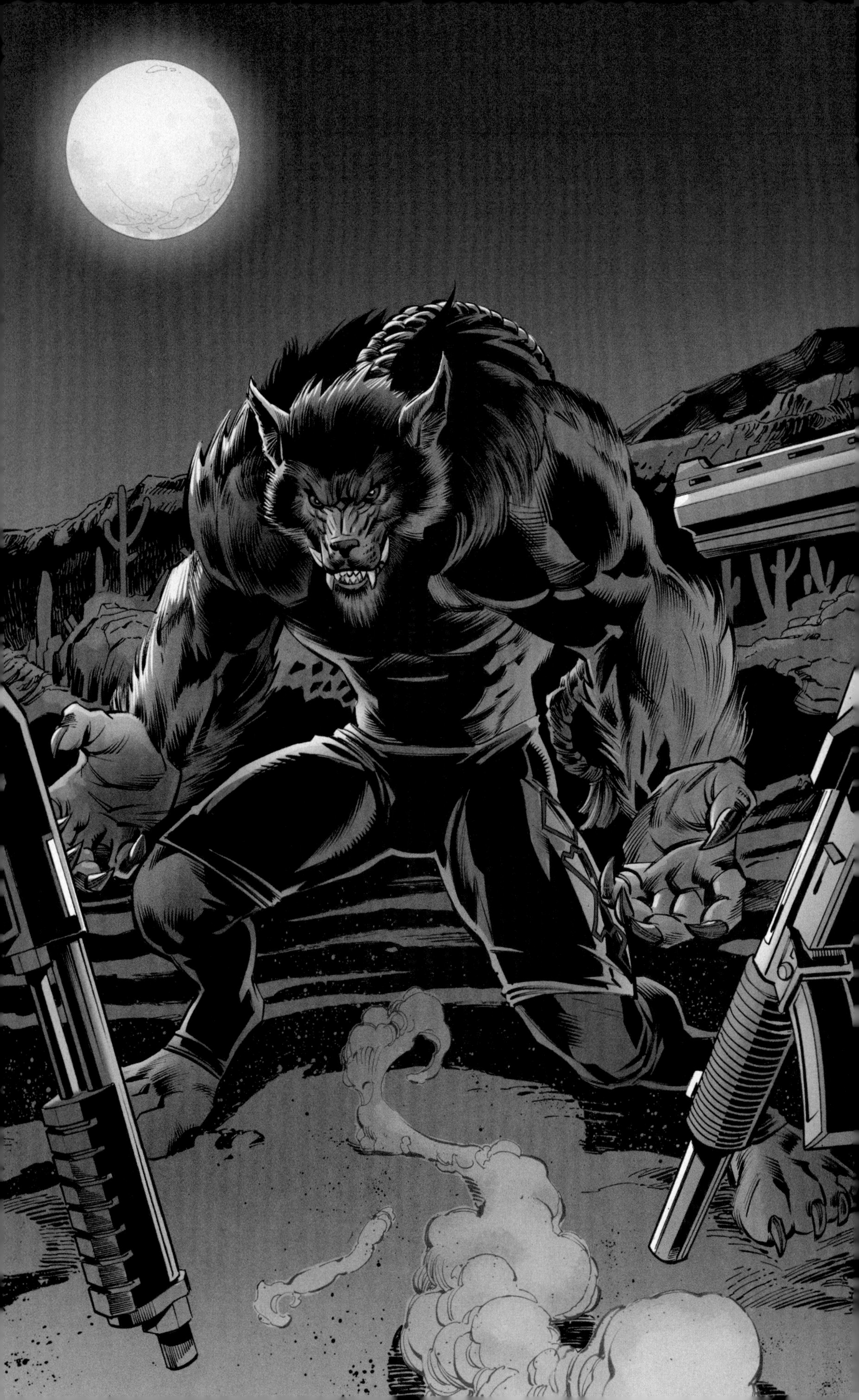

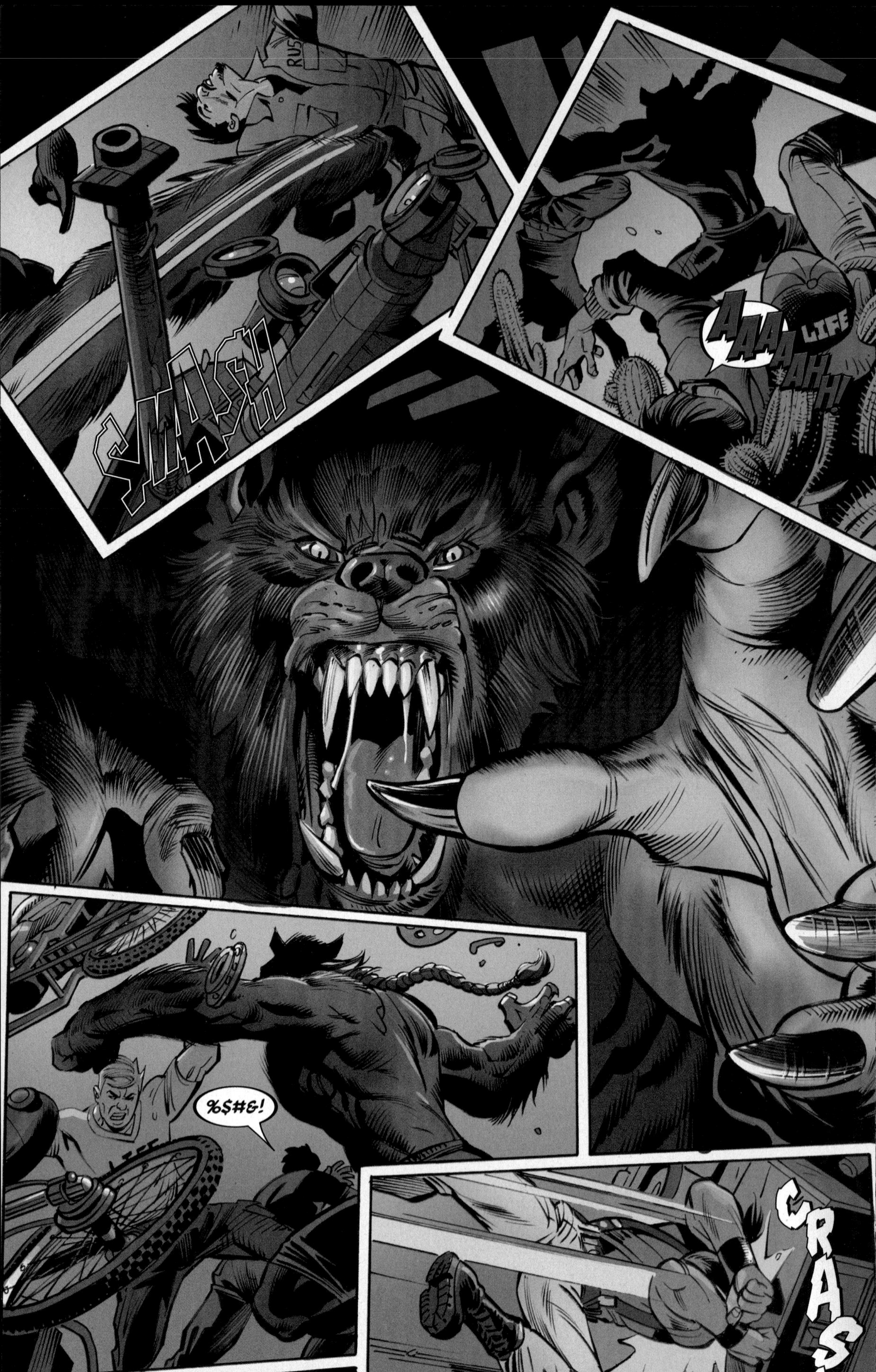
SMASH
AAAAAHH!
LIFE
%$#&!
CRASH

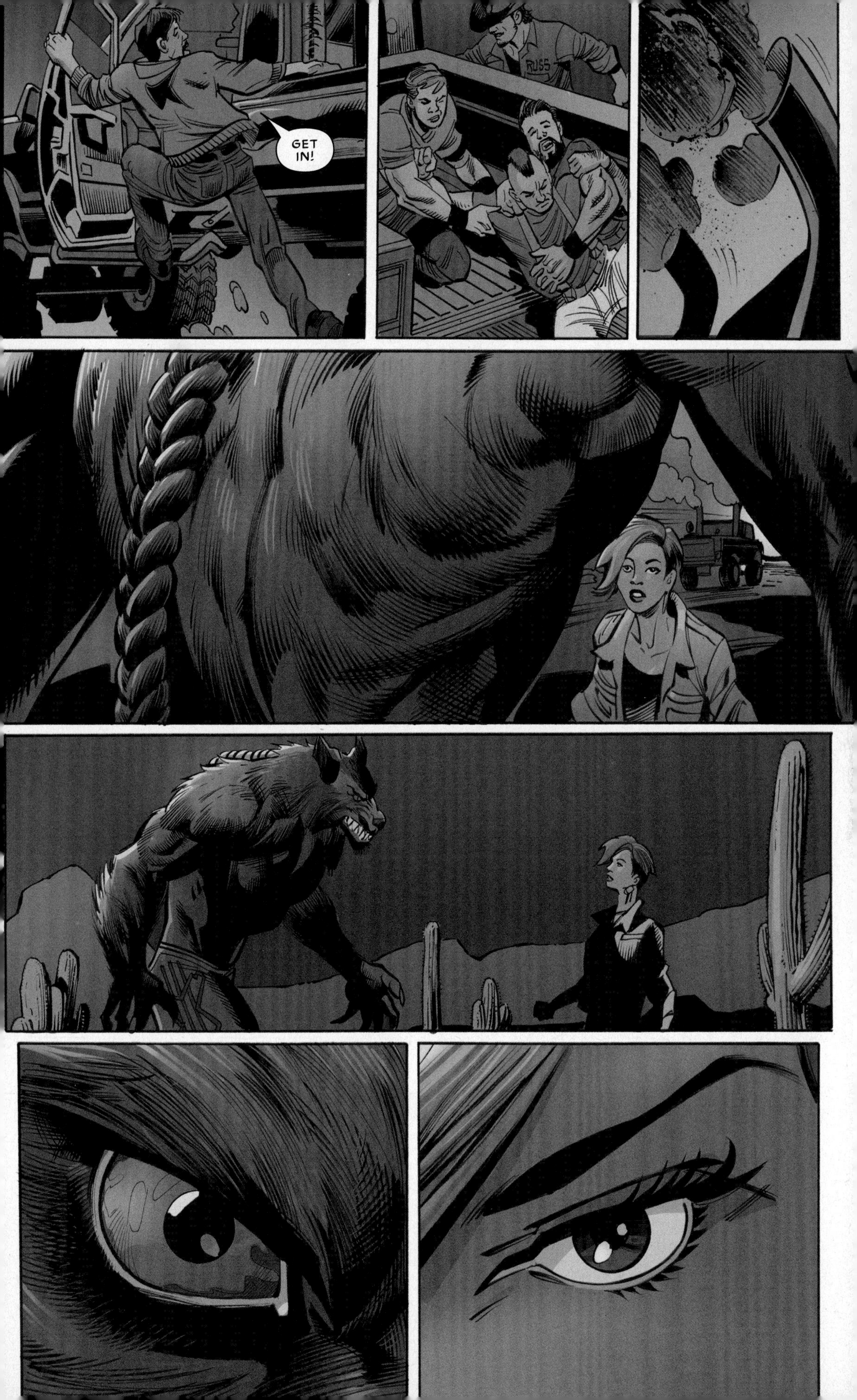
GET IN!

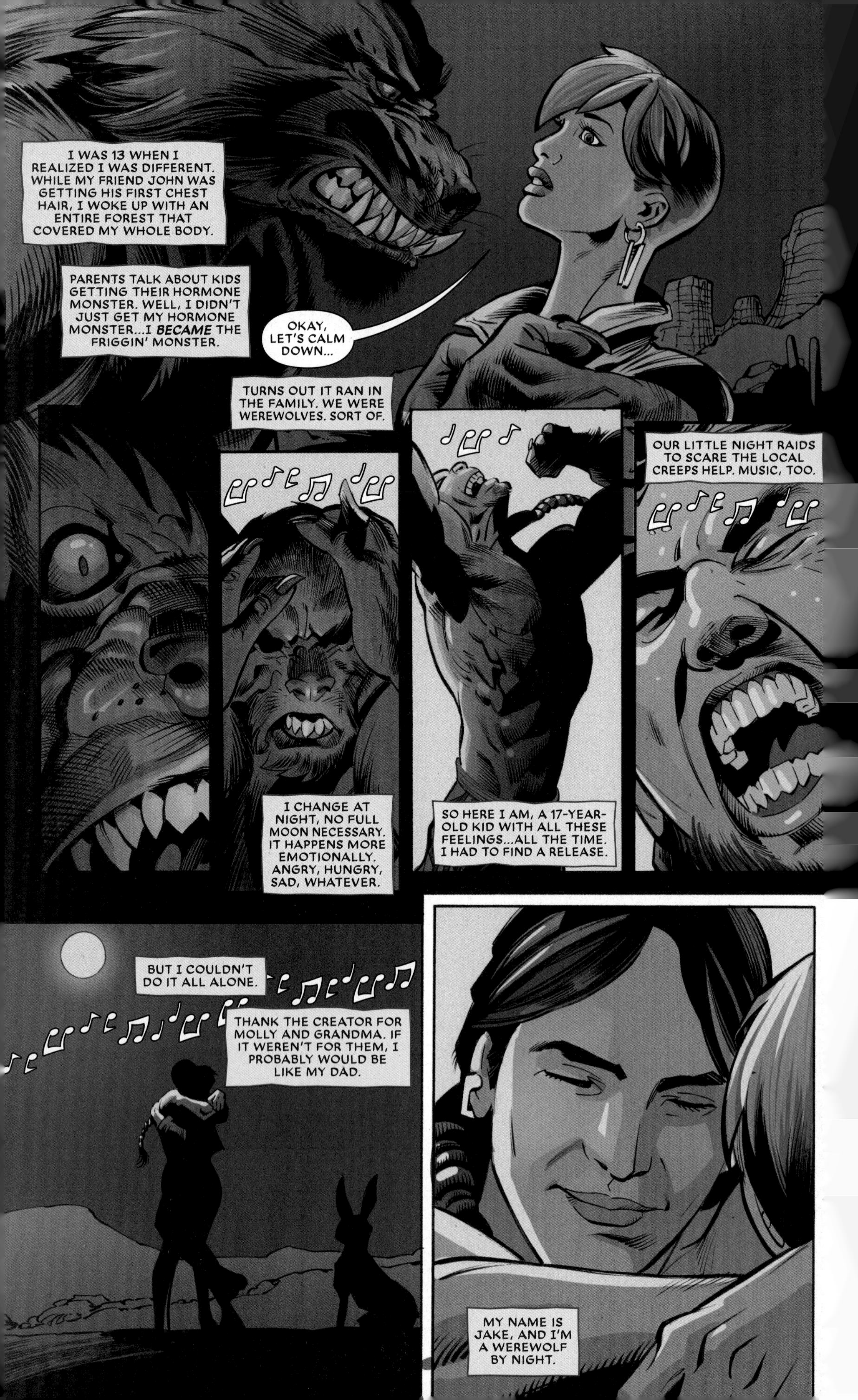
I WAS 13 WHEN I REALIZED I WAS DIFFERENT. WHILE MY FRIEND JOHN WAS GETTING HIS FIRST CHEST HAIR, I WOKE UP WITH AN ENTIRE FOREST THAT COVERED MY WHOLE BODY.
PARENTS TALK ABOUT KIDS GETTING THEIR HORMONE MONSTER. WELL, I DIDN'T JUST GET MY HORMONE MONSTER...I *BECAME* THE FRIGGIN' MONSTER.
OKAY, LET'S CALM DOWN...
TURNS OUT IT RAN IN THE FAMILY. WE WERE WEREWOLVES. SORT OF.
I CHANGE AT NIGHT, NO FULL MOON NECESSARY. IT HAPPENS MORE EMOTIONALLY. ANGRY, HUNGRY, SAD, WHATEVER.
SO HERE I AM, A 17-YEAR-OLD KID WITH ALL THESE FEELINGS...ALL THE TIME. I HAD TO FIND A RELEASE.
OUR LITTLE NIGHT RAIDS TO SCARE THE LOCAL CREEPS HELP. MUSIC, TOO.
BUT I COULDN'T DO IT ALL ALONE.
THANK THE CREATOR FOR MOLLY AND GRANDMA. IF IT WEREN'T FOR THEM, I PROBABLY WOULD BE LIKE MY DAD.
MY NAME IS JAKE, AND I'M A WEREWOLF BY NIGHT.

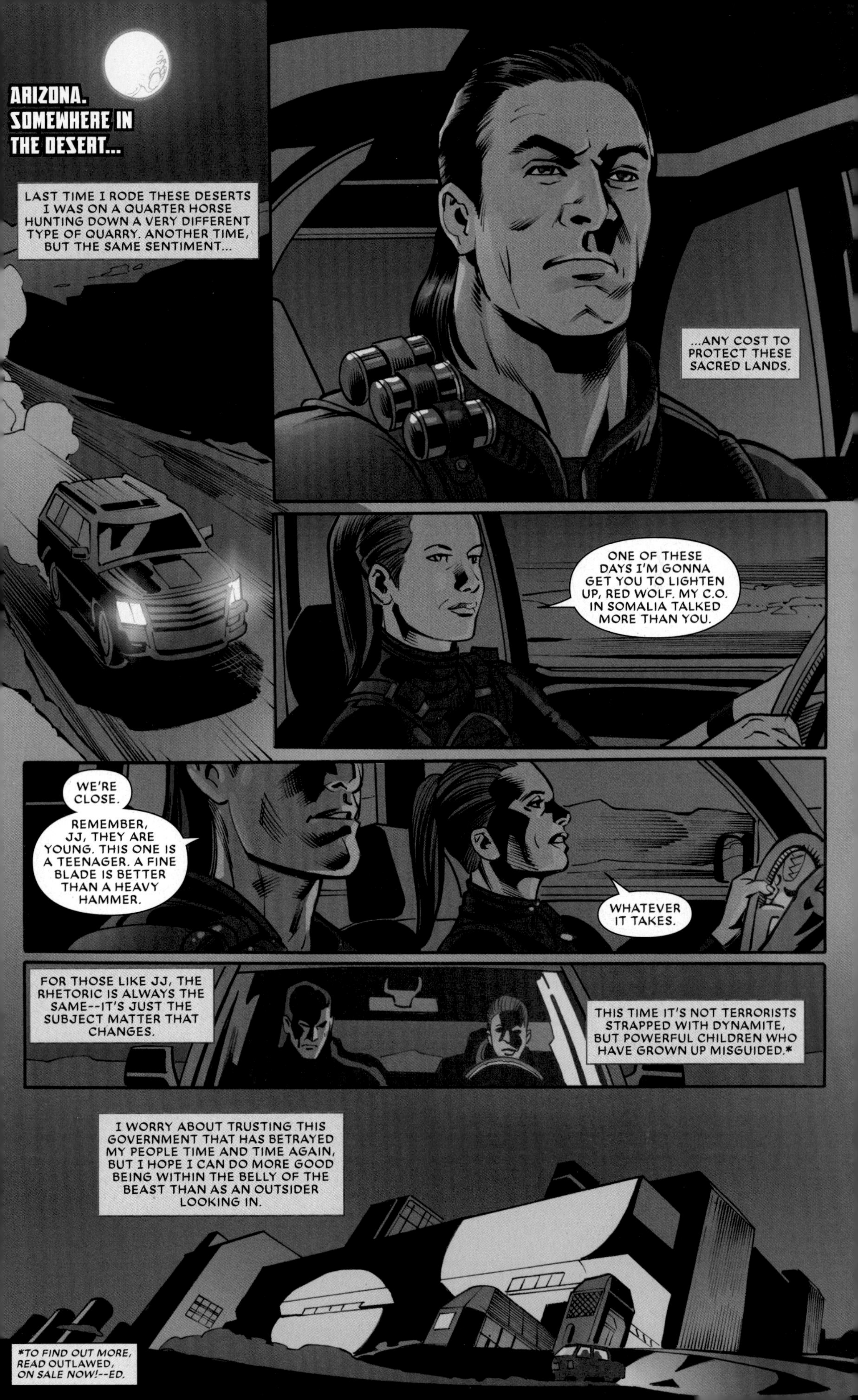
ARIZONA. SOMEWHERE IN THE DESERT...
LAST TIME I RODE THESE DESERTS I WAS ON A QUARTER HORSE HUNTING DOWN A VERY DIFFERENT TYPE OF QUARRY. ANOTHER TIME, BUT THE SAME SENTIMENT...
...ANY COST TO PROTECT THESE SACRED LANDS.
ONE OF THESE DAYS I'M GONNA GET YOU TO LIGHTEN UP, RED WOLF. MY C.O. IN SOMALIA TALKED MORE THAN YOU.
WE'RE CLOSE.
REMEMBER, JJ, THEY ARE YOUNG. THIS ONE IS A TEENAGER. A FINE BLADE IS BETTER THAN A HEAVY HAMMER.
WHATEVER IT TAKES.
FOR THOSE LIKE JJ, THE RHETORIC IS ALWAYS THE SAME--IT'S JUST THE SUBJECT MATTER THAT CHANGES.
THIS TIME IT'S NOT TERRORISTS STRAPPED WITH DYNAMITE, BUT POWERFUL CHILDREN WHO HAVE GROWN UP MISGUIDED.*
I WORRY ABOUT TRUSTING THIS GOVERNMENT THAT HAS BETRAYED MY PEOPLE TIME AND TIME AGAIN, BUT I HOPE I CAN DO MORE GOOD BEING WITHIN THE BELLY OF THE BEAST THAN AS AN OUTSIDER LOOKING IN.
*TO FIND OUT MORE, READ OUTLAWED, ON SALE NOW!--ED.

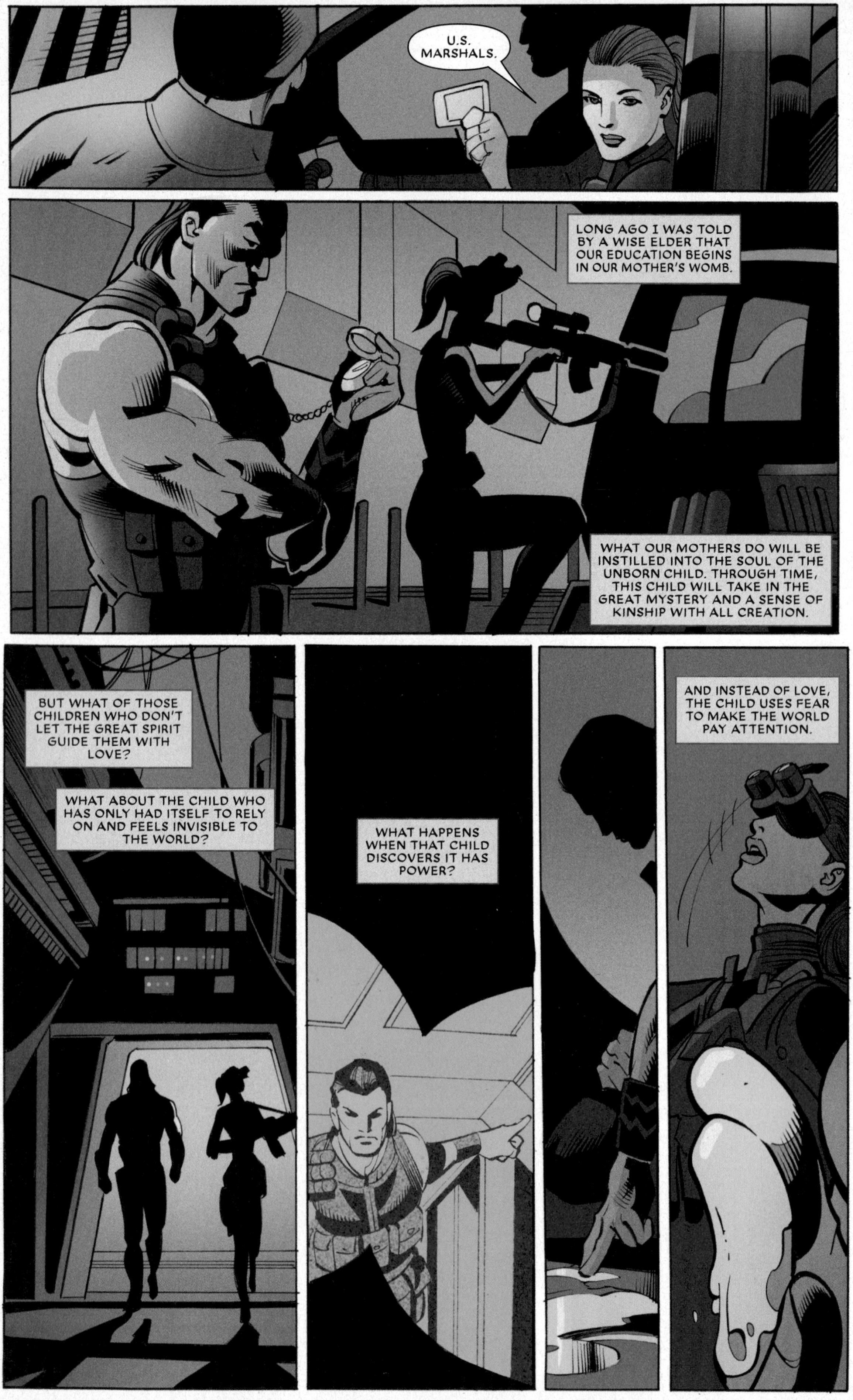
U.S. MARSHALS.
LONG AGO I WAS TOLD BY A WISE ELDER THAT OUR EDUCATION BEGINS IN OUR MOTHER'S WOMB.
WHAT OUR MOTHERS DO WILL BE INSTILLED INTO THE SOUL OF THE UNBORN CHILD. THROUGH TIME, THIS CHILD WILL TAKE IN THE GREAT MYSTERY AND A SENSE OF KINSHIP WITH ALL CREATION.
BUT WHAT OF THOSE CHILDREN WHO DON'T LET THE GREAT SPIRIT GUIDE THEM WITH LOVE?
WHAT ABOUT THE CHILD WHO HAS ONLY HAD ITSELF TO RELY ON AND FEELS INVISIBLE TO THE WORLD?
WHAT HAPPENS WHEN THAT CHILD DISCOVERS IT HAS POWER?
AND INSTEAD OF LOVE, THE CHILD USES FEAR TO MAKE THE WORLD PAY ATTENTION.

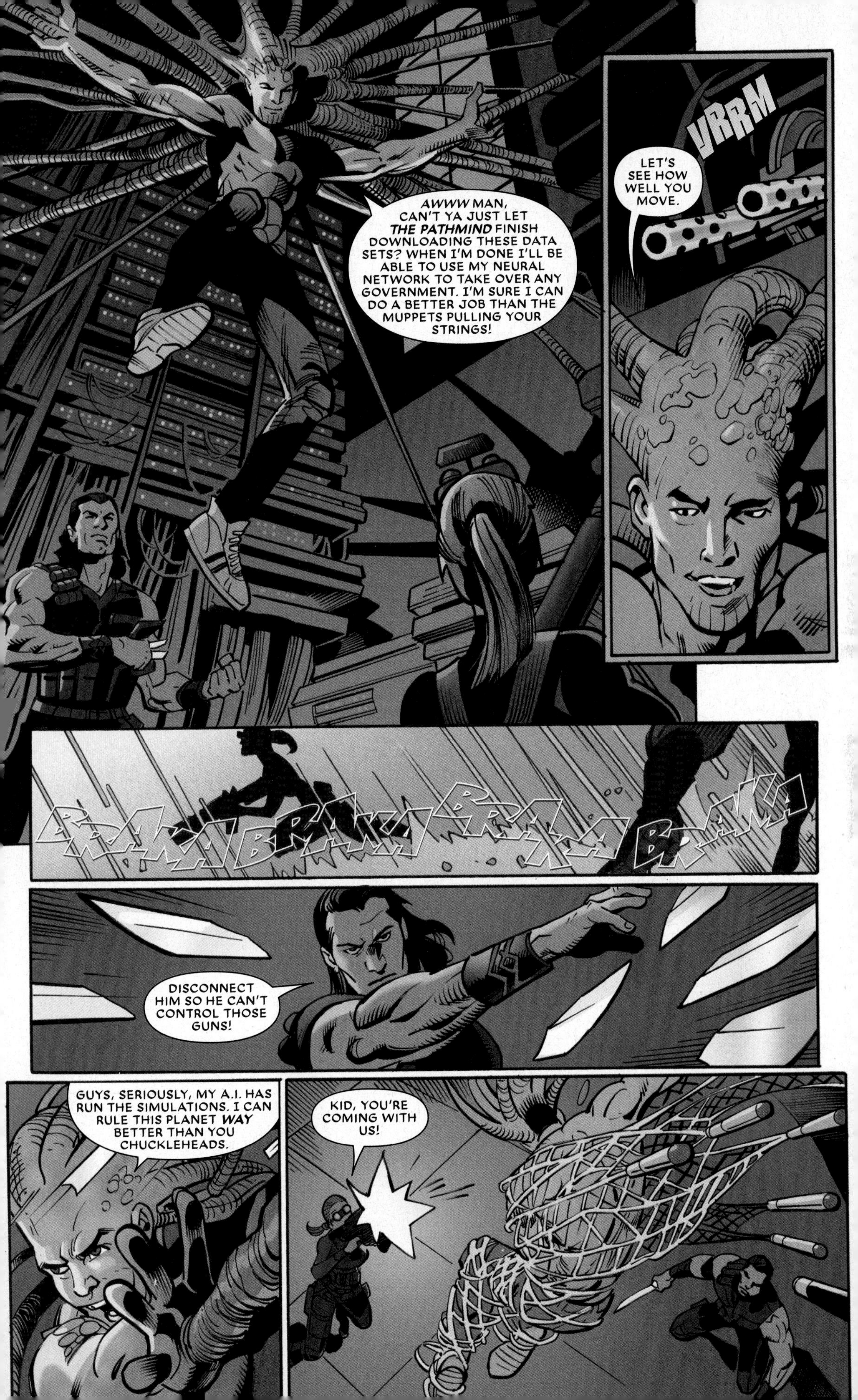
AWWW MAN, CAN'T YA JUST LET THE PATHMIND FINISH DOWNLOADING THESE DATA SETS? WHEN I'M DONE I'LL BE ABLE TO USE MY NEURAL NETWORK TO TAKE OVER ANY GOVERNMENT. I'M SURE I CAN DO A BETTER JOB THAN THE MUPPETS PULLING YOUR STRINGS!
VRRM
LET'S SEE HOW WELL YOU MOVE.
BRAKA BRAKA BRAKA BRAKA
DISCONNECT HIM SO HE CAN'T CONTROL THOSE GUNS!
GUYS, SERIOUSLY, MY A.I. HAS RUN THE SIMULATIONS. I CAN RULE THIS PLANET WAY BETTER THAN YOU CHUCKLEHEADS.
KID, YOU'RE COMING WITH US!

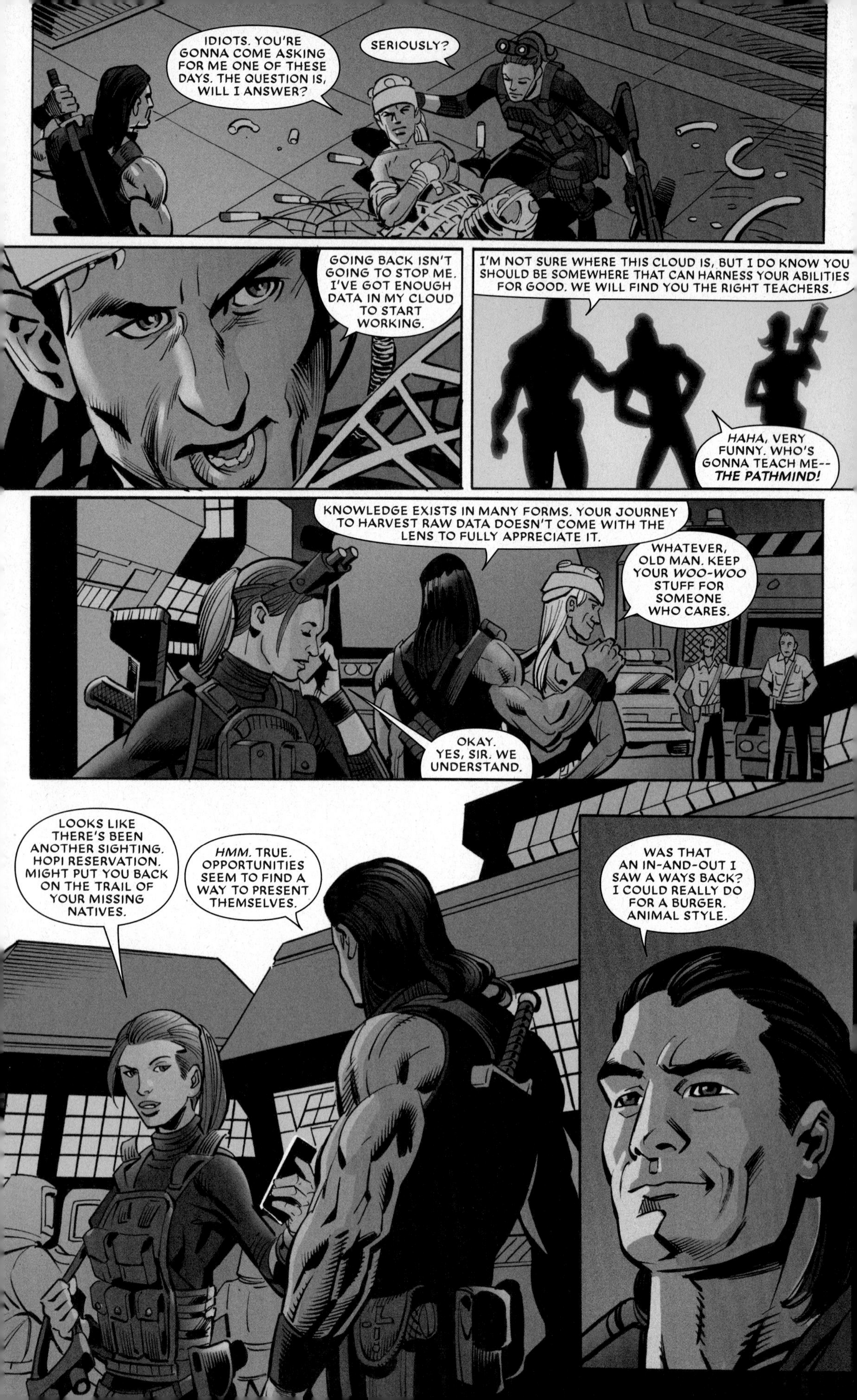
IDIOTS. YOU'RE GONNA COME ASKING FOR ME ONE OF THESE DAYS. THE QUESTION IS, WILL I ANSWER?
SERIOUSLY?
GOING BACK ISN'T GOING TO STOP ME. I'VE GOT ENOUGH DATA IN MY CLOUD TO START WORKING.
I'M NOT SURE WHERE THIS CLOUD IS, BUT I DO KNOW YOU SHOULD BE SOMEWHERE THAT CAN HARNESS YOUR ABILITIES FOR GOOD. WE WILL FIND YOU THE RIGHT TEACHERS.
HAHA, VERY FUNNY. WHO'S GONNA TEACH ME-- ***THE PATHMIND!***
KNOWLEDGE EXISTS IN MANY FORMS. YOUR JOURNEY TO HARVEST RAW DATA DOESN'T COME WITH THE LENS TO FULLY APPRECIATE IT.
WHATEVER, OLD MAN. KEEP YOUR *WOO-WOO* STUFF FOR SOMEONE WHO CARES.
OKAY. YES, SIR. WE UNDERSTAND.
LOOKS LIKE THERE'S BEEN ANOTHER SIGHTING. HOPI RESERVATION. MIGHT PUT YOU BACK ON THE TRAIL OF YOUR MISSING NATIVES.
HMM. TRUE. OPPORTUNITIES SEEM TO FIND A WAY TO PRESENT THEMSELVES.
WAS THAT AN IN-AND-OUT I SAW A WAYS BACK? I COULD REALLY DO FOR A BURGER. ANIMAL STYLE.

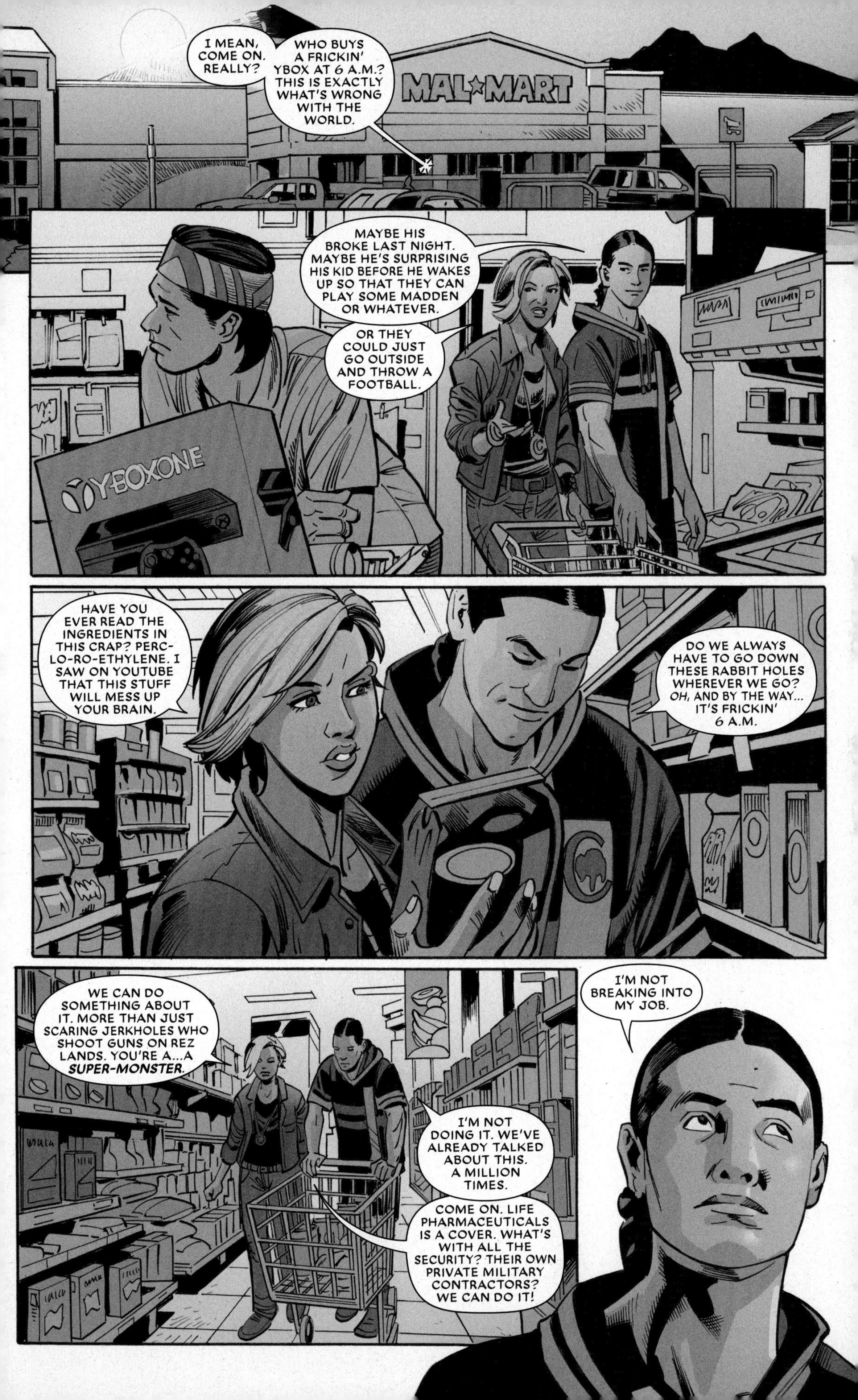
MAL★MART
I MEAN, COME ON. REALLY?
WHO BUYS A FRICKIN' YBOX AT 6 A.M.? THIS IS EXACTLY WHAT'S WRONG WITH THE WORLD.
YBOXONE
MAYBE HIS BROKE LAST NIGHT. MAYBE HE'S SURPRISING HIS KID BEFORE HE WAKES UP SO THAT THEY CAN PLAY SOME MADDEN OR WHATEVER.
OR THEY COULD JUST GO OUTSIDE AND THROW A FOOTBALL.
HAVE YOU EVER READ THE INGREDIENTS IN THIS CRAP? PERC-LO-RO-ETHYLENE. I SAW ON YOUTUBE THAT THIS STUFF WILL MESS UP YOUR BRAIN.
DO WE ALWAYS HAVE TO GO DOWN THESE RABBIT HOLES WHEREVER WE GO? *OH,* AND BY THE WAY... IT'S FRICKIN' 6 A.M.
WE CAN DO SOMETHING ABOUT IT. MORE THAN JUST SCARING JERKHOLES WHO SHOOT GUNS ON REZ LANDS. YOU'RE A...A ***SUPER-MONSTER.***
I'M NOT DOING IT. WE'VE ALREADY TALKED ABOUT THIS. A MILLION TIMES.
COME ON. LIFE PHARMACEUTICALS IS A COVER. WHAT'S WITH ALL THE SECURITY? THEIR OWN PRIVATE MILITARY CONTRACTORS? WE CAN DO IT!
I'M NOT BREAKING INTO MY JOB.

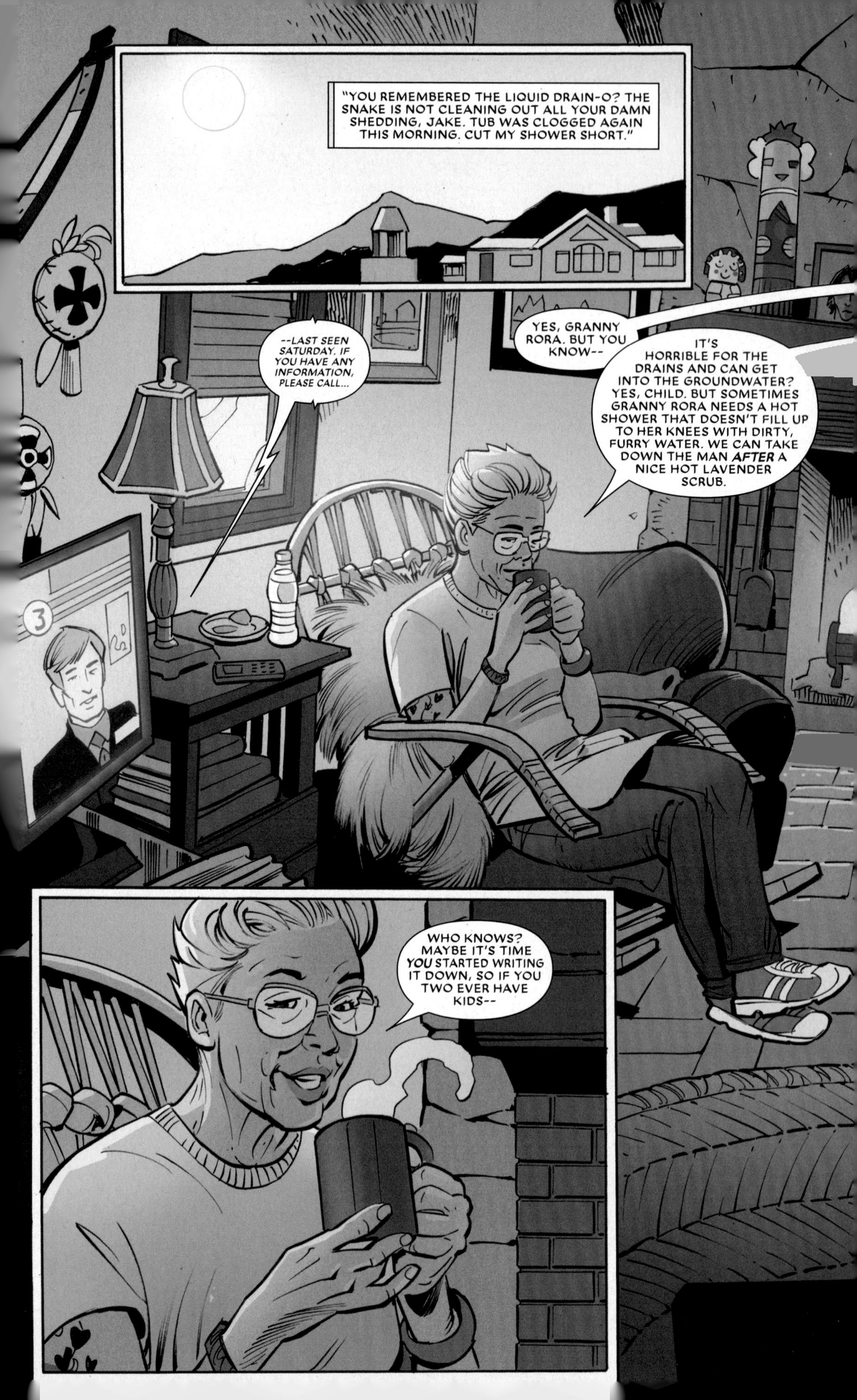
"YOU REMEMBERED THE LIQUID DRAIN-O? THE SNAKE IS NOT CLEANING OUT ALL YOUR DAMN SHEDDING, JAKE. TUB WAS CLOGGED AGAIN THIS MORNING. CUT MY SHOWER SHORT."
--LAST SEEN SATURDAY. IF YOU HAVE ANY INFORMATION, PLEASE CALL...
YES, GRANNY RORA. BUT YOU KNOW--
IT'S HORRIBLE FOR THE DRAINS AND CAN GET INTO THE GROUNDWATER? YES, CHILD. BUT SOMETIMES GRANNY RORA NEEDS A HOT SHOWER THAT DOESN'T FILL UP TO HER KNEES WITH DIRTY, FURRY WATER. WE CAN TAKE DOWN THE MAN *AFTER* A NICE HOT LAVENDER SCRUB.
3
WHO KNOWS? MAYBE IT'S TIME *YOU* STARTED WRITING IT DOWN, SO IF YOU TWO EVER HAVE KIDS--

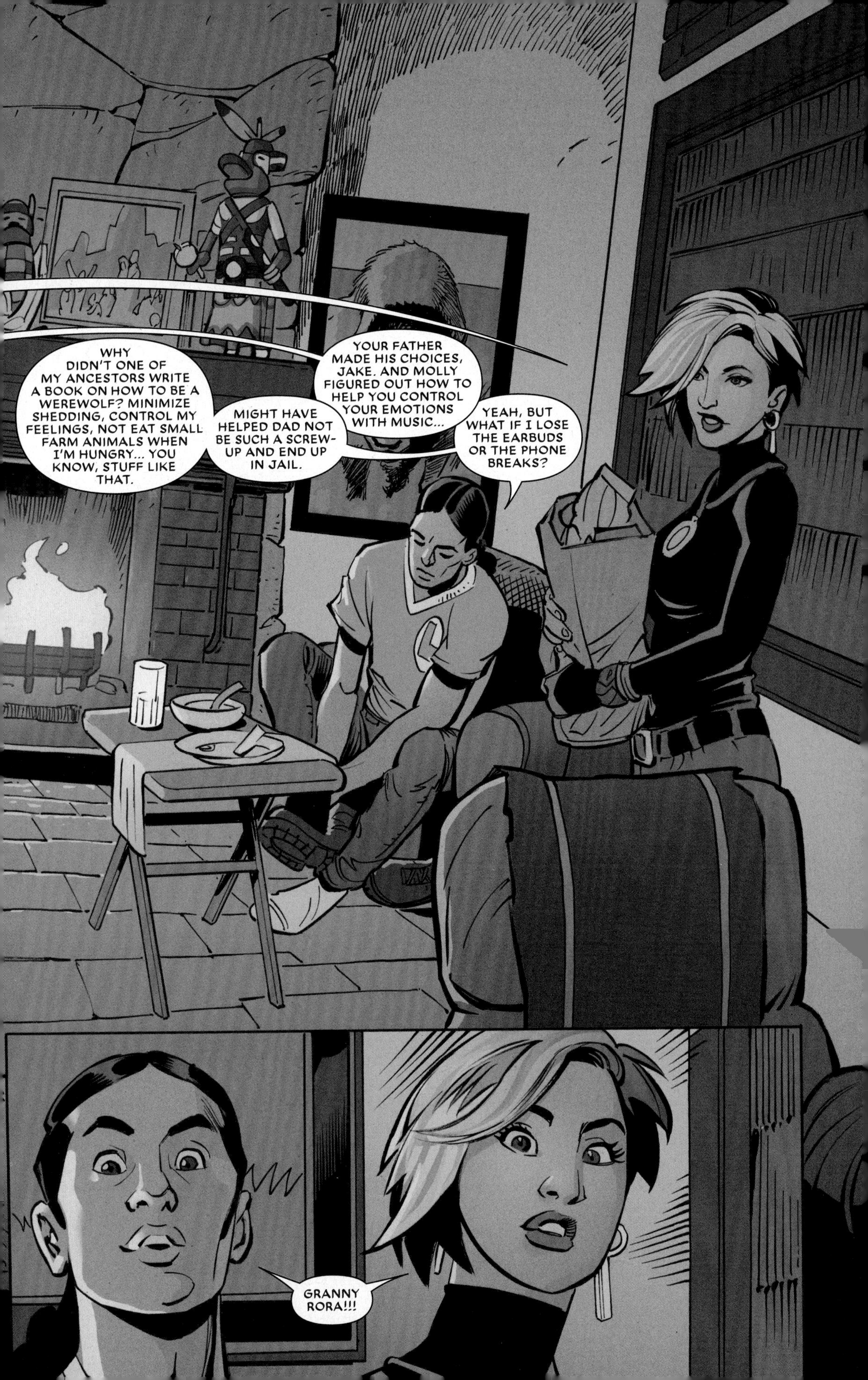
WHY DIDN'T ONE OF MY ANCESTORS WRITE A BOOK ON HOW TO BE A WEREWOLF? MINIMIZE SHEDDING, CONTROL MY FEELINGS, NOT EAT SMALL FARM ANIMALS WHEN I'M HUNGRY... YOU KNOW, STUFF LIKE THAT.
MIGHT HAVE HELPED DAD NOT BE SUCH A SCREW-UP AND END UP IN JAIL.
YOUR FATHER MADE HIS CHOICES, JAKE. AND MOLLY FIGURED OUT HOW TO HELP YOU CONTROL YOUR EMOTIONS WITH MUSIC...
YEAH, BUT WHAT IF I LOSE THE EARBUDS OR THE PHONE BREAKS?
GRANNY RORA!!!

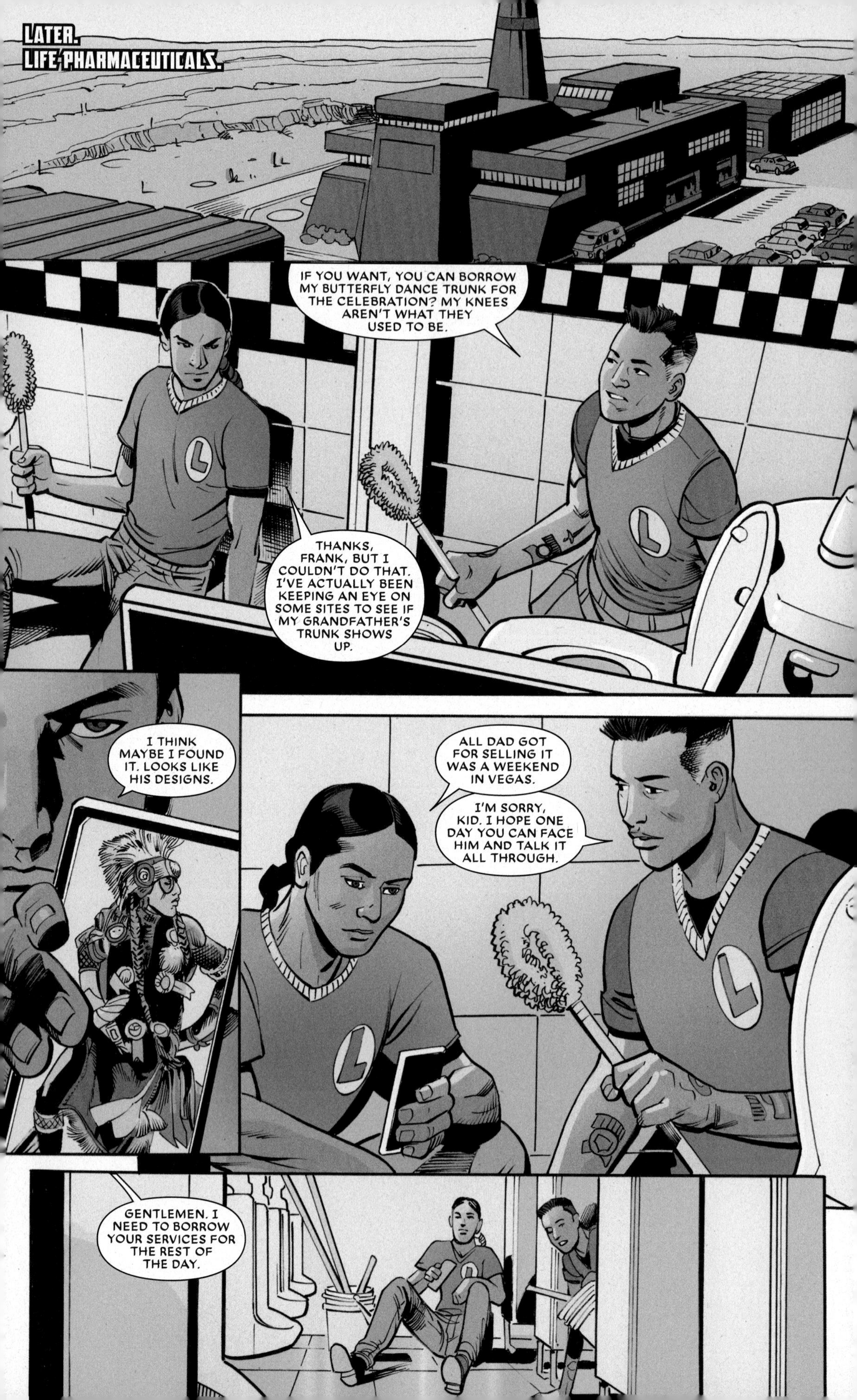
LATER.
LIFE PHARMACEUTICALS.
IF YOU WANT, YOU CAN BORROW MY BUTTERFLY DANCE TRUNK FOR THE CELEBRATION? MY KNEES AREN'T WHAT THEY USED TO BE.
THANKS, FRANK, BUT I COULDN'T DO THAT. I'VE ACTUALLY BEEN KEEPING AN EYE ON SOME SITES TO SEE IF MY GRANDFATHER'S TRUNK SHOWS UP.
I THINK MAYBE I FOUND IT. LOOKS LIKE HIS DESIGNS.
ALL DAD GOT FOR SELLING IT WAS A WEEKEND IN VEGAS.
I'M SORRY, KID. I HOPE ONE DAY YOU CAN FACE HIM AND TALK IT ALL THROUGH.
GENTLEMEN. I NEED TO BORROW YOUR SERVICES FOR THE REST OF THE DAY.

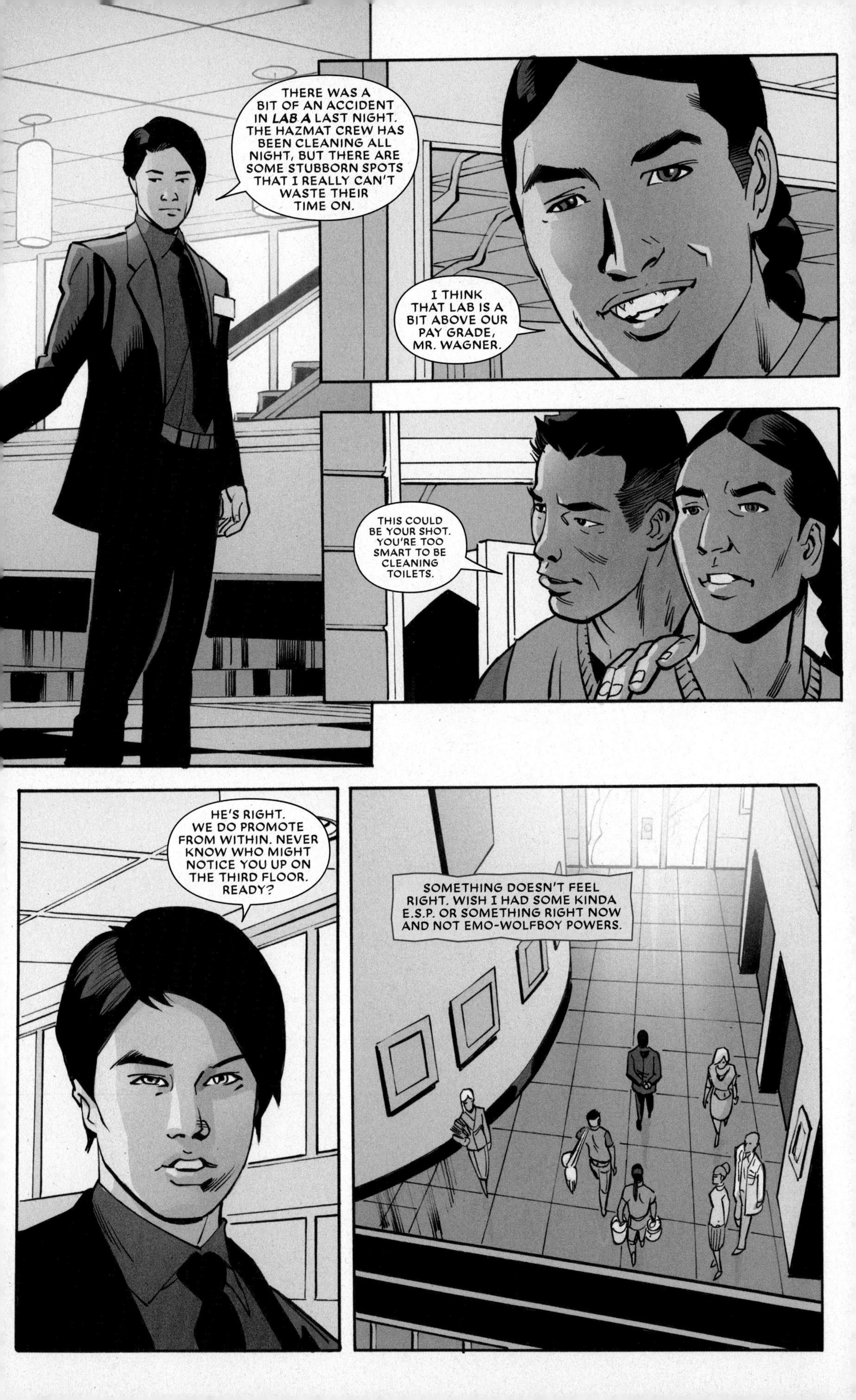
THERE WAS A BIT OF AN ACCIDENT IN *LAB A* LAST NIGHT. THE HAZMAT CREW HAS BEEN CLEANING ALL NIGHT, BUT THERE ARE SOME STUBBORN SPOTS THAT I REALLY CAN'T WASTE THEIR TIME ON.
I THINK THAT LAB IS A BIT ABOVE OUR PAY GRADE, MR. WAGNER.
THIS COULD BE YOUR SHOT. YOU'RE TOO SMART TO BE CLEANING TOILETS.
HE'S RIGHT. WE DO PROMOTE FROM WITHIN. NEVER KNOW WHO MIGHT NOTICE YOU UP ON THE THIRD FLOOR. READY?
SOMETHING DOESN'T FEEL RIGHT. WISH I HAD SOME KINDA E.S.P. OR SOMETHING RIGHT NOW AND NOT EMO-WOLFBOY POWERS.

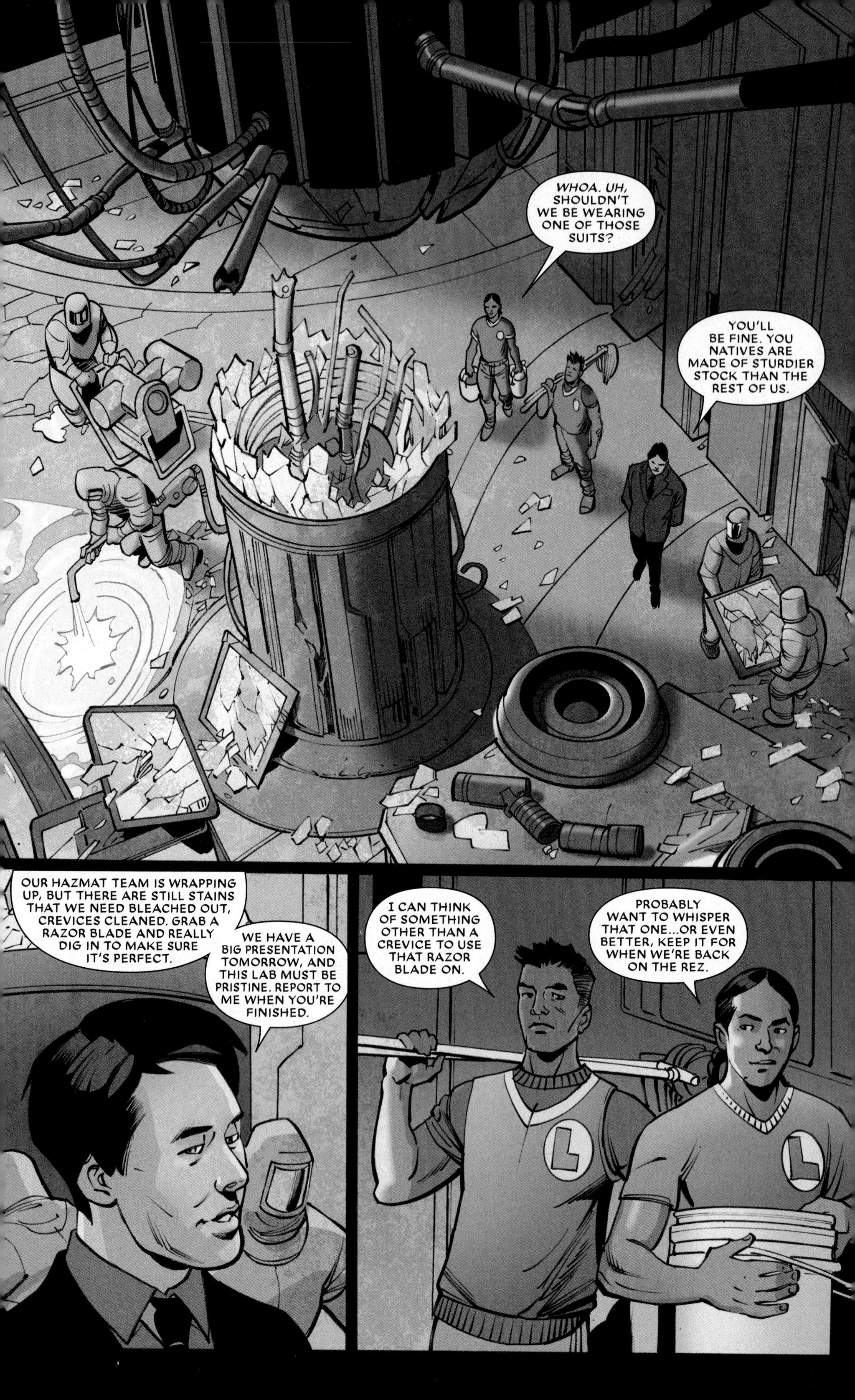
WHOA. UH, SHOULDN'T WE BE WEARING ONE OF THOSE SUITS?
YOU'LL BE FINE. YOU NATIVES ARE MADE OF STURDIER STOCK THAN THE REST OF US.
OUR HAZMAT TEAM IS WRAPPING UP, BUT THERE ARE STILL STAINS THAT WE NEED BLEACHED OUT, CREVICES CLEANED. GRAB A RAZOR BLADE AND REALLY DIG IN TO MAKE SURE IT'S PERFECT.
WE HAVE A BIG PRESENTATION TOMORROW, AND THIS LAB MUST BE PRISTINE. REPORT TO ME WHEN YOU'RE FINISHED.
I CAN THINK OF SOMETHING OTHER THAN A CREVICE TO USE THAT RAZOR BLADE ON.
PROBABLY WANT TO WHISPER THAT ONE...OR EVEN BETTER, KEEP IT FOR WHEN WE'RE BACK ON THE REZ.

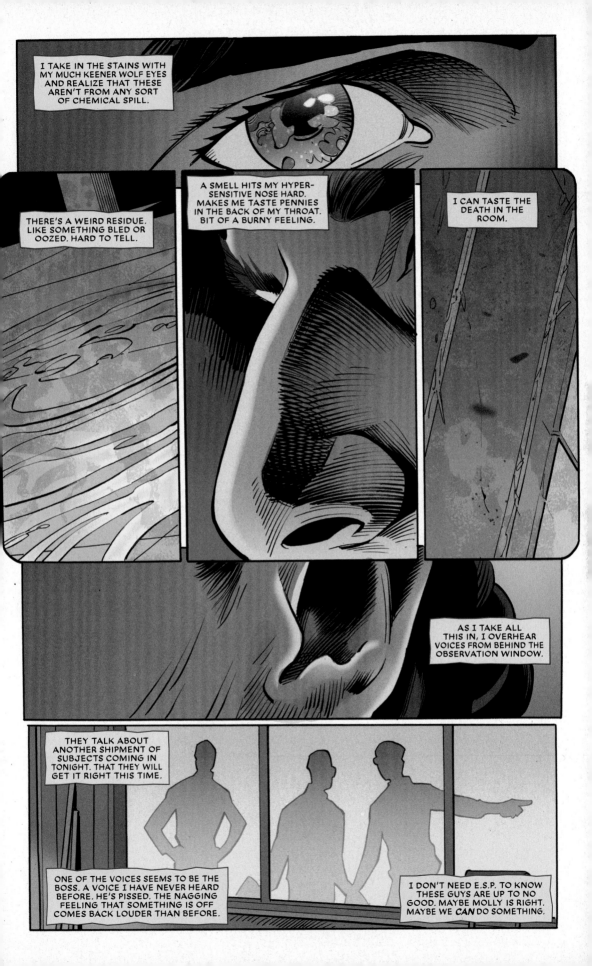

I TAKE IN THE STAINS WITH MY MUCH KEENER WOLF EYES AND REALIZE THAT THESE AREN'T FROM ANY SORT OF CHEMICAL SPILL.

THERE'S A WEIRD RESIDUE. LIKE SOMETHING BLED OR OOZED. HARD TO TELL.

A SMELL HITS MY HYPER-SENSITIVE NOSE HARD. MAKES ME TASTE PENNIES IN THE BACK OF MY THROAT. BIT OF A BURNY FEELING.

I CAN TASTE THE DEATH IN THE ROOM.

AS I TAKE ALL THIS IN, I OVERHEAR VOICES FROM BEHIND THE OBSERVATION WINDOW.

THEY TALK ABOUT ANOTHER SHIPMENT OF SUBJECTS COMING IN TONIGHT. THAT THEY WILL GET IT RIGHT THIS TIME.

ONE OF THE VOICES SEEMS TO BE THE BOSS. A VOICE I HAVE NEVER HEARD BEFORE. HE'S PISSED. THE NAGGING FEELING THAT SOMETHING IS OFF COMES BACK LOUDER THAN BEFORE.

I DON'T NEED E.S.P. TO KNOW THESE GUYS ARE UP TO NO GOOD. MAYBE MOLLY IS RIGHT. MAYBE WE *CAN* DO SOMETHING.

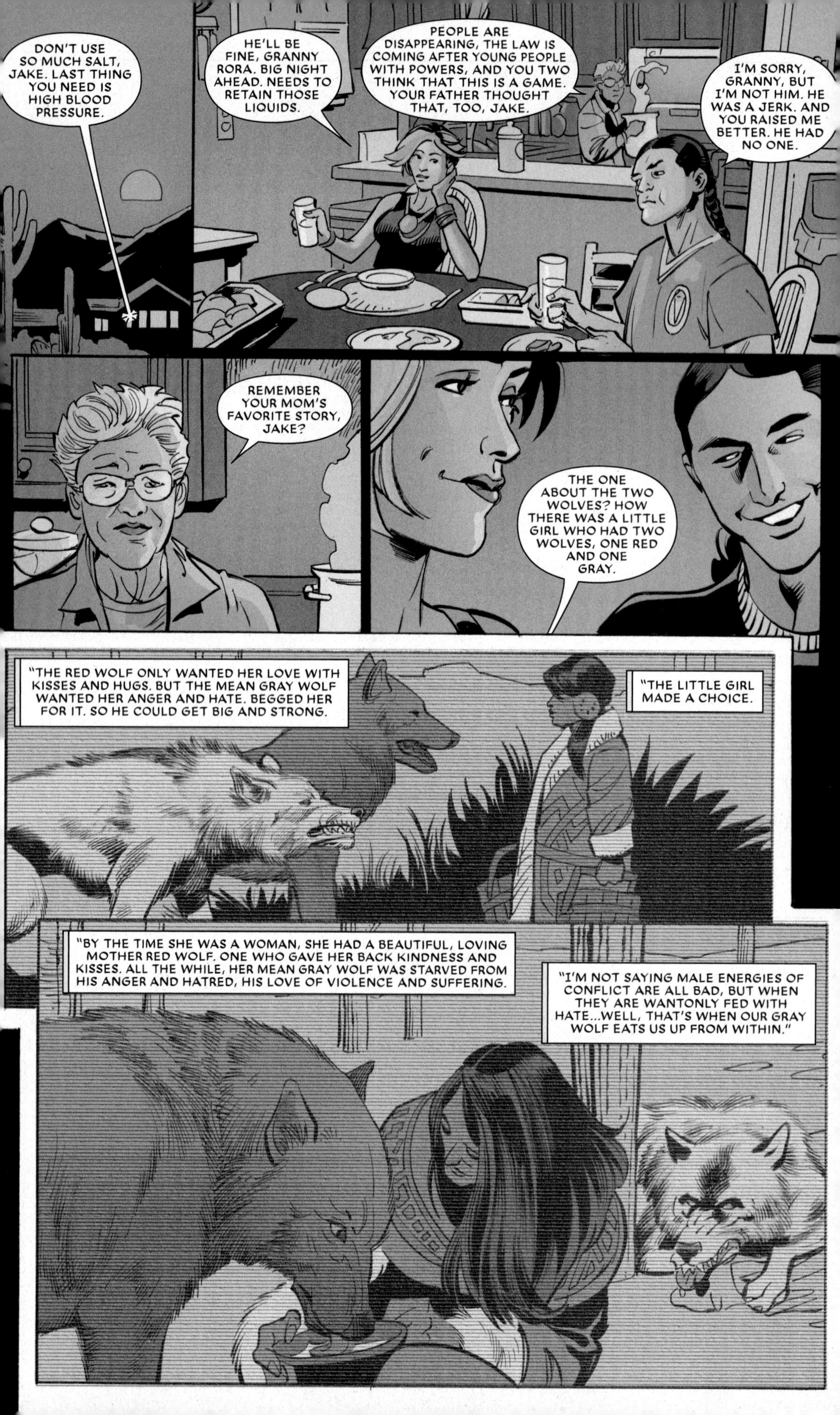
DON'T USE SO MUCH SALT, JAKE. LAST THING YOU NEED IS HIGH BLOOD PRESSURE.
HE'LL BE FINE, GRANNY RORA. BIG NIGHT AHEAD. NEEDS TO RETAIN THOSE LIQUIDS.
PEOPLE ARE DISAPPEARING, THE LAW IS COMING AFTER YOUNG PEOPLE WITH POWERS, AND YOU TWO THINK THAT THIS IS A GAME. YOUR FATHER THOUGHT THAT, TOO, JAKE.
I'M SORRY, GRANNY, BUT I'M NOT HIM. HE WAS A JERK. AND YOU RAISED ME BETTER. HE HAD NO ONE.
REMEMBER YOUR MOM'S FAVORITE STORY, JAKE?
THE ONE ABOUT THE TWO WOLVES? HOW THERE WAS A LITTLE GIRL WHO HAD TWO WOLVES, ONE RED AND ONE GRAY.
"THE RED WOLF ONLY WANTED HER LOVE WITH KISSES AND HUGS. BUT THE MEAN GRAY WOLF WANTED HER ANGER AND HATE. BEGGED HER FOR IT. SO HE COULD GET BIG AND STRONG.
"THE LITTLE GIRL MADE A CHOICE.
"BY THE TIME SHE WAS A WOMAN, SHE HAD A BEAUTIFUL, LOVING MOTHER RED WOLF. ONE WHO GAVE HER BACK KINDNESS AND KISSES. ALL THE WHILE, HER MEAN GRAY WOLF WAS STARVED FROM HIS ANGER AND HATRED, HIS LOVE OF VIOLENCE AND SUFFERING.
"I'M NOT SAYING MALE ENERGIES OF CONFLICT ARE ALL BAD, BUT WHEN THEY ARE WANTONLY FED WITH HATE...WELL, THAT'S WHEN OUR GRAY WOLF EATS US UP FROM WITHIN."

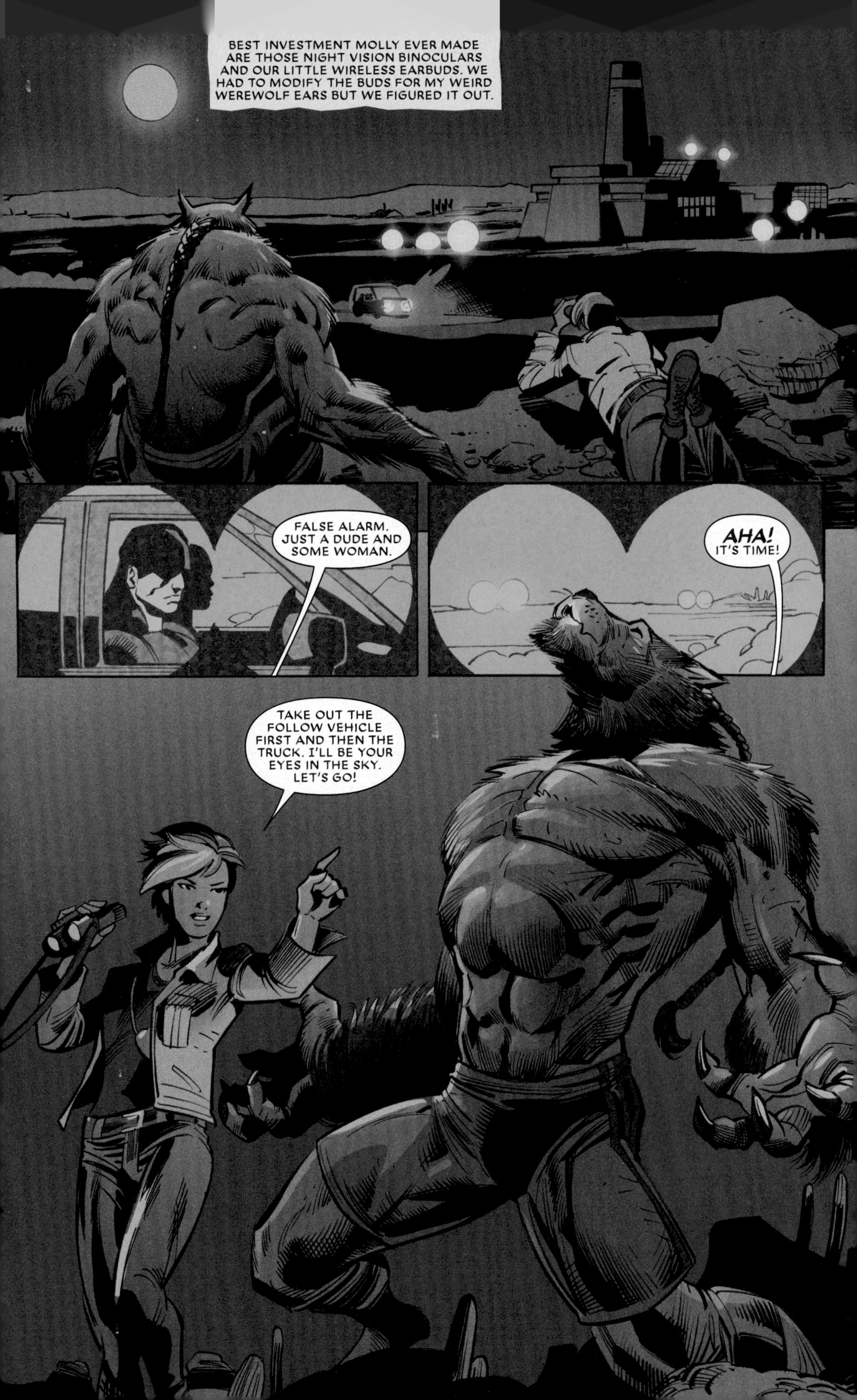
BEST INVESTMENT MOLLY EVER MADE ARE THOSE NIGHT VISION BINOCULARS AND OUR LITTLE WIRELESS EARBUDS. WE HAD TO MODIFY THE BUDS FOR MY WEIRD WEREWOLF EARS BUT WE FIGURED IT OUT.
FALSE ALARM. JUST A DUDE AND SOME WOMAN.
AHA! IT'S TIME!
TAKE OUT THE FOLLOW VEHICLE FIRST AND THEN THE TRUCK. I'LL BE YOUR EYES IN THE SKY. LET'S GO!

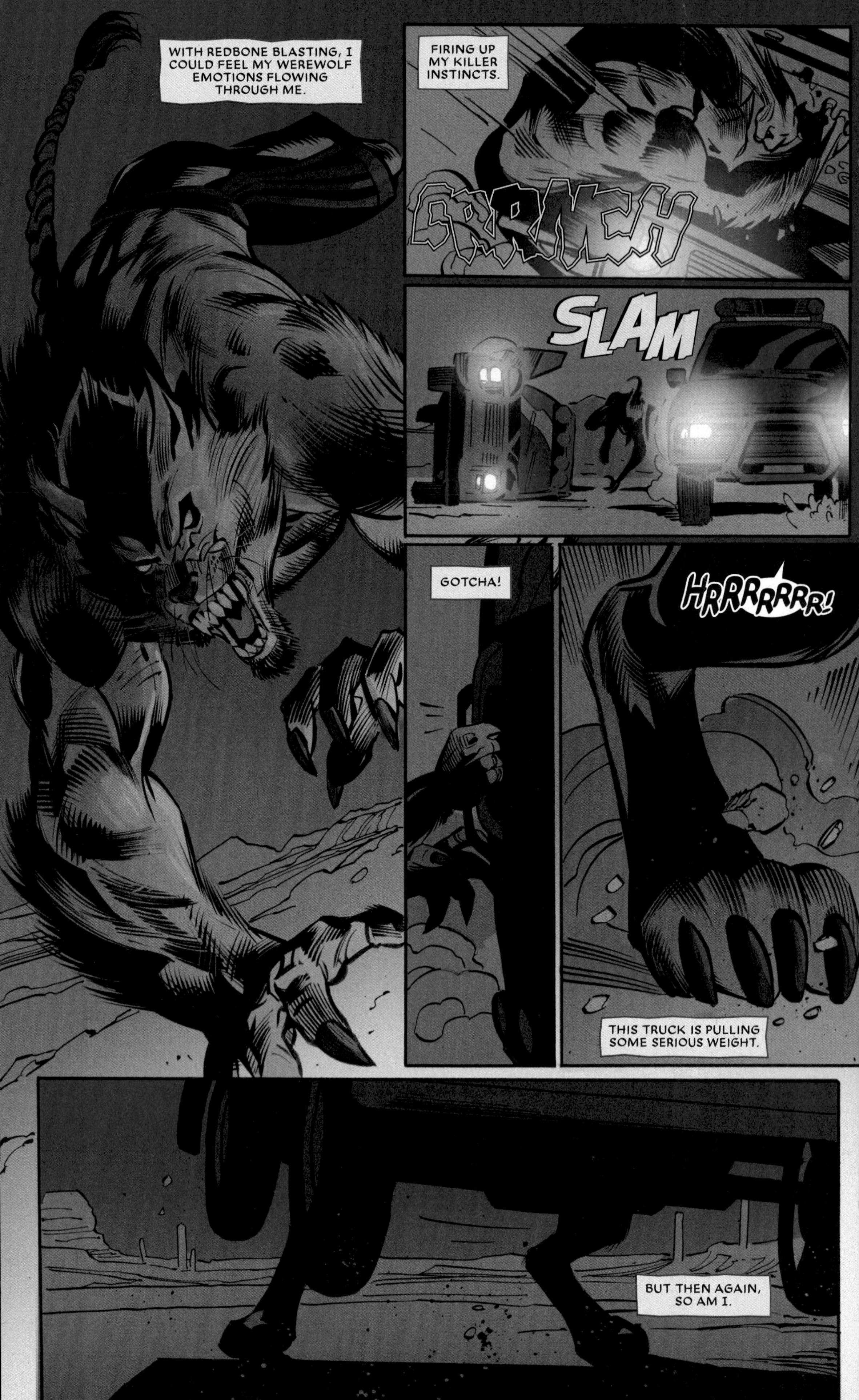
WITH REDBONE BLASTING, I COULD FEEL MY WEREWOLF EMOTIONS FLOWING THROUGH ME.
FIRING UP MY KILLER INSTINCTS.
CRUNCH
SLAM
GOTCHA!
HRRRRRRR!
THIS TRUCK IS PULLING SOME SERIOUS WEIGHT.
BUT THEN AGAIN, SO AM I.

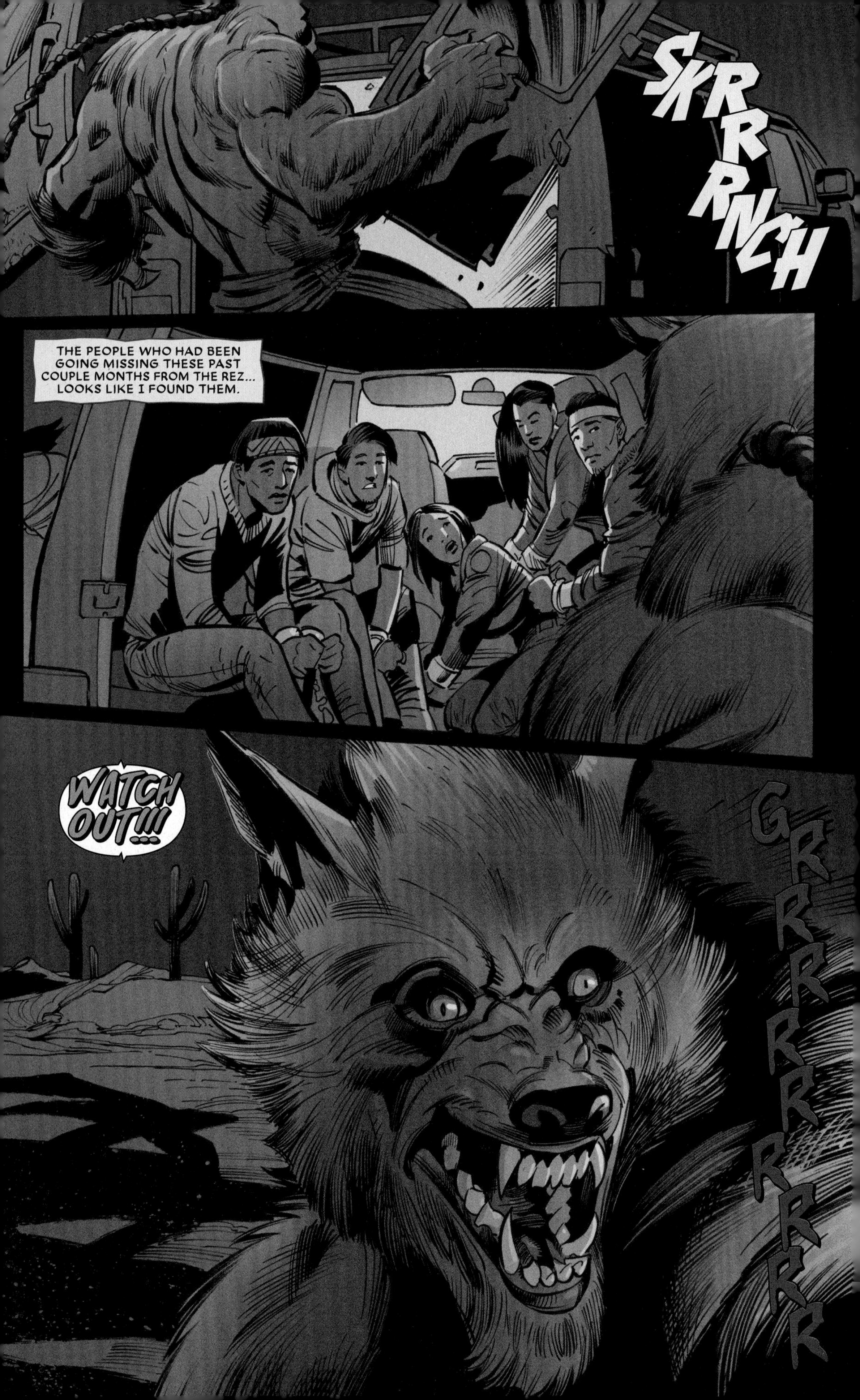
SKRRRNCH
THE PEOPLE WHO HAD BEEN GOING MISSING THESE PAST COUPLE MONTHS FROM THE REZ... LOOKS LIKE I FOUND THEM.
WATCH OUT!!!
GRRRRRRRRRR

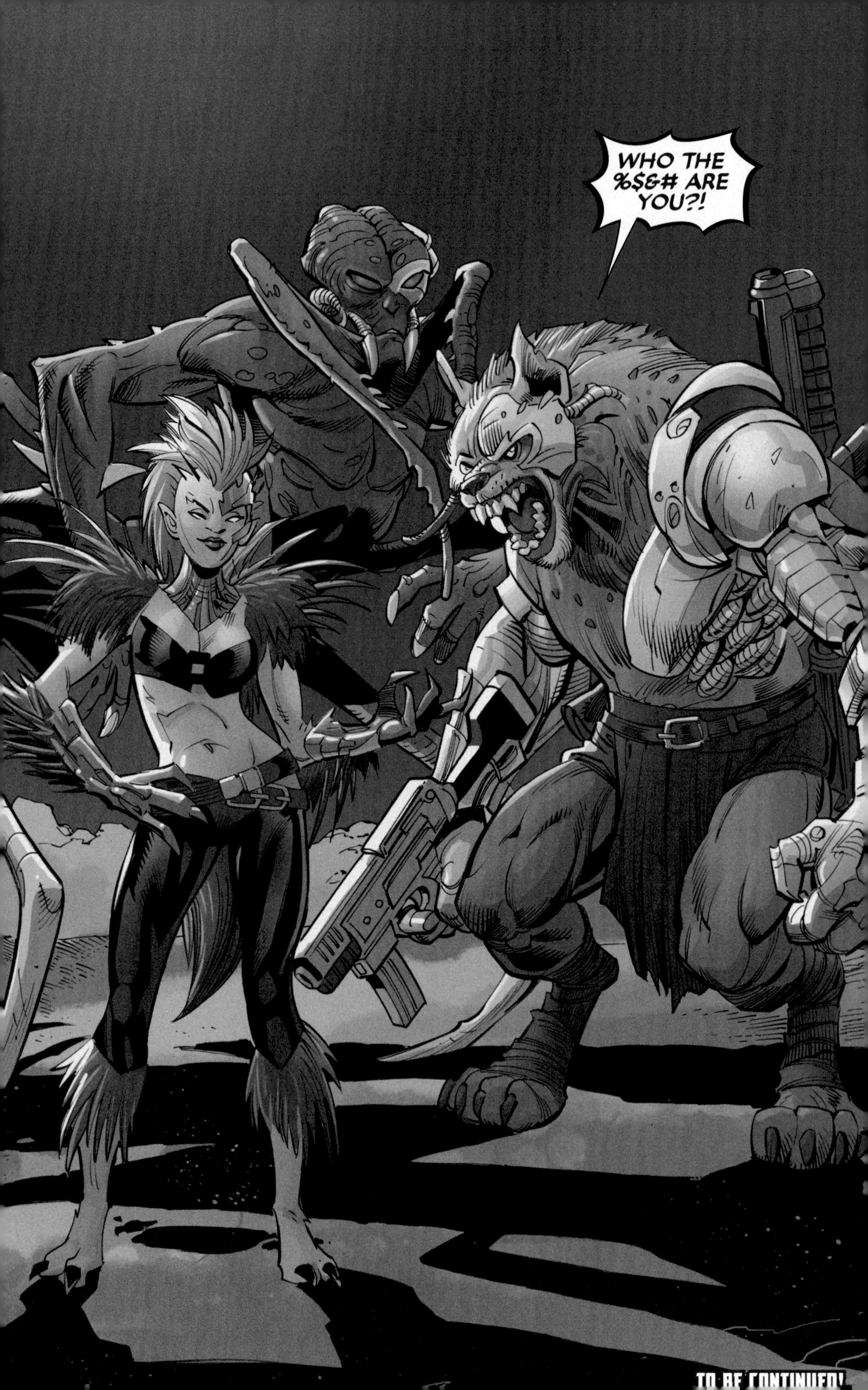
WHO THE %$&# ARE YOU?!
TO BE CONTINUED!

DURING THE DAY HE MAY APPEAR AS A NORMAL MAN, BUT WHEN THE SUN SETS AND DARKNESS FALLS, HE BECOMES A...

WEREWOLF BY NIGHT

WRITTEN BY
TABOO & B. EARL

ART BY
SCOT EATON

INKS BY
SCOTT HANNA

COLOR ART BY
MIROSLAV MRVA

LETTERER
VC's JOE SABINO

COVER BY
MIKE McKONE & JASON KEITH

VARIANT COVERS BY
TAKASHI OKAZAKI & EDGAR DELGADO;
JEFFREY VEREGGE; MIKE PLOOG & MORRY HOLLOWELL

PRODUCTION DESIGN	ASSISTANT EDITOR	EDITOR	EDITOR IN CHIEF
NICK RUSSELL	**LINDSEY COHICK**	**JAKE THOMAS**	**C.B. CEBULSKI**

WORDS FROM THE WOLF PACK

HELLO, TRUE BELIEVERS!

First off, a big thanks to Jake and Lindsey, our editors on this book, and to everyone at Marvel who took a chance on us to re-invent the iconic and legendary character Werewolf by Night. And, of course, a big shout out to the art team, Scot, Scott, Miroslav, and Joe, who took the words we wrote and visually brought them to life on the page! And last but most certainly not least, Vince and Dolores Schilling and Jay C. Shelton, Jr., with whom we consulted to make sure that this story authentically represented Indian Country. Their blessing means the world to us as storytellers. All in all, we couldn't be more proud and honored to be a part of the Marvel family for the creation of a new Native American hero.

As we write this letter, the world is in the grip of the COVID-19 pandemic. The aisles have been wiped clean of toilet paper and hand sanitizer. The NBA, NHL, and Broadway are all shut down.

With all that going on, we are really excited that you picked up this story. You could have spent your hard-earned bucks on that last roll of toilet paper. Hopefully as you read this, the craze for white butt-gold will have died down! Joking aside, this is a time where our world needs to find some common ground and start discussions to heal all the past harm.

Under our skin we all have the same blood and bones. We are all made of the same stardust. But we have let certain people and institutions divide us for their own gains at the cost of the whole. No one has felt this betrayal greater than the Natives, from America to Australia.

Everywhere we find indigenous folks we see this "othering" in order to take that which we can never own: Nature.

Nature doesn't care about our NBA games. Nature doesn't care about our borders. Nature doesn't care about our feelings. Nature just is.

Natives have always understood that. They have always had an awe and respect for Nature. Unfortunately, that was lost in translation when the colonizers first came to Turtle Island (the name given to the Americas by the First People). Not to get all pedantic and blah blah blah, but we have lost this awe. We have lost this respect. We have taken it into our tiny little hands and said, "No, we are the masters of this domain, and it's ours to control."

This story is about that and a lot of other stuff. Monsters and monsters and more monsters. The illusion of control. Analog versus digital. Music as frequency and vibrations. Believing technology makes us gods... Our digital simulacrums of Nature. A young Native kid who's been stuck with his family's werewolf curse has to face off against a bunch of monsters created by a futurist who believes Nature must merge with human technology to form the Singularity. Not so crazy an idea at a moment when our phones have more computing power than the machine that sent the first rocket into space. The dizzying speeds our technology is evolving at is exponential!

It's a crazy time, but in truth, it's always been a crazy time. In order for us to move into the future, we must look to the past to heal our present. And a friendly reminder: A roll of toilet paper probably won't stop any future viruses. That said, thanks for checking out our story, and we hope you enjoy these four issues as we introduce Jake Gomez, a kid who never asked to be a... WEREWOLF BY NIGHT!

Taboo would like to thank his wife Jaymie and their four kids Jett, Journey, Jalen, and Joshua Gomez. Also, Paulette Jordan, the inspiration for Molly!

Benjamin wants to thank his son Liam Earl and Liam's mom Tanya Earl Buer, along with his parents Nancy Earl Jackendoff and Harry "Sparky" Jackendoff.

Taboo & Ben
March 13, 2020
Los Angeles

I was a huge fan of Jack Russell and the original WEREWOLF BY NIGHT series that Marvel ran in the 1970s. At the time, there were a bunch of weird, surreal Marvel comics like GHOST RIDER, THE FRANKENSTEIN MONSTER, MORBIUS: THE LIVING VAMPIRE, TOMB OF DRACULA, MAN-THING and WEIRDWORLD on the stands, and they were a perfect place for horror fans, fantasy fans, and kids who were into monsters.

It always seemed to me all of those books would resonate today. Hollywood has shown that we really love super heroes in the real world—villains, too. How about monsters?

When Jake and Lindsey invited me to do the art for a new, 2020 version of WWBN, said yes immediately, but had no idea what I was getting into. Then I read Ben and Tab's notes and ideas and was sold! Or more like drafted. Jake Gomez is a funny, headstrong kid, growing up on the reservation, with his grandma and girlfriend as his strongest influences. At the same time, he's trying to make sense of his werewolf legacy. That seemed amazing enough, but they added in one of my all-time favorite heroes, Red Wolf. I was all in! Bouncing ideas off of those two has been a pleasure and reading what they have planned is great. Capturing it all is the only challenge I have.

Ben and Taboo want to build larger-than-life monsters in the real world. Not a super hero comic but a monster rally. Amazing creatures that are cursed or created, contrasted with the real world, real people, and smashed into real situations. All with a tiny bit of the WWE, MMA, and a lot of pop culture thrown in. There's a lot to fit in, but they provide plenty of help.

To close, I secretly hope that at some point we can contrast some of the thumbnails Ben has provided along with the scripts to the finished art. Early on I teased him about that, but people might be surprised how much beat for beat they made it to the final page. Taboo has also based a lot of Jake on his own life and personality. He's put a tremendous amount of himself into this book, and it shows, but I also think he's the type of guy who will keep that to himself. I hope he talks about that at some point.

Most of all I hope everyone enjoys the show.

Scot Eaton

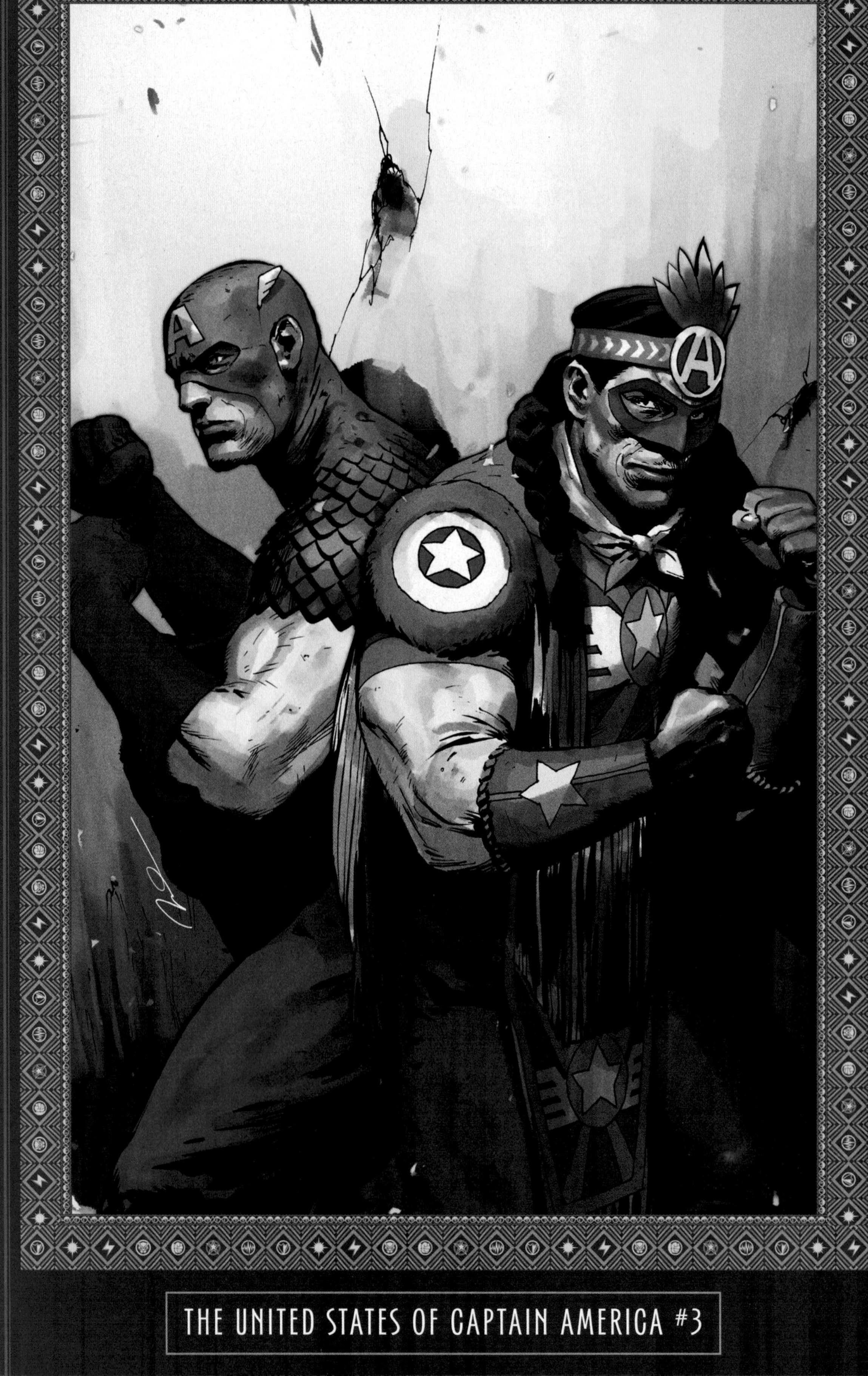

THE UNITED STATES OF CAPTAIN AMERICA #3

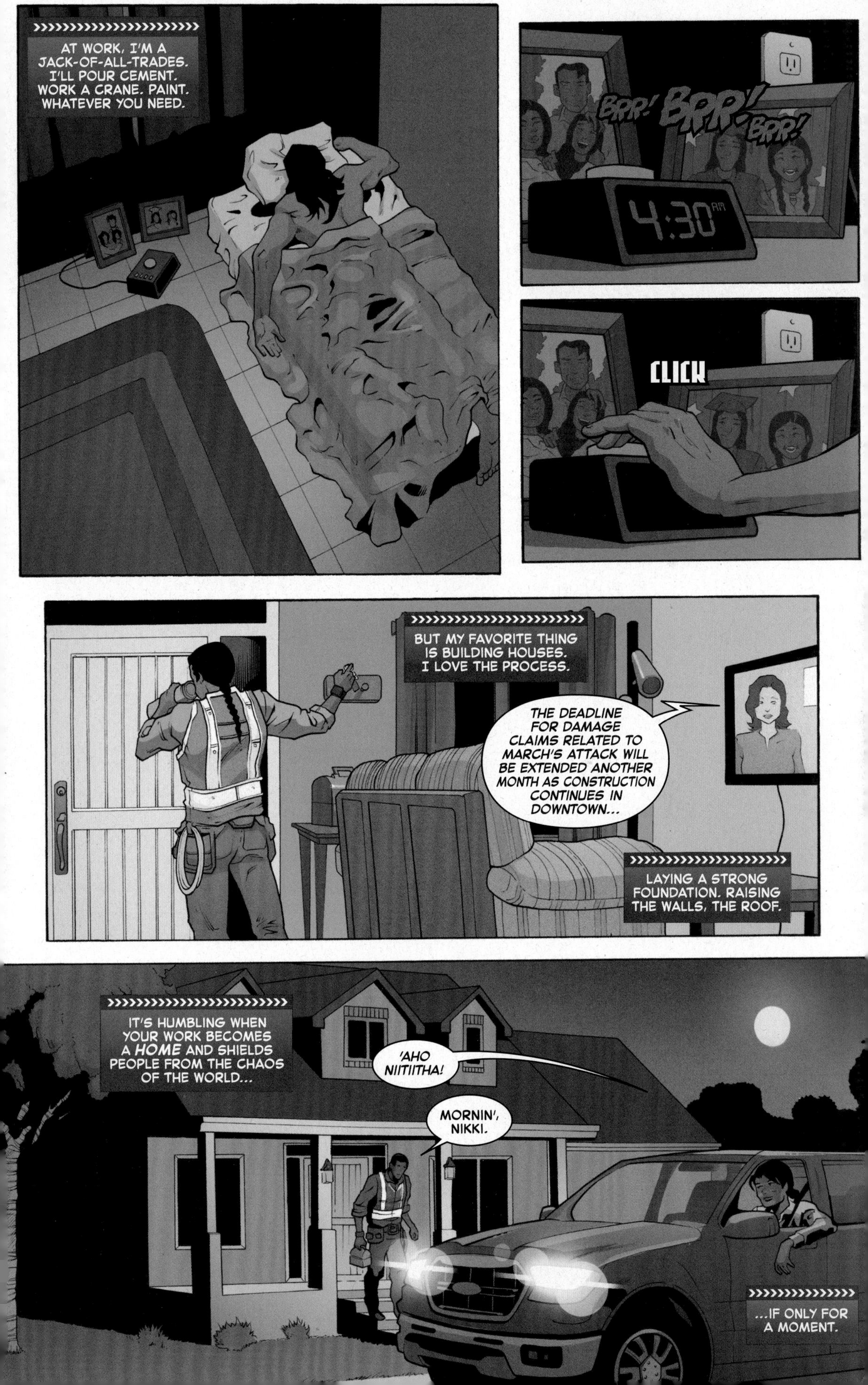
AT WORK, I'M A JACK-OF-ALL-TRADES. I'LL POUR CEMENT. WORK A CRANE. PAINT. WHATEVER YOU NEED.
BRR! BRR! BRR!
4:30 AM
CLICK
BUT MY FAVORITE THING IS BUILDING HOUSES. I LOVE THE PROCESS.
THE DEADLINE FOR DAMAGE CLAIMS RELATED TO MARCH'S ATTACK WILL BE EXTENDED ANOTHER MONTH AS CONSTRUCTION CONTINUES IN DOWNTOWN...
LAYING A STRONG FOUNDATION. RAISING THE WALLS, THE ROOF.
IT'S HUMBLING WHEN YOUR WORK BECOMES A HOME AND SHIELDS PEOPLE FROM THE CHAOS OF THE WORLD...
'AHO NIITIITHA!
MORNIN', NIKKI.
...IF ONLY FOR A MOMENT.

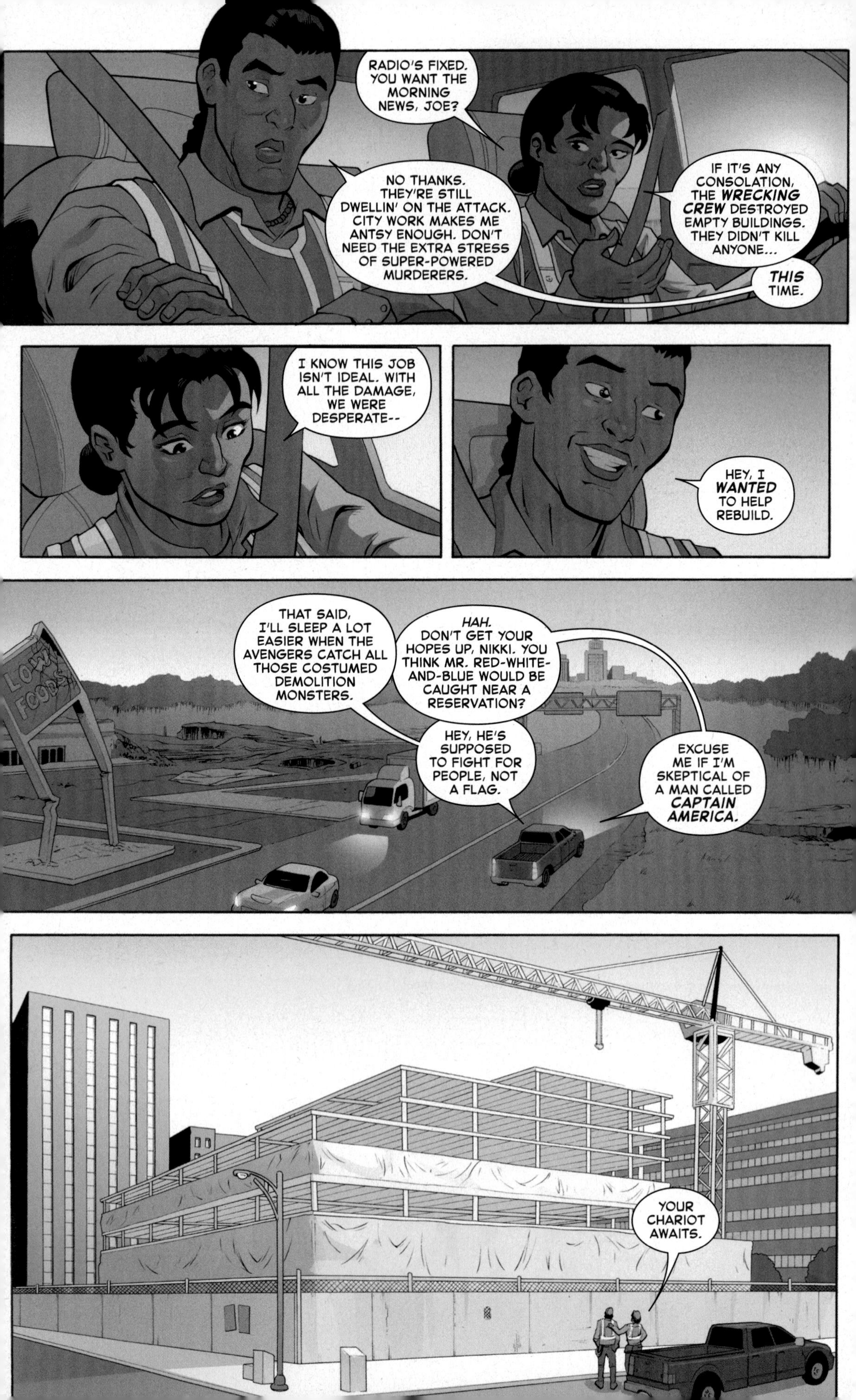
RADIO'S FIXED. YOU WANT THE MORNING NEWS, JOE?
NO THANKS. THEY'RE STILL DWELLIN' ON THE ATTACK. CITY WORK MAKES ME ANTSY ENOUGH. DON'T NEED THE EXTRA STRESS OF SUPER-POWERED MURDERERS.
IF IT'S ANY CONSOLATION, THE **WRECKING CREW** DESTROYED EMPTY BUILDINGS. THEY DIDN'T KILL ANYONE...
THIS TIME.
I KNOW THIS JOB ISN'T IDEAL. WITH ALL THE DAMAGE, WE WERE DESPERATE--
HEY, I **WANTED** TO HELP REBUILD.
THAT SAID, I'LL SLEEP A LOT EASIER WHEN THE AVENGERS CATCH ALL THOSE COSTUMED DEMOLITION *MONSTERS.*
HAH. DON'T GET YOUR HOPES UP, NIKKI. YOU THINK MR. RED-WHITE-AND-BLUE WOULD BE CAUGHT NEAR A RESERVATION?
HEY, HE'S SUPPOSED TO FIGHT FOR PEOPLE, NOT A FLAG.
EXCUSE ME IF I'M SKEPTICAL OF A MAN CALLED **CAPTAIN AMERICA.**
YOUR CHARIOT AWAITS.

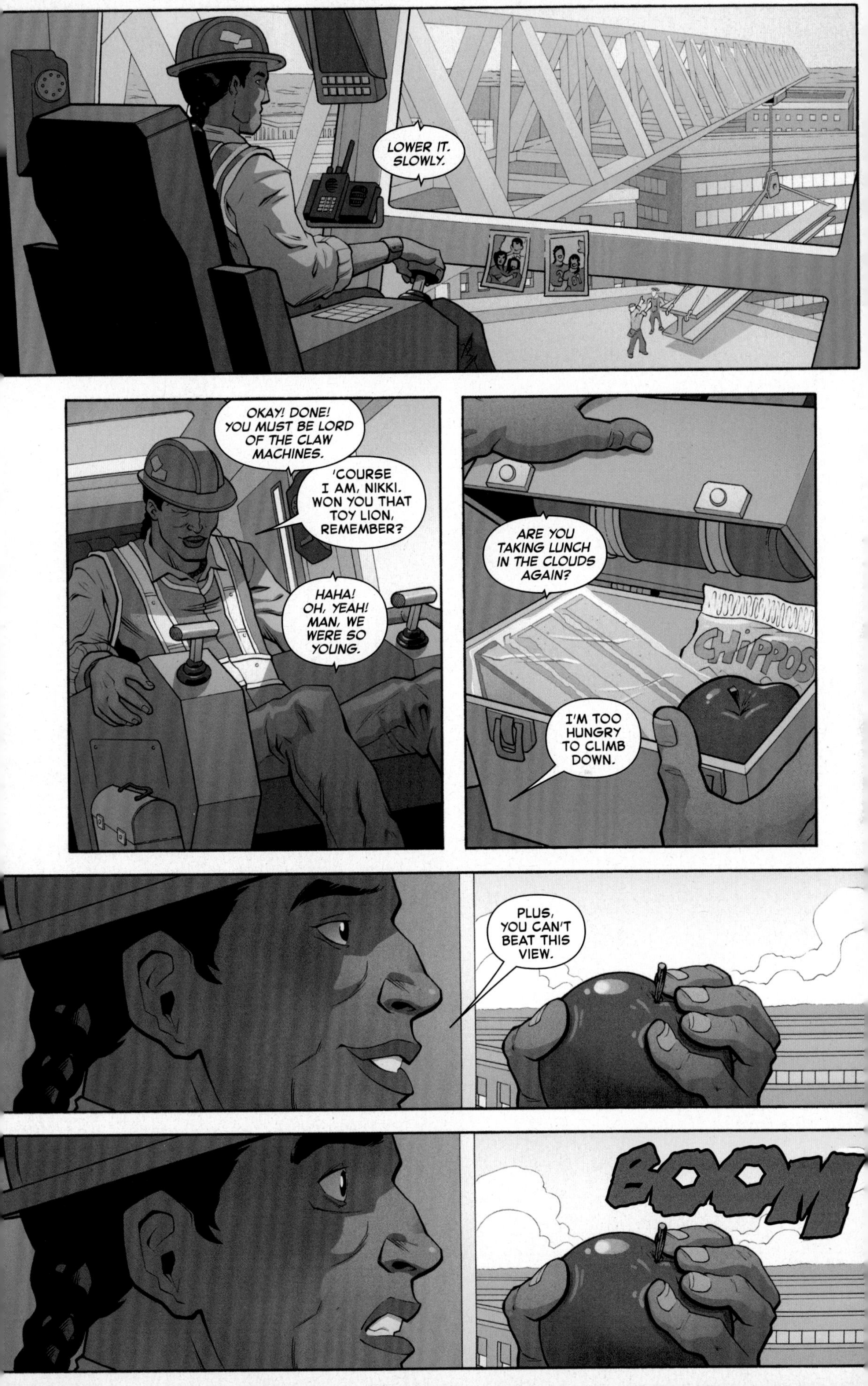
LOWER IT. SLOWLY.
OKAY! DONE! YOU MUST BE LORD OF THE CLAW MACHINES.
'COURSE I AM, NIKKI. WON YOU THAT TOY LION, REMEMBER?
HAHA! OH, YEAH! MAN, WE WERE SO YOUNG.
ARE YOU TAKING LUNCH IN THE CLOUDS AGAIN?
CHIPPOS
I'M TOO HUNGRY TO CLIMB DOWN.
PLUS, YOU CAN'T BEAT THIS VIEW.
BOOM

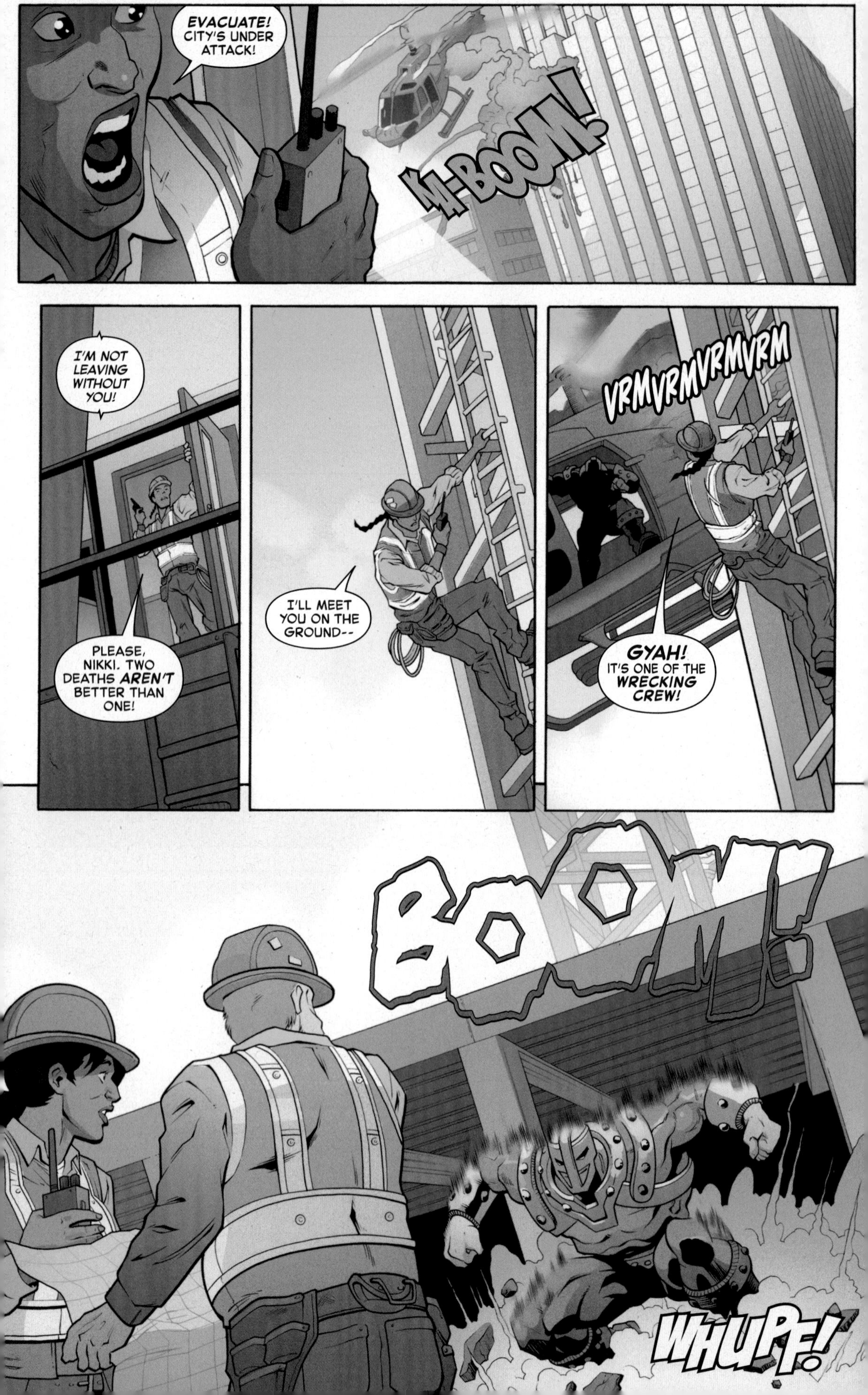
EVACUATE! CITY'S UNDER ATTACK!
KA-BOOM!
I'M NOT LEAVING WITHOUT YOU!
PLEASE, NIKKI. TWO DEATHS AREN'T BETTER THAN ONE!
I'LL MEET YOU ON THE GROUND--
VRMVRMVRMVRM
GYAH! IT'S ONE OF THE WRECKING CREW!
BOOM!
WHUMF!

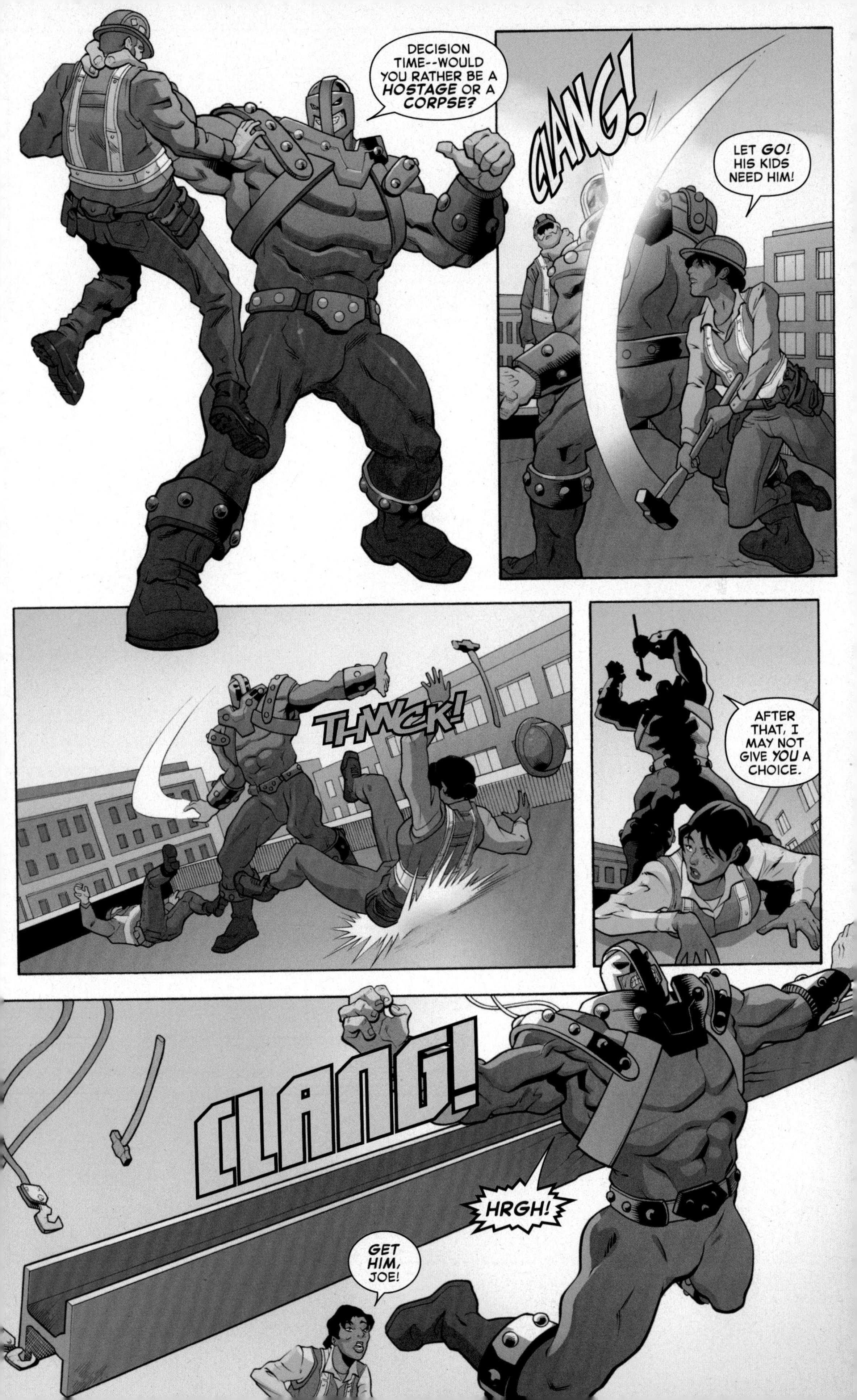
DECISION TIME--WOULD YOU RATHER BE A HOSTAGE OR A CORPSE?
CLANG!
LET GO! HIS KIDS NEED HIM!
THWCK!
AFTER THAT, I MAY NOT GIVE YOU A CHOICE.
CLANG!
HRGH!
GET HIM, JOE!

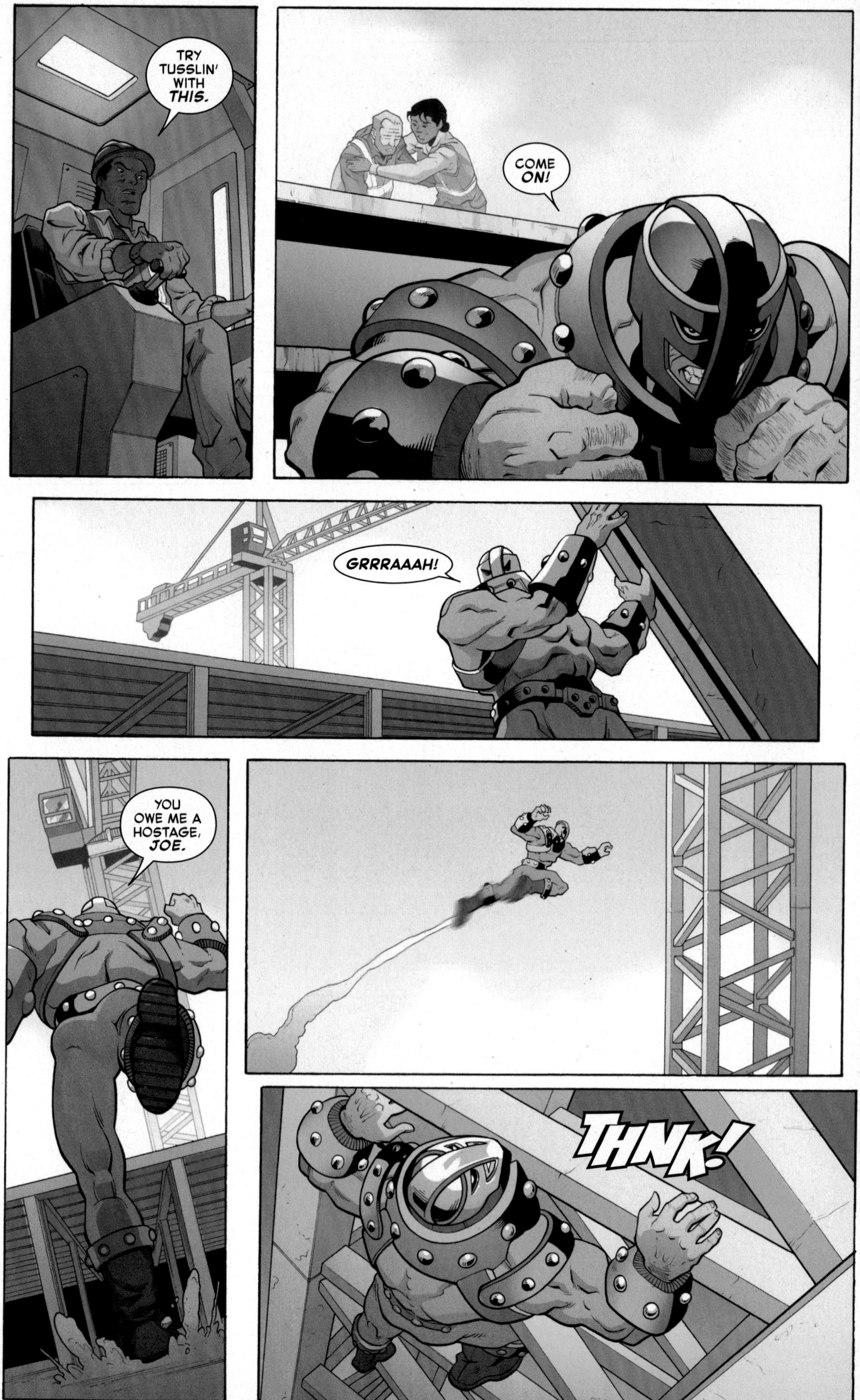
TRY TUSSLIN' WITH THIS.
COME ON!
GRRRAAAH!
YOU OWE ME A HOSTAGE, JOE.
THNK!

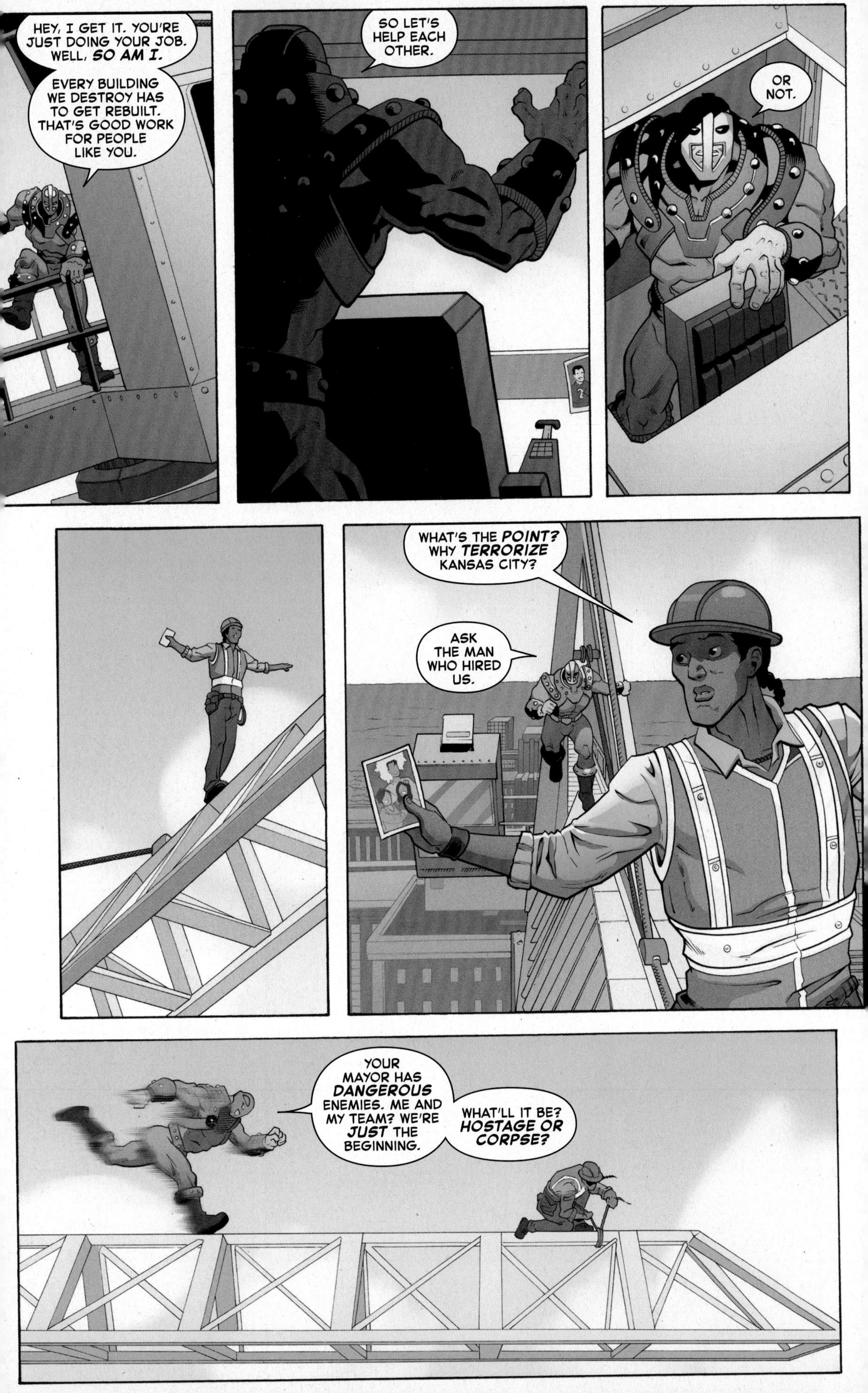
HEY, I GET IT. YOU'RE JUST DOING YOUR JOB. WELL, SO AM I.
EVERY BUILDING WE DESTROY HAS TO GET REBUILT. THAT'S GOOD WORK FOR PEOPLE LIKE YOU.
SO LET'S HELP EACH OTHER.
OR NOT.
WHAT'S THE POINT? WHY TERRORIZE KANSAS CITY?
ASK THE MAN WHO HIRED US.
YOUR MAYOR HAS DANGEROUS ENEMIES. ME AND MY TEAM? WE'RE JUST THE BEGINNING.
WHAT'LL IT BE? HOSTAGE OR CORPSE?

NEITHER!

AAAAAH!

THE FULL SAYING GOES: JACK OF ALL TRADES, MASTER OF NONE. I CAN TIE A BOWLINE--

C'MON...

--BUT IN A RUSH, MY KNOTS AREN'T THE BEST.

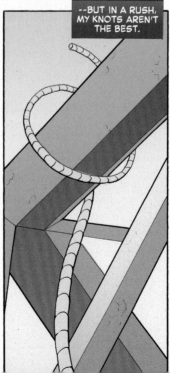

I TRIED TO HOPE.

THE AVENGERS PLUCK A HUNDRED BYSTANDERS OUTTA THE AIR EVERY YEAR. SO WHY NOT ME?

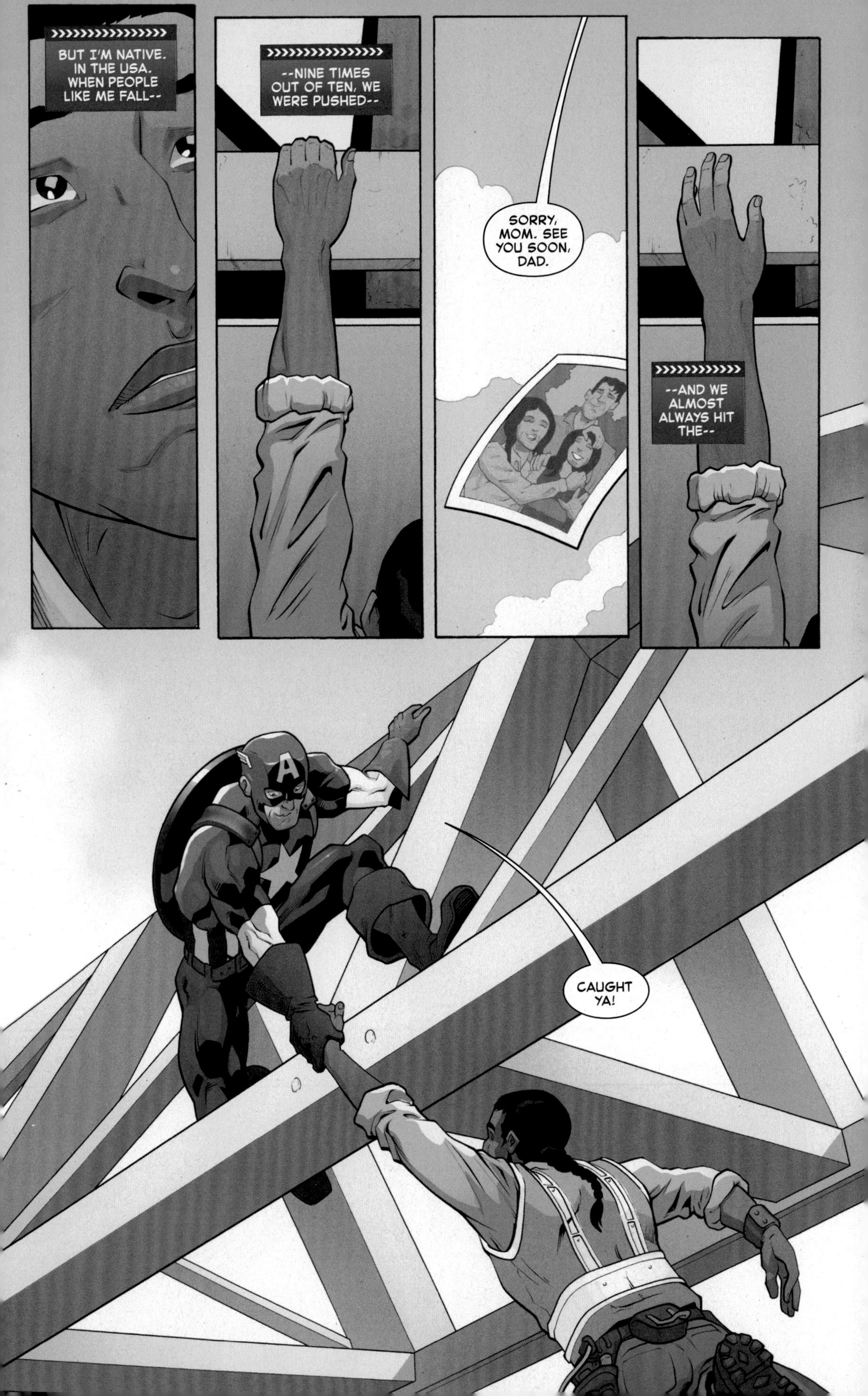
BUT I'M NATIVE. IN THE USA. WHEN PEOPLE LIKE ME FALL--
--NINE TIMES OUT OF TEN, WE WERE PUSHED--
SORRY, MOM. SEE YOU SOON, DAD.
--AND WE ALMOST ALWAYS HIT THE--
CAUGHT YA!

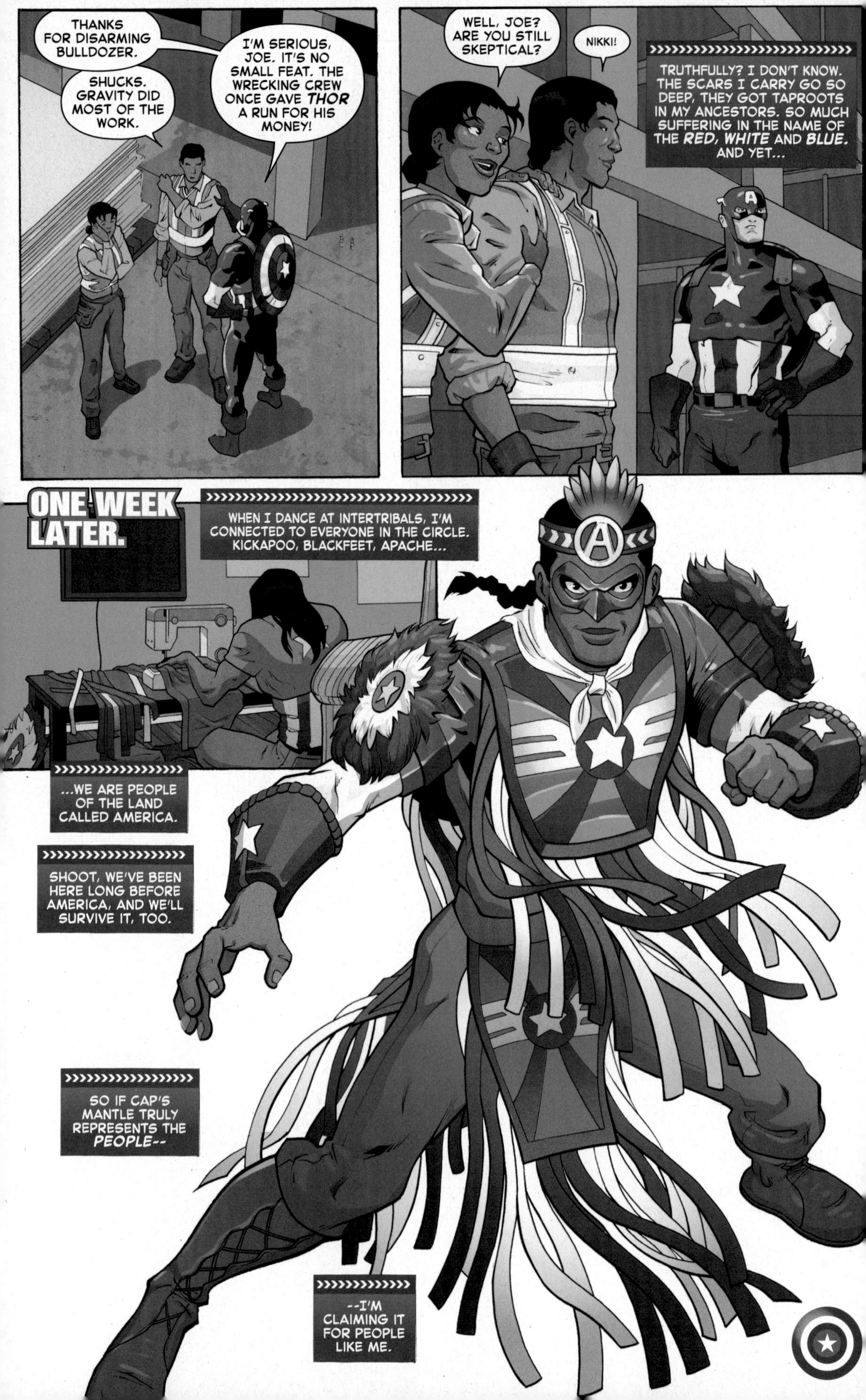
THANKS FOR DISARMING BULLDOZER.
SHUCKS. GRAVITY DID MOST OF THE WORK.
I'M SERIOUS, JOE. IT'S NO SMALL FEAT. THE WRECKING CREW ONCE GAVE THOR A RUN FOR HIS MONEY!
WELL, JOE? ARE YOU STILL SKEPTICAL?
NIKKI!
TRUTHFULLY? I DON'T KNOW. THE SCARS I CARRY GO SO DEEP, THEY GOT TAPROOTS IN MY ANCESTORS. SO MUCH SUFFERING IN THE NAME OF THE RED, WHITE AND BLUE. AND YET...
ONE WEEK LATER.
WHEN I DANCE AT INTERTRIBALS, I'M CONNECTED TO EVERYONE IN THE CIRCLE. KICKAPOO, BLACKFEET, APACHE...
...WE ARE PEOPLE OF THE LAND CALLED AMERICA.
SHOOT, WE'VE BEEN HERE LONG BEFORE AMERICA, AND WE'LL SURVIVE IT, TOO.
SO IF CAP'S MANTLE TRULY REPRESENTS THE PEOPLE--
--I'M CLAIMING IT FOR PEOPLE LIKE ME.

CAPTAINS NETWORK

THE CAPTAIN AMERICA OF THE KICKAPOO TRIBE

Notes compiled by Steve Rogers and Sam Wilson

Name: Joe Gomez
Kickapoo Name: Chiitaaska (Thunder That Jumps Across The Sky)
Clan: Thunder

AGE: 43

LAST KNOWN LOCATION: Kickapoo Reservation, Kansas

DATA: A construction worker and handyman who took up the mantle of Captain America to protect his reservation. Champions the overlooked and underserved in his community and elsewhere.

NOTE FROM STEVE: Everybody we met had only nice things to say about this guy. Seems like he's fixed an air conditioner or leaky sink for about everyone on his street.

NOTE FROM SAM: Giving you any ideas, Steve? You gonna come over and fix my air conditioner?

NOTE FROM STEVE: As if I know how air conditioners work...

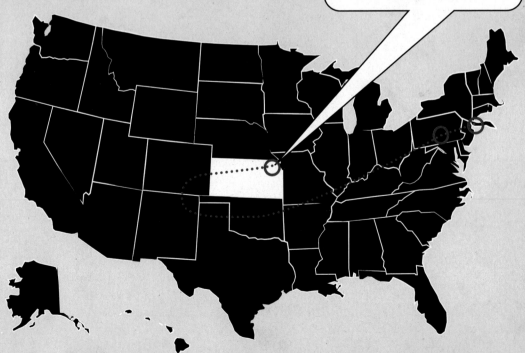

Special thanks to Kickapoo consultants Keith Bluecloud and Mosiah Bluecloud.

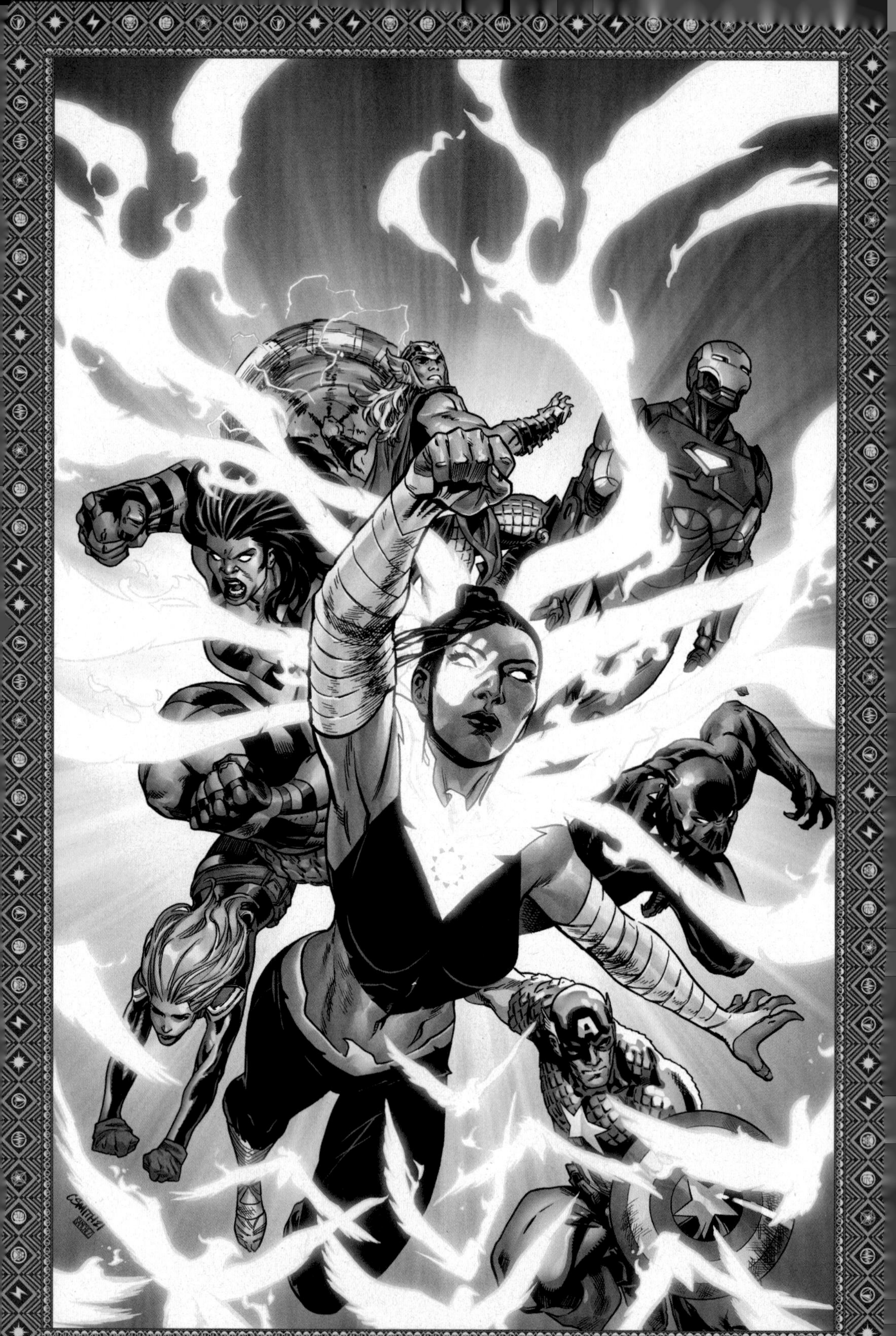

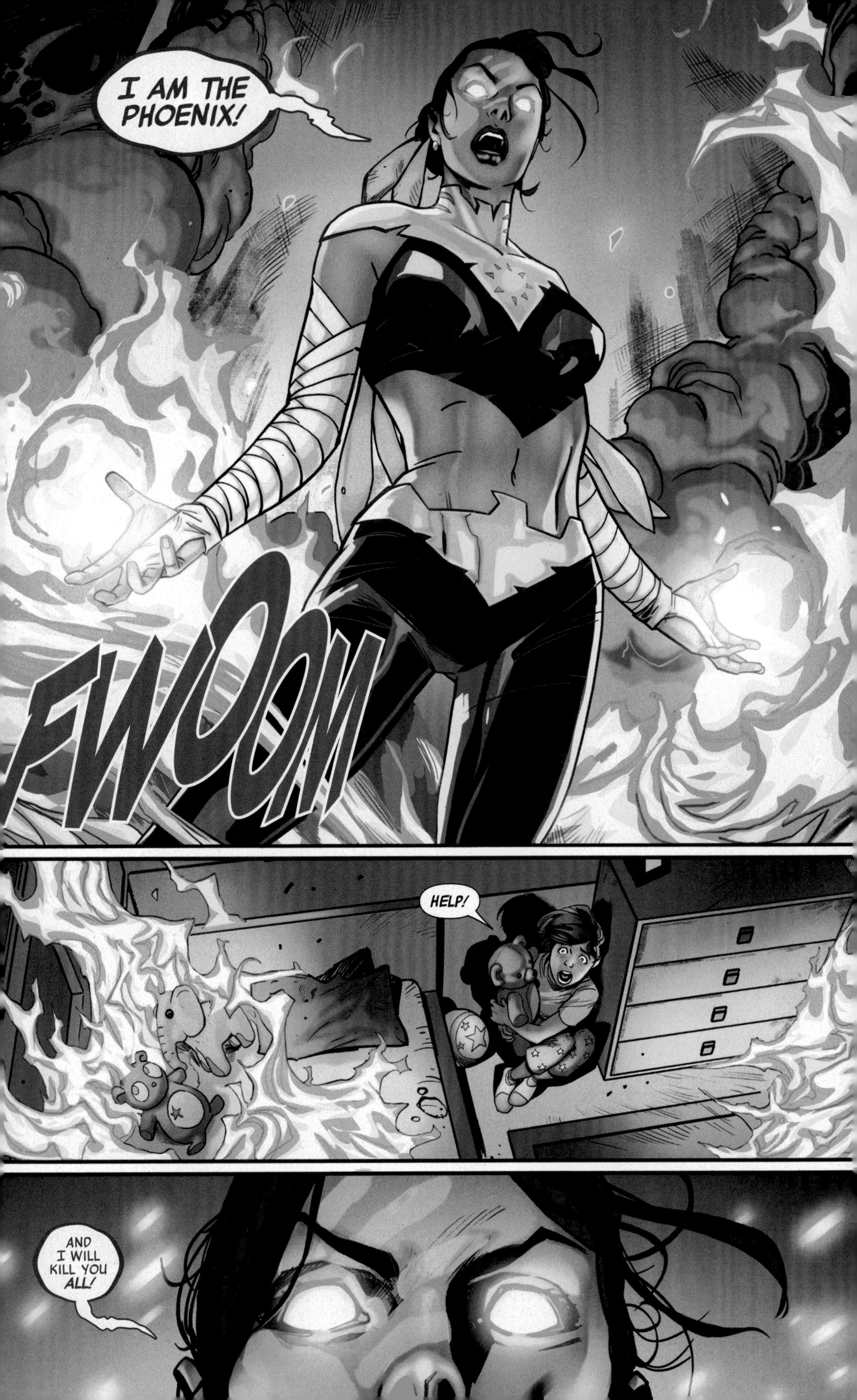
I AM THE PHOENIX!
FWOOM
HELP!
AND I WILL KILL YOU ALL!

deaf, **Maya Lopez**, A.K.A. **Echo**, was an otherwise happy child **Kingpin** murdered her father and blamed it on **Daredevil**, aya as his own daughter for years. Maya eventually learned rejected her adoptive father, and joined the ranks of super hanks to the photographic reflexes that make her an led dancer and hand-to-hand combatant.

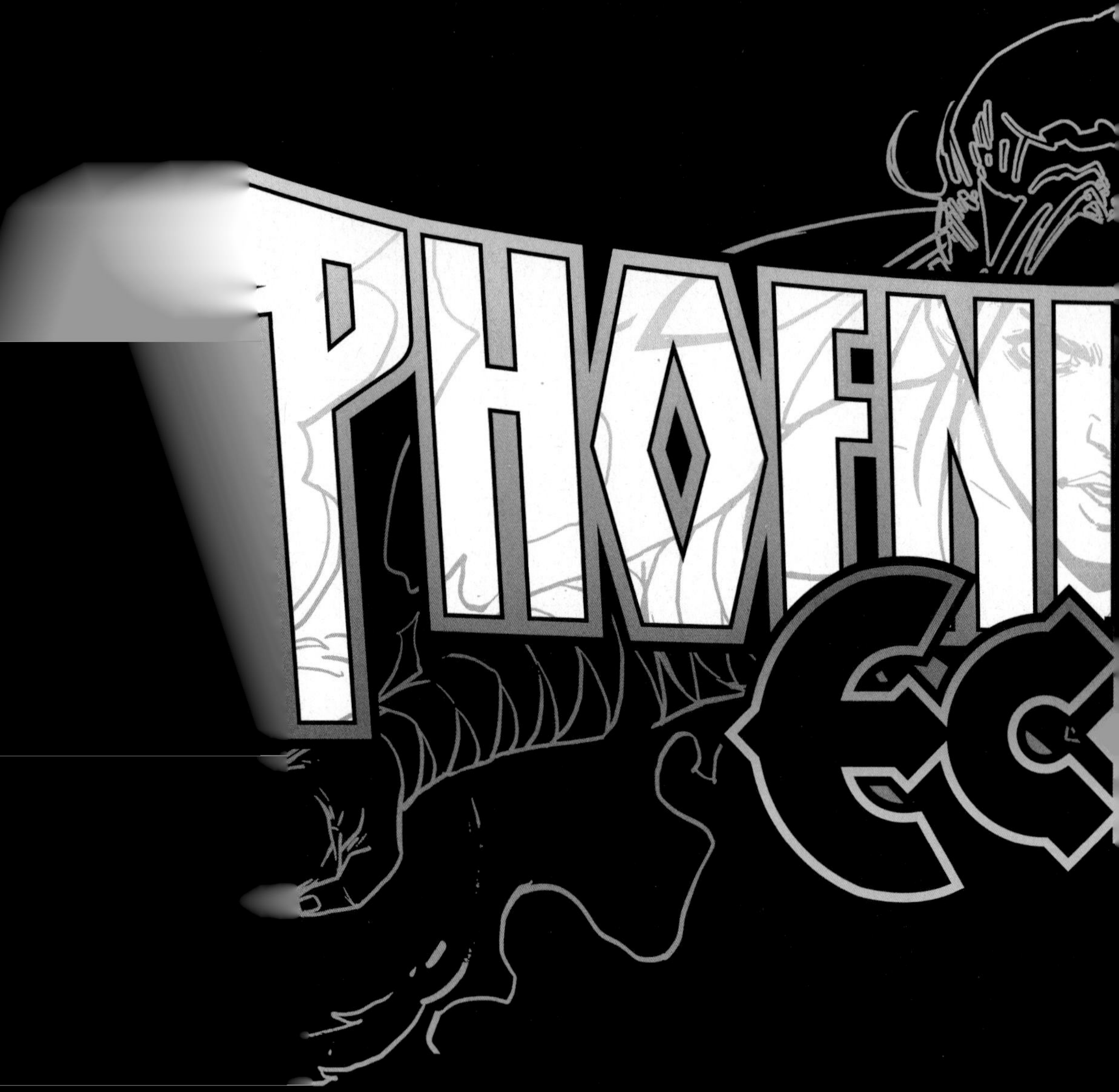

WRITER **REBECCA ROANHORSE**
COLOR ARTIST **CARLOS LOPEZ**

COVER ARTISTS **CORY SMITH & ALEJANDRO SÁNCHEZ**

RIANT COVER ARTISTS **CARMEN CARNERO & MATTHEW WILSON; TODD NAUCK & RACHELLE ROSENBERG; OSCAR VEGA; LEINIL FRANCIS YU & SUNNY GHO**

Still, she was the backup, the stealth agent...until the **Phoenix Force** came searching for a champion and pitted heroes against one another. It chose Maya as its new host, even though Maya lost her fight against **Namor**. No one really understands why, least of all Maya, but she must have a purpose in this cosmos...

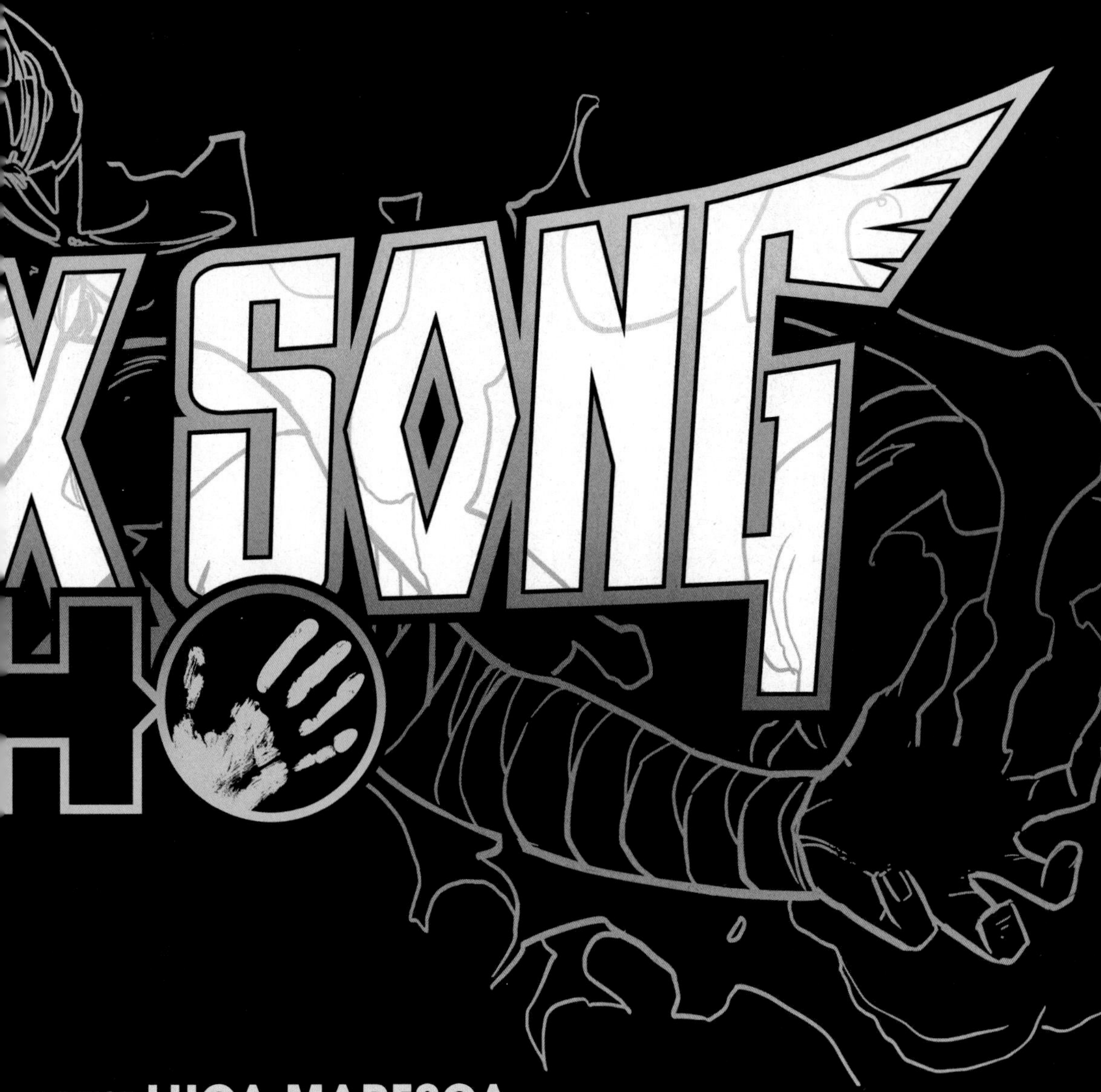
X SONG

ARTIST **LUCA MARESCA**
LETTERER **VC's ARIANA MAHER**

LOGO **JAY BOWEN**
PRODUCTION DESIGN **NICK RUSSELL**

EDITOR **SARAH BRUNSTAD**
EXECUTIVE EDITOR **TOM BREVOORT**
EDITOR IN CHIEF **C.B. CEBULSKI**

SPECIAL THANKS
JASON AARON

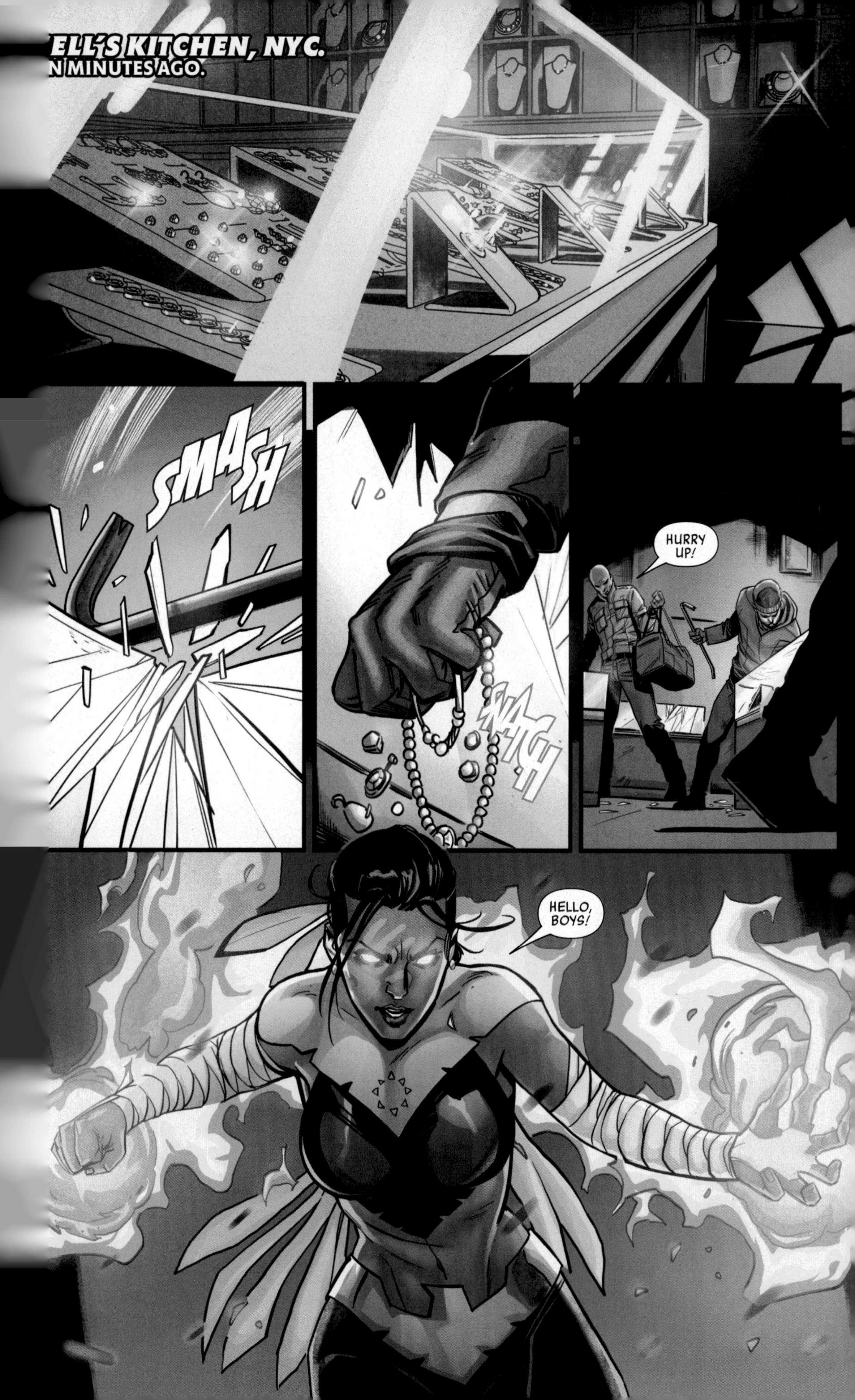
ELL'S KITCHEN, NYC.
N MINUTES AGO.
SMASH
SNATCH
HURRY UP!
HELLO, BOYS!

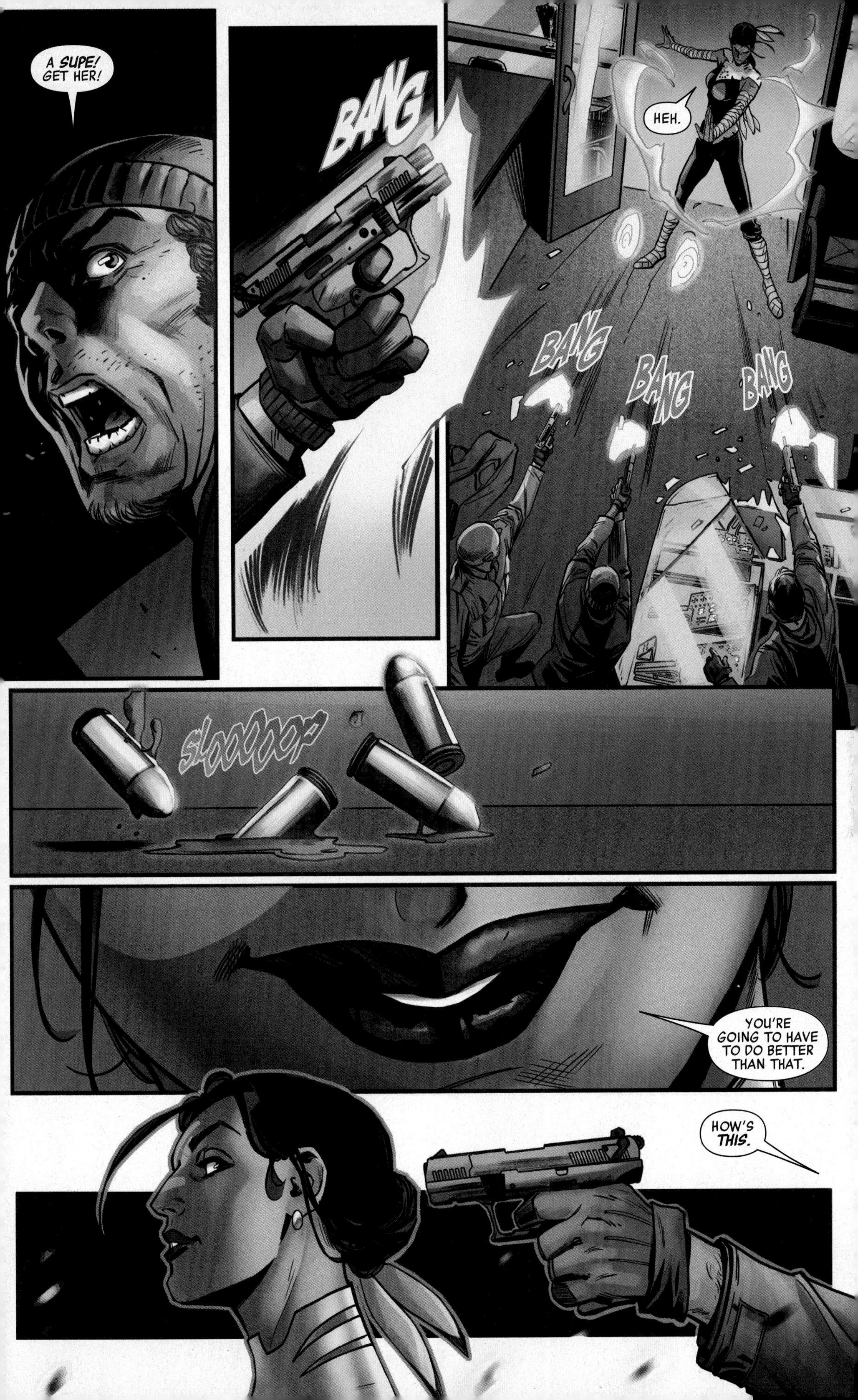
A SUPE! GET HER!
BANG
HEH.
BANG
BANG
BANG
SLOOOOOP
YOU'RE GOING TO HAVE TO DO BETTER THAN THAT.
HOW'S THIS.

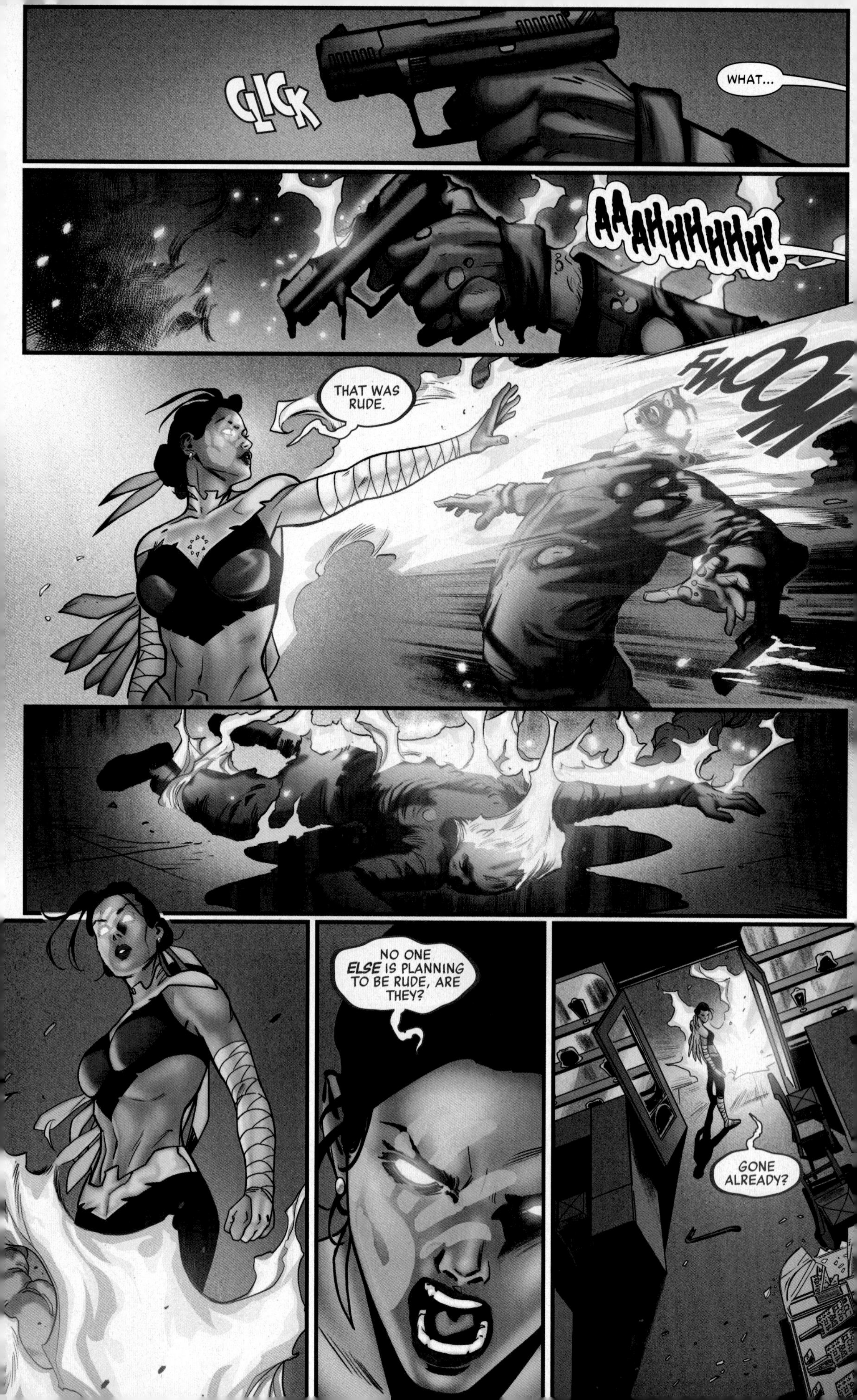
CLICK
WHAT...
AAAHHHHHH!
FWOOM
THAT WAS RUDE.
NO ONE *ELSE* IS PLANNING TO BE RUDE, ARE THEY?
GONE ALREADY?

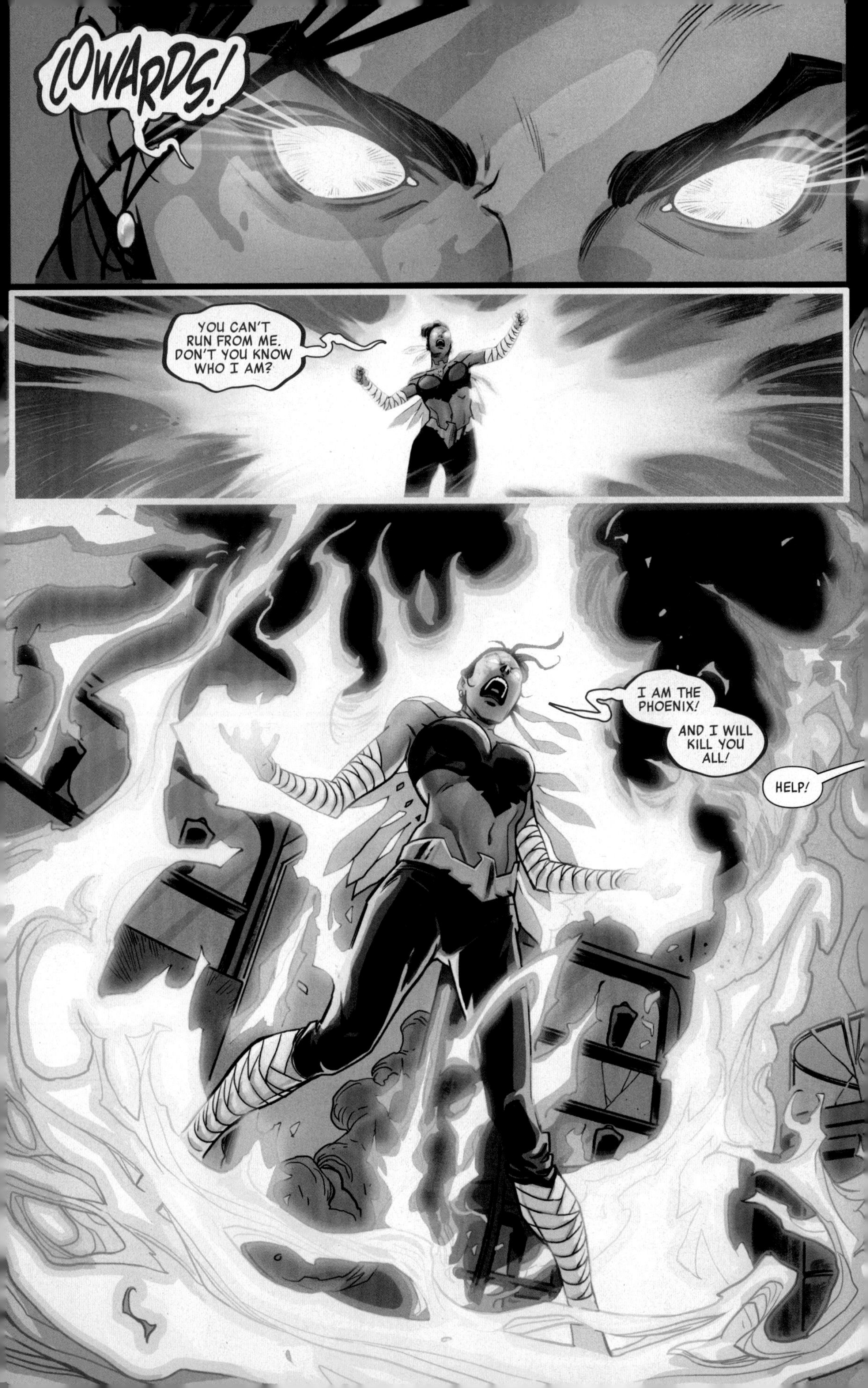
COWARDS!
YOU CAN'T RUN FROM ME. DON'T YOU KNOW WHO I AM?
I AM THE PHOENIX!
AND I WILL KILL YOU ALL!
HELP!

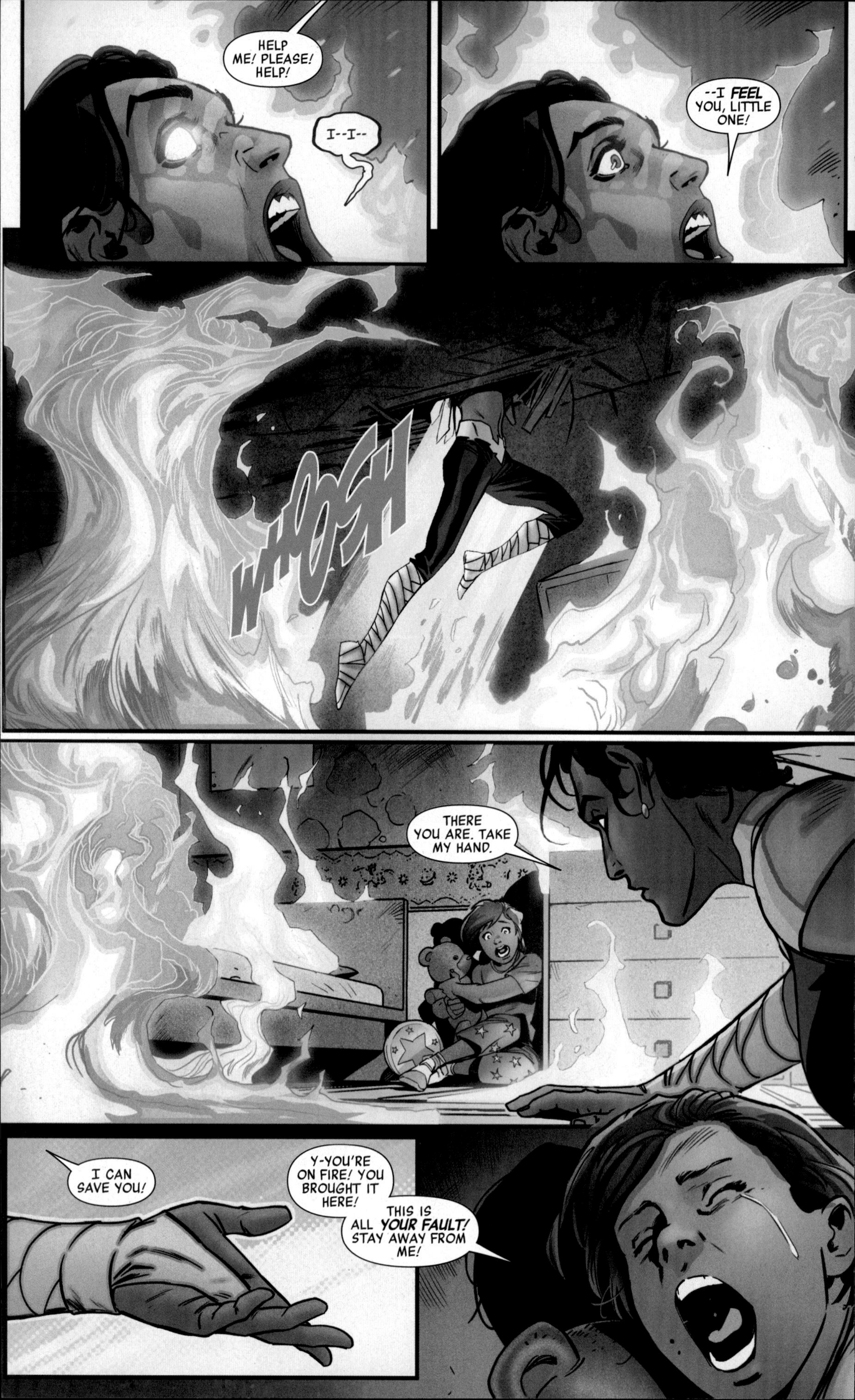
HELP ME! PLEASE! HELP!
I--I--
--I FEEL YOU, LITTLE ONE!
WHOOSH
THERE YOU ARE. TAKE MY HAND.
I CAN SAVE YOU!
Y-YOU'RE ON FIRE! YOU BROUGHT IT HERE!
THIS IS ALL YOUR FAULT! STAY AWAY FROM ME!

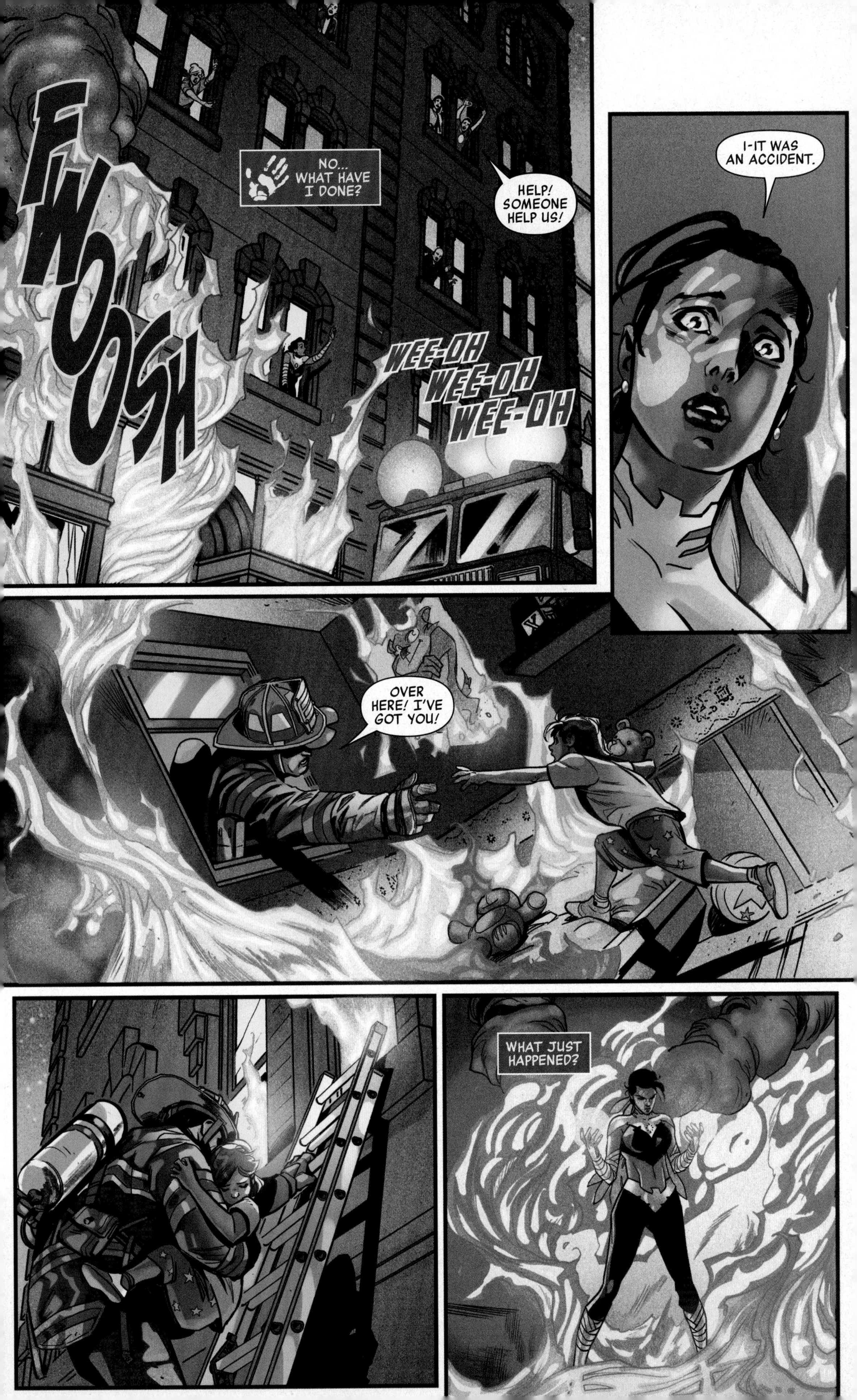
FWOOSH
NO... WHAT HAVE I DONE?
HELP! SOMEONE HELP US!
WEE-OH WEE-OH WEE-OH
I-IT WAS AN ACCIDENT.
OVER HERE! I'VE GOT YOU!
WHAT JUST HAPPENED?

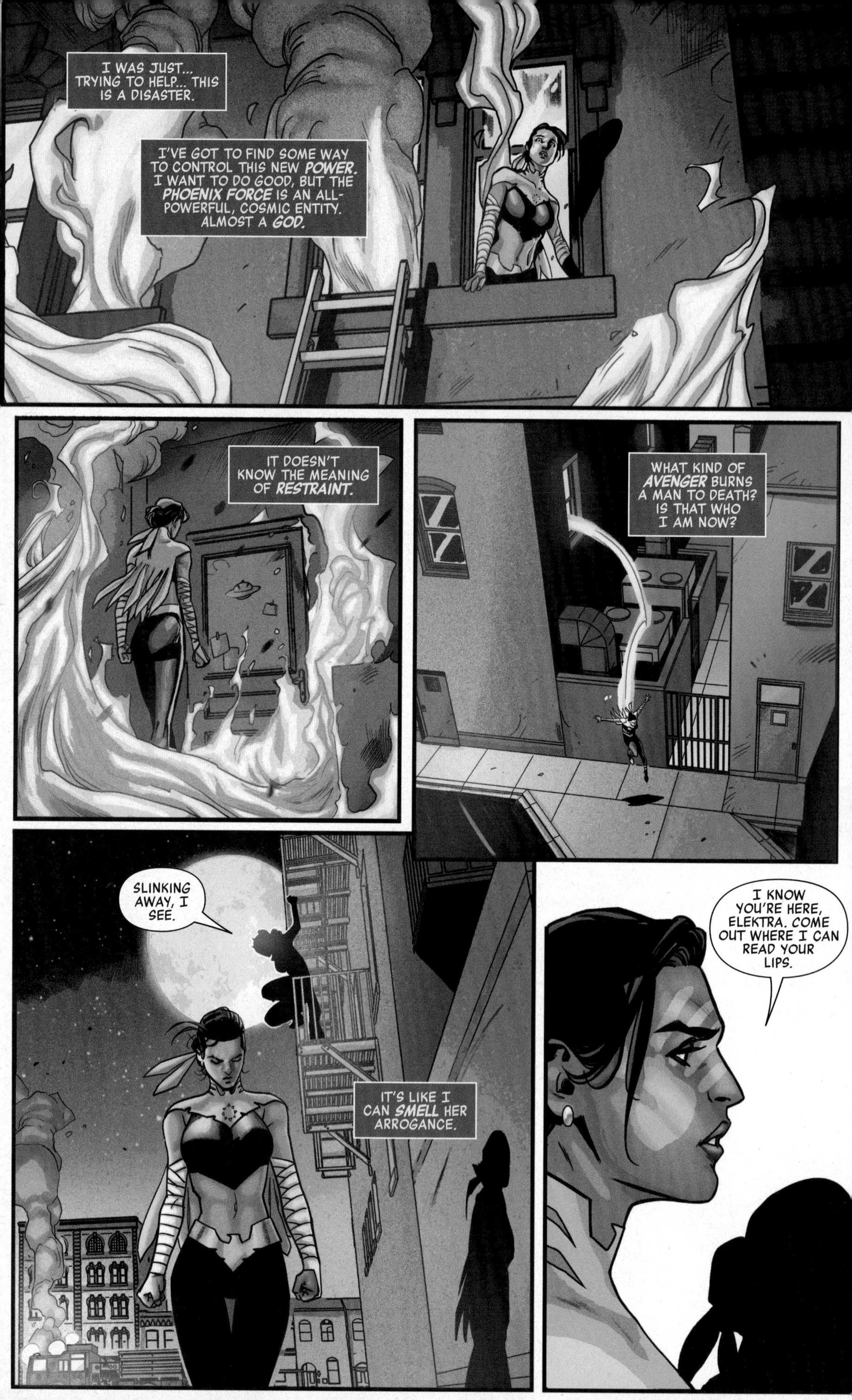
I WAS JUST... TRYING TO HELP... THIS IS A DISASTER.
I'VE GOT TO FIND SOME WAY TO CONTROL THIS NEW POWER. I WANT TO DO GOOD, BUT THE PHOENIX FORCE IS AN ALL-POWERFUL, COSMIC ENTITY. ALMOST A GOD.
IT DOESN'T KNOW THE MEANING OF RESTRAINT.
WHAT KIND OF AVENGER BURNS A MAN TO DEATH? IS THAT WHO I AM NOW?
SLINKING AWAY, I SEE.
IT'S LIKE I CAN SMELL HER ARROGANCE.
I KNOW YOU'RE HERE, ELEKTRA. COME OUT WHERE I CAN READ YOUR LIPS.

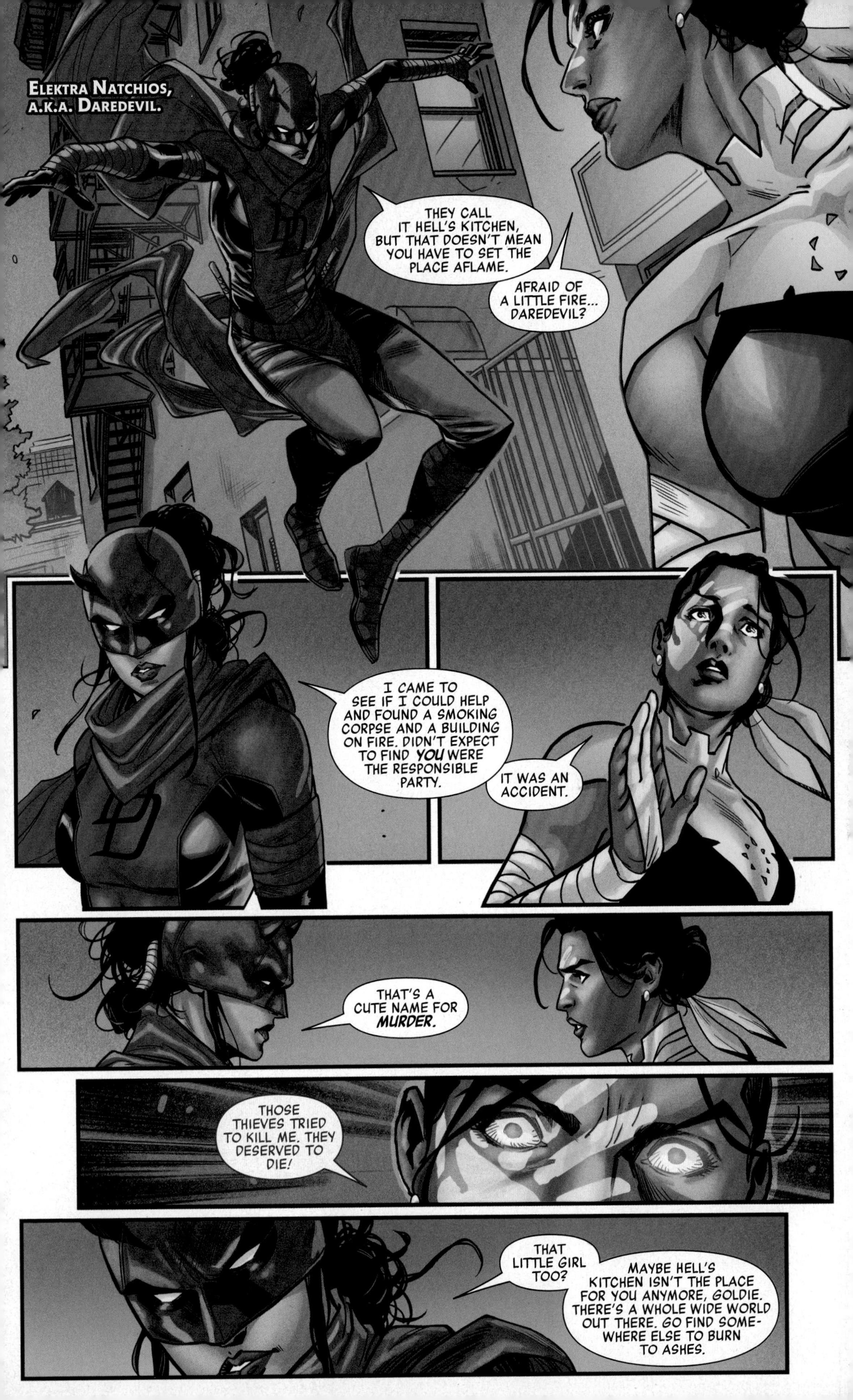
ELEKTRA NATCHIOS, A.K.A. DAREDEVIL.
THEY CALL IT HELL'S KITCHEN, BUT THAT DOESN'T MEAN YOU HAVE TO SET THE PLACE AFLAME.
AFRAID OF A LITTLE FIRE... DAREDEVIL?
I CAME TO SEE IF I COULD HELP AND FOUND A SMOKING CORPSE AND A BUILDING ON FIRE. DIDN'T EXPECT TO FIND YOU WERE THE RESPONSIBLE PARTY.
IT WAS AN ACCIDENT.
THAT'S A CUTE NAME FOR MURDER.
THOSE THIEVES TRIED TO KILL ME. THEY DESERVED TO DIE!
THAT LITTLE GIRL TOO?
MAYBE HELL'S KITCHEN ISN'T THE PLACE FOR YOU ANYMORE, GOLDIE. THERE'S A WHOLE WIDE WORLD OUT THERE. GO FIND SOME-WHERE ELSE TO BURN TO ASHES.

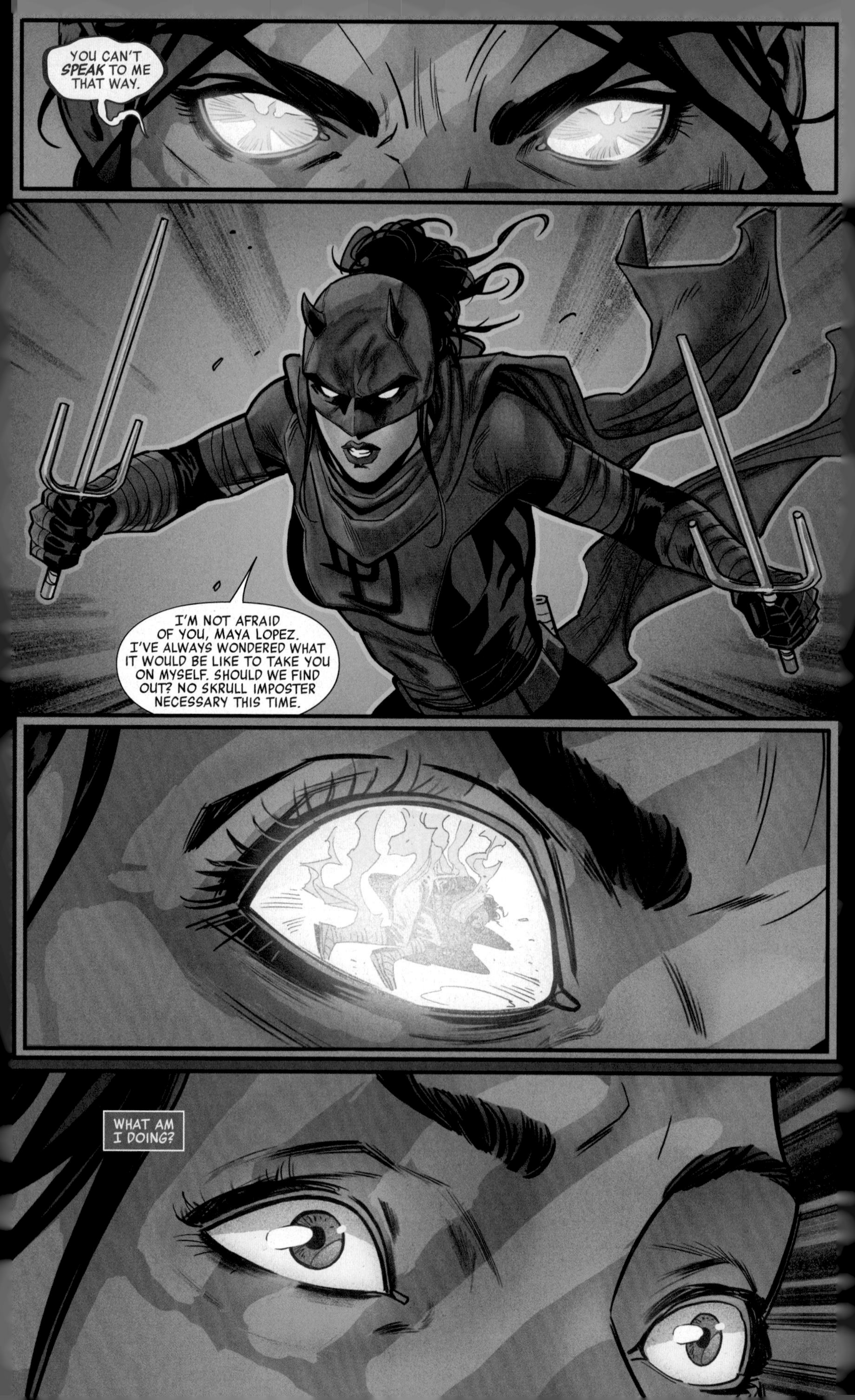
YOU CAN'T SPEAK TO ME THAT WAY.
I'M NOT AFRAID OF YOU, MAYA LOPEZ. I'VE ALWAYS WONDERED WHAT IT WOULD BE LIKE TO TAKE YOU ON MYSELF. SHOULD WE FIND OUT? NO SKRULL IMPOSTER NECESSARY THIS TIME.
WHAT AM I DOING?

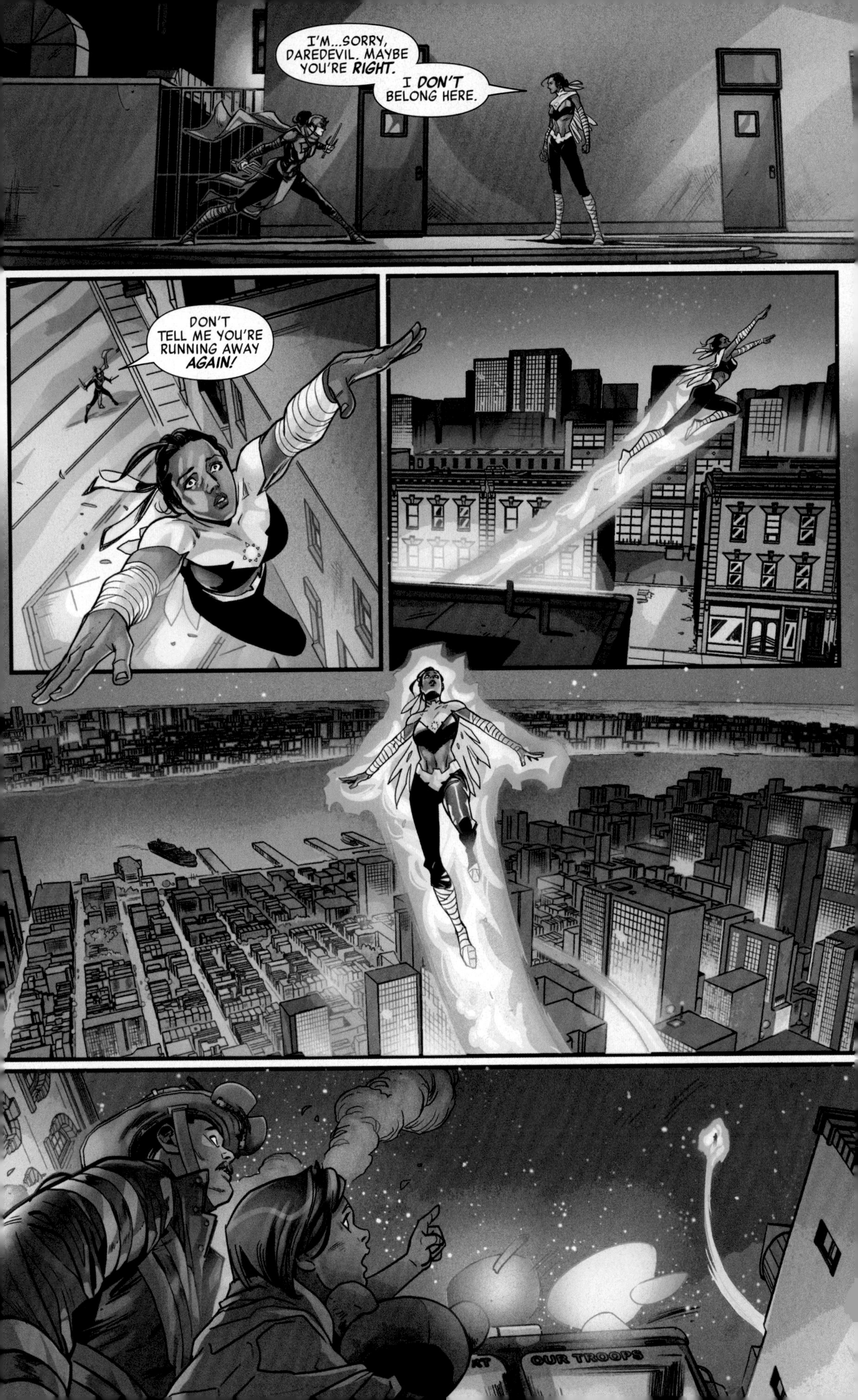
I'M...SORRY, DAREDEVIL. MAYBE YOU'RE **RIGHT.**
I **DON'T** BELONG HERE.
DON'T TELL ME YOU'RE RUNNING AWAY **AGAIN!**
OUR TROOPS

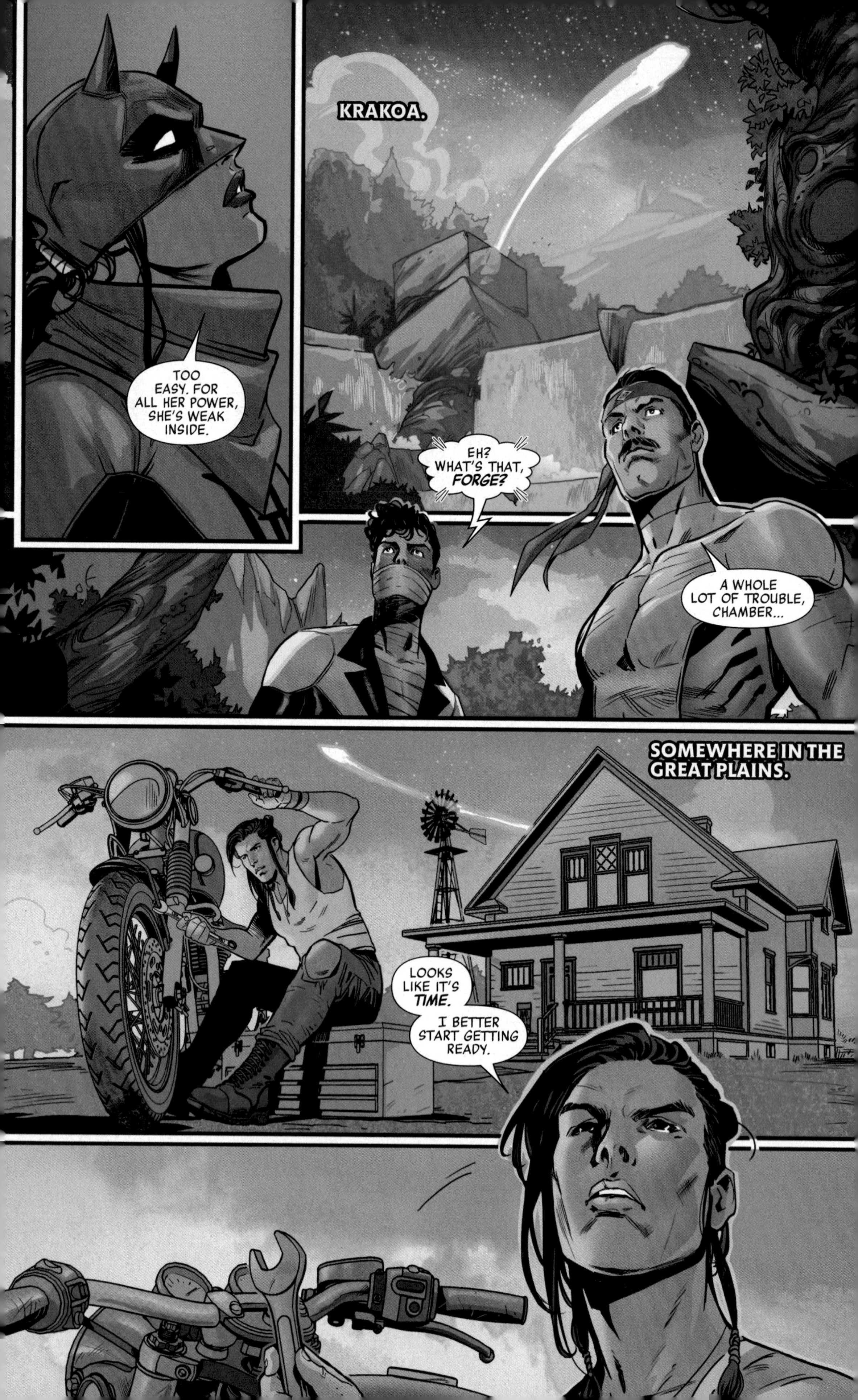
TOO EASY. FOR ALL HER POWER, SHE'S WEAK INSIDE.
KRAKOA.
EH? WHAT'S THAT, FORGE?
A WHOLE LOT OF TROUBLE, CHAMBER...
SOMEWHERE IN THE GREAT PLAINS.
LOOKS LIKE IT'S TIME.
I BETTER START GETTING READY.

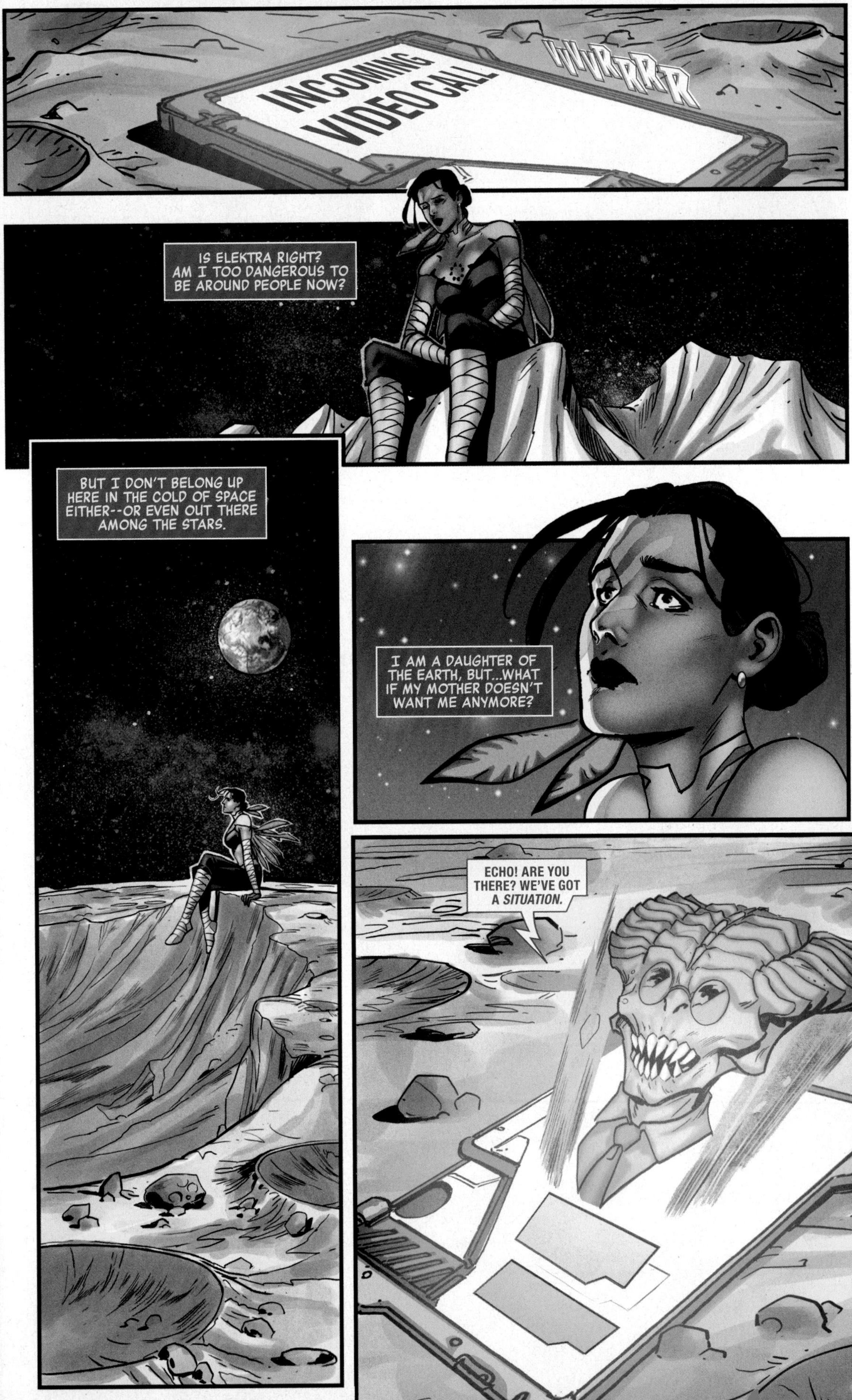
INCOMING VIDEO CALL
WRRRRR
IS ELEKTRA RIGHT? AM I TOO DANGEROUS TO BE AROUND PEOPLE NOW?
BUT I DON'T BELONG UP HERE IN THE COLD OF SPACE EITHER--OR EVEN OUT THERE AMONG THE STARS.
I AM A DAUGHTER OF THE EARTH, BUT...WHAT IF MY MOTHER DOESN'T WANT ME ANYMORE?
ECHO! ARE YOU THERE? WE'VE GOT A *SITUATION.*

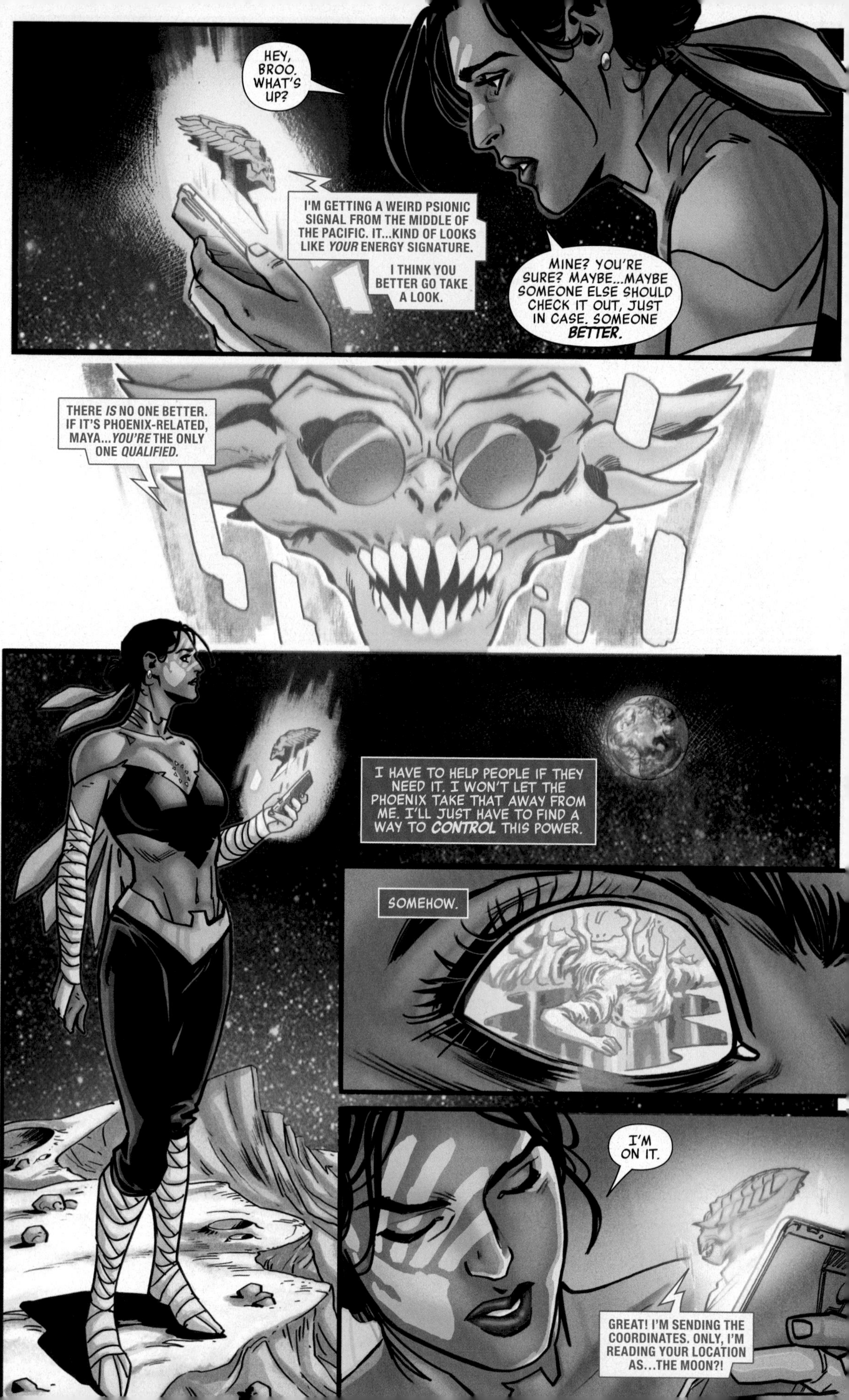
HEY, BROO. WHAT'S UP?
I'M GETTING A WEIRD PSIONIC SIGNAL FROM THE MIDDLE OF THE PACIFIC. IT...KIND OF LOOKS LIKE *YOUR* ENERGY SIGNATURE.
I THINK YOU BETTER GO TAKE A LOOK.
MINE? YOU'RE SURE? MAYBE...MAYBE SOMEONE ELSE SHOULD CHECK IT OUT, JUST IN CASE. SOMEONE ***BETTER.***
THERE *IS* NO ONE BETTER. IF IT'S PHOENIX-RELATED, MAYA...*YOU'RE* THE ONLY ONE *QUALIFIED.*
I HAVE TO HELP PEOPLE IF THEY NEED IT. I WON'T LET THE PHOENIX TAKE THAT AWAY FROM ME. I'LL JUST HAVE TO FIND A WAY TO ***CONTROL*** THIS POWER.
SOMEHOW.
I'M ON IT.
GREAT! I'M SENDING THE COORDINATES. ONLY, I'M READING YOUR LOCATION AS...THE MOON?!

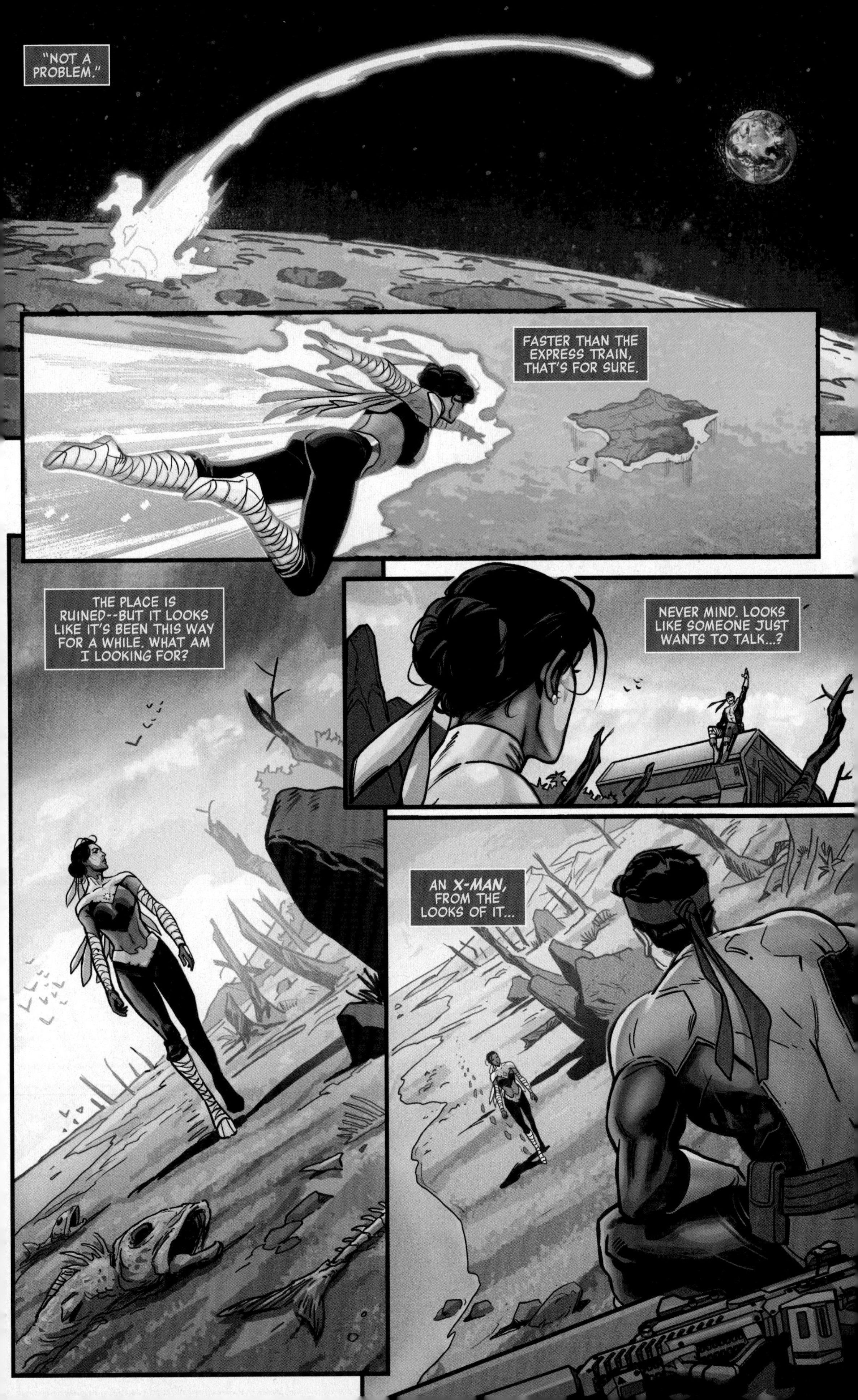
"NOT A PROBLEM."
FASTER THAN THE EXPRESS TRAIN, THAT'S FOR SURE.
THE PLACE IS RUINED--BUT IT LOOKS LIKE IT'S BEEN THIS WAY FOR A WHILE. WHAT AM I LOOKING FOR?
NEVER MIND. LOOKS LIKE SOMEONE JUST WANTS TO TALK...?
AN X-MAN, FROM THE LOOKS OF IT...

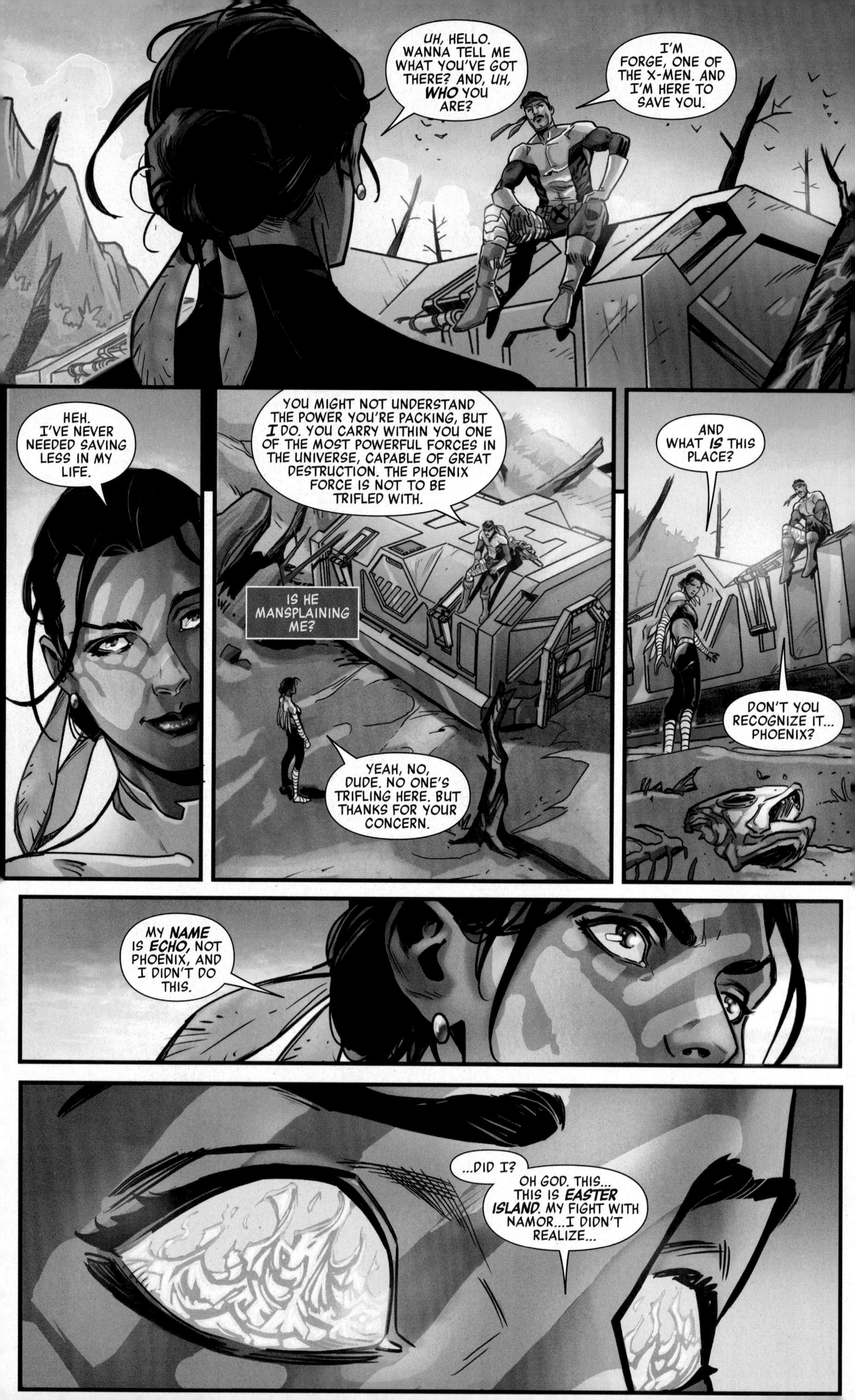
UH, HELLO. WANNA TELL ME WHAT YOU'VE GOT THERE? AND, UH, WHO YOU ARE?
I'M FORGE, ONE OF THE X-MEN. AND I'M HERE TO SAVE YOU.
HEH. I'VE NEVER NEEDED SAVING LESS IN MY LIFE.
YOU MIGHT NOT UNDERSTAND THE POWER YOU'RE PACKING, BUT I DO. YOU CARRY WITHIN YOU ONE OF THE MOST POWERFUL FORCES IN THE UNIVERSE, CAPABLE OF GREAT DESTRUCTION. THE PHOENIX FORCE IS NOT TO BE TRIFLED WITH.
IS HE MANSPLAINING ME?
YEAH, NO, DUDE. NO ONE'S TRIFLING HERE. BUT THANKS FOR YOUR CONCERN.
AND WHAT IS THIS PLACE?
DON'T YOU RECOGNIZE IT... PHOENIX?
MY NAME IS ECHO, NOT PHOENIX, AND I DIDN'T DO THIS.
...DID I?
OH GOD. THIS... THIS IS EASTER ISLAND. MY FIGHT WITH NAMOR...I DIDN'T REALIZE...

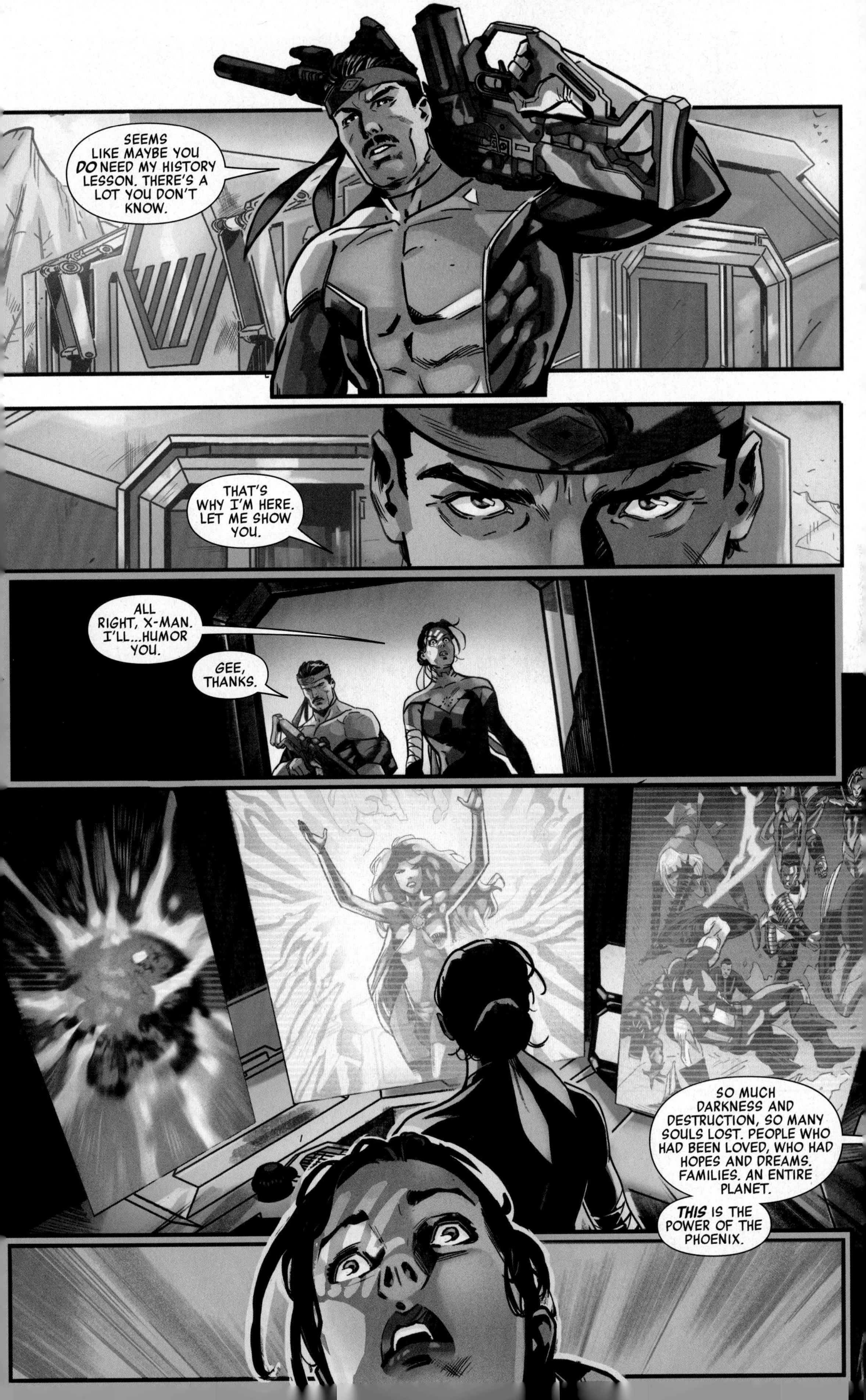
SEEMS LIKE MAYBE YOU DO NEED MY HISTORY LESSON. THERE'S A LOT YOU DON'T KNOW.
THAT'S WHY I'M HERE. LET ME SHOW YOU.
ALL RIGHT, X-MAN. I'LL...HUMOR YOU.
GEE, THANKS.
SO MUCH DARKNESS AND DESTRUCTION, SO MANY SOULS LOST. PEOPLE WHO HAD BEEN LOVED, WHO HAD HOPES AND DREAMS. FAMILIES. AN ENTIRE PLANET.
THIS IS THE POWER OF THE PHOENIX.

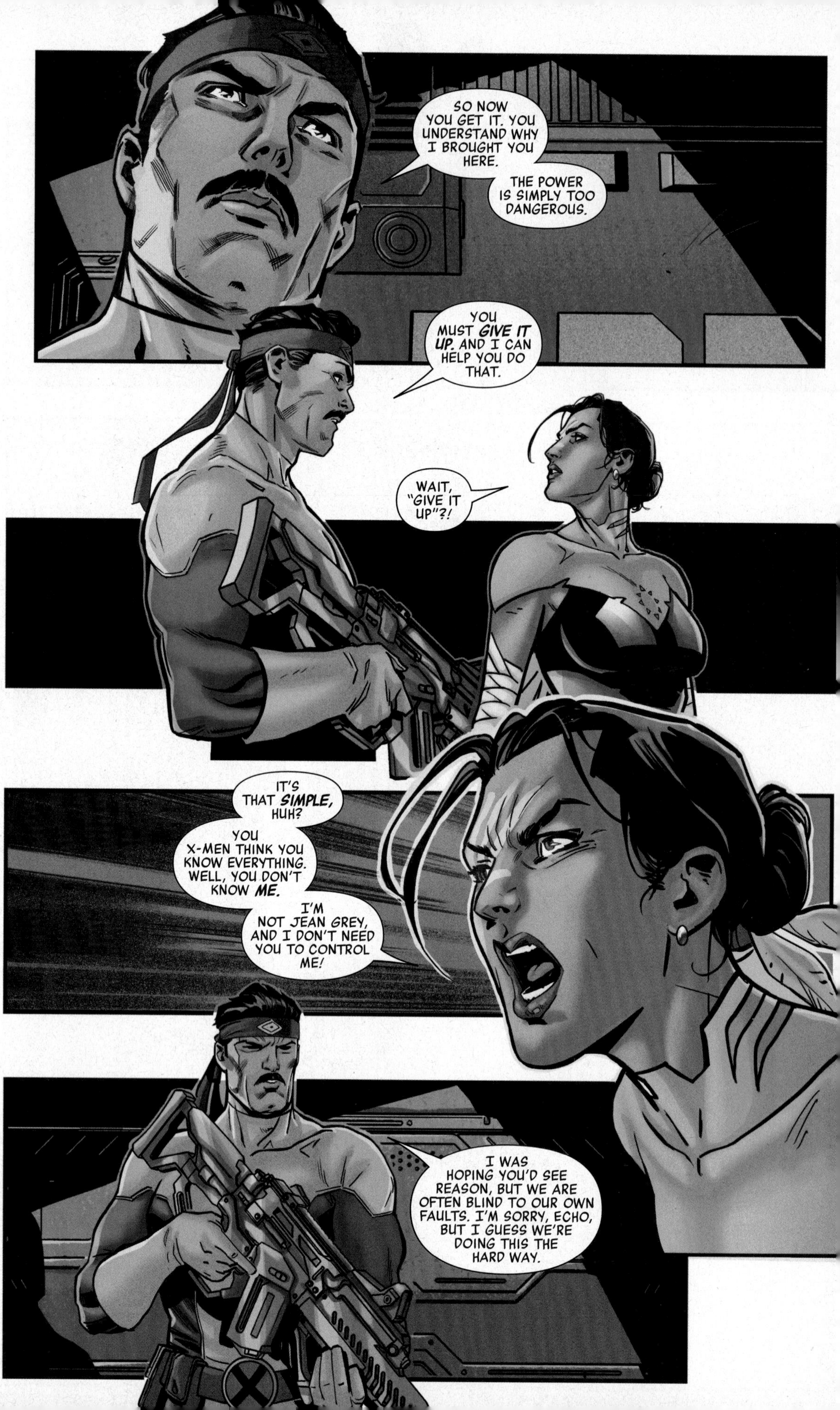
SO NOW YOU GET IT. YOU UNDERSTAND WHY I BROUGHT YOU HERE.
THE POWER IS SIMPLY TOO DANGEROUS.
YOU MUST *GIVE IT UP.* AND I CAN HELP YOU DO THAT.
WAIT, "GIVE IT UP"?!
IT'S THAT *SIMPLE,* HUH?
YOU X-MEN THINK YOU KNOW EVERYTHING. WELL, YOU DON'T KNOW *ME.*
I'M NOT JEAN GREY, AND I DON'T NEED YOU TO CONTROL ME!
I WAS HOPING YOU'D SEE REASON, BUT WE ARE OFTEN BLIND TO OUR OWN FAULTS. I'M SORRY, ECHO, BUT I GUESS WE'RE DOING THIS THE HARD WAY.

AGH!

BZZGHRT

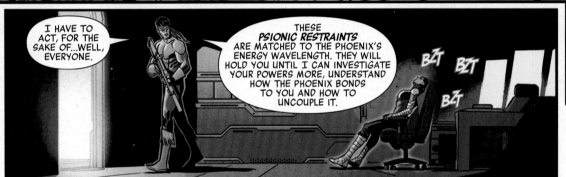

I HAVE TO ACT, FOR THE SAKE OF...WELL, EVERYONE.

THESE **PSIONIC RESTRAINTS** ARE MATCHED TO THE PHOENIX'S ENERGY WAVELENGTH. THEY WILL HOLD YOU UNTIL I CAN INVESTIGATE YOUR POWERS MORE, UNDERSTAND HOW THE PHOENIX BONDS TO YOU AND HOW TO UNCOUPLE IT.

BZT   BZT

BZT

THIS ISN'T FOREVER, ECHO. WITH TIME, I'LL FIND A WAY TO RELEASE YOU, FROM ALL OF IT. I PROMISE.

RUMBLE

XAVIER WON'T LIKE THIS, BUT SOMEONE HAD TO DO SOMETHING WHILE WE STILL COULD. HAVEN'T WE MUTANTS SEEN THIS HAPPEN OVER AND OVER AGAIN? STILL, I DO...

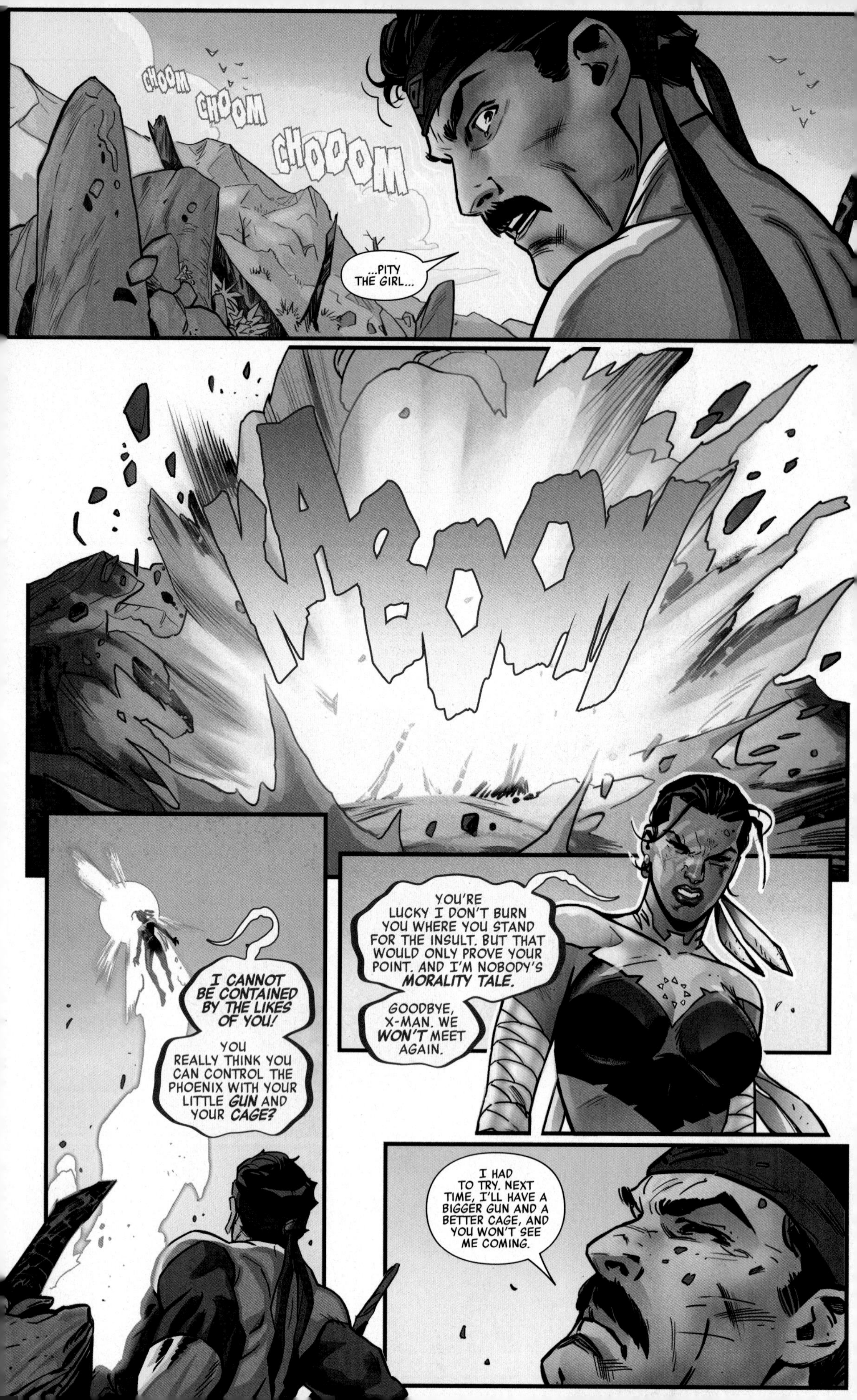
CHOOM
CHOOM
CHOOOM
...PITY THE GIRL...
KABOOM
I CANNOT BE CONTAINED BY THE LIKES OF YOU!
YOU REALLY THINK YOU CAN CONTROL THE PHOENIX WITH YOUR LITTLE GUN AND YOUR CAGE?
YOU'RE LUCKY I DON'T BURN YOU WHERE YOU STAND FOR THE INSULT. BUT THAT WOULD ONLY PROVE YOUR POINT. AND I'M NOBODY'S MORALITY TALE.
GOODBYE, X-MAN. WE WON'T MEET AGAIN.
I HAD TO TRY. NEXT TIME, I'LL HAVE A BIGGER GUN AND A BETTER CAGE, AND YOU WON'T SEE ME COMING.

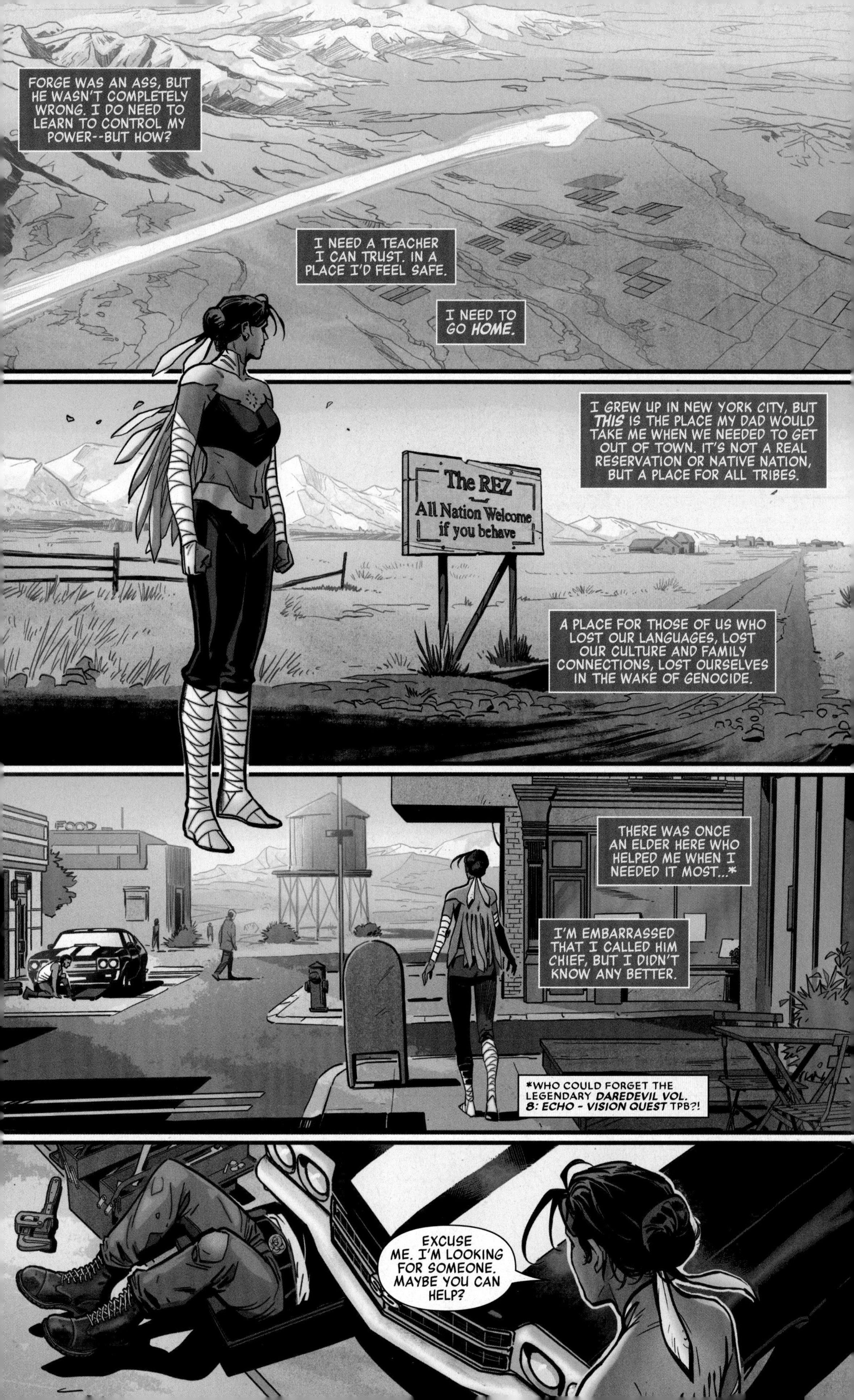
FORGE WAS AN ASS, BUT HE WASN'T COMPLETELY WRONG. I DO NEED TO LEARN TO CONTROL MY POWER--BUT HOW?
I NEED A TEACHER I CAN TRUST. IN A PLACE I'D FEEL SAFE.
I NEED TO GO *HOME.*
I GREW UP IN NEW YORK CITY, BUT *THIS* IS THE PLACE MY DAD WOULD TAKE ME WHEN WE NEEDED TO GET OUT OF TOWN. IT'S NOT A REAL RESERVATION OR NATIVE NATION, BUT A PLACE FOR ALL TRIBES.
The REZ
All Nation Welcome if you behave
A PLACE FOR THOSE OF US WHO LOST OUR LANGUAGES, LOST OUR CULTURE AND FAMILY CONNECTIONS, LOST OURSELVES IN THE WAKE OF GENOCIDE.
FOOD
THERE WAS ONCE AN ELDER HERE WHO HELPED ME WHEN I NEEDED IT MOST...*
I'M EMBARRASSED THAT I CALLED HIM CHIEF, BUT I DIDN'T KNOW ANY BETTER.
*WHO COULD FORGET THE LEGENDARY *DAREDEVIL VOL. 8: ECHO - VISION QUEST* TPB?!
EXCUSE ME. I'M LOOKING FOR SOMEONE. MAYBE YOU CAN HELP?

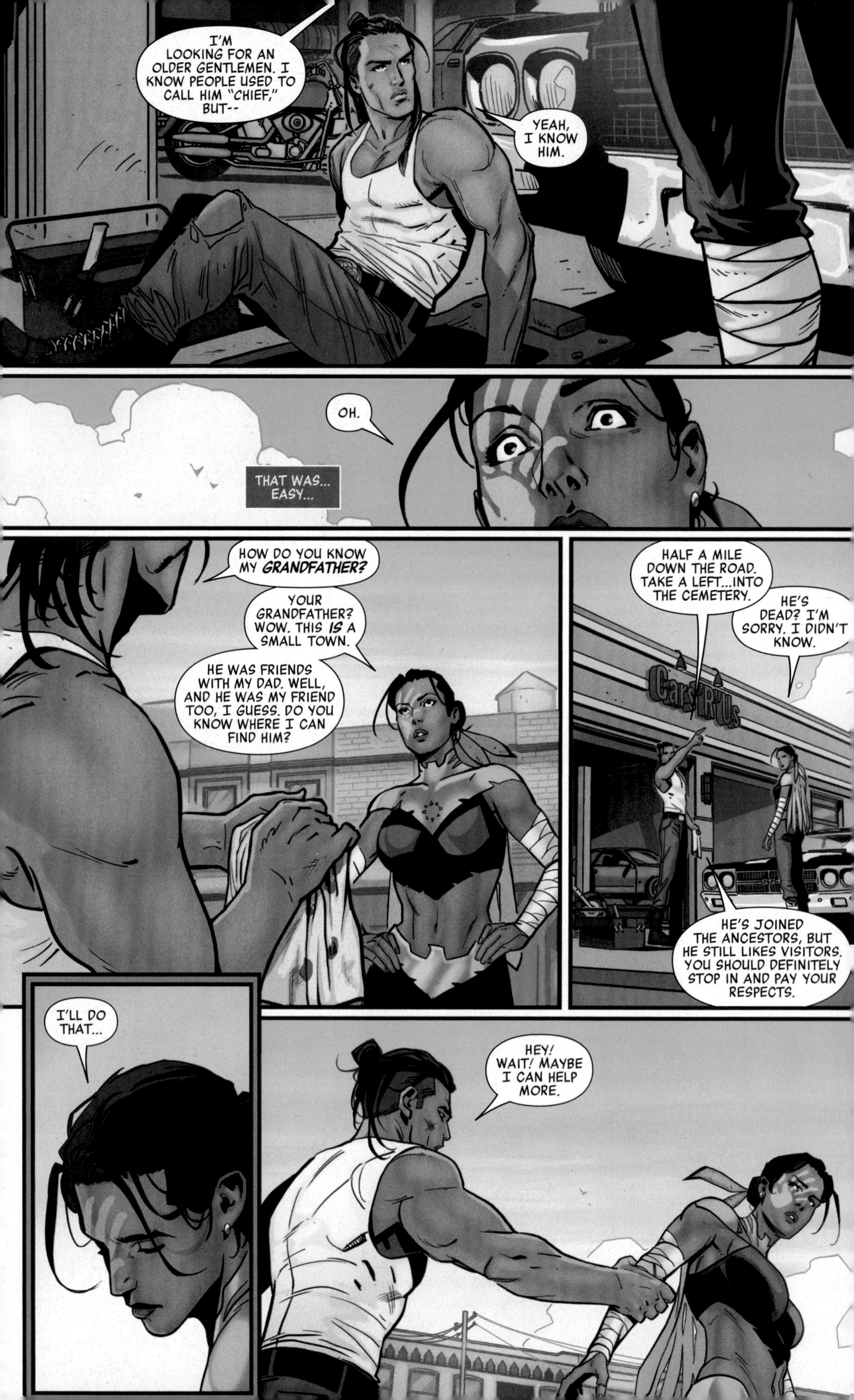

I'M LOOKING FOR AN OLDER GENTLEMEN. I KNOW PEOPLE USED TO CALL HIM "CHIEF," BUT--
YEAH, I KNOW HIM.
OH.
THAT WAS... EASY...
HOW DO YOU KNOW MY GRANDFATHER?
YOUR GRANDFATHER? WOW. THIS IS A SMALL TOWN.
HE WAS FRIENDS WITH MY DAD. WELL, AND HE WAS MY FRIEND TOO, I GUESS. DO YOU KNOW WHERE I CAN FIND HIM?
HALF A MILE DOWN THE ROAD. TAKE A LEFT...INTO THE CEMETERY.
HE'S DEAD? I'M SORRY. I DIDN'T KNOW.
Cars "R" Us
HE'S JOINED THE ANCESTORS, BUT HE STILL LIKES VISITORS. YOU SHOULD DEFINITELY STOP IN AND PAY YOUR RESPECTS.
I'LL DO THAT...
HEY! WAIT! MAYBE I CAN HELP MORE.

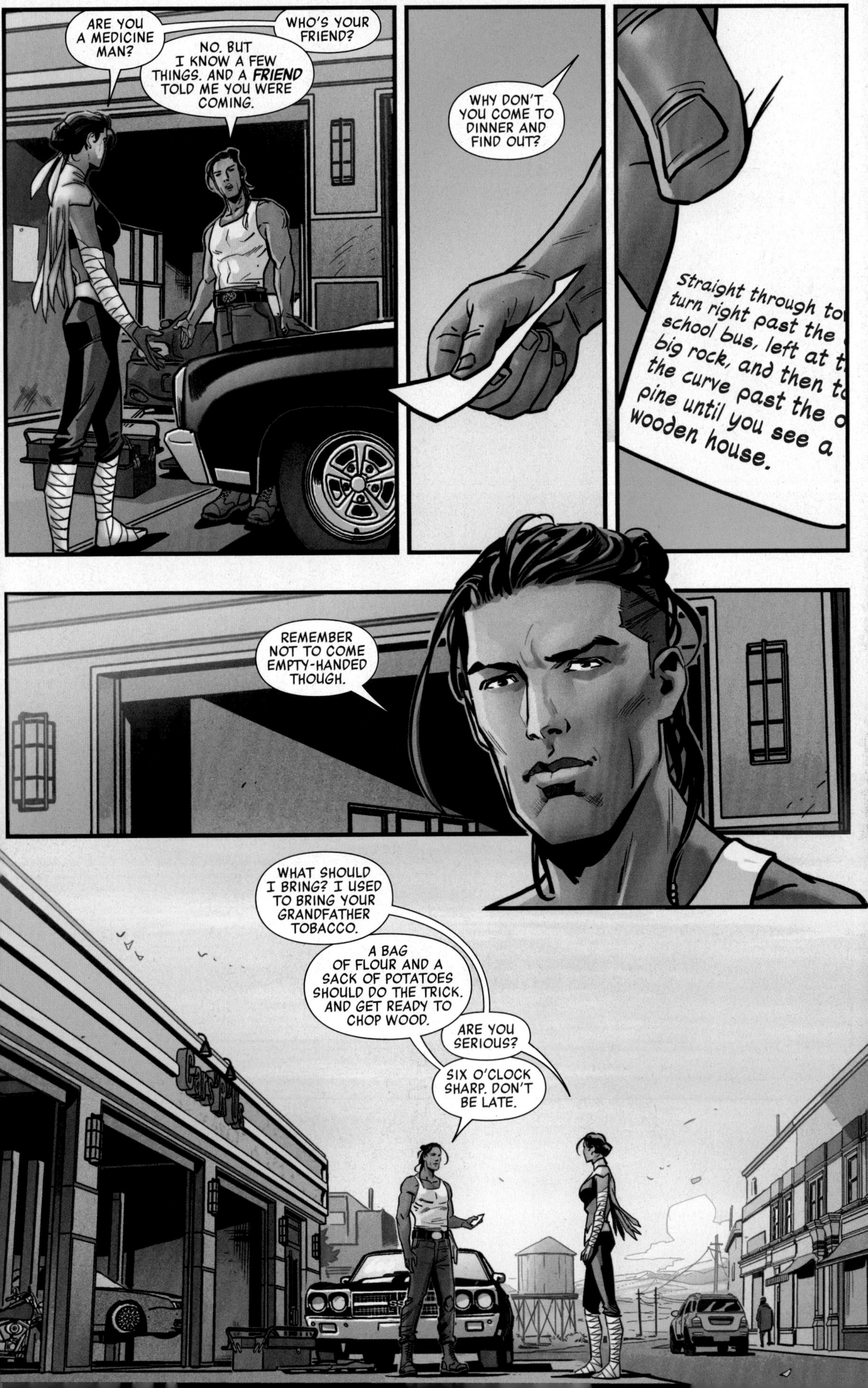
ARE YOU A MEDICINE MAN?
WHO'S YOUR FRIEND?
NO. BUT I KNOW A FEW THINGS. AND A **FRIEND** TOLD ME YOU WERE COMING.
WHY DON'T YOU COME TO DINNER AND FIND OUT?
Straight through to
turn right past the
school bus, left at t
big rock, and then to
the curve past the o
pine until you see a
wooden house.
REMEMBER NOT TO COME EMPTY-HANDED THOUGH.
WHAT SHOULD I BRING? I USED TO BRING YOUR GRANDFATHER TOBACCO.
A BAG OF FLOUR AND A SACK OF POTATOES SHOULD DO THE TRICK. AND GET READY TO CHOP WOOD.
ARE YOU SERIOUS?
SIX O'CLOCK SHARP. DON'T BE LATE.

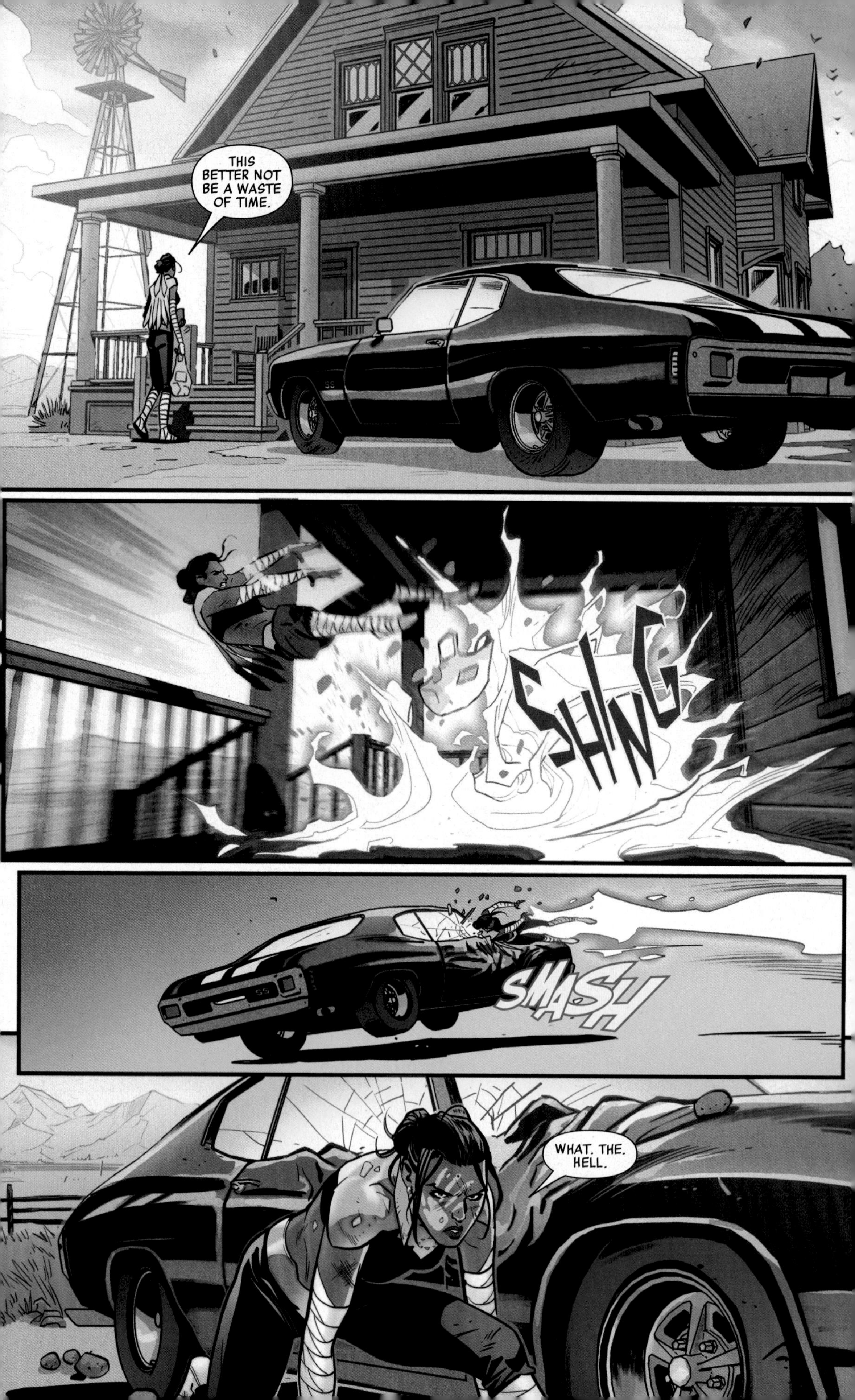
THIS BETTER NOT BE A WASTE OF TIME.
SHING
SMASH
WHAT. THE. HELL.

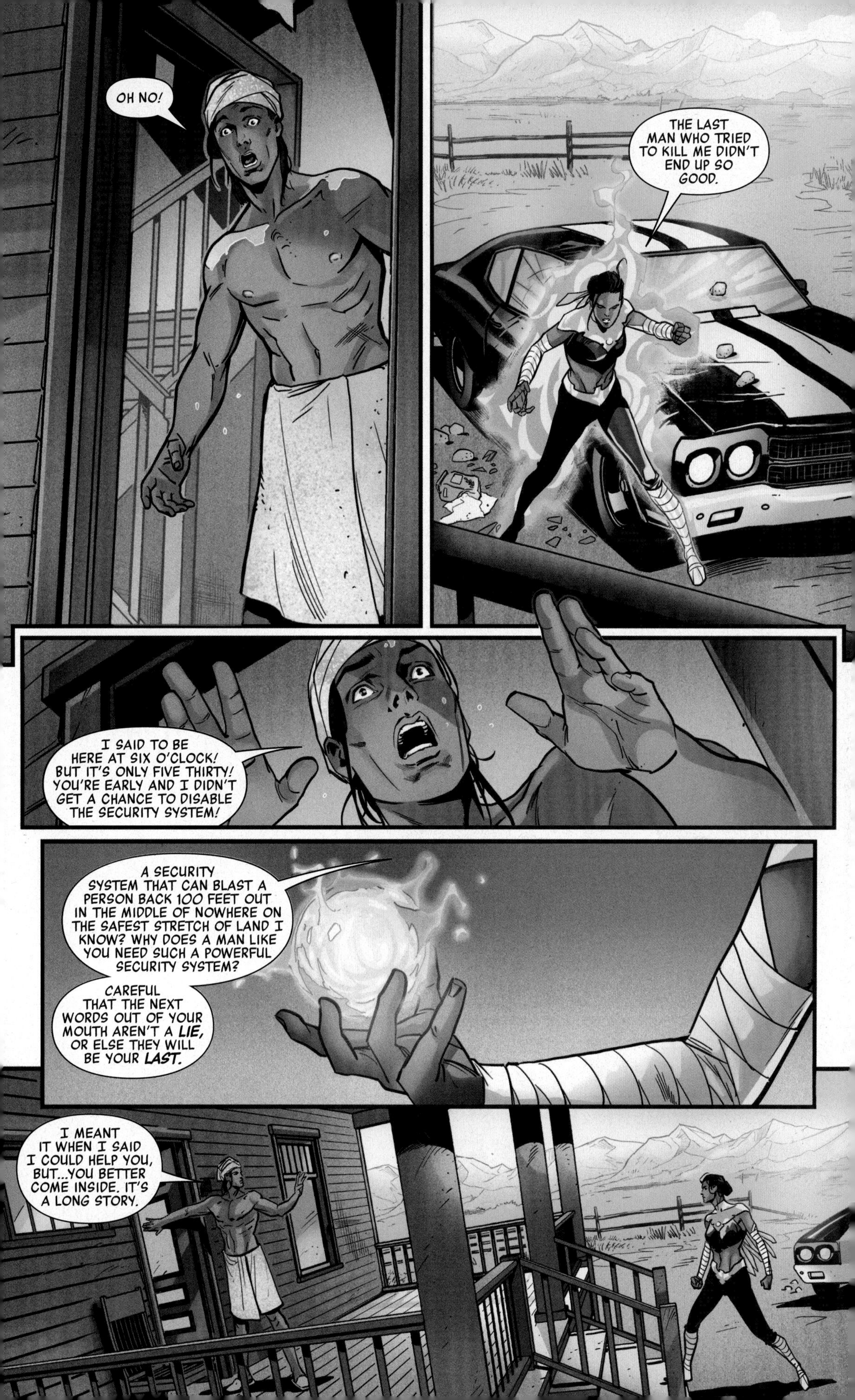
OH NO!
THE LAST MAN WHO TRIED TO KILL ME DIDN'T END UP SO GOOD.
I SAID TO BE HERE AT SIX O'CLOCK! BUT IT'S ONLY FIVE THIRTY! YOU'RE EARLY AND I DIDN'T GET A CHANCE TO DISABLE THE SECURITY SYSTEM!
A SECURITY SYSTEM THAT CAN BLAST A PERSON BACK 100 FEET OUT IN THE MIDDLE OF NOWHERE ON THE SAFEST STRETCH OF LAND I KNOW? WHY DOES A MAN LIKE YOU NEED SUCH A POWERFUL SECURITY SYSTEM?
CAREFUL THAT THE NEXT WORDS OUT OF YOUR MOUTH AREN'T A *LIE*, OR ELSE THEY WILL BE YOUR *LAST*.
I MEANT IT WHEN I SAID I COULD HELP YOU, BUT...YOU BETTER COME INSIDE. IT'S A LONG STORY.

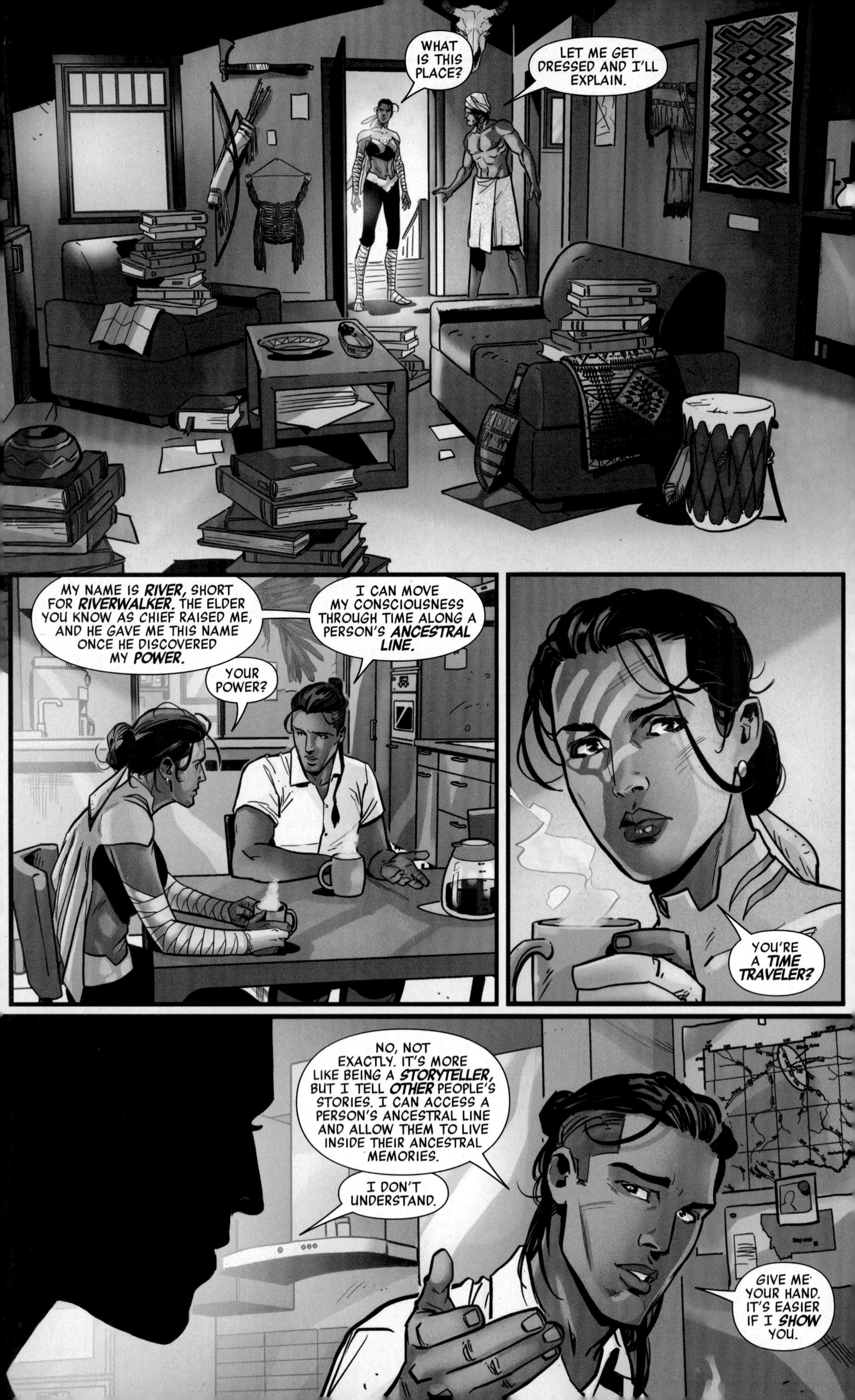
WHAT IS THIS PLACE?
LET ME GET DRESSED AND I'LL EXPLAIN.
MY NAME IS RIVER, SHORT FOR RIVERWALKER. THE ELDER YOU KNOW AS CHIEF RAISED ME, AND HE GAVE ME THIS NAME ONCE HE DISCOVERED MY POWER.
YOUR POWER?
I CAN MOVE MY CONSCIOUSNESS THROUGH TIME ALONG A PERSON'S ANCESTRAL LINE.
YOU'RE A TIME TRAVELER?
NO, NOT EXACTLY. IT'S MORE LIKE BEING A STORYTELLER, BUT I TELL OTHER PEOPLE'S STORIES. I CAN ACCESS A PERSON'S ANCESTRAL LINE AND ALLOW THEM TO LIVE INSIDE THEIR ANCESTRAL MEMORIES.
I DON'T UNDERSTAND.
GIVE ME YOUR HAND. IT'S EASIER IF I SHOW YOU.

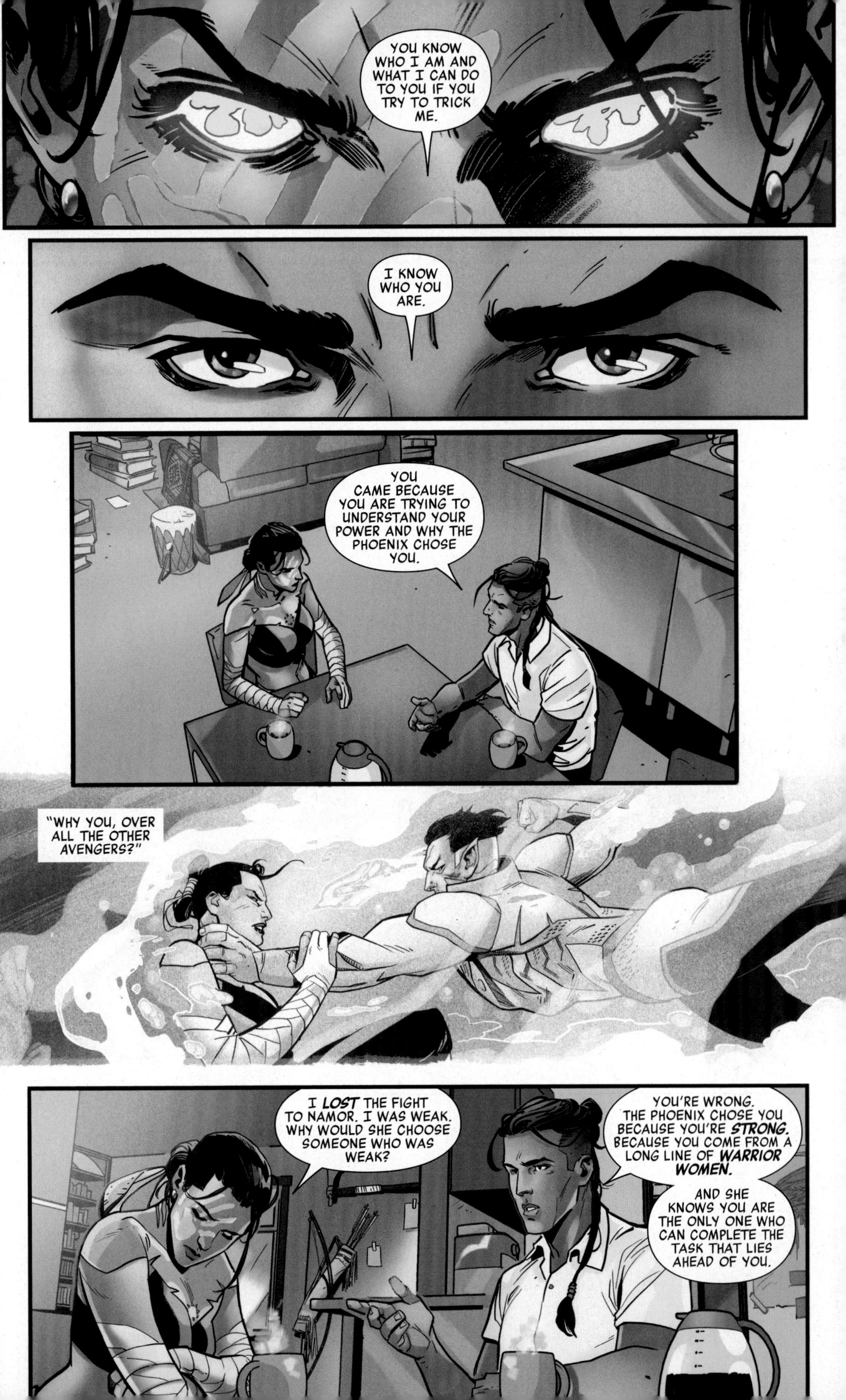
YOU KNOW WHO I AM AND WHAT I CAN DO TO YOU IF YOU TRY TO TRICK ME.
I KNOW WHO YOU ARE.
YOU CAME BECAUSE YOU ARE TRYING TO UNDERSTAND YOUR POWER AND WHY THE PHOENIX CHOSE YOU.
"WHY YOU, OVER ALL THE OTHER AVENGERS?"
I LOST THE FIGHT TO NAMOR. I WAS WEAK. WHY WOULD SHE CHOOSE SOMEONE WHO WAS WEAK?
YOU'RE WRONG. THE PHOENIX CHOSE YOU BECAUSE YOU'RE STRONG. BECAUSE YOU COME FROM A LONG LINE OF WARRIOR WOMEN.
AND SHE KNOWS YOU ARE THE ONLY ONE WHO CAN COMPLETE THE TASK THAT LIES AHEAD OF YOU.

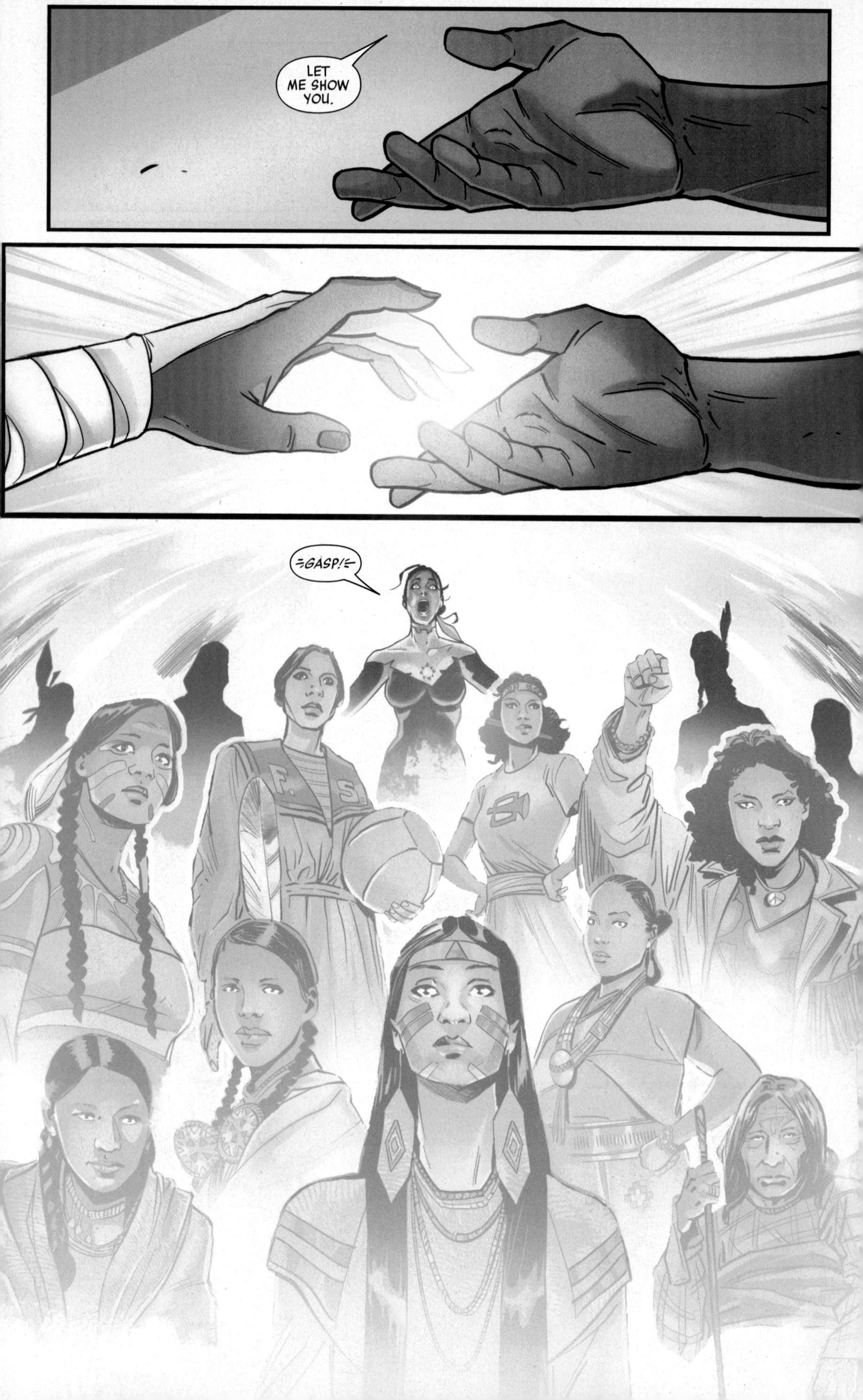
LET ME SHOW YOU.
GASP!

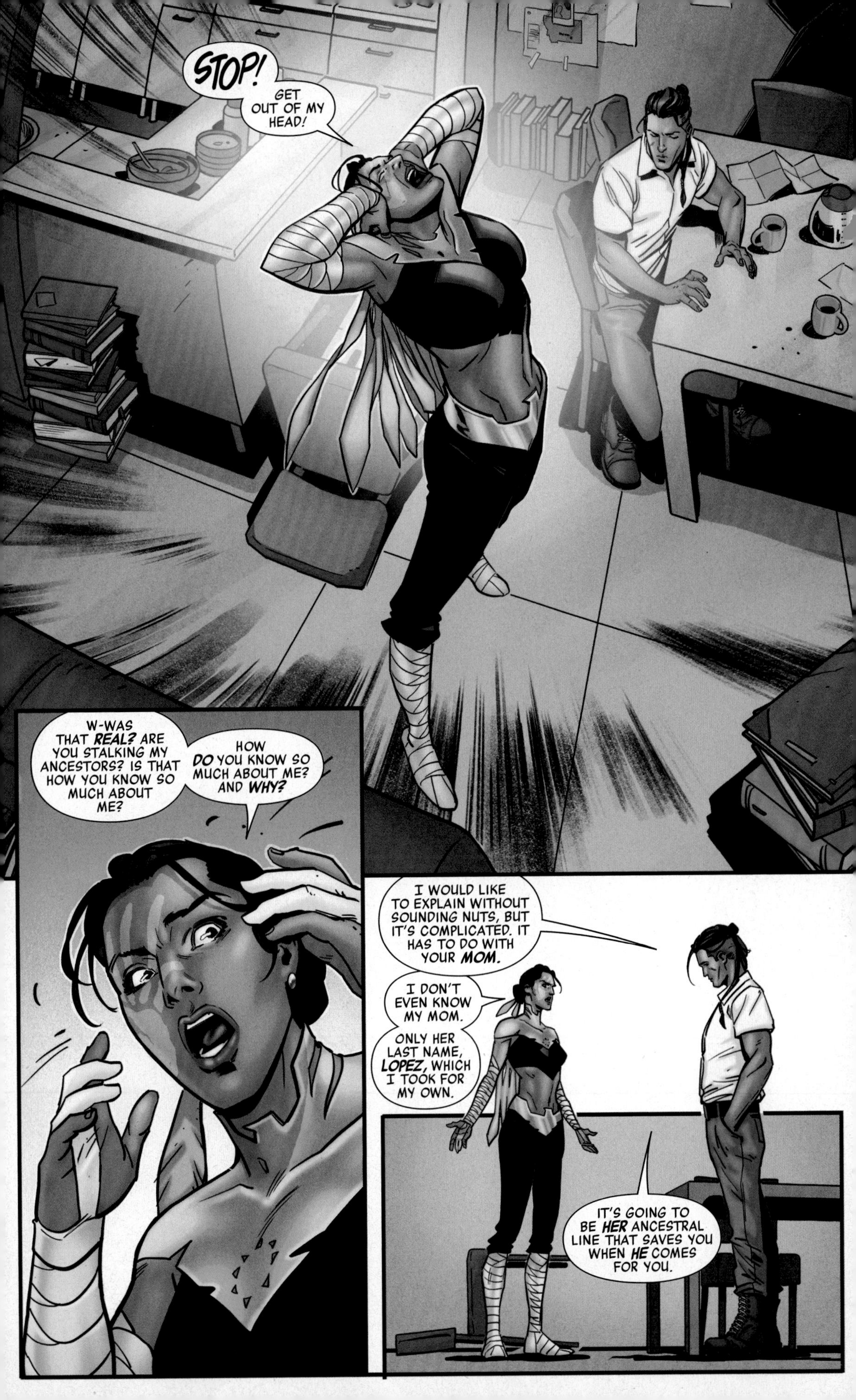
STOP!
GET OUT OF MY HEAD!
W-WAS THAT REAL? ARE YOU STALKING MY ANCESTORS? IS THAT HOW YOU KNOW SO MUCH ABOUT ME?
HOW DO YOU KNOW SO MUCH ABOUT ME? AND WHY?
I WOULD LIKE TO EXPLAIN WITHOUT SOUNDING NUTS, BUT IT'S COMPLICATED. IT HAS TO DO WITH YOUR MOM.
I DON'T EVEN KNOW MY MOM.
ONLY HER LAST NAME, LOPEZ, WHICH I TOOK FOR MY OWN.
IT'S GOING TO BE HER ANCESTRAL LINE THAT SAVES YOU WHEN HE COMES FOR YOU.

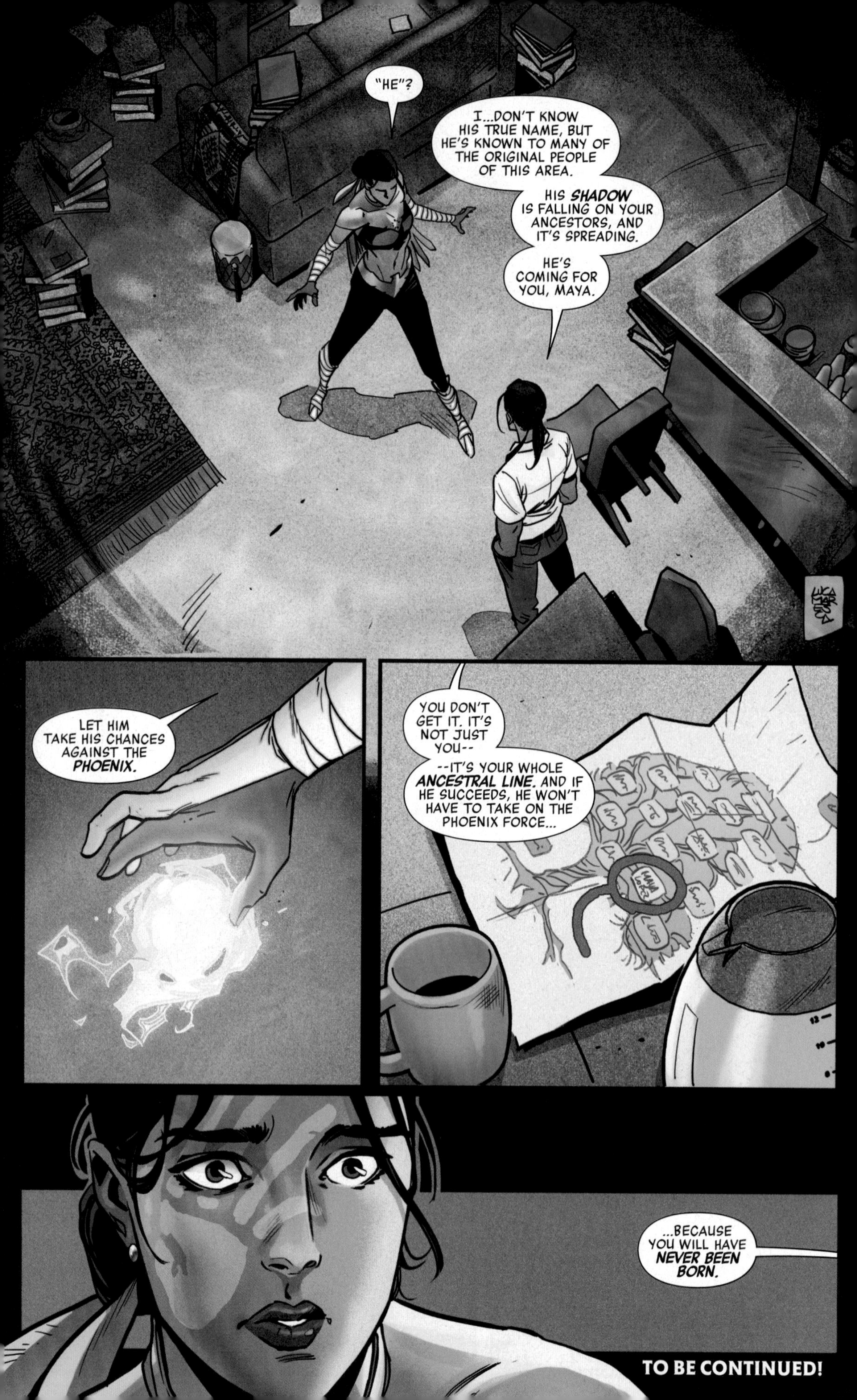
"HE"?
I...DON'T KNOW HIS TRUE NAME, BUT HE'S KNOWN TO MANY OF THE ORIGINAL PEOPLE OF THIS AREA.
HIS SHADOW IS FALLING ON YOUR ANCESTORS, AND IT'S SPREADING.
HE'S COMING FOR YOU, MAYA.
LET HIM TAKE HIS CHANCES AGAINST THE PHOENIX.
YOU DON'T GET IT. IT'S NOT JUST YOU--
--IT'S YOUR WHOLE ANCESTRAL LINE. AND IF HE SUCCEEDS, HE WON'T HAVE TO TAKE ON THE PHOENIX FORCE...
...BECAUSE YOU WILL HAVE NEVER BEEN BORN.
TO BE CONTINUED!

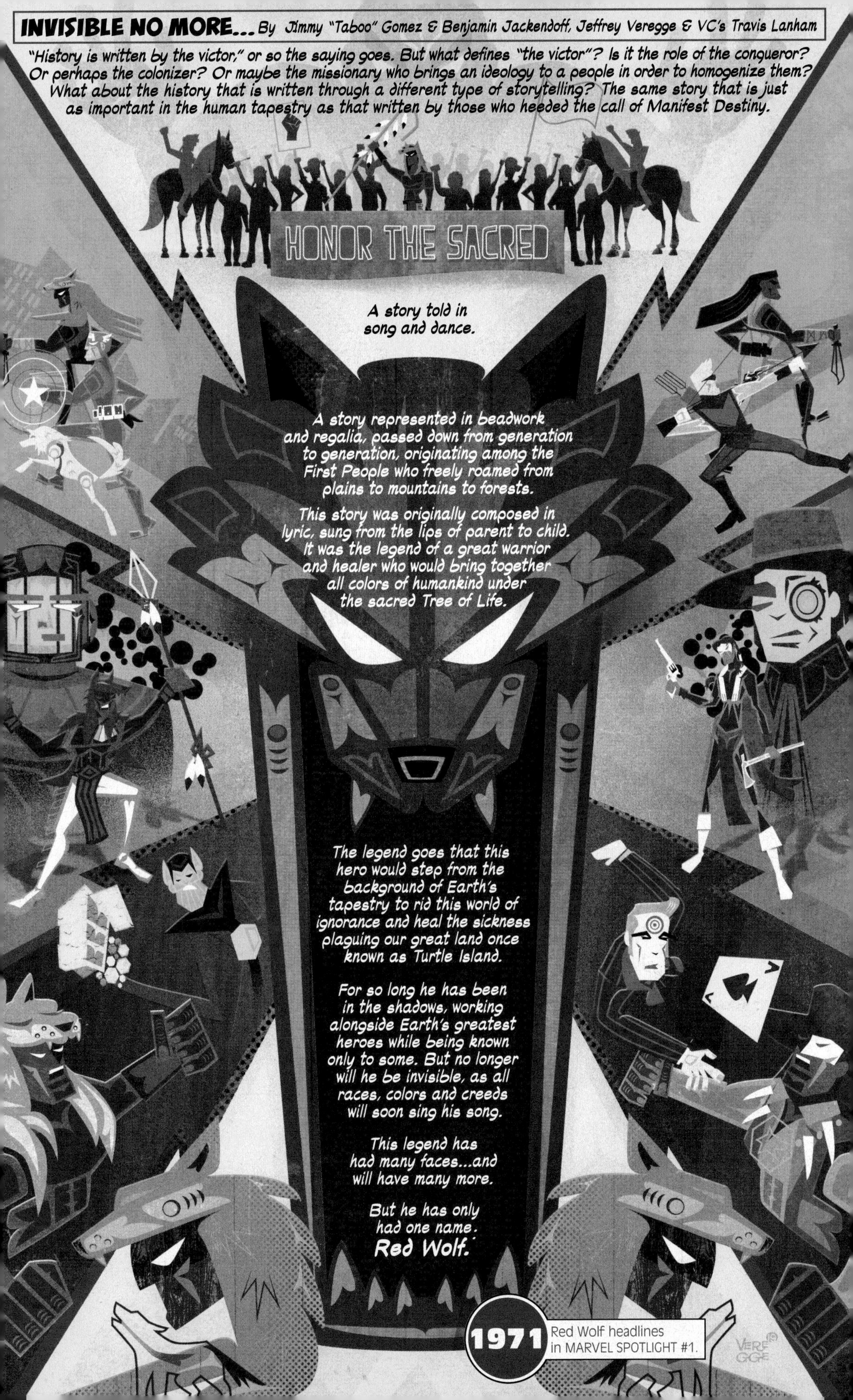
INVISIBLE NO MORE... By Jimmy "Taboo" Gomez & Benjamin Jackendoff, Jeffrey Veregge & VC's Travis Lanham
"History is written by the victor," or so the saying goes. But what defines "the victor"? Is it the role of the conqueror? Or perhaps the colonizer? Or maybe the missionary who brings an ideology to a people in order to homogenize them? What about the history that is written through a different type of storytelling? The same story that is just as important in the human tapestry as that written by those who heeded the call of Manifest Destiny.
HONOR THE SACRED
A story told in song and dance.
A story represented in beadwork and regalia, passed down from generation to generation, originating among the First People who freely roamed from plains to mountains to forests.
This story was originally composed in lyric, sung from the lips of parent to child. It was the legend of a great warrior and healer who would bring together all colors of humankind under the sacred Tree of Life.
The legend goes that this hero would step from the background of Earth's tapestry to rid this world of ignorance and heal the sickness plaguing our great land once known as Turtle Island.
For so long he has been in the shadows, working alongside Earth's greatest heroes while being known only to some. But no longer will he be invisible, as all races, colors and creeds will soon sing his song.
This legend has had many faces...and will have many more.
But he has only had one name. Red Wolf.
1971 Red Wolf headlines in MARVEL SPOTLIGHT #1.
VEREGGE

"MARVEL'S VOICES" ESSAY

BY DARCIE LITTLE BADGER

As a contributor to *Marvel's Voices: Indigenous Voices #1*, I was thrilled to write a story about a character near and dear to my comic-loving heart: Dani Moonstar, A.K.A. Mirage of the X-Men.

I've previously waxed poetic about all the qualities that make Dani such an awesome hero. For example, her mutant abilities are both unique and psychologically compelling (true to the name Mirage, Dani can connect to a person's psyche and project their greatest fears or desires as illusions). That said, Dani has vast storytelling potential, far more than ten pages—or even ten thousand pages—can contain. Therefore, in order to find a focus, I took a moment to consider the importance of voice.

That's when a disorienting childhood memory immediately came to mind. How old was I? Young. Maybe 4 or 5. At the time, my parents, brother, and I lived in Iowa, half a country away from our extended family, my aunts, uncles, cousins, and grandparents. In other words, I knew in theory that Mom had sisters; I'd seen their faces in photo albums. But I'd never heard them speak.

Anyway, I was playing in a park, the kind with more grass and trees than anything else, when a voice called, "Darcie! Darcie! Come here!"

My mother was sitting nearby, and the voice

on. But I recognized at an instinctual level that the call did not come from my mother. It lacked her warmth. Her affection. The accent was slightly off. It was as if a doppelgänger with my mother's shape had called my name, but the mimic could not imitate everything that made her voice unique.

Fortunately, my aunt stepped into view. Not quite the monster I'd feared. Still, the experience left me unsettled.

It also highlights an important element of voices. A complete stranger might sound familiar. Maybe it's their accent or idioms or the stories they tell. Simultaneously, individual voices carry elements that make them unique. After all, humans are complex. A multitude of elements piece together our identities and personalities.

That's the beauty of Dani Moonstar. In junior high school, shortly after a rack of assorted comic books in a village convenience store introduced me to *X-Men* comics, I started reading *New Mutants*. That was my first encounter with Dani, a Cheyenne woman. It was also my first encounter with a Native main character in any comic book—heck, make that in any speculative book, movie, or TV show

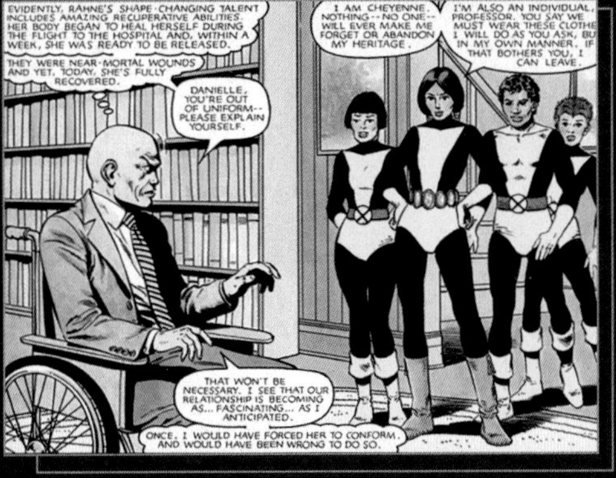
EVIDENTLY, RAHNE'S SHAPE-CHANGING TALENT INCLUDES AMAZING RECUPERATIVE ABILITIES. HER BODY BEGAN TO HEAL HERSELF DURING THE FLIGHT TO THE HOSPITAL AND, WITHIN A WEEK, SHE WAS READY TO BE RELEASED.
THEY WERE NEAR-MORTAL WOUNDS AND YET, TODAY, SHE'S FULLY RECOVERED.
DANIELLE, YOU'RE OUT OF UNIFORM-- PLEASE EXPLAIN YOURSELF.
I AM CHEYENNE. NOTHING--NO ONE-- WILL EVER MAKE ME FORGET OR ABANDON MY HERITAGE.
I'M ALSO AN INDIVIDUAL, PROFESSOR. YOU SAY WE MUST WEAR THESE CLOTHE I WILL DO AS YOU ASK, BU IN MY OWN MANNER. IF THAT BOTHERS YOU, I CAN LEAVE.
THAT WON'T BE NECESSARY. I SEE THAT OUR RELATIONSHIP IS BECOMING AS... FASCINATING... AS I ANTICIPATED.
ONCE, I WOULD HAVE FORCED HER TO CONFORM, AND WOULD HAVE BEEN WRONG TO DO SO.

Marvel Graphic Novel No. 4
The New Mutants (1982)

In many ways, I immediately related to Dani's perspective as an Indigenous woman. I'm Lipan Apache. Dani is Cheyenne. There are hundreds of Indigenous peoples in this country—we're not a monolith by any means! But we are all the descendants of people who survived the brutal colonization of our homelands.

Perhaps that's why Dani's first showdown with death made such a great impact on me as a young reader. See, shortly after gaining Valkyrie powers, Dani returned to her home on the rez. There, she tried to save the life of Pat, a man who used to be her friend (unfortunately, he grew into a hateful person; I recommend reading the whole issue—*New Mutants #41*—for context). When Death came for Pat, it took the form of a cowboy gunslinger. From a storytelling perspective, allowing Dani to challenge Cowboy Death, a figure from the "old west" mythos, was powerful. Cowboys vs. Indians. Colonization and genocide vs. resistance and survival. Of course, Dani won the fight. As a young Native reader, I cheered her victory.

What is more, within Dani, culture and heritage coexist with the other important facets of her personality. From the get-go, she made that exceptionally clear to Professor Charles Xavier. After joining Xavier's institute, a teenage Dani paired her standard yellow uniform with a pair of leather boots and a turquoise-embellished belt. When the professor demanded, "Danielle, you're out of uniform. Please explain yourself," she said, "I am Cheyenne. Nothing—no one—will ever make me forget or abandon my heritage. I am also an individual." That piece of dialogue endeared me to Dani for life because it's so similar to what I feel every day of my life.

Who is Dani Moonstar? Well, she's a Cheyenne woman. A mutant hero. A vehemently loyal friend, an independent thinker, a successful teacher, an effective leader, and—as mentioned previously—an on-again, off-again Valkyrie. Like all Native folks, she's many things simultaneously. Dani's character is not made to minimize or compromise her indigeneity in pursuit of individuality or complexity. She reflects elements of myself I seldom see in popular fiction, while also demonstrating the fantastic variety and potential of Native voices. That, as well as the spirit of the classic New Mutant adventures, are what ultimately inspired my story in *Indigenous Voices*.

"MARVEL'S VOICES" ESSAY

BY KARLA PACHECO

"So...where are you from, exactly?"
"Kansas, mostly! Though I've also lived in Chicago, New York, Washington—"
"No. You know. Originally."
"Oh."

It's a question you get a lot when your physical appearance and features confuse people. To be clear, the people asking are rarely looking for my thoughts on trends from my home state or town. They see my features, my complexion, my last name, and because they don't immediately know what box of "other" to put me in, they probe to find answers. When I was younger, I would joke, "Part of my family came over on the *Pinta*, the *Niña*, and the *Santa María*; part came over on the *Mayflower*. The rest were already here!"

As I got older, I got tired of explaining a family history and heritage that, for much of my life, I'd been cut off from. At some point, I went back to just saying "Kansas," followed by staring at people until they felt as uncomfortable as I did.
For most multiracial or multiethnic folks identity can be complicated. Family life didn't help clear anything up. When I was at maternal family reunions in Kansas, I could see bits of myself reflected in my cousins' faces, but only bits. We had the same chin, the same cackling laugh, but I stuck out like a brown thumb. Many of us have been asked in various ways "What are you?" our entire lives. Personally, my answer has always been, "*It's complicated.*"

That sentiment of complicated identities and even more complicated family histories and heritages is also why I related to the stories and characters in Marvel Comics.

Mutants, scientific accidents, medical experiments gone wrong, aliens, and gods—regardless of race or species—are my favorite characters. I have always loved characters like Wolverine, Spider-Woman, Jessica Jones, and Deadpool, characters who don't necessarily belong on either side of the human equation. Some assume secret identities, others conceal themselves, while others are pulled into organizations with a

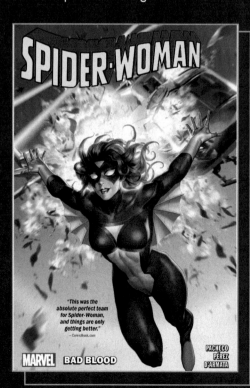

SPIDER-WOMAN

"This was the absolute perfect team for Spider-Woman, and things are only getting better."
—ComicBook.com

MARVEL   BAD BLOOD

PACHECO
PEREZ
D'ARMATA

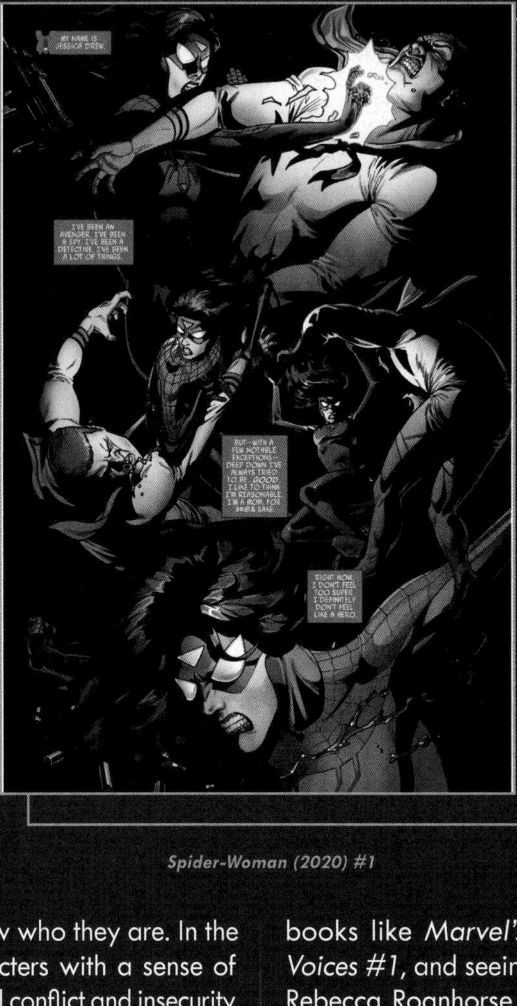
MY NAME IS JESSICA DREW
I'VE BEEN AN AVENGER. I'VE BEEN A SPY. I'VE BEEN A DETECTIVE. I'VE BEEN A LOT OF THINGS.
BUT--WITH A FEW NOTABLE EXCEPTIONS--DEEP DOWN I'VE ALWAYS TRIED TO BE... *GOOD.* I LIKE TO THINK I'M REASONABLE. I'M A MOM, FOR $#@& SAKE.
RIGHT NOW, I DON'T FEEL TOO SUPER. I DEFINITELY DON'T FEEL LIKE A HERO.

Spider-Woman (2020) #1

mission to protect people with less power than them. Like me, these characters are smart-mouthed badasses who don't always know where they belong, but they know who they are. In the end, these are characters with a sense of complexity, of personal conflict and insecurity, and core rage regarding their circumstances.

That is one of the reasons it's been amazing to bring my identity and lived experiences as a BIPOC creator into my writing. From taking a frustrated Misty Knight on the run and finding a community of fellow outsiders in *Secret Empire: Brave New World #4*, to funneling my personal struggles with physical disabilities into *Fearless #2*. I have been able to be a part of the expansion of the Marvel Universe writing the stories of characters from different backgrounds and making their identities a natural part of the story, reflecting the world around us—even when it's a dystopian future in *Fantastic Four 2099*.

Today, I'm so proud and delighted to see not just my work but the work of so many BIPOC creators reflecting their culture, their stories, and their backgrounds in the comics we all know and love. For example, having books like *Marvel's Voices: Indigenous Voices #1*, and seeing BIPOC creators like Rebecca Roanhorse, Darcie Little Badger, and my Pacific Northwest "cousin" Jeffrey Veregge bring their incredible take on my favorite heroes not only entertains but, for me, provides a sense of pride and the feeling of community that I have always felt cut off from. That is truly the power of not just storytelling but representation.

So...to answer the question:

"*Where are you from?*" Kansas, yes. But also Wundagore, Asgard, Krakoa, Latveria, and Wakanda.

"*What are you?*" I'm the one making your world bigger, more colorful, more painful, and joyful, and real—and that includes the Marvel Universe and the characters I love so much.

My family is a Marvel family. My eldest daughter is an Iron Man loyalist. My son believes no super hero tops Peter Parker, A.K.A. Spider-Man. My youngest daughter is in love with the brilliant Riri Williams, A.K.A. Ironheart. While my husband has his share of faves, including Gambit and Scott Lang, A.K.A. Ant-Man. Me? It's layered. While Black Widow stands out as a symbol of woman force, I love the ever-charming Groot and am simply in awe of brother and sister heroes T'Challa and Shuri. Needless to say, our family has some intense conversations and heated debates over Marvel's story arcs. But my most cherished moments are when we stop to **dream on the possibilities of Native-centered Marvel stories, imagining and playing with Native characters and experiences in the Marvel Universe**. Because, as much as we love and adore these characters, much of Marvel does not include the complex richness of Native lives.

In 2018, when my family first finished watching *Marvel Studios' Black Panther*, we dissected and highlighted the epic scenes and creative cinematography. While a number of things stood out, the line that had us rolling in ironic amusement was Shuri's iconic comment, **"Don't scare me like that, colonizer!"** I felt those words so intensely. As a mother in our vibrant Navajo family, I deeply understand the ongoing ways colonization and settler colonization has been a part of our peoples' livelihood for centuries and into the present. Shuri was

not just showing us "the world outside our window," as Stan Lee proclaimed—Shuri was opening the door to Indigenous/Black realism and futures. That afternoon, I asked my family, *what would a Marvel story look like if it was from our Native perspectives?* As we dreamed, I could never have imagined that dream would become a reality.

What a surprising gift it is, years later, to hold the pages of *Marvel's Voices: Heritage* in our hands in what feels like a direct response to our family's discussions. Without a doubt, there are many more Native families dreaming up these comics. The stories in this series offer a doorway into the realities of Native lives and imagined futures, inviting us to panels of entrance into Native genius and creativity. And I didn't skip a beat—I entered.

As an educator, researcher and storyteller, I—alongside my colleagues—have advocated and written about the absence of and damaging views of Native presence in school settings and society for years. In my book *Native Presence and Sovereignty in College: Sustaining Indigenous Weapons to Defeat Systemic Monsters*, I share stories of ten Navajo teenagers who confront a world that does not know them for who they are, having harmful effects on how they see themselves and the world around them. The reality of "not knowing" or **the window of erasure is the story that too often is told and retold, limiting possible views**

...and futures for indigenous peoples. That window must change.

Marvel's Voices: Heritage is changing the narrative. With each panel, every page, **indigenous presence is aesthetically and literally showing that *we are here!* These stories are building the worlds that we deserve and are empowered by and giving us permission to dream of the possibilities of imagined futures in all their complexity and glorious brilliance.**

Seeing and reading about ourselves as Native peoples across these pages acknowledges our existence, which is incredibly important in a society where laws and policies were signed with ink and blood to erase (and replace) us. The implications of such policies have had devastating effects, continuing to this day. Research in 2020 found that Native representation in film ranges from 0.3–0.5% and is nearly nonexistent in television.[1] Of course, Native representation in 2021 shifted significantly, with shows such as *Rutherford Falls* and *Reservation Dogs* and a growing excitement over the soon-to-be-released *Marvel Studios' Echo* series on Disney+, which stars Native actress Alaqua Cox and features a number of Native writers in the writers' room, including acclaimed novelist and *Phoenix Song: Echo* (2020) and *Marvel's Voices: Heritage* writer Rebecca Roanhorse.

Little by little, the window is changing. As a deaf Cheyenne and Latina badass, Echo opens the door of possibilities while wrestling with the harshness of not just her past but that of her people. For many Native peoples, Echo's storyline is relatable as, in many ways, the harshness of the past is connected to the sociopolitical realities of today. In addition to Echo, we see other Native heroes reflect our realities. Snowguard, an Inuk hero empowered by ancestral traditions and super hero powers, works to help the young Native people in the village of Nunavut. Her story reminds us of the mighty Indigenous weapons that Native peoples are equipped with that have been passed down from generation to generation. And like a true Native auntie, Danielle "Dani" Moonstar, A.K.A. Mirage, a Cheyenne hero, speaks words of wisdom to a young mutant super hero, Julian, by saying, "We can be many things, Julian... and have many families," acknowledging the complexity of identity and belonging in Native communities.

It is clear that Marvel is catching up to where Indigenous presence has always been and should be. We have held and continue to hold stories of warriors, monsters and more-than-human relatives who teach and protect us. We have long traveled on rainbows, lightning bolts and webs. Timelessness is respected and understood. Indigenous writers and artists alike know of these stories. These **stories are our survival for futures. Imagination is our weapon for futures**. We exist today because of stories. These pages assert self-determination and possibilities of Indigenous presence and imagined futures. *Now these stories, our stories,* are part of the Marvel Universe. Let's open the door and windows to reality and possible futures and welcome more beauty and more brilliance. *Yéego!*

DR. AMANDA R. TACHINE is Navajo from Ganado, Arizona. She is an Assistant Professor in Educational Leadership and Innovation at Arizona State University. She is the author of *Native Presence and Sovereignty in College* and co-editor of *Weaving an Otherwise: In-relations Methodological Practice*. She has been published in the *Huffington Post, Al Jazeera, The Hill, Teen Vogue, Indian Country Today, Inside Higher Ed* and *Navajo Times* where she advances ideas regarding discriminatory actions, educational policies and inspirational movements

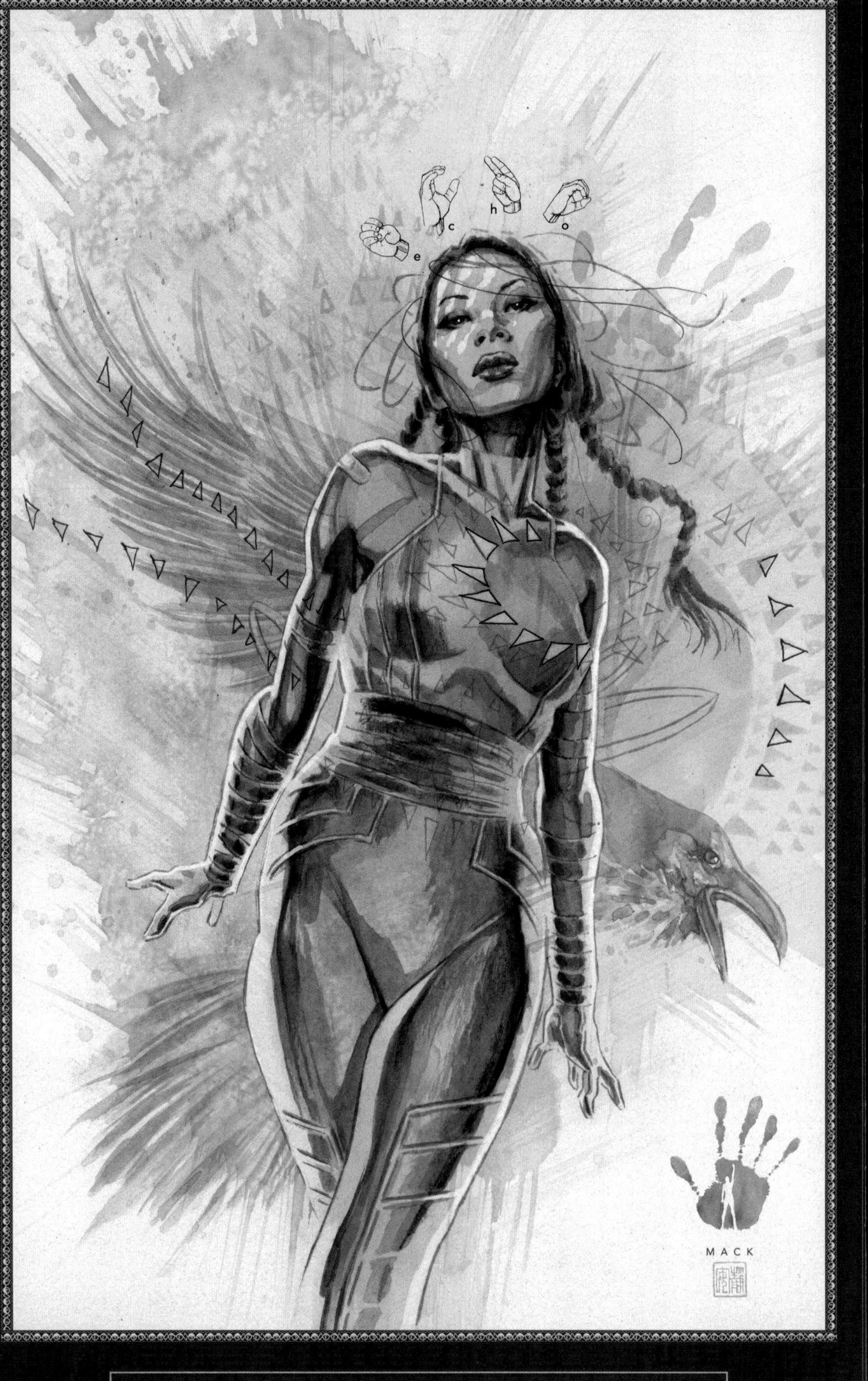
e
c
h
o
MACK

MARVEL'S VOICES: INDIGENOUS VOICES VARIANT BY **DAVID MACK**

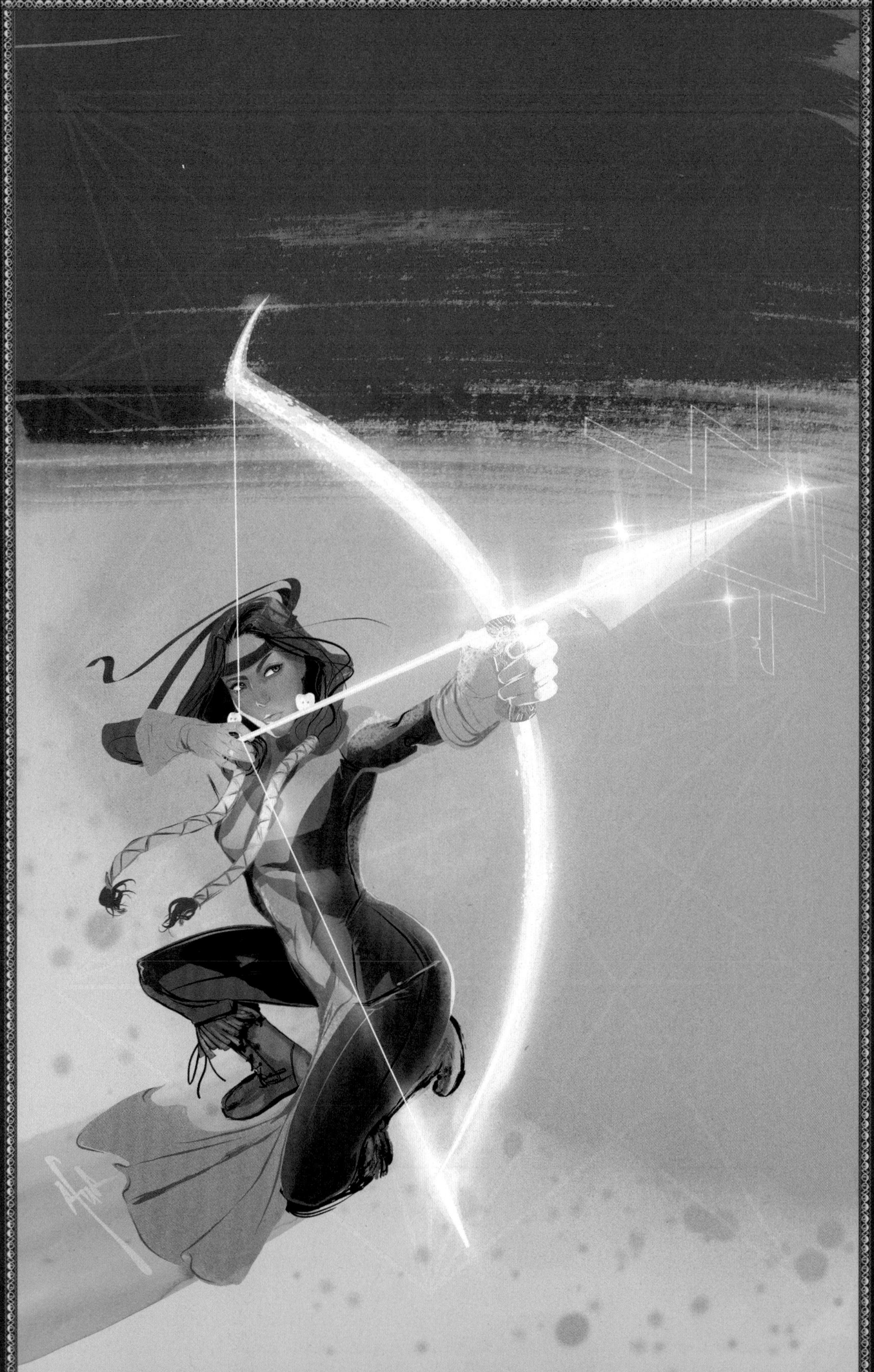

MARVEL'S VOICES: INDIGENOUS VOICES VARIANT BY **AFUA RICHARDSON**

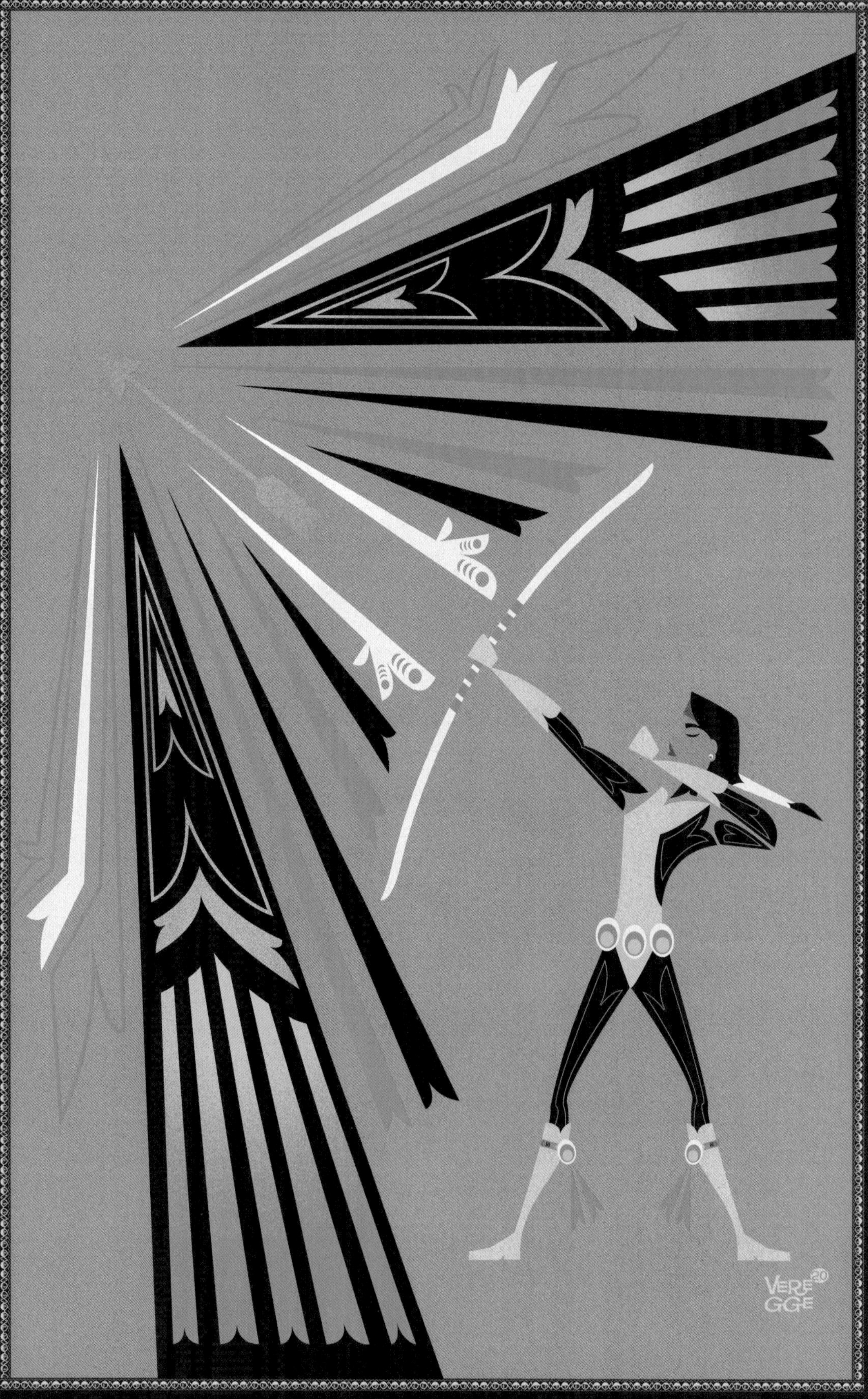
VEREGGE 20

MARVEL'S VOICES: INDIGENOUS VOICES VARIANT BY **JEFFREY VEREGGE**

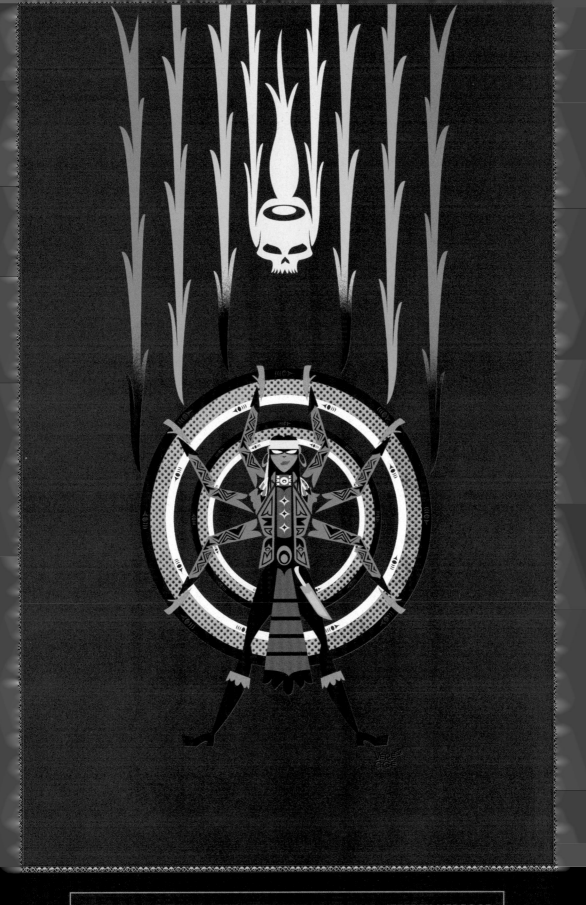

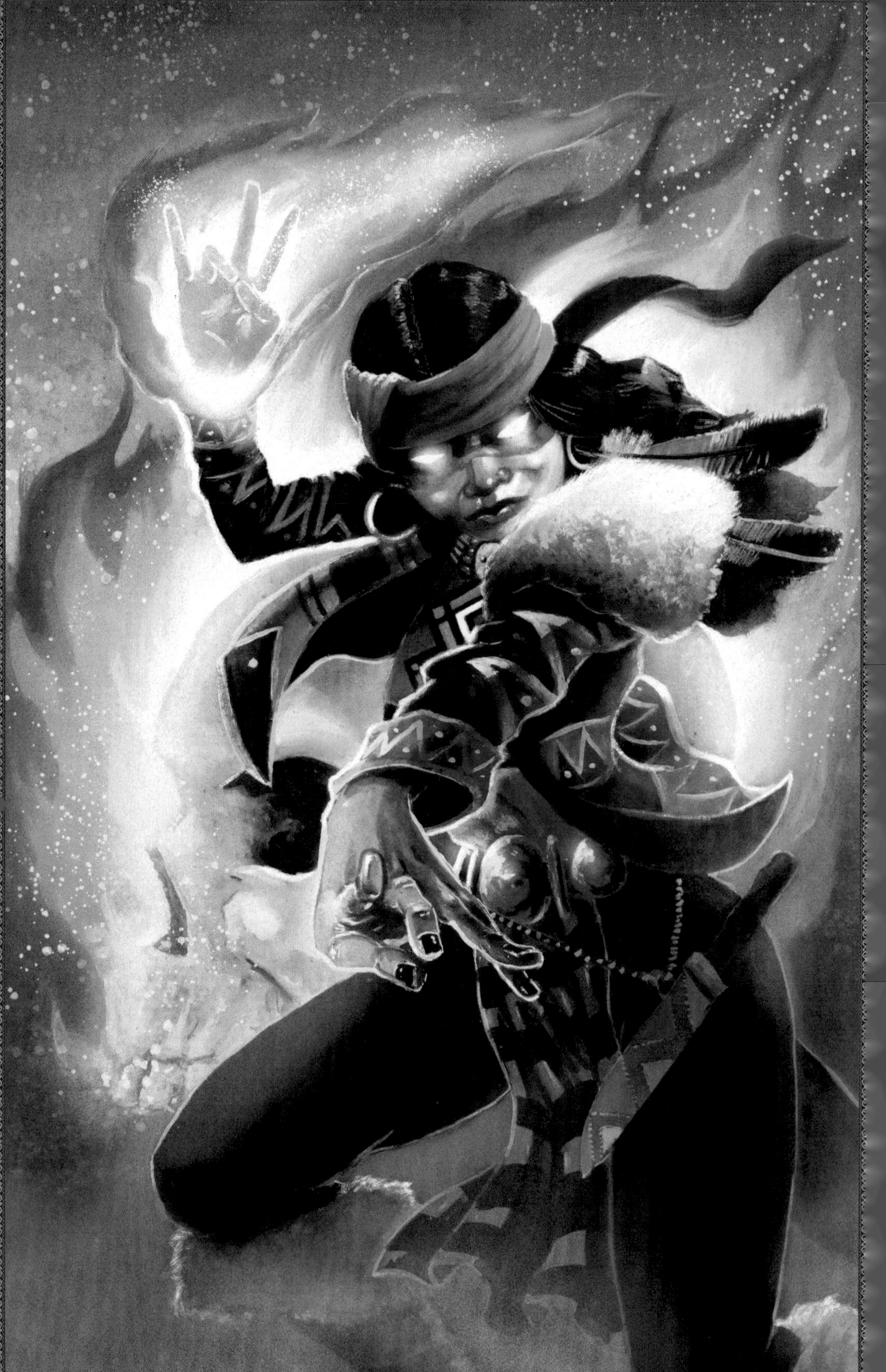

MARVEL'S VOICES: HERITAGE VARIANT BY **ROY BONEY**

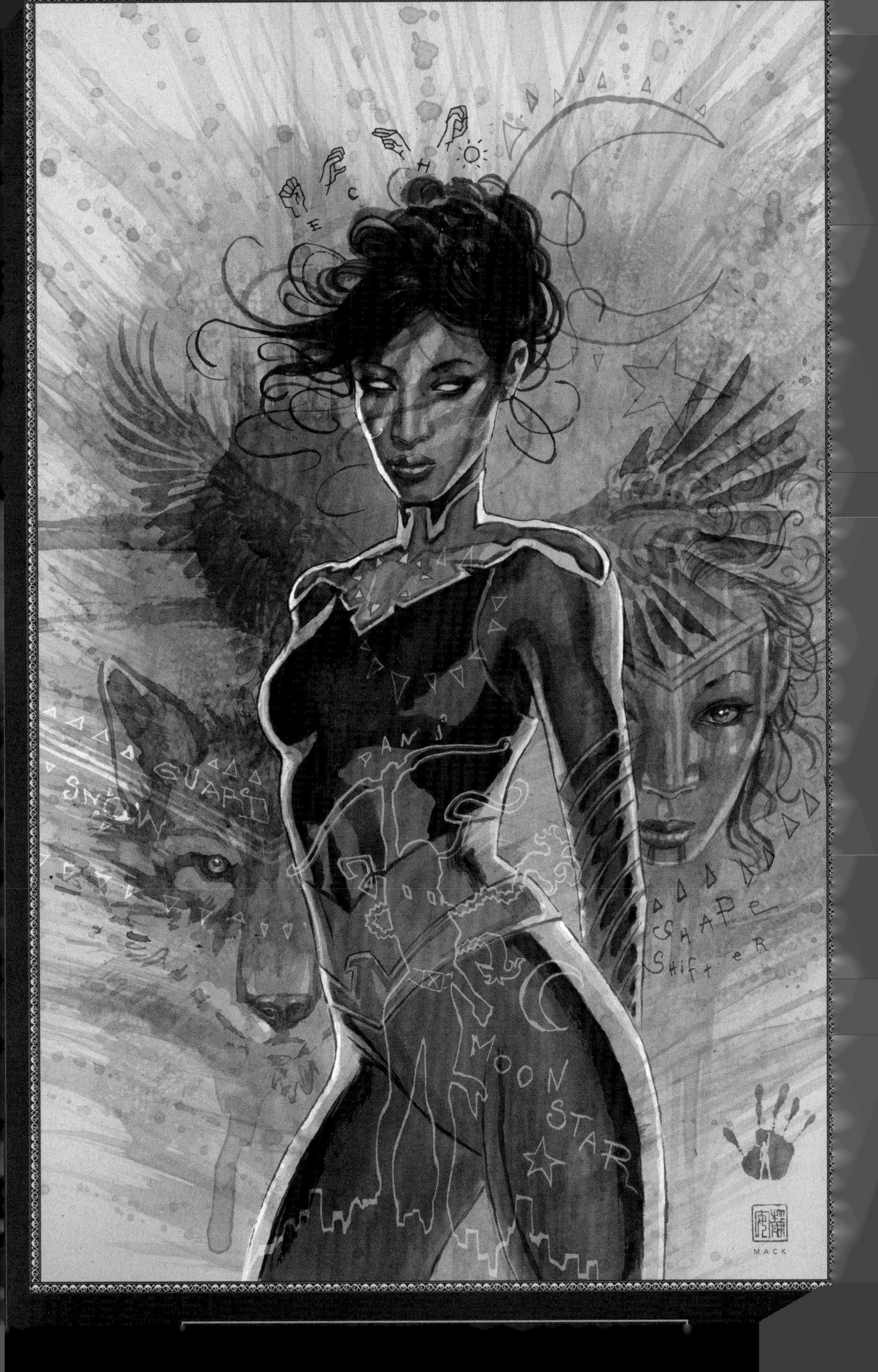
DANI
SNOW
GUARD
SHAPE
SHIFTER
MOON
STAR
MACK

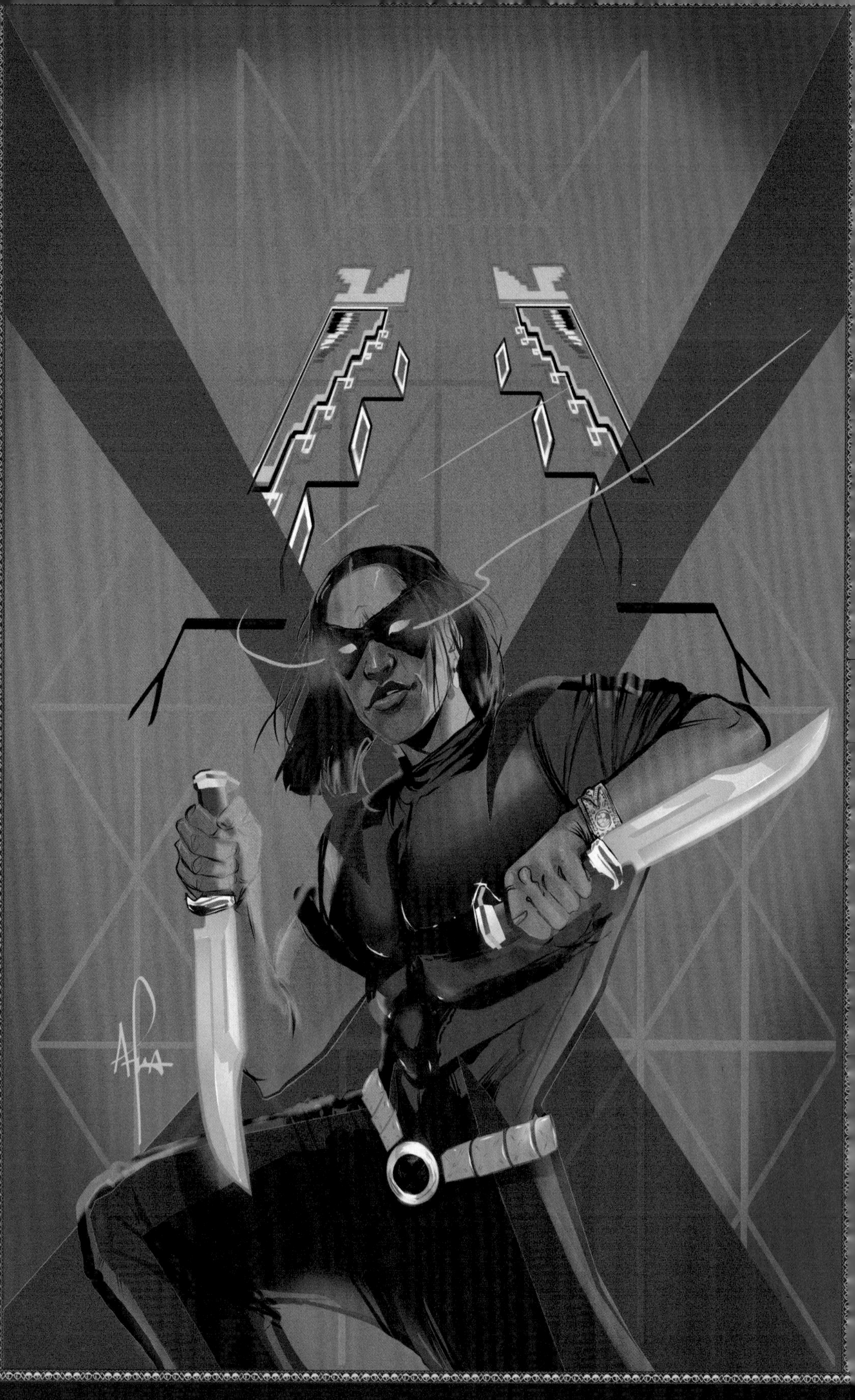
Afua

MARVEL'S VOICES: HERITAGE VARIANT BY AFUA RICHARDSON

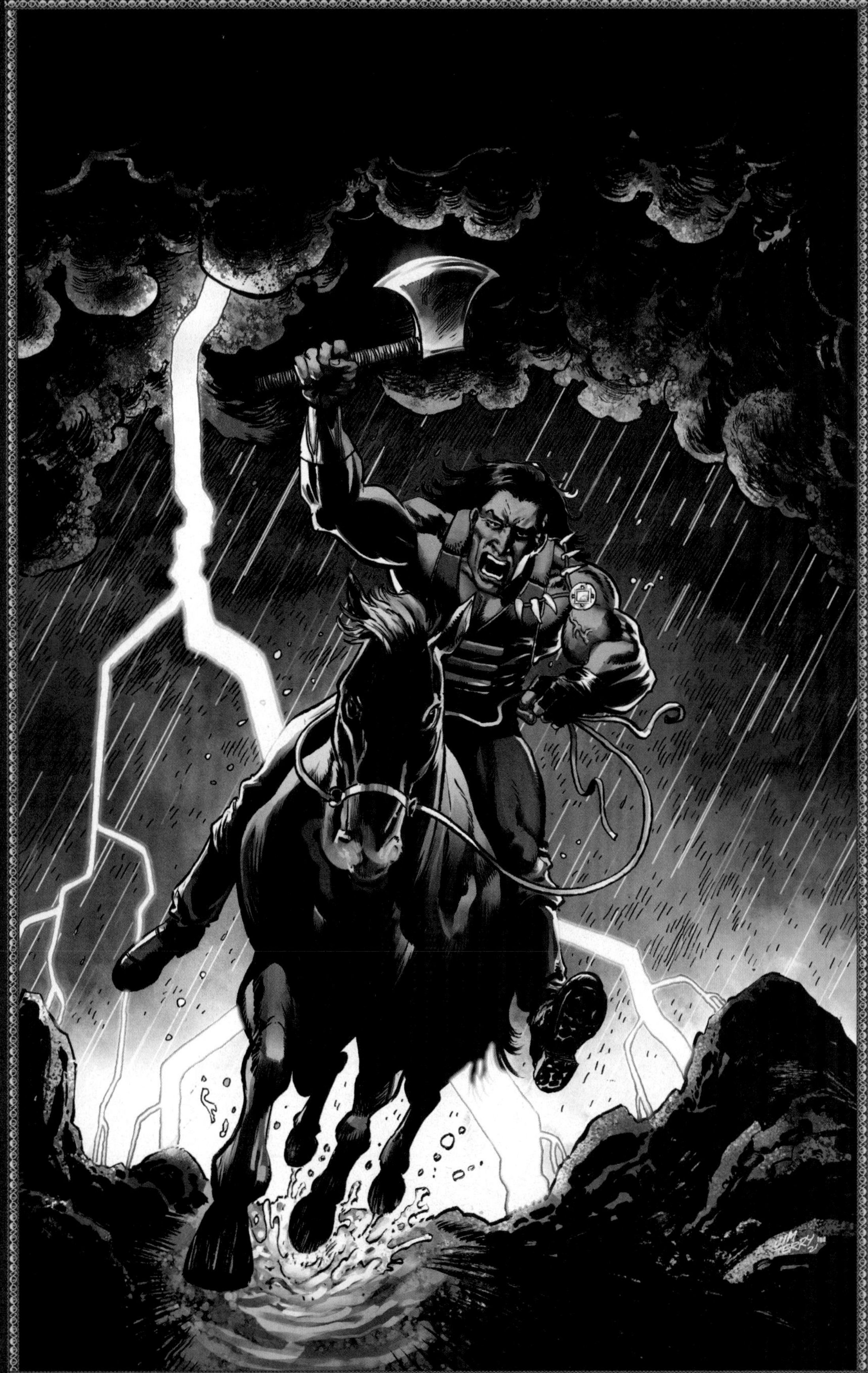
JIM TERRY

MARVEL'S VOICES: HERITAGE VARIANT BY **JIM TERRY & FRANK D'ARMATA**

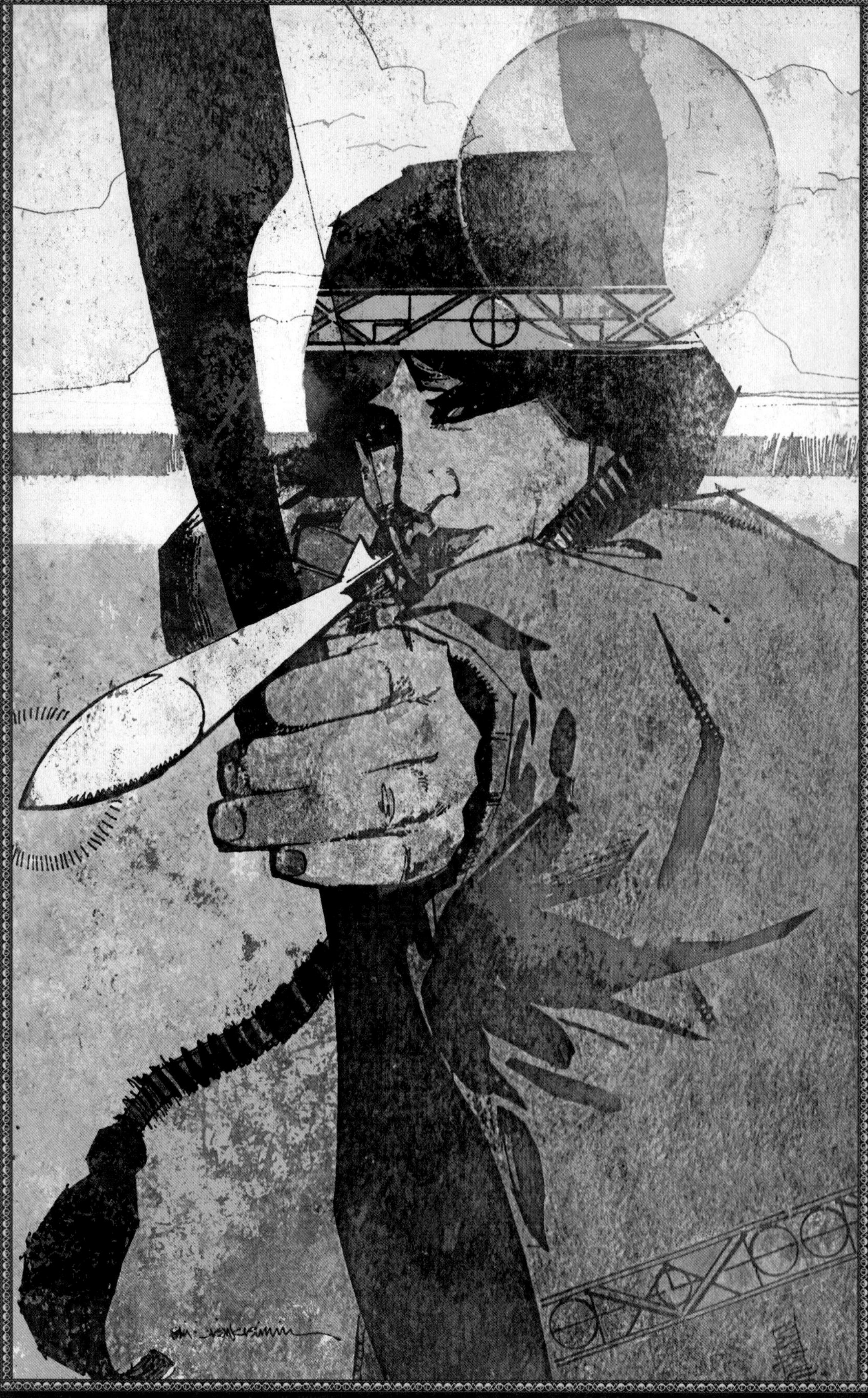

MARVEL'S VOICES: HERITAGE HIDDEN GEM VARIANT BY **BILL SIENKIEWICZ**

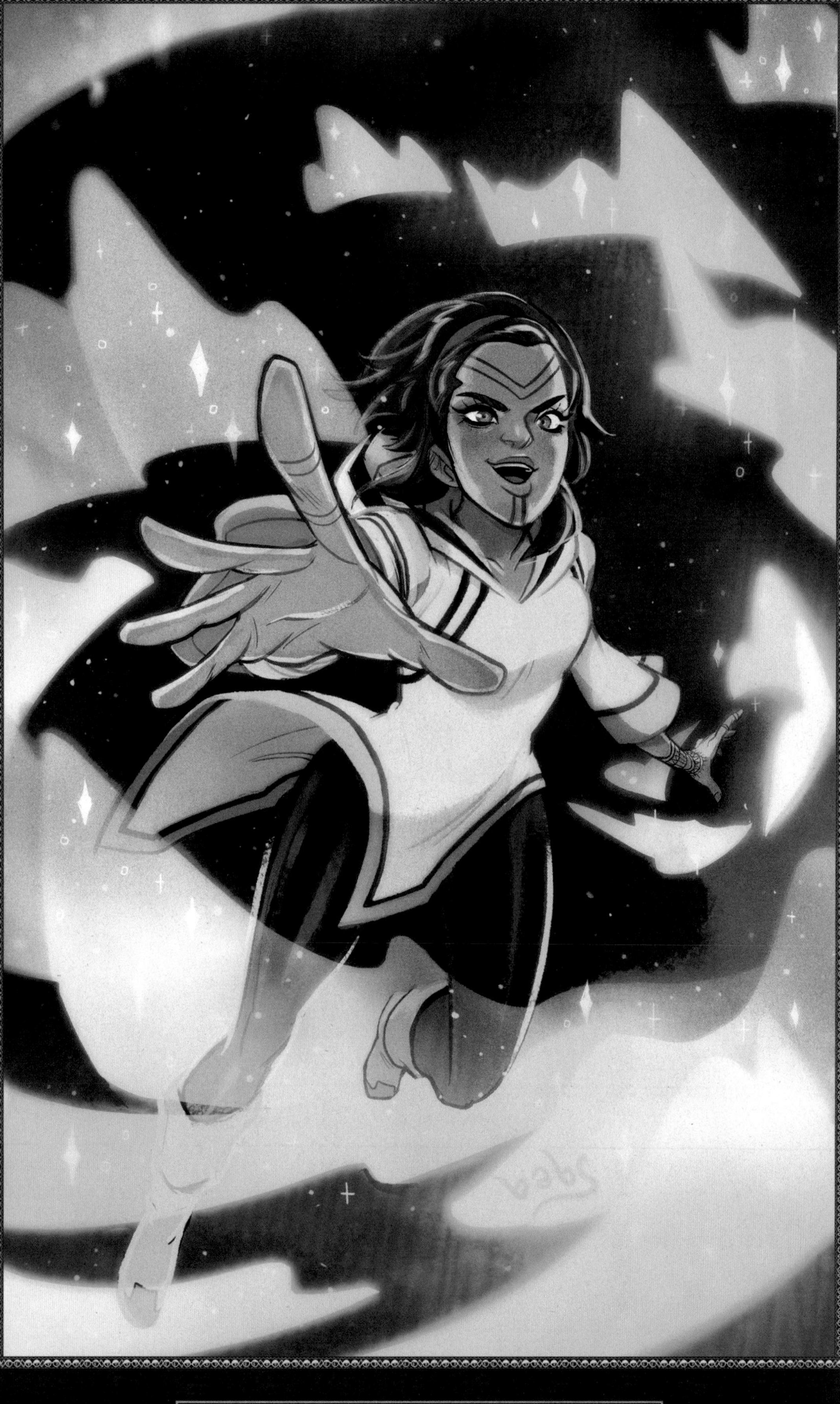

CHAMPIONS ANNUAL #1 VARIANT BY **BABS TARR**

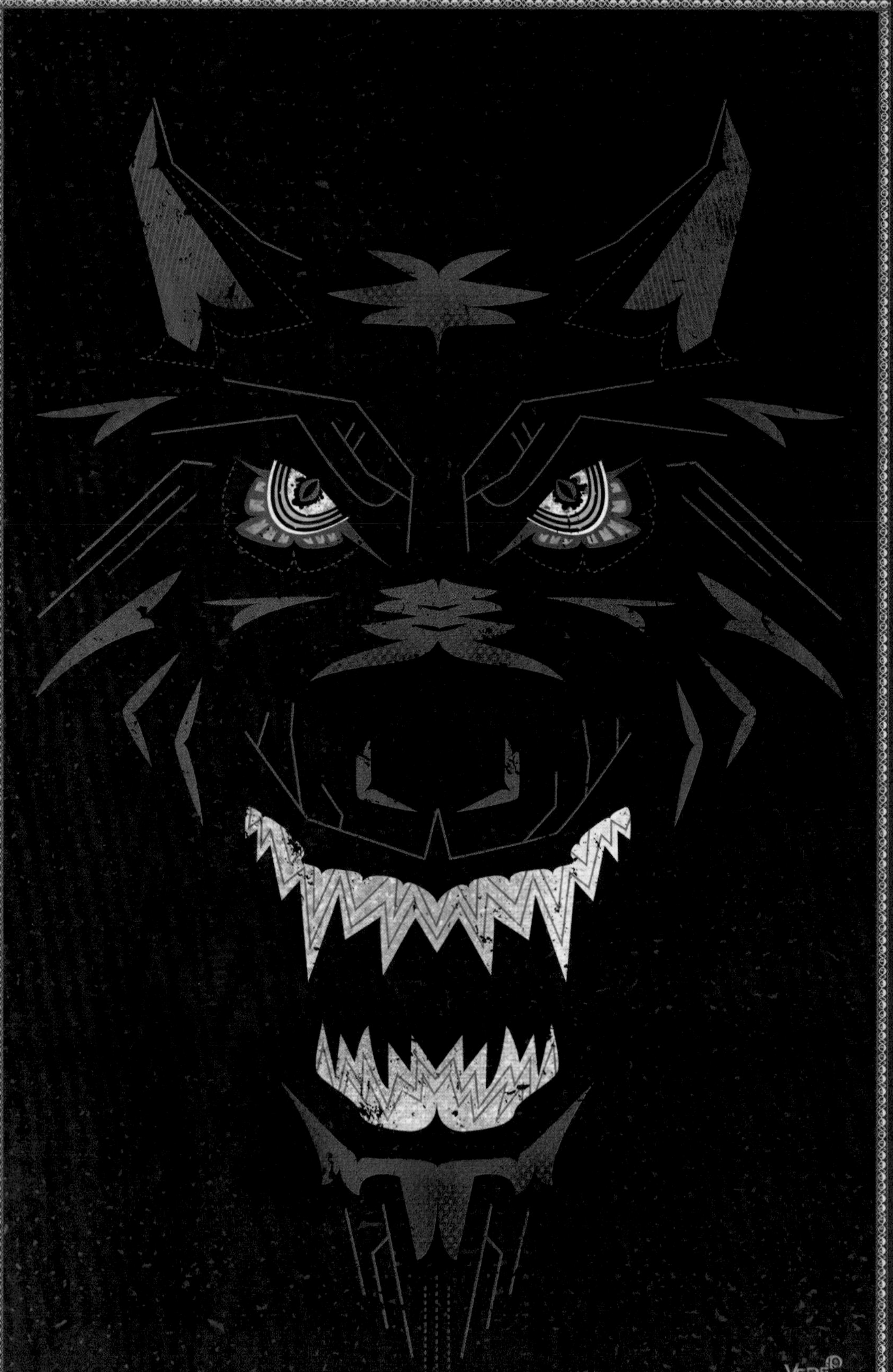
VEREGGE

***WEREWOLF BY NIGHT* #1** VARIANT BY **JEFFREY VEREGGE**

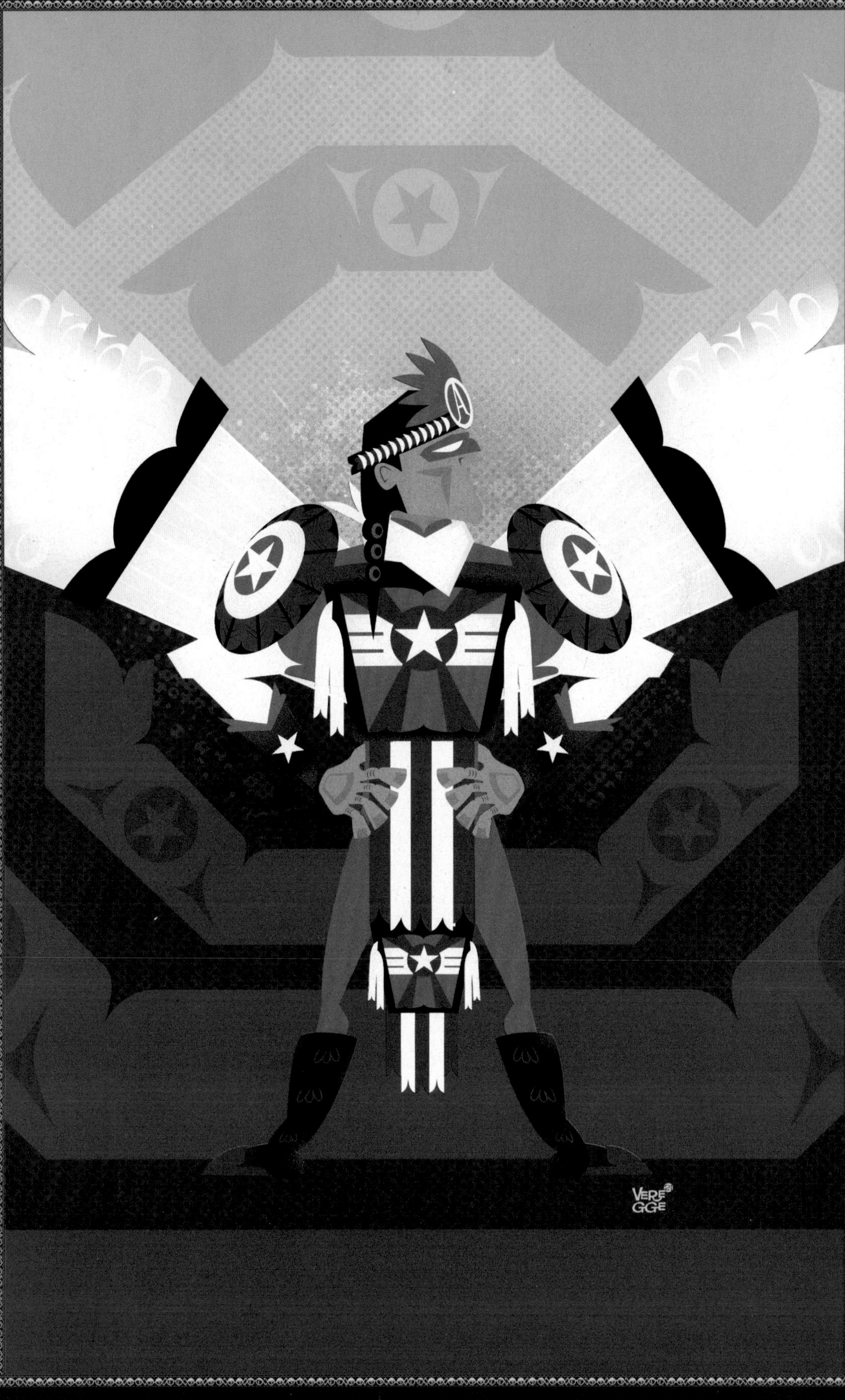
VEREGGE

THE UNITED STATES OF CAPTAIN AMERICA #3 VARIANT BY **JEFFREY VEREGGE**

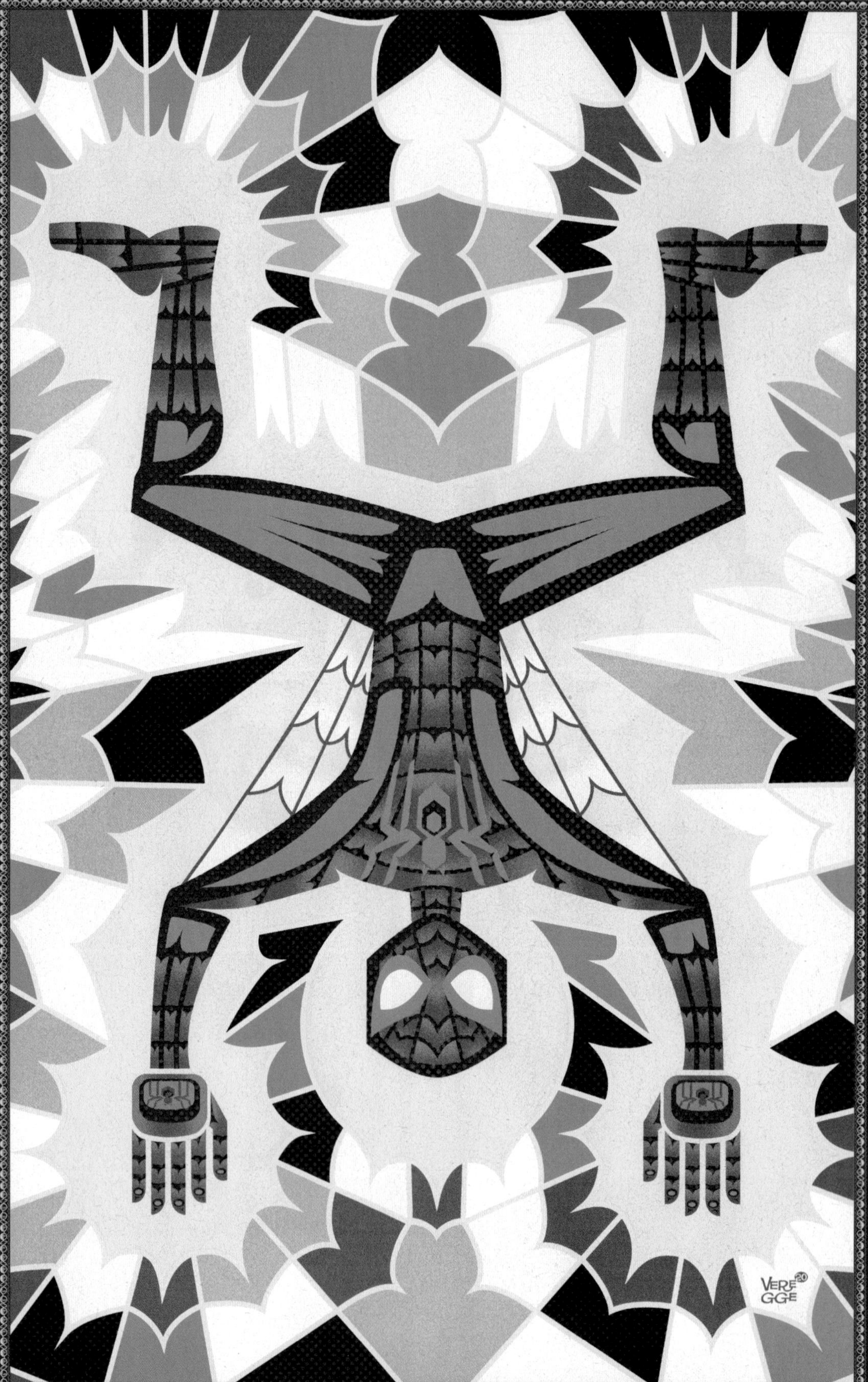

AMAZING SPIDER-MAN #52 VARIANT BY **JEFFREY VEREGGE**

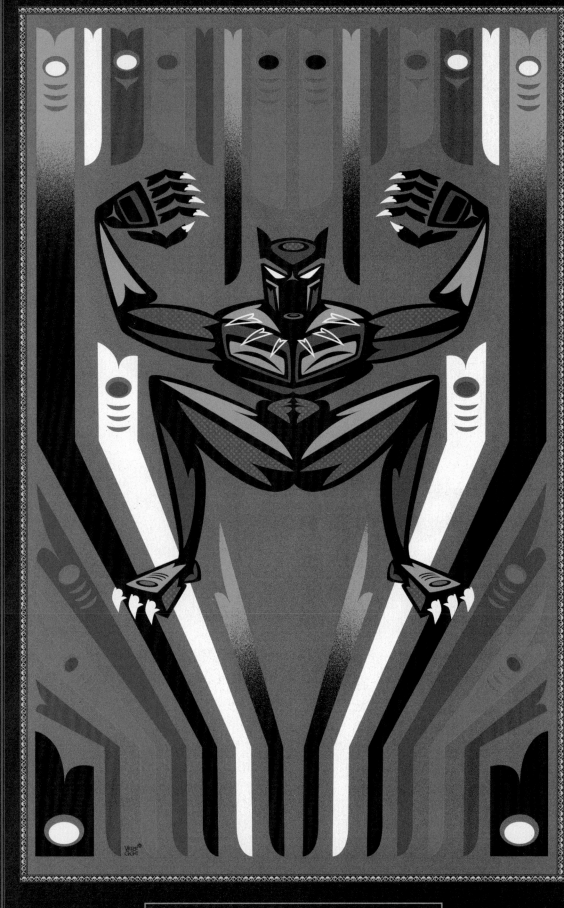

AVENGERS #38 VARIANT BY JEFFREY VEREGGE

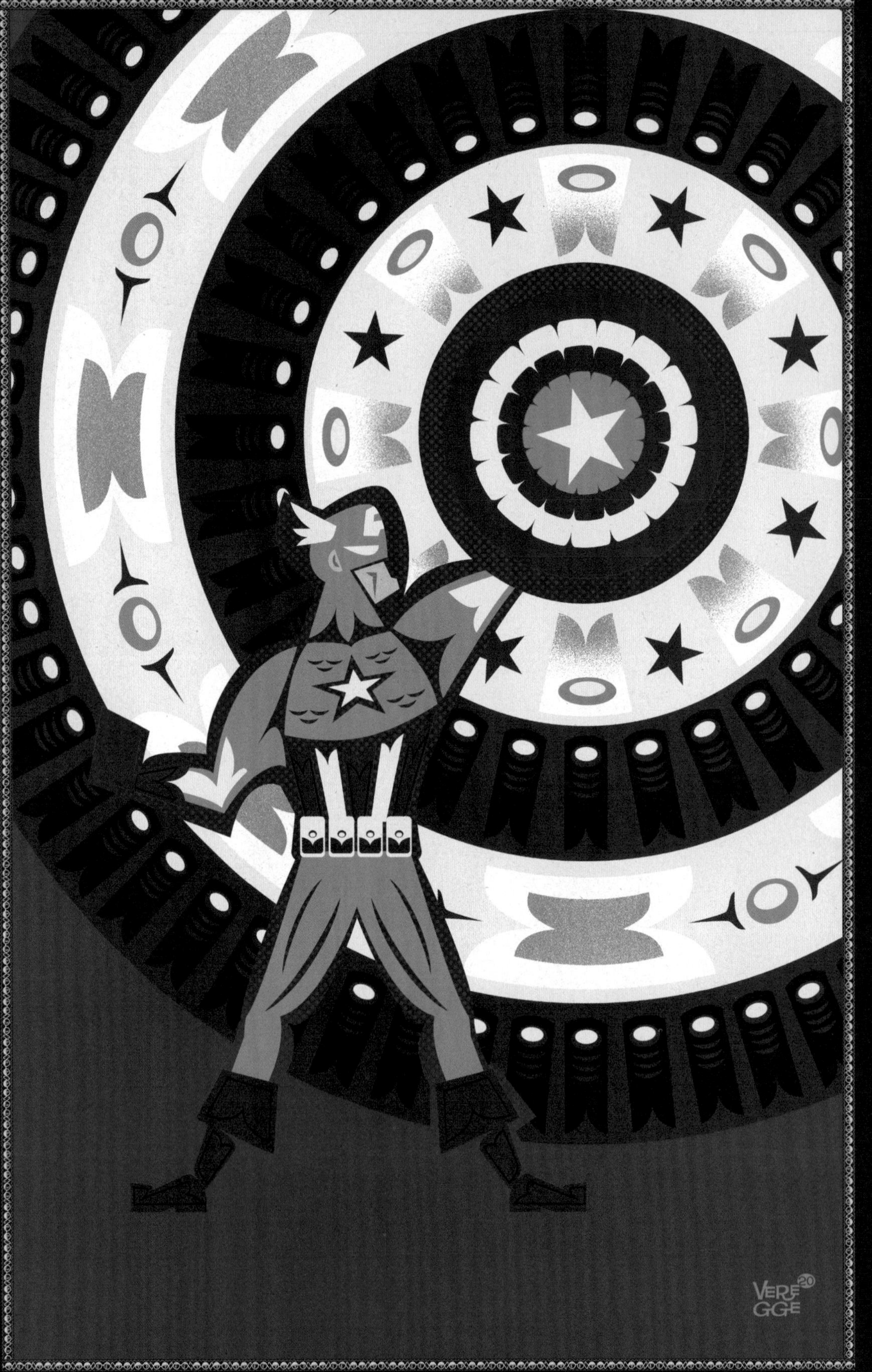
VEREGGE 20

CAPTAIN AMERICA #25 VARIANT BY **JEFFREY VEREGGE**

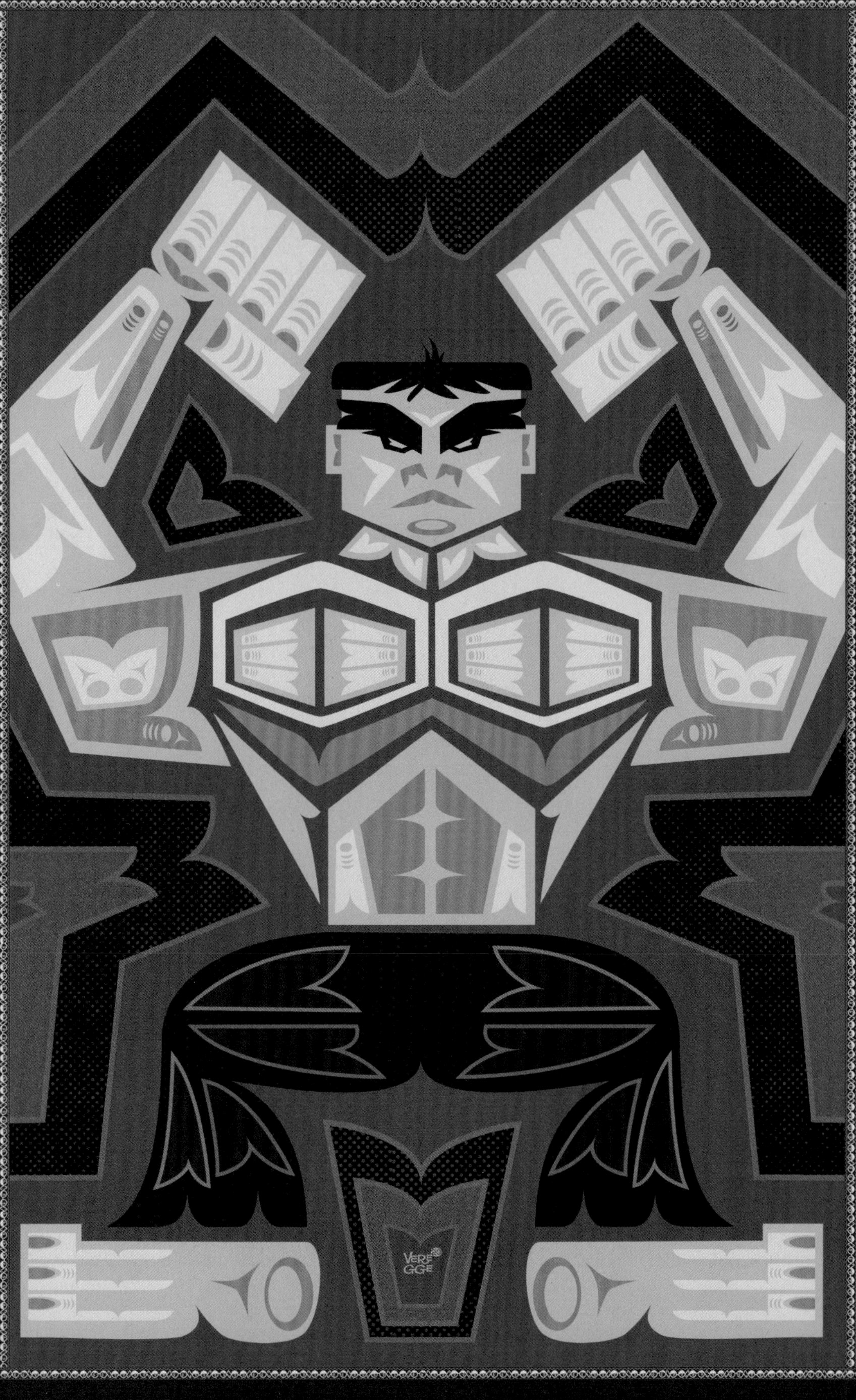
VEREGGE

IMMORTAL HULK #40 VARIANT BY **JEFFREY VEREGGE**

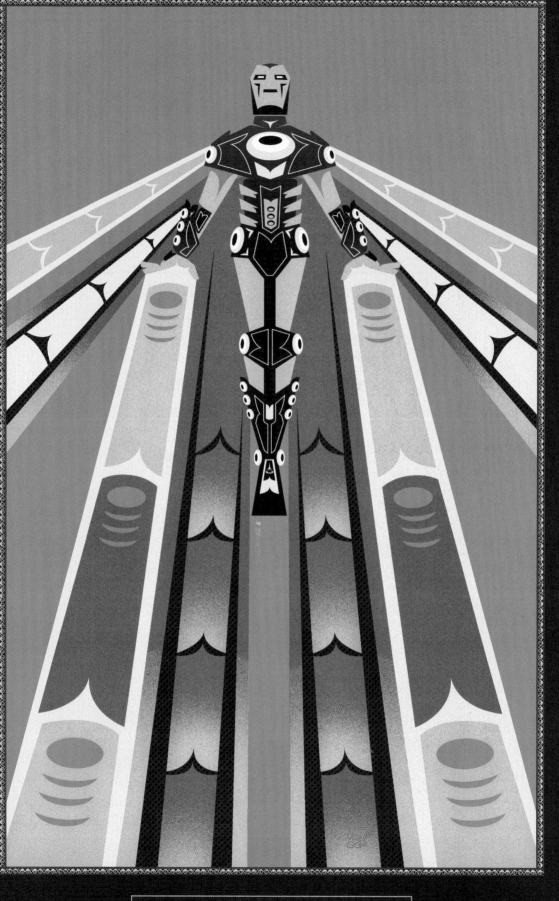

IRON MAN #3 VARIANT BY **JEFFREY VEREGGE**

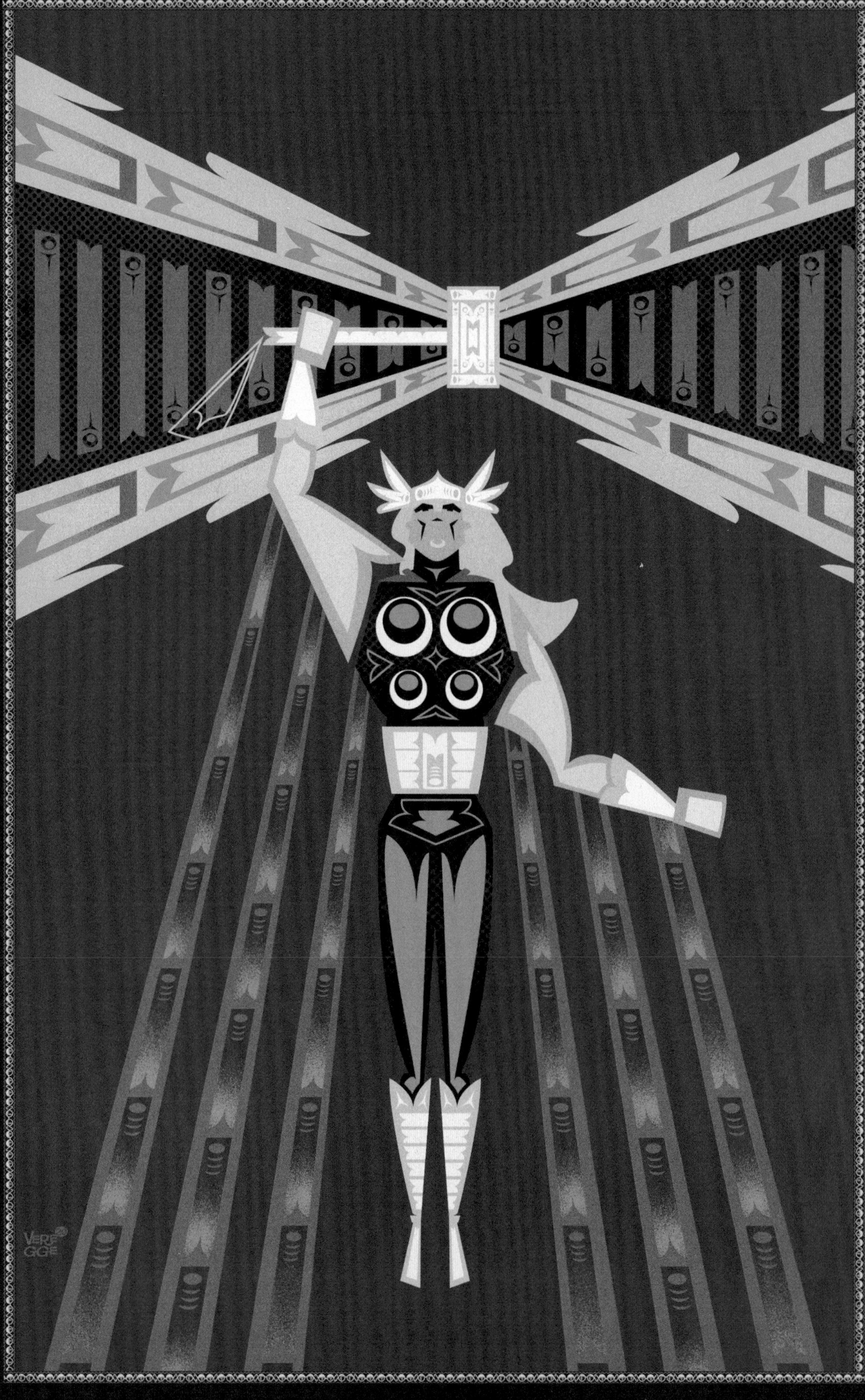
VERREGGE

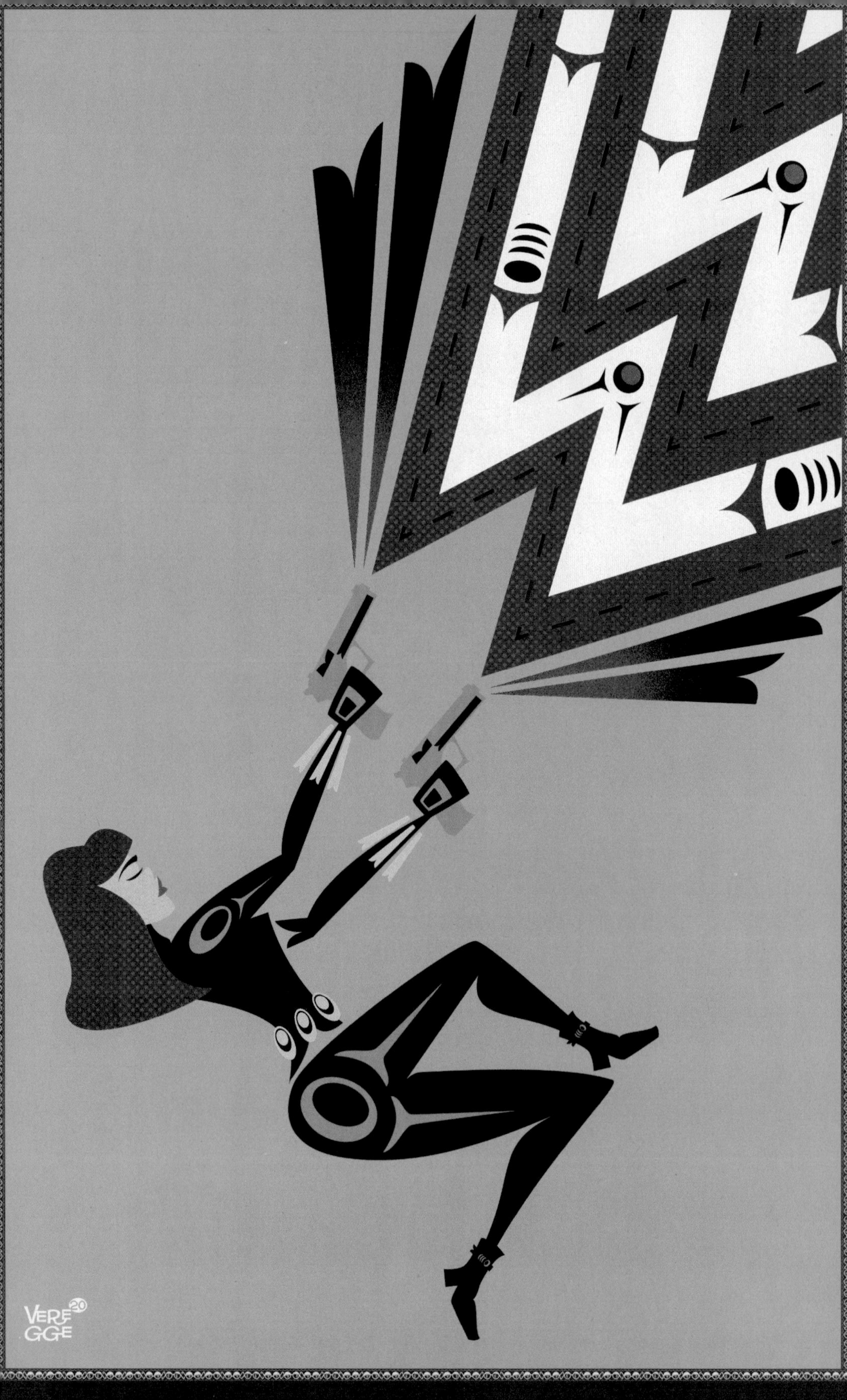
VEREGGE 20

WIDOWMAKERS: RED GUARDIAN AND YELENA BELOVA VARIANT BY **JEFFREY VEREGGE**

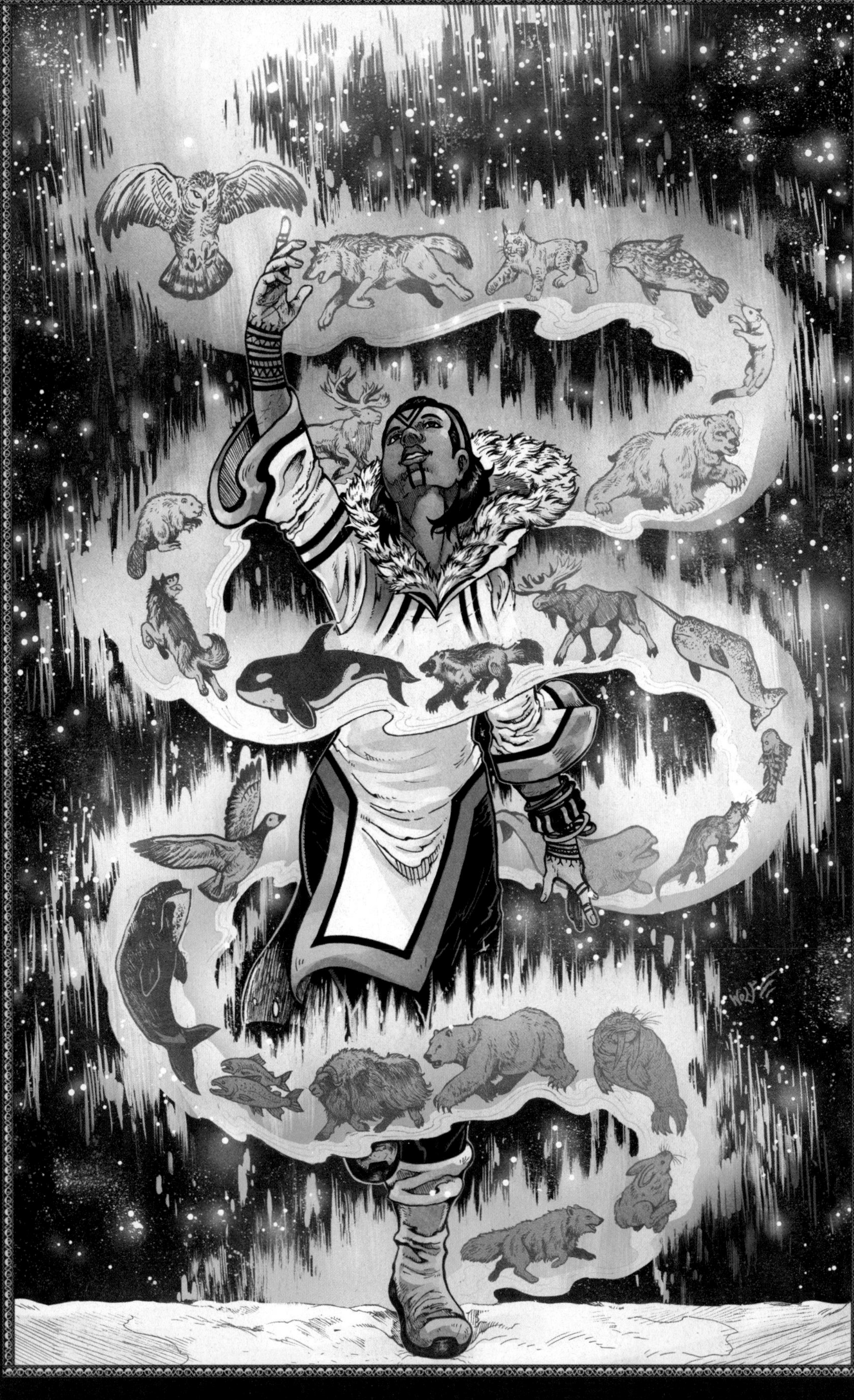
WOLF

MOON KNIGHT #5 NATIVE AMERICAN HERITAGE VARIANT BY **MARIA WOLF** & **MIKE SPICER**

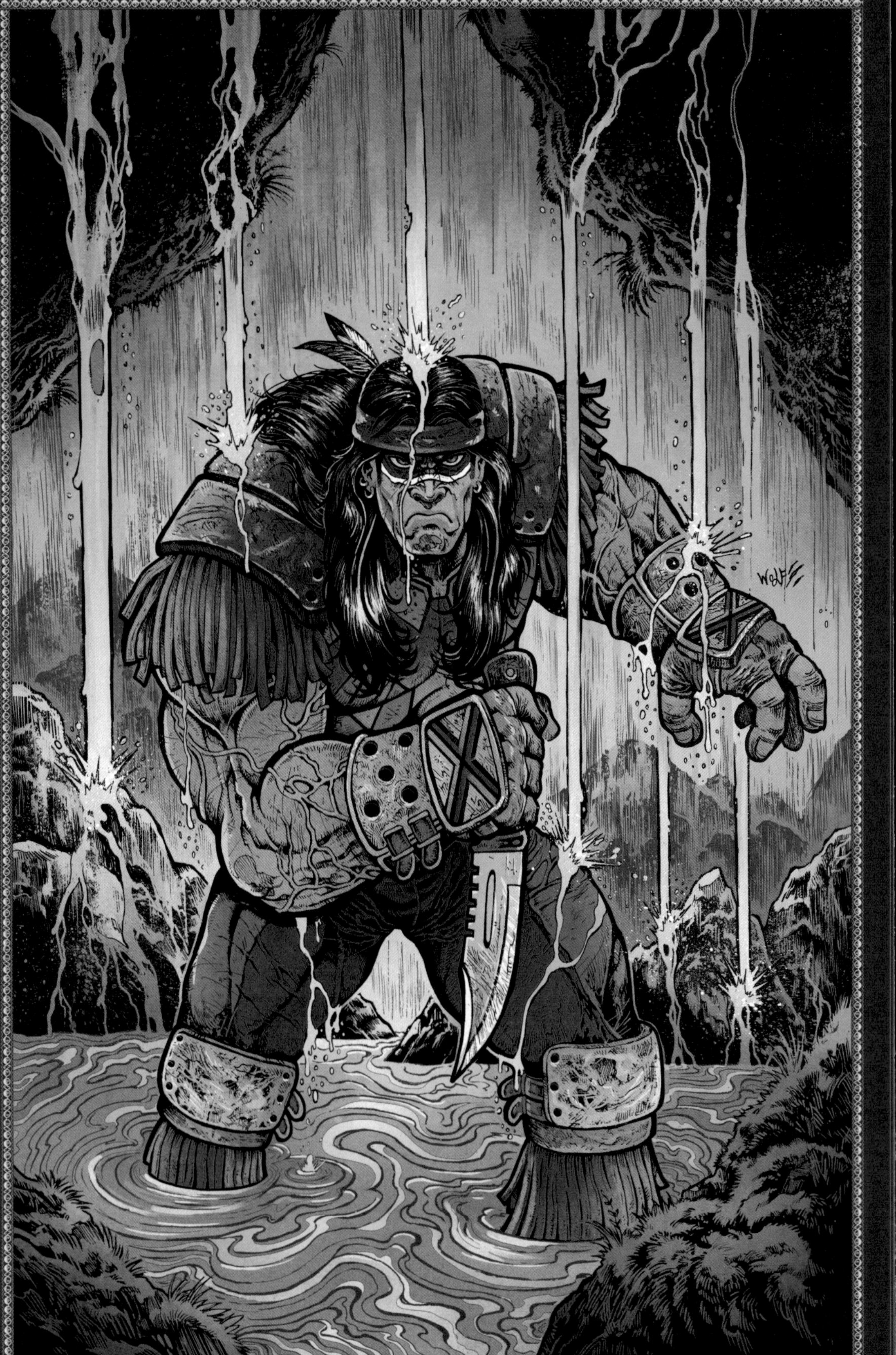

***X-FORCE* #25** NATIVE AMERICAN HERITAGE VARIANT BY **MARIA WOLF** & **MIKE SPICER**

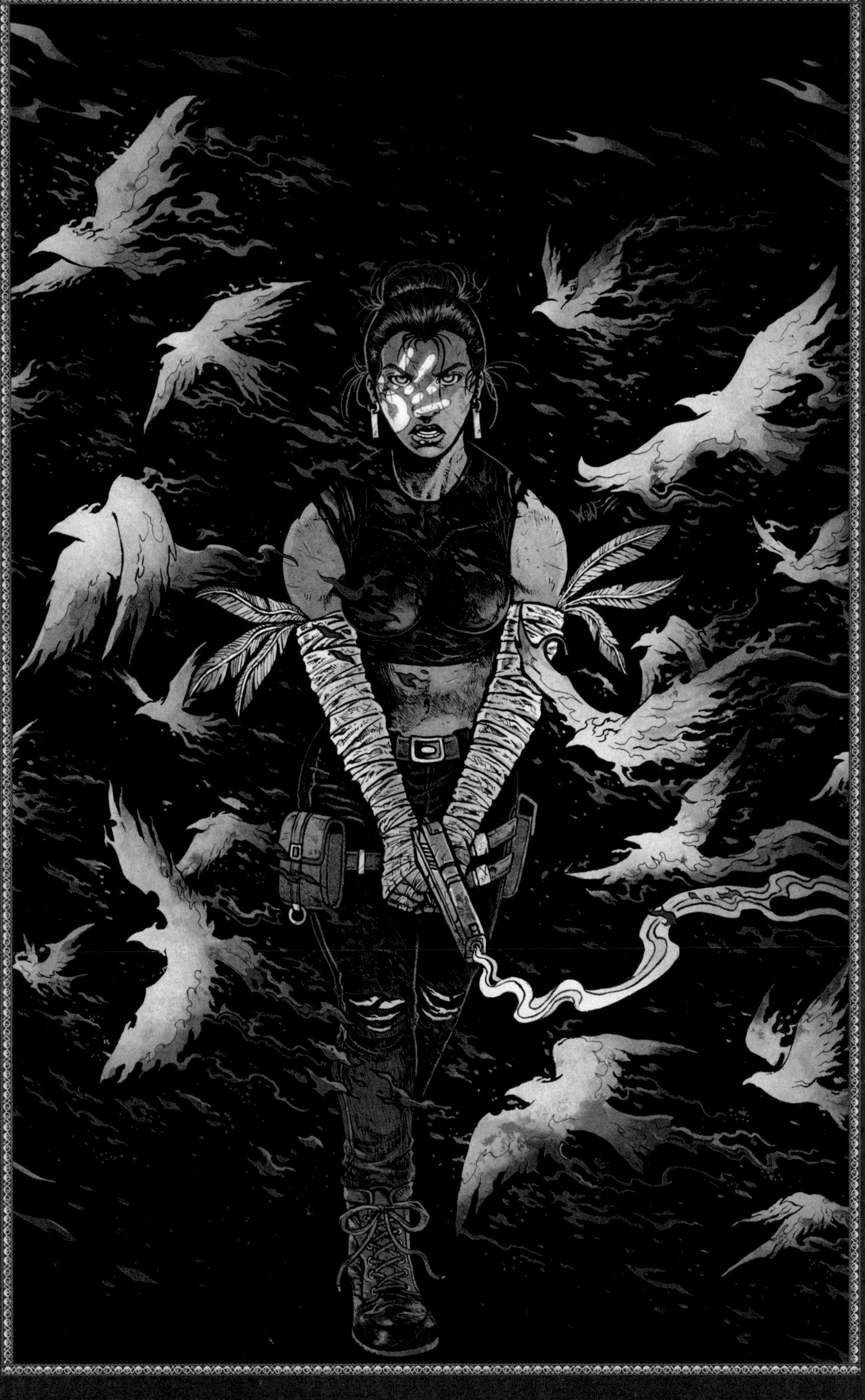

PHOENIX SONG: ECHO **#5** VARIANT BY **MARIA WOLF** & **MIKE SPICER**

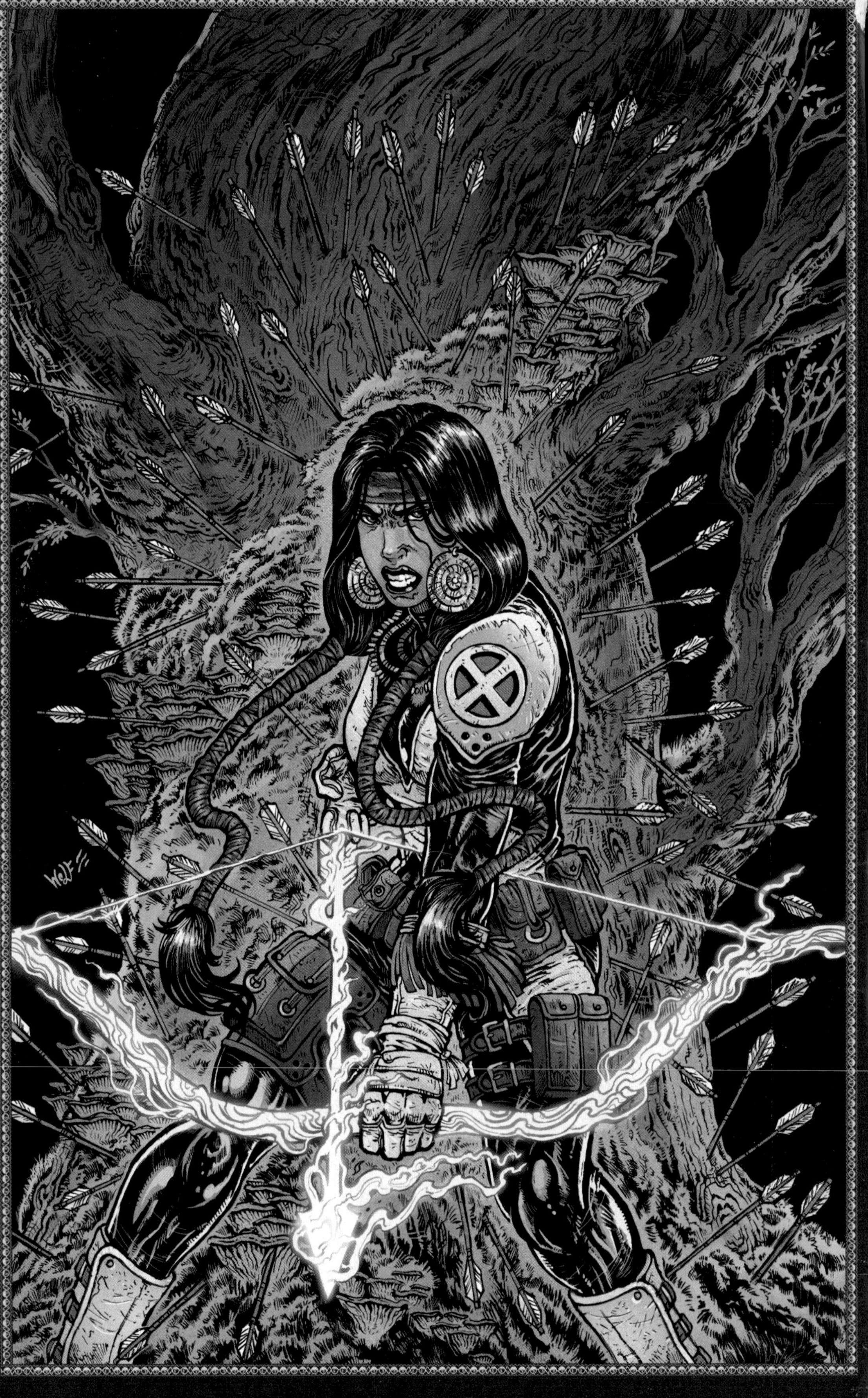

NEW MUTANTS #26 VARIANT BY **MARIA WOLF**